The German Lyric of the Baroque in English Translation

UNC | COLLEGE OF ARTS AND SCIENCES
Germanic and Slavic Languages and Literatures

From 1949 to 2004, UNC Press and the UNC Department of Germanic & Slavic Languages and Literatures published the UNC Studies in the Germanic Languages and Literatures series. Monographs, anthologies, and critical editions in the series covered an array of topics including medieval and modern literature, theater, linguistics, philology, onomastics, and the history of ideas. Through the generous support of the National Endowment for the Humanities and the Andrew W. Mellon Foundation, books in the series have been reissued in new paperback and open access digital editions. For a complete list of books visit www.uncpress.org.

The German Lyric of the Baroque in English Translation

GEORGE C. SCHOOLFIELD

UNC Studies in the Germanic Languages and Literatures
Number 29

Copyright © 1961

This work is licensed under a Creative Commons CC BY-NC-ND license. To view a copy of the license, visit http://creativecommons.org/licenses.

Suggested citation: Schoolfield, George C. *The German Lyric of the Baroque in English Translation*. Chapel Hill: University of North Carolina Press, 1961. DOI: https://doi.org/10.5149/9781469658322_Schoolfield

Library of Congress Cataloging-in-Publication Data
Names: Schoolfield, George C.
Title: The German lyric of the baroque in English translation / by George C. Schoolfield.
Other titles: University of North Carolina Studies in the Germanic Languages and Literatures ; no. 29.
Description: Chapel Hill : University of North Carolina Press, [1961] Series: University of North Carolina Studies in the Germanic Languages and Literatures.
Identifiers: LCCN 61064204 | ISBN 978-0-8078-8029-6 (pbk: alk. paper) | ISBN 978-1-4696-5832-2 (ebook)
Subjects: German poetry — Early modern, 1500-1700. | German poetry — Translations into English.
Classification: LCC PD25 .N6 NO. 29 | DCC 831/ .082

To
EDWIN H. ZEYDEL
si canimus silvas, silvae sint consule dignae

PREFACE

The present book has been written to serve three ends. First, it is meant to introduce the German lyric of the seventeenth century to people who, while perhaps interested in European literary matters, cannot read German well enough to make out Baroque texts, and who, most likely, are not aware that Germany possessed a literature in the seventeenth century. The German Baroque, so well known to cultured Americans in its musical and architectural manifestations, deserves to be made accessible from its literary side as well.

In the second place, the book is intended to aid those undergraduates who have decided to concentrate in German. It may help them to understand Baroque German a little better; it may make them realize that, despite the evidence of Gryphius' tragedies and Opitz's *Buch von der deutschen Poeterei*, the seventeenth century can offer genuine reading pleasure.

Finally, the book has been written because the author enjoyed writing it, a confession, to be sure, which may cause his dishonorable discharge from even the disciplinary battalions of scholarship.

The reader's attention is called to a matter at which, if he will, he may take umbrage. All texts have been reprinted just as they appear in the listed source, which means that some poems appear with modernized spelling while others do not. Since the book had a pedagogical purpose, it seemed better not to modernize the texts taken from original or unrevised printings: thus the student should learn to cope with some of the peculiarities of the preclassical language.

It will be noted, too, that the author has, except in a very few cases, avoided the use of feminine rhyme. The poems containing the "very few cases" represent the germ-cell of the book, translations made at the beginning of the undertaking. Very soon the author saw that the gain in music to be had from the use of English feminine rhyme could not make up for the loss in sense. In abandoning feminine rhyme, he joined good company, as one can tell by a glance at Shakespeare's sonnets or at Weckherlin's attempts to write English poetry.

The author's special gratitude must go to Professor Ernst Oppenheimer of Carleton University, Ottawa, who suggested the idea of the book some years back. Since then, Professor Oppenheimer, by polite inquiry about his godchild, has prodded the lazy author into activity more than once.

Warm thanks must also go to Professor Curt von Faber du Faur, who has allowed the author to use the German Literature Collection at Yale University, and to quote poems from some of its holdings.

Three other scholars have also distinguish themselves by remarkable goodness of heart: Professor Klaus Jonas of the University of Pittsburgh, Professor Blake Lee Spahr of the University of California at Berkeley, and Professor George de Capua of Cornell University. Professor Spahr was particularly kind in his provision of Birken material to the author.

Everyone knows that all scholarly books owe their completion to some preceptor, muse, or Maecenas; this position of honor, for the present book, is held by three typists: Miss Estellie Smith, Mrs. Daniel Johnston, and Mrs. Robert Harris.

Finally, the author's thanks must be expressed to Professor Frederic Coenen of the University of North Carolina, for his sympathetic interest in the undertaking, and to the Council on Research of Duke University, which provided generous financial support of the book's publication.

As an envoy, the author would like to say of his book what Aurora Königsmarck said of Charles XII after her defeat at Altrannstädt: "Kanske har han bara nödmynt i pungen, men jag älskar honom ändå."

GEORGE C. SCHOOLFIELD

Durham, North Carolina
December 17, 1960

INTRODUCTION

In Strindberg's story, *The White Mountain*, the Swedish cavalry general, Hans Kristoffer von Königsmarck, leads a small band of troopers toward Prague. The expedition will end in glorious success; Königsmarck, aided by the Austrian deserter, Odowalsky, will capture the "Kleinseite" of the Golden City and thus win the last great prize of the Thirty Years' War: "Königsmarck is said to have sent five wagons with gold and silver to the northwest." Yet riding through the Bohemian Forest, Königsmarck has beheld a sight which all the gold of the Hradschin will never erase from his mind; he has seen "men, women and children sitting in a ring around a bake-oven, the last remnant of a village.... Within the bake-oven, on an iron shovel, a piece of game, which could be a gigantic hare but was not, was being roasted. Like a hare, it was very small in the legs and thin across its back and chest, and its backside alone seemed to be well-developed; it had its head stuck between its front paws... No, they were not paws, but rather two five-fingered hands, human hands, and around the neck a half-charred rope was knotted. It was a human being, a hanged man who had been cut down that he might be devoured."

The seventeenth century in the lands of German tongue might have as its insignia the magnificent general and the turncoat, the gilded roofs of the Hradschin and the corpse in the oven; in it, humanity reached such extremes, of grandeur and of misery, that the poets, the beholders of this world of peaks and abysses, could either be dazzled or horrified by what they saw. They could in no case write of it with serenity. There is no calm in the age of the baroque; its poets cannot say, like Goethe's Lynkeus:

> Zum Sehen geboren, zum Schauen bestellt,
> Dem Turme geschworen, gefällt mir die Welt.

While, in their festive poetry, they expressed a huge delight with the good things of the world, the circumstances of their lives would not let them forget that their happiness was fragile, and their pleasures transitory. The wheel of fortune, revolving, made princes into beggars and beggars into princes, but its final turn was sure to be into darkness. In the Jesuit Biedermann's Latin tragedy, Belisaurius, who but lately has heard his armies cry "Laudemus Belisaurium," dies blinded and alone in the streets of Constantinople. The fireworks of even the Nürnberg poets are dampened by the remembrance of ruin's imminence; Gustav Adolf had shown the town's patricians that, had it not been for his protecting hand, they would have been defenseless against Wallenstein. Gustav Adolf himself fell at Lützen, perhaps by treachery, and, a little more than three years later, Wallenstein was murdered at Eger by his own officers. The possession of goods or power counted at the moment for much, in the long run for little.

The horrors and the incertitudes of war did not end for Germany with the Peace of Westphalia. The Swedes, long since forgetful of the religious ideals which presumably had brought them to the continent, continued to turn the north of Germany into a dark and bloody ground, and the Elector of Brandenburg issued a proclamation to "all right-thinking Germans": "Let him who'll not eat Swedish bread consider what he must do for the honor of the German name." Frederick William himself struck a valiant blow for the German name at Fehrbellin in the Havelland (1675), when he routed a Swedish force having twice the strength of the Brandenburgers. Meanwhile, however, France nibbled away at Germany's western reaches, and here there was no Fehrbellin. Grimmelshausen, who had managed to survive the countless perils of the Thirty Years' War, had his old age darkened by Turenne's invasion of Baden; Heidelberg, whose surroundings had once inspired some of Martin Opitz's best poetry, was ravaged twice by the French (in 1689 and 1692), and in the first of these sacks, Mélac won a kind of immortality by blowing up the Castle. In the same campaign of 1689, the old city of Speyer was so dreadfully devastated that "the wolves found nothing in its streets." The horrors of the Thirty Years' War returned to a community that, fifty-seven years before, had been taken by both Swedes and Spaniards.

Nor was life in the southeast any more secure. A Protestant revolt against Austrian Catholic despotism had occurred in Hapsburg Hungary, and Kara Mustafa, taking advantage of a situation which had been exacerbated by the *agents provocateurs* of France, invaded the Empire's unhappy march, won some easy victories, and pressed on to Vienna, thinking to succeed where Soliman the Magnificent had failed. This second Turkish siege of Vienna was carried out with a cruelty and a pomp the like of which the baroque century had not beheld before. Kara Mustafa's master of ceremonies recorded a minor incident of camp life in his diary of the expedition: "As it was announced to the Grand Vizier that one of the prisoners, who were employed in the army as drudges, had murdered his master, the Grand Vizier issued a command that all such prisoners be killed. The command was made known everywhere by the criers, and in that very hour one-hundred-and-fifty prisoners were beheaded before the executioner's tent. On the two following days, about one thousand prisoners were beheaded in the rest of the army." The blood baths which are a literary staple in works like Heinrich Anselm von Zigler und Klipphausen's *Die asiatische Banise oder das blutige, doch mutige Pegu (Asiatic Banise, or Bloody yet Brave Pegu,* 1689) or Lohenstein's Turkish and Roman tragedies, had their counterpart in fact.

The forces of Ernst Rüdiger von Starhemberg turned back the Turks, and the armies of the Emperor Leopold swept first into Hungary (where they triumphed not only over the Turks but over the rebellious Calvinists), then eastward to Transylvania and south toward the Balkans. Belgrade was captured by Ludwig of Baden in 1688, and it became apparent to the western world that Turkish power was on the decline. Not that the Turks gave way easily; Mustafa Köprili retook the city, despite a heroic defense by Count Aspremonte, in 1690, and it remained in their hands until "Prince Eugene, the Noble Knight" captured it in 1717. With the Peace of Passarowitz, Austria had won the heart of the Balkans; it had taken the Iron Gate and gone beyond it. The baroque age of the hero was drawing to a close, the age of southeastern colonization had begun. Johann Christian Günther's bombastic but moving "Gedicht auf den Passarowitzer Frieden" is one of the last pieces of baroque heroic poetry.

Prince Eugene is the happiest of the baroque's great heroes. He knew neither betrayal nor defeat, but was able to invest the financial rewards of his victories in splendid architecture: on his commission, Lukas von Hildebrandt designed the Upper and Lower Belvedere at Vienna. In the north, Prince Eugene had a contemporary of still sterner courage and with still nobler plans. Charles XII of Sweden did not leave palaces to serve as his memorial; Växjö's simple library is an example of the architecture that Charles gave Sweden. Instead, Charles gave his own life as a model not only to his countrymen – who indeed grew heartily tired of their king's overweening ambition – but to all non-Slavic Europe. Germany, in the course of Charles's campaigns against Augustus of Saxony, had suspected that the soldier-king would revive the old Swedish terror, yet Charles was not a freebooter, as men like Johan Banér had been; and when Charles began his march through Russia, the good wishes of Germany went with him: Leibniz addressed a poem to him and Barthold Feind, the Hamburg poet, wrote a drama on his exploits. At Poltava, Charles was defeated and, nine years later, he fell at the siege of Fredrikshall in Norway.

The ball which killed Charles was perhaps a Swedish one; it is possible that the last of baroque heroes – figures of monolithic will who fought not, in the end, for wealth or power but for glory – died at the hands of his own men. The heroic age and the age of faith died together in Charles, a most devout Lutheran who had the crusader's concept of his war against Peter of Russia. Charles was the last of his kind, and soon his name was used merely "to point a moral or adorn a tale." Men were becoming politic rather than grand and foolhardy; they had read a little book by a Jesuit which, although published in Spain in 1647, had its impact on the German baroque mind toward the end of the seventeenth century: Balthasar Gracian's little guide for the clever courtier, the *Oráculo manual*. Leibniz and Wolff were uttering cogent and attractive arguments for reason and optimism, and the reading public was slowly ceasing to care how one remained constant in the face of torture, despair, and death, that problem which had so disturbed the great baroque lyricists, Fleming, Gryphius, and Greiffenberg. The public began to worry instead about the methods of leading a wise life. At first, the wise man was seen as the statesman and leader (the subject, for example, of Lohenstein's courtly novel, *Der grossmüthige Feldherr Arminius: The Magnanimous General Arminius*, 1689-1690), and thus the grand proportions of the baroque were for a time preserved; but soon magnanimity, however politic, gave way to a concern with mere correctness of behavior. The German novel, which lately had been giving birth to masterpieces like Grimmelshausen's picaresque tales, now brought forth Christian Weise's *Die drei ärgsten Erznarren in der ganzen Welt (The Three Worst Arch-Fools in the Whole World)*. Weise's book was first published in 1672, and its popularity did not decrease as the rationalistic current in German thought grew ever stronger. The *Arch-Fools* were enjoying their tenth edition when, in 1710, Leibniz published his *Essais de théodicée sur la bonté de Dieu, la liberté de l'homme et l'origine du mal*, and gave the quietus to the baroque tension between good and evil, light and darkness, spirit and flesh. Germans, recovering at last from the wounds of the preceding century's wars, were happy to believe the Leibnizian postulation about the best of all possible worlds.

Although the literary baroque was drawing to a close – some of the last flashes of the old tension are to be found in the cutting epigrams of the Danish diplomatist, Christian Wernicke, and the strangely old-fashioned religious lyrics of the Prague Jesuit, Oppelt – the grandeur of the baroque style was not so easily eradicated from those arts, music and architecture, which for practical reasons could not flower in the midst of war. There were important composers who flourished during the Thirty Years' War: Heinrich

Schütz, born in 1585, a year after Georg Weckherlin, found refuge at courts like Copenhagen and Dresden, spared by the conflict; Dietrich Buxtehude, though a German, grew up in the quiet of Hälsingborg and obtained his first post there. Yet the great masters of baroque music came to maturity in an age when the literary baroque was dying. Händel and Bach were born in 1685, Georg Philipp Telemann was four years older than they and Reinhard Keiser, the operatic composer, eleven; but their music gives expression to the spiritual attitudes of the literary baroque. Händel treated distinctly baroque subjects like Samson, Joseph, and Hercules, Bach drew constant inspiration from the work of Paul Gerhardt (1607-1676), the finest writer of Lutheran church songs, Telemann served an apprenticeship with Kaspar Printz, composer and writer of picaresque novels; but beyond these connections of fact between old literature and new music lie the more intangible resemblances of style. Händel, a hundred years younger than Weckherlin, has precisely the same monumental dignity as the lyricist who graced both Stuttgart and London; Bach composes with the same religious conviction that informs the poems of Greiffenberg. Such resemblances may rest, one is aware, partly on illusion. However, nothing is more erroneous than to believe that the same style must appear simultaneously in all the major arts. German literary Romanticism, to take an example from another age, begins almost twenty-five years before its musical counterpart can be fairly called established.

The time-lag between the arts is still more evident if one examines the history of baroque architecture and painting. The baroque style in the plastic arts, as in music, flourishes in the last quarter of the seventeenth and the first two quarters of the eighteenth century. One can write poetry in the midst of war or under the threat of invasion; it is less likely that one will compose oratorios and operas, or build even a house, let alone a church or a palace. War, too, is a benefactor to the architect lucky enough to come after it; wreckage must be cleared away and new buildings built, and – in the baroque age, at any rate – the captains and the sutlers, grown wealthy from conflict, liked nothing better than to give their power a permanent form in stone. Men who had learned much of the vagaries of the baroque goddess, Fortuna, they tried to cheat her in the only way they knew. Reading Horace, they reflected that it was all very well to have a glorious reputation for their "monumentum aere perennius," but that a *Stadtpalais* was insurance taken out on glory. Likewise, the Roman Catholic Church, resting from its missionary labors during the Counter-Reformation, felt that it could at last afford the luxury of new churches; nor only luxury: these churches would be the outward sign of security newly re-won. The Church, happily, demonstrated in this time of construction a short memory;

forgetting that similar building programs had helped create the necessity for the Counter-Reformation, it gave Gaetano Pisoni the chance to build the cathedral of Saint Urs at Solothurn in Switzerland, and Jentsch von Hirschberg the cloister-church at Grüssau in Silesia. The south and the middle German lands, from the Aare to the Oder, received a priceless architectural gift from the *ecclesia triumphans*.

There arose a band of artists who took advantage of the situation to the fullest of their genius: architects like Fischer von Erlach, the master-builder of baroque Austria, Jakob Prandtauer, the creator of St. Florian, and Lukas von Hildebrandt, who, having served such Caesars as the Auerspergs, the Kinskys, and Prince Eugene, paid his debt to God with Cloister Göttweih; fresco-painters like Cosmos Damian Asam and his brother Egid Quirin, the designers and decorators of Weltenburg's heroic church; sculptors like Raphael Donner and Balthasar Permoser, the one of whom adorned Vienna, Graz, and Salzburg, the other Dresden, with statue upon statue. It is only artistic justice that the Roman Catholic Church and the Hapsburgs should have stood Maecenas to these workers and all their many contemporaries. During the baroque age, there was such a dearth of literary production in the Roman Catholic lands where German was spoken, that Herbert Cysarz, writing in the nineteen-twenties, could coin the famous and almost accurate aperçu on the division of artistic labor: north German baroque was, he said, "word-baroque," south German baroque, "image-baroque."

Why was the German North a breeding ground of the word, the South of the image? Or, more specifically, why did the Protestant culture of the German baroque produce poets, while the Catholic brought forth architects, sculptors, and painters? The answers to these questions seem easy enough to give. The Lutheran tradition respected the word, the Lutheran society, for all its intolerance – Jakob Böhme, the Silesian mystic, had to promise his pastor that he would write no more heresy – did not put that intolerance into effect with quite the savage force employed by Catholic prelates or temporal rulers. On the other hand, the Lutheran, and the Reformed, Churches had no use for decoration in the temple: had the Asams been born, say, on Brandenburg's sandy plain, they would have found small outlet for their peculiar genius. The greatest of the Northern plastic artists (and the North, despite Cysarz, did have artists in stone and oil, just as the South had some poets) was compelled to put his wine in secular bottles: Andreas Schlüter built palaces, not churches, and left an epitome of his work in the equestrian statue of the Great Elector at Berlin. The North had no princes of the church who would buy themselves wonderful domiciles, like the Residenz which Balthasar Neumann designed for the prince-bishops of Würzburg, or the castle at Pommersfelden, built by Dietzenhofer and Welsch to the taste of Lothar Franz von Schönborn, archbishop of Mainz. In North Germany, even secular princes were poor; the Hohenzollerns spent more money on their armies than their dwellings, and Schlüter finally had to seek a living from Slavic potentates with bigger pocketbooks and more flamboyant natures: Poniatowski in Warsaw and Peter of Russia in his new city on the Finnish Gulf. In the affluent South, there were the wealthy men of God, the soldiers who had profited from the Turkish Wars, the new "money-nobility" (of which Strauss's and Hofmannsthal's Herr von Faninal is an example) – and there was the Hapsburg court at Vienna, which, as Günther Müller has pointed out, served as model and spur to all the rulers of the South and Middle German lands, even before Louis XIV's Versailles had stimulated the imaginations of Germany's duodecimo sun-kings.

Nevertheless, having explained "word-baroque" and "image-baroque" thus easily, one is still troubled by the feeling that the reasons for the Catholic South's literary failure have not been sufficiently explored. There existed, obviously, no inherent fault in the Southern nature which prevented the development of literary genius: neither Bavaria nor the Austrian lands had heretofore played a Boeotian part. The great poets both of the high and the declining middle ages had come from south of the Main, even from the Alpine provinces, Charles IV's Prague had been the first home of German humanism, the University of Vienna, on the eve of the Reformation, attracted such free spirits as Conrad Celtis, Joachim von Waadt, and Ulrich Zwingli. But the events of the early sixteenth century changed the course of German literary history to an extent which, as Karl Viëtor's essay, "Luthertum, Katholizismus, und deutsche Literatur," demonstrates, has never been fully appreciated. Nations where Protestantism won but a few followers, nations like Spain, Italy, and France, continued to produce literature of the first rank; the German "Catholic" lands, where Protestantism had made great initial successes, did not. A strong foe in Germany, Protestantism frightened the Roman Church into the most repressive measures. Every effort was made to keep the disease of heresy from spreading, every effort was made to erect a wall between Protestant and Catholic German. The curtain was only paper, to be sure, but still effective. Luther's bible had given a part of Germany a national language, a language above dialects, but the German Catholic was forbidden to use it. Meanwhile, literature and learning passed more and more into the hands of the militant orders, whose members used Latin for their serious literary production, and German dialect for their sermons. "From now on there were not only two separate Christian churches; from the middle of the sixteenth century until the end of the eighteenth century there were also two different languages and literatures in Germany (and only here): a Protestant and a Catholic."

The literary spokesmen of German baroque Catholicism are: Jesuits and Benedictines who write Latin plays and verse, a handful of churchmen using the vernacular, and a few converts. The student of the baroque can only feel bitterness at the waste of genius occasioned by the use of Latin; here one finds virtuoso-compositions for an instrument long since obsolete. Jakob Balde, the Jesuit Horace, possessed one of the supreme lyric talents of his century; Herder attempted to save his *Carmina* from oblivion by translating them into German, but even he could not succeed, of course, in making Balde a part of German literature. As for Balde's few verses originally composed in German, they, like the German doggerel of Simon Rettenbacher, Salzburg's and Kremsmünster's Benedictine Latinist, but prove Viëtor's point: the German Catholic's native tongue was hopelessly unsuited to the demands of baroque verse. If the dramatists Jakob Bidermann and Nikolaus Avancinus had possessed a literary German, and had elected to write in it, there might exist German baroque drama still stageworthy today; certainly Bidermann's *Cenodoxus*, even in the wooden translation of Bidermann's contemporary, Joachim Meichel, is the liveliest play in the baroque canon.

The Catholic poets who wrote in their own language make dismal reading. With one exception, Friedrich Spee (who lived in the Rhineland and died in Trier, far from the Hapsburg center of Catholic power), the Catholic poet in German is neither the intellectual nor the artistic equal of the Latinist. Procopius von Templin composes dull songs to the Virgin Mary. Johann Martin (Laurentius von Schnüffis), court actor to the Archduke Karl Ferdinand of the Tyrol and later a Capuchin, is a poet now ridiculous, now witty. Ulrich Megerle (Abraham a Santa Clara), a Badenser who became Leopold I's court preacher, is fascinating by the inventiveness of his style; yet he, like Martin, is perhaps daring because he is cut off from a living tradition of good German – and perhaps because he may not be daring in his thought. The converts to Catholicism are literary men of a higher order. In some cases they remind one of the Romantic converts, who entered the Church as, in E. T. A. Hoffmann's words, "a sure harbor, which no storm may threaten." Johann Scheffler, "Angelus Silesius," became a Catholic and a priest only after the most painful spiritual crisis had exhausted him, Anton Ulrich of Brunswick-Wolfenbüttel joined the church at the end of a life filled with political tribulation. Lessing's favorite baroque poet, the Silesian Andreas Scultetus, appears to have pledged himself to Rome for another reason; he was not a religious thinker but rather painted religious scenes in verse, a talent which Scultetus' Catholic teachers evidently encouraged during their pupil's brief life: he died, twenty-five years old, at Troppau's Jesuit college. The most interesting *quaestio conversionis*, however, is provided by Grimmelshausen. Certainly that novelist, although he spent most of his lengthy military service with the Imperial forces, did not believe that "Catholic" troops were incapable of atrocities: the Emperor's faithful Croats were as bad as the marauding Swedes. One suspects that Grimmelshausen, having seen the suffering caused by intolerance from both sides, did not make too fine a distinction between the faiths, and that he must have been converted for some practical aim: he cared for Christianity, not sect. In *Simplicius Simplicissimus*, the hero discusses religion with the (Reformed) pastor at Lippstadt. "Jesus Maria," the soldier has said, and the horrified pastor rebukes him for calling on Mary's aid. Simplicius replies: "Should it then not become a Christian to name the mother of his Redeemer?" The pastor hastens to the counterattack with the observation that his young friend has taken communion neither at the Reformed church nor with the Lutherans. Simplicius replies with homespun nobility: "I confess that I am neither Petrine nor Pauline, but rather that I believe *simpliciter* what the twelve articles of the general holy Christian faith contain.... Will you not behold (but with my impartial eyes) what Konrad Vetter and Johannes Nas have publicly printed against Luther, and, on the other hand, what Luther and his followers have publicly printed against the Pope, but most especially what Spangenberg printed against Saint Francis, who some hundred years ago was regarded as a holy and a blessed man? Which side shall I join then, if each cries out about the other that it has not a speck of good in it?... and besides, there exist still more religions than those in Europe alone – the Armenians, Abyssinians, Greeks, Georgians, and the like."

How many baroque men felt as Simplicius did? One cannot be sure; the bitterness with which the Thirty Years' War was fought indicates that, for all the economic, diplomatic, and personal motivations involved, there were many indeed who believed that Luther was the devil incarnate, and just as many who shared Weckherlin's opinion, expressed in one of his sonnets on current events, that a priest, burned alive when some fireworks in a Jesuit drama got out of control, had reached hell a little earlier than he otherwise might. Yet, remembering the religious hatreds into which the partisans of both sides could excite themselves, remembering the bestialities committed in Christ's name by Catholic and Lutheran alike, remembering the persecutions of the Lutheran intelligentsia in the Austrian lands (a phenomenon with no precise analogy in Lutheran Germany: such however can be found in England, both

Anglican and Puritan): then one must conclude that the century's poets, though encouraged to intolerance by friend's and foe's deed, possessed either Grimmelshausen's somewhat ironic forbearance or an even finer tolerance. The baroque poets but rarely give expression to the sectarian rages of their time.

The history of the Counter Reformation in Austria is of particular importance for the study of the German baroque: its events help to answer the riddle of "Austria non cantat" posed above, and it illuminates, albeit by a kind of reflected light, the remarkable tolerance of the baroque poet. By the end of the third quarter of the sixteenth century, the majority of the townspeople in the Austrian duchies had become Lutheran, with a good part of the nobility and the peasantry following suit. The Emperor Maximilian II himself had in his salad days shown certain Protestant leanings; he even screwed up his courage enough to give his Lutheran citizens not inconsiderable privileges – no small thing for a man who had a chance of inheriting the Spanish throne. Christoph von Schallenberg (1561-1597), an Upper Austrian nobleman and a poet of the pre-baroque, served, despite his Lutheranism and his Tübingen training, as Maximilian's governor in Lower Austria and admiral of the Danube fleet. Outstanding figures from German Lutheranism were vied for by the excellent new Lutheran gymnasiums. Nicodemus Frischlin, rejecting a call to Graz, went instead to Laibach, but the burghers of Graz had their feelings assuaged when they captured Johannes Kepler, a young man of twenty-three, for their institution. Kepler's fate in the Austrian schools demonstrates what was happening to the Lutheran cause and, more important, to the cause of intellectual freedom. After the death in 1590 of Styria's liberal Archduke Karl, and six years of government by guardianship, Karl's son Ferdinand, destined to be emperor during the Thirty Years' War, brought a new spirit into the Graz Hofburg. Ferdinand surrounded himself with troops, sent "commissions" through the duchy to convert peasantry and bourgeoisie, and saw to it that Graz's Lutheran gymnasium was closed. It was still possible, to be sure, for young men to obtain an education in Styria: the Jesuits had founded a university in 1585, and a gymnasium the following year. Kepler left Graz in 1600, following a call to the imperial court at Prague, where he acted first as Tycho Brahe's assistant, then his successor. At length ,having failed to obtain the salary agreed upon, he departed for the gymnasium at Linz in Upper Austria. Kepler never went back to Styria, the starting point of his Austrian misadventures; only the nobility in that unhappy province was allowed to preserve its freedom of conscience, and the nobility, wishing to retain its lucrative posts as army provisioners and border officials, found that it could easily be persuaded to return to the old confession. Some noblemen were made of harder stuff, of course. Johann Wilhelm von Stubenberg, the Lutheran lord of Kapfenberg on the Mürz, retained his iron-rich lands, but published his important translations of contemporary Romance literature at Nürnberg. Understandably, he found it desirable to live the most of his days in Germany, too. However, one trace of the Protestant humanistic spirit remained alive and useful in the Austrian southeast. The celebrated Turkish grammar of Hieronymus Megiser, a Stuttgarter, pupil of Frischlin, and rector of the "Ständeschule" at Klagenfurt, was a necessary handbook for all officers on Balkan service,

Upper Austria was the most strongly Protestant province at the beginning of the seventeenth century, and the province which maintained a Protestant culture, despite oppression, for the longest time. The land above the Enns was in greater proximity to Protestant Germany than its sister duchies, it was safe from the Turkish peril, it had noblemen powerful and brave enough to struggle for their rights. The Jesuits arrived in Linz comparatively late, in 1600, and the Protestant opposition was so well organized that Kepler could retain his gymnasium post for fourteen years, from 1612 until 1626; there was, then, the opportunity for the development of a literature in no wise worse than that of Germany proper. Yet the great authors of Upper Austria, like the Irish masters of the twentieth century, all spent a part of their lives in exile; none died on his native soil. The case of Wolfgang Helmhard von Hohberg (1612-1688) is typical. Hohberg could say, with Heinrich Julius in Grillparzer's *Ein Bruderzwist in Hapsburg*: "Lord, I am a Protestant. In faith alone and not in opposition," for he had served bravely in the Imperial armies during the Thirty Years' War. In 1664, the very year in which he gave up the battle against religious oppression, sold his properties, and moved to Regensburg, he published his principal work and the chief verse epic of the baroque, *Der Hapsburgsche Ottobert*. In this poem, Hohberg glorified not only his titular hero, the fictitious ancestor of the Hapsburg family, but also, in an *Aeneid*-like prophecy, all future Hapsburgs, including the reigning and bigoted Leopold. Two years earlier, Catharina Regina von Greiffenberg, one of the baroque's supreme lyric geniuses, had elected to publish her *Geistliche Sonette, Lieder, und Gedichte* in Nürnberg, and from that time on she regarded the Franconian city as her home; although it was not until 1674 that she could bring herself to sell Castle Seyssenegg, her Upper Austrian birthplace [1], to a person of less heretical beliefs than hers. Thus Austria had succeeded in ridding itself of its epicist and its lyricist; the novelist was to follow. Johann Beer (1655-1700), the picaresque writer whose rediscovery is owed to Richard Alewyn, was twenty years younger than Greiffenberg and some forty-three years the junior of Hohberg; but he left his Upper Austrian homeland during those same hopeless 'sixties which saw the departure of the older poets. Beer's father, an innkeeper at Sankt Georg in the Attergau and a Lutheran, fled with his family to Regensburg, where Hohberg and many another Austrian refugee resided. After studies in his adopted city, Beer went to Leipzig, Halle, and finally, Weissenfels, at whose court he served as chief musician. Beer is the last major Austrian-born author before Grillparzer, who saw the light of day in 1791, and Grillparzer, in his turn, is the first major poet from a Catholic home since Friedrich von Spee (1591-1635). The Counter Reformation had done its work well.

Nonetheless, the literary victims of the Hapsburg persecutions seldom complained at the injustice of their lot, and in their forbearance they followed the tolerant pattern of their Silesian colleagues, who had also suffered, although by no means so severely, from the pressures that Vienna exerted. Baroque literature has few examples of anti-papistic feeling to be compared with those produced during the *Kulturkampf*, the rather artificial religious crisis produced by Bismarck's political ambitions on the one hand and Pius IX's obscurantism on the other. Baroque poets rarely indulge in the distasteful bigotry which mars the work of some of the nineteenth century's most admirable artists: like Theodor Fontane, who implied, in *Cécile* and *Graf Petöfy* ,that there was a connection between Roman Catholicism and sexual immorality, or like C. F. Meyer, with his protracted jibe at Catholic perfidy *(Das Amulett)* and his wolf-faced Jesuit *(Das Leiden eines Knaben)*. Instead, in one of the best baroque novels, *Die adriatische Rosemund* (1645), Philipp von Zesen discusses, fairly and dispassionately, the tragedy growing out of a love affair between a Protestant Silesian nobleman and a beautiful Venetian Catholic maiden. Sünnebald, Rosemund's father, will not allow his daughter to change her faith for Markhold's sake, and so she pines away and dies. Neither Sünnebald, Markhold, nor poor Rosemund is depicted as a bigot; Sünnebald, indeed, is the most charming and urbane of men. The tragedy arises from the time, not from the actors and actresses placed against its harsh backdrop.

Zesen and Grimmelshausen are not the only novelists to have addressed themselves to the problems of sectarianism. Johann Beer's *Narren-Spital* (1681) is as coarse a book as Zesen's *Rosemund* is refined; yet it continues the probing of bigotry, begun by Zesen and continued by Grimmelshausen, to a conclusion which prepares, as it were, for the religious indifference of the *Aufklärung*. Hans, Beer's picaro, argues religion with his master, Lorenz, and learns that Lorenz has far more interest in priests' housekeepers and pastors' wives than in the clergymen's faith. But Hans persists: "'Which minister has pleased you best, the Lutheran, the Catholic, or the Calvinist?' 'Ha,' he replied, 'There was nothing special about any of the three. They stood on their legs and struck out with both fists; I thought they'd give me a box on the ear if I got any closer to them. Yet the Lutherans had big books lying beside them, and so I thought: *ex libro doctus quilibet esse potest* (anyone can become learned from a book).'" A generation before, Logau had asked:

Lutheran, Popish, Calvinistic, all of these confessions three
Stand before us, yet we wonder where then Christendom may be.

Lorenz, and Beer, have ceased to look for it.

Thus apathy and contempt took possession of the artist's mind; it was well for baroque literature that this final slackening of the religious nerve came so late. Despicable as religious bickering is, and as little productive of good literature (who can read the polemics of the Reformation?), religious passion has always sown lyric and dramatic seeds: no period of German literature has produced religious poetry even remotely comparable, in range and in strength, to that of the baroque. The baroque poets do not channel their religious fervor into recriminations against Vienna or Rome, however severe the wounds they or their homelands have been dealt. Greiffenberg speaks no ill of pope or Hapsburg; instead, while not failing to lament the misery of the human condition, she devotes her best energies to fathoming and celebrating the ways of God. Gryphius, for all the woes which religious strife visited upon his divided Silesia, behaved as Greiffenberg did: he lamented man's lot and celebrated God's splendor, but, even in the careless days before he became an official, sent only the bluntest of arrows at the colossi in the south.

It would be an injustice to suspect Greiffenberg and Gryphius of being vaguely enthusiastic "God-seekers," baroque equivalents of that type which proliferated in German literature at the beginning of the twentieth century; daughter and son of the seventeenth century, they knew scripture and they knew dogma, but they placed the religious ecstasy above the sect. Spiritually, they are the immediate forebears of the pietists, who were so eager to contemplate the face of God that they employed every instrument, Lutheran, Calvinist, and Catholic, to achieve that special vision. If faith reduced to the absurd could produce indifference in satirical observers like Beer (and in finely strung lyricists, too: a stoic anti-Christianity can be detected in Hofmannswaldau and, more especially, in Lohenstein), the same faith could inspire stronger spirits to lift themselves above the warfare of factions – nominally religious but as often political – to a higher and purer realm.

Greiffenberg, Gryphius, and some of their contemporaries suffered from a sublime blindness to the seamier sides of the religious life, a blindness which makes them, to the modern reader, appear perhaps more "tolerant" than they in truth were. The sublime blindness was born of faith, just as a good many of the century's dreadful enormities were; faith penetrated every corner of the baroque psyche in an astonishing measure – the more astonishing because it was so soon to vanish. Faith was a real thing, a food without which life could scarcely be lived, a food which the perils of war made seem still more desirable. "Your cause is God's. March to that end/ And to His hand yourself commend!/ Thus you need fear no peril," runs the "field psalm" of Gustav Adolf's troops, and they believed its promise to the letter. Faith, into whatever ugly shapes it might be twisted, was not lightly to be cast aside; and when at last it did begin to fall into disrepute, the Turkish armies were on the retreat, and the soldiery which so often plundered the German west had given way to the better disciplined French troops of the eighteenth century: the unspeakable Mélac was the last of his kind.

Indispensable faith, then, raised the baroque poets above religious factions, and other, cultural influences were at work upon them too, keeping them from the intransigeance into which pastor and priest were frozen. Few periods of German literature have been more influenced by foreign cultures (and of all the major literatures, the German most readily accepts influences from abroad): the influences came, by and large, from Catholic lands and Catholic poets. To be sure, many of the artists who unwittingly helped to form the German baroque were almost as unwitting in their Catholicism; what is strikingly Catholic about Ronsard or du Bellay? Yet others, like the Spaniards Cervantes, Lope de Vega, and Calderon, certainly had *animae naturaliter catholicae*, and that playwright who made the greatest impact upon the development of the Silesian dramatic school was a convert to Catholicism: Joost van den Vondel became a member of the Roman Church in 1641, at the very time when Gryphius was in Holland, studying, among other things, the plays of the "Dutch Shakespeare." Save for the writers of Lutheran church songs – for the most part, Lutheran churchmen themselves – no non-Catholic poet of the baroque kept free from contact with the Catholic world. Many a young author traveled in Italy and Spain, and the Silesians, whose works compose the main part of the baroque corpus, lived in a milieu where they were daily confronted with Catholics and Catholic thought. The Church in Silesia was not in a position of undisputed power; it had to put a better foot forward than it did in Austria. Likewise, Martin Opitz did not think it incongruous with his fathers' faith when he took service with a rabid anti-Lutheran, Burggraf Karl Hannibal von Dohna, at Breslau, and later became the official historiographer of His Catholic Majesty,

Vladislav IV of Poland. Lohenstein served as Imperial Councillor, and flattered Leopold both in the choruses of his *Sophonisbe* and in *Arminius*, while his co-religionists were being driven from Upper Austria; Lohenstein's fellow Breslauer, Hofmannswaldau, although not as frequent a visitor in Vienna, had no compunctions about being an Imperial Councillor, too.

Other factors also kept the baroque poets from making religious mischief. The language societies, those organizations for the purification of the mother tongue modeled after the Florentine "Accademia della crusca," had among their rules one expressly forbidding religious controversy at their meetings or among their members. The members of the baroque Parnassus, however religious they were, ranked art above sect. Leibniz wrote an elegy on the Jesuit Spee, Moscherosch, a militant Protestant who in his *Gesichte Philanders von Sittewald* paints the Swedish troops in brightest colors, took the trouble to edit the works of Jakob Wimpheling (1450-1528), priest, Latin dramatist, and opponent of the Reformation. The Protestant authors had to look backward for their Catholic "friendships," to be sure; the orders had succeeded in ruining the crop of lay Catholic poets. Otherwise, one could well imagine that there might, in the midst of all the religious strain, have come to pass relationships like those in American intellectual history of the nineteenth century, when Henry Adams, straight from Boston's Unitarian stronghold, had the artist John Lafarge, Fordham graduate and leading Catholic layman, as his best friend and traveling companion.

There were, marvelous to say, states, rulers, and even churchmen that indulged in syncretic practices or visions. Curiously, it was from Calvinist soil that much seventeenth century tolerance sprang. The reasons for this development, which surely must have made the gloomy Genevan turn over in his grave, are far too complicated to be investigated here: perhaps it occurred, in part at least, because the Calvinists were compelled by their creed to avoid the involvement with temporal power which darkens both Lutheran and Catholic history in the German lands. Calvinism, in its pure form, denied every unlimited earthly rule, because only God Himself was omnipotent. Thus, Calvinism could not become the tool of the absolutist prince to the same extent that Lutheranism and Catholicism did. Even Cromwell, the Calvinist dictator, believed that he had established a theocracy; and Calvinism flourished precisely in those lands where the nobility, or a strong burgher-class, was attempting to throw off an absolutist yoke, in the Netherlands, Scotland, Hungary, and, to a lesser extent, in France and Poland. Holland is the classical example of the Calvinist state where, for every citizen and every visitor, complete freedom of conscience pertained; here, rather than in the Lutheran states of Germany, Luther's wonderful formula, the basis of Protestantism, had come true: "Each man is free and is as if his own conscience." Many of Germany's baroque poets received a part – often the most important part – of their intellectual training in the Netherlands. Gryphius is the best-known example, but scarcely the only one: Zincgref, Opitz, Fleming, Lauremberg, Schottel, Zesen, Harsdörffer, Birken, Hofmannswaldau, Assmann von Abschatz, Scheffler, Kuhlmann, and Canitz all sojourned in the Netherlands, be it as student, traveler, or (as in Kuhlmann's case) peregrinating religious fanatic. Nor were the Estates-General, which provided not only a training ground for Germany's poets but a sanctuary for such unlike souls as the wise Amos Comenius, the rakehell Charles II of England, and the intrigant Korfitz Ulfeld, the only land where Calvinism fostered tolerance. Even in Geneva, once the bloody days of Calvin himself were over, an unusual gentleness of spirit began to reign. The Jesuit Edmund Campion passed through Geneva in 1580, on his way to England and martyrdom. Despite the fact that Campion and his party confessed their faith and their mission to the town's magistrates, they were treated with exquisite courtesy. Thereupon, Campion and his friend Persons, pressing their luck, sought out the venerable Theodore Beza, Calvin's successor, and badgered him with religious questions. Beza, after having given them a patient hearing, sent them two Anglicans, with whom they argued far into the night. Miguel Servetus, it seems, had made the mistake of visiting Geneva a quarter of a century too soon.

The few Calvinist princes in Germany also distinguished themselves by their unique broadmindedness. Johann Friedrich, Electoral Prince of Brandenburg, was a Lutheran, but sent his son, Johann Sigismund to study at Heidelberg, the intellectual center of German Calvinism. In 1613, Johann Sigismund, becoming a Calvinist ruler over a Lutheran land, did not exercise his prerogative of "cujus regio, ejus religio" against his subjects in Brandenburg, just as he would not put it into force against the Catholics of Jülich-Cleve. His grandson, the Great Elector (who spent much of his youth in Holland), forbade the preachers of both the Reformed and the Lutheran churches to curse one another in their sermons; in the same noble tradition he welcomed the refugees from the Edict of Nantes to Berlin, Brandenburg-Prussia became, religiously, the most tolerant of the German states; Bismarck's anti-Catholic policies were distinctly at variance with the age-old custom of his nation.

The Electors of Brandenburg were not the only German Calvinist rulers to show what good stuff they were made of. Karl Ludwig of the Palatinate, son of the unhappy "Winter King," should have fallen heir to some strong resentments against his father's rapacious Catholic foes and false Lutheran friends; yet when he received his lands again at the Peace of Westphalia, he saw to it that Catholics and Lutherans had the same rights as members of the Reformed Church. In Mannheim, Karl Ludwig founded the "Kirche zur heiligen Eintracht" (Church of Holy Harmony), where members of all three confessions might worship. However, this last flowering of Calvinist tolerance in the Palatinate was short-lived; the House of Simmern was succeeded by the Catholic Neuburgs, and during the reigns of the bigot brothers, Johann Wilhelm (1690-1716) and Karl Philipp (1716-1742), Catholicism was propagated with a sternness that would have made the Hapsburgs blush – and that helped to populate North America. Nevertheless, it must not be thought that only Calvinist rulers were capable of tolerance; when Anton Ulrich of Brunswick-Wolfenbüttel embraced the Roman faith, he let his subjects stay Lutheran.

Beside the miracle of the tolerant ruler stood the miracle of the tolerant churchman. A Spaniard, Cristoforo Rojas de Spinola, a general of the Franciscan Order who served from 1685 until 1695 as Bishop of Wiener Neustadt, acted in a way quite at odds with recent Hapsburg policy. In co-operation with Leibniz, Spinola worked out a plan for the reunion of Catholics and Protestants; the latter had only to recognize the Pope as an administrative head of the newly reconstituted church. Despite Cardinal Bossuet's approval of the scheme, Louis XIV, who had every reason to encourage dissension in Germany, helped bring the efforts of the bishop and the philosopher to naught. Truth to tell, dreams of spiritual unity had as active enemies within Germany as without. The Lutheran church, placed on guard by the Catholic resurgence, threatened by imperial troops, was thus put by external happenings into a mood of rigid dogmatism. Internally, it had passed the age of experiment, when Melanchthon's gentle irony had softened the stubborn self-righteousness of Luther, and had entered a period of crystallization, when Wittenbergian infallibility was set over against Roman. The tradition of Melanchthon did survive, however, in Georg Calixtus, born Jörgen Callisen at Medelby in Slesvig and, from 1614 until his death in 1656, professor of theology at Helmstedt. Calixtus, whose father had been Melanchthon's pupil, kept the humanistic strain in Lutheranism alive; returning, as a good humanist, to the sources, he argued that a common concept of Christianity might be drawn from the church fathers; upon this concept, a reunion of Lutheranism, Calvinism, and Catholicism might be based. Among unselfish statesmen and non-theologians, the opinions of Calixtus were well received; but soon the poor man found himself waging theological war on two fronts. He was attacked from the one side by Catholics, from the other by his fellow Lutherans, who contemptuously dismissed his theories as "syncretism," a word which even today is often used pejoratively in theological circles. Calixtus' chief opponent was Abraham Calovius, professor at Wittenberg and the very model of an orthodox Lutheran theologian of the baroque: immensely learned, hateful to a fault, and zealous pursuer of "heresy." Calixtus is remembered for himself and his works; Calovius is remembered because he epitomizes that inflexibility which caused German Lutheranism's inward death. Under Calovius and his small imitators, Lutheranism ceased to be a home for the Protestant who believed "each man is free."

Here lies still another cause for the apparent tolerance prevalent among the Lutheran-born poets of the baroque. They suspected that the mighty fortress of orthodox Lutheranism was not worth holding; certainly, they would not make any very savage sallies from its walls. The poets of the Lutheran persuasion did not turn their backs completely on their faith, as the great figures of German classicism did, a century later and more. They were not yet prepared to abandon Lutheranism, but, once the initial enthusiasms of the Thirty Years' War had passed, they could not even wax excessively hot about its defense. They were, as Burckhardt later said, caught between "two orthodoxies."

The Protestant spirit in religion, once aroused, was not to be easily suppressed by men of Calovius' ilk. There had existed in Germany since the middle ages a strong mystical current, the bearers of which attempted to find an individual and personal way to God; the Dominican Master Eckhart, with his "innermost ground of soul" which was directly one with the Godhead, died just in time to avoid considerable embarrassment from the Inquisition's tribunals, and, two hundred years later, Thomas Münzer, the leader of the Anabaptists, fell mortally afoul of Martin Luther by listening to an "inner word." Sebastian Franck, a contemporary of Münzer who harkened to an "inner voice," conceived of a Christianity at once tolerant and practical; unlike the pugnacious Münzer, Franck had the good sense to seek sanctuary in Basel, and suffered no fate worse than being called a "devil's mouth" by Luther. Franck, in his turn, coined an apter phrase; he spoke of the "old and the new papacy." In the course of the sixteenth century, as the old and the new papacies first sparred, then prepared for battle, other figures appeared who, like Franck, sought salvation, or tried to fathom the divine mysteries, according to procedures of their own devising. Franck himself, though trained as a priest, had abandoned any clerical office; instead he made his living as a printer, all the while busily communing with God. In Franck's wake there came ambiguous vagabonds, like the Swiss physician Paracelsus, or, with his real name, Theophrastus Bombastus von Hohenheim. The dictum of Paracelsus, that "man is not only flesh and blood, but in addition a body that is too transparent for coarse eyes," gave ammunition not only to baroque pansophists but to Carl Gustav Jung himself. There were vaguely sinister students of the occult like Agrippa von Nettesheim, there were astrologists like the Cantabrigian, Dr. John Dee, who, after advising Good Queen Bess of the stars' wisdom, tried to make gold for Rudolf II at Prague. Finally, there were noble spirits like Valentin Weigel, pastor at Zschoppau in Saxony, who quietly planted a bomb in the walls of Lutheranism. Twenty years after Weigel's death (1588), his works were published – much to the horror of his bereaved colleagues, for Weigel had proclaimed that the theologian, that customs-man between God and man, was quite useless: "For this indeed we theologians should have learned from Christ, that Paradise or Heaven or the Kingdom of God or the Father or the Son is not to be sought or to be found outside of us... but rather we shall become blessed within us, and behold God and see Him face to face, and not at all outside of us."

With these words, in the *Dialogus de Christianismo*, Weigel has postulated one of the two basic tenets on which baroque mystical poetry is built, and in *Morgenröte im Aufgang (The Dawn Ascending*, 1612), Jakob Böhme, a shoemaker from Görlitz in the forests of western Silesia, postulated the other: "Each man is free, and as if his own God, he may transform himself in this life into wrath or into light; whatever dress each man puts on, that dress transfigures him." The mystic poet of the baroque becomes a hero, the favorite figure of the age; for, without the aid and protection of dogma and dogma's executor, the pastor or priest, the mystic poet is free to approach God as he likes, and to succeed or fail as he can. The road is fraught with peril: Böhme, like the poets, and the plastic artists, who followed him, beheld a world in which good and evil, light and darkness, are in constant and eternal battle; indeed, Böhme skirted depths of which a baroque dramatist like Gryphius, with his monolithic Christian heroes and heroines, did not dream. "One cannot say of God that he is good or bad, or is this or that"; God, this "Urkraft," this "Ungrund," contains all possibilities.

While the Lutheran hymnists of the baroque century wrote their mighty hymns of awe at God's power and trust in His might, such as Rist's "O Ewigkeit, du Donnerwort" and Gerhardt's "Befiehl du deine Wege/ Und was dein Hertze kränkt" (familiar to American Lutheran audiences in, strangely enough, John Wesley's translation: "Commit thou all thy griefs/ And ways into His hands"), the Silesian mystic poets wrote epigrams which bespoke a far greater religious daring. First came Abraham von Frankenberg, a country gentleman who wrote two biographies of Böhme; he was followed by Daniel von Czepko, a member of the Frankenberg circle in whom wit and religiosity had a happy marriage, and finally by Frankenberg's protégé, the physician Johann Scheffler. Each of the trio carried the spiritual foolhardiness of Böhme a little farther. Frankenberg put Böhme's inseparable opposites, good and evil, into his verse:

> Naught has in the wisdom of God been lit
> That did not in that hour devise its opposite.

Czepko, both a secular and a mystic poet, leads his readers into the puzzles of theosophy:

> Who sees God, sees a naught. That which cannot be told,
> That same naught he does see, and Him does all behold.

Johann Scheffler, "Angelus Silesius," less sophisticated than Czepko, takes more daring flights than he, writing those famous epigrams of identification with God (an identification which is the final goal of the mystic experience) before he falls back into Catholicism's protecting arms. In 1653 Scheffler became a convert and, eight years later, a priest, passing thus from the outlawry of extreme mysticism to the army of extreme orthodoxy. A militant Catholic, Scheffler spent his later years issuing hateful polemics against Protestantism – which, indeed, had failed to provide a spiritual home for him or his kind – and even called the Turkish invasions God's way of punishing Germany for the Lutheran heresy. Scheffler had one of the conceivable fates of the mystic; Quirinus Kuhlmann, the mad Breslauer who thought to found a new world empire, "das Kuhlmannstum," had another. He was burned alive at Moscow, by order of that city's patriarch, after he had made a nuisance of himself in such different places as Leyden and Constantinople. Böhme's heroism of the spirit had degenerated into a lunatic's chiliasm, religious individualism into religious madness. Mysticism had destroyed itself, as it must; but the best of it lived on in pietism, whose followers believed simply that Christianity was not a body of knowledge but a continual act of love.

It was perhaps in pietism that the syncretic visions of Calixtus came closest to realization; it was principally in pietism's form that the religious fervor of the baroque was transmitted to the eighteenth century. Like mysticism, pietism grew out of Lutheranism; unlike mysticism, with which it has many points of contact and agreement, it did not consume itself in paradox, but threw its energies into a practical expression of Christian love. Johann Arndt, its forerunner (1555-1626), was a prominent Lutheran churchman who attained the lofty post of "Generalsuperintendent" at Celle in Lower Saxony. With his *Vier Bücher vom wahren Christentum* (1605), an "Imitatio Christi" for those who would rather live as Christ than merely contemplate Him, Arndt prepared for the good deeds of the pietists to come: "all that is treated in theology has life as its aim," wrote his disciple, Johann Gerhard. Still another Lutheran churchman is called "pietism's father": the Alsatian Philipp Jakob Spener, who was reared in the semi-Calvinistic atmosphere of Alsatian Lutheranism, and indeed studied in Geneva, where he got to know Jean de Labadie, sometime Jesuit and present Calvinist. Even at the time of the meeting between young Spener and Labadie, the latter had begun to think that Calvinism, too, had perverted the idea of the true Christian community (the mystic thinks as an individual, the pietist in terms of the community). In 1668, after having served as spiritual shepherd to a Walloon congregation in the Netherlands, Labadie withdrew from the Reformed church, organizing his own "pure community." Some of Labadie's notions – he called marriages between "unbelievers" null and void – were too much even for the celebrated tolerance of the Dutch, and Labadie's band fled first to Herford in Westphalia, then to Altona, and finally to the wastes of Dutch Frisia, where, in the eighteenth century, it dwindled and died. Labadie's followers suffered what was to be the classic fate of later pietistic groups: their community was too pure in its intent and, eventually, too weak against the wiles of the world.

Spener, it may be, perceived in Labadie the dangers awaiting a man who would organize a Christian community outside a recognized church. At any event, Spener stayed a Lutheran minister all his days, devoting himself to a reformation of his faith from within. In 1666, the year that Labadie assumed his final Calvinist post, Spener became "Senior der Geistlichkeit" at Frankfurt am Main, and there wrote the *Pia Desideria*, in which he recommended, before all things, simplicity as a cure to Lutheranism's faults: simplicity of church organization, of oratory from the chancel, of belief itself. But of Spener's recommended reforms the most fateful was the suggestion that private individuals conduct bible-hours and house-services in their own homes: Spener's fellow ministers were mightily suspicious of this apparent surrender of authority. Despite the damage done Spener by his over-zealous followers, who demanded a clean separation of the "collegia pietatis" from the mother church, Spener succeeded in obtaining for himself excellent posts at Dresden and Berlin. In Berlin he had the support of the Reformed court, which revealed, as ever, a keen interest in practical Christianity; it was under Spener's leadership that the University of Halle was founded (1694), receiving the pietistic stamp which it retained throughout the eighteenth century.

While Spener was struggling for pietistic interests in Berlin, a young Lutheran theologian from Lübeck, August Hermann Francke, found that his own pietistic enthusiasms – he had undergone a marvelous conversion to "living Christianity" in 1687 – were getting him into trouble not with his fellow Protestants but with their Catholic rivals. As deacon at Erfurt's Augustinerkirche, Francke made Christianity such a lively matter that he won many converts among Erfurt's Catholic citizens. The prince-archbishop of Mainz, under whose control Erfurt lay, got wind of Francke's success and gave the young man forty-eight hours to leave the city. Spener, wirh characteristic directness, got Francke the chair of oriental languages at Halle, whose faculty immediately received an object lesson in the application of charity to education. Francke founded a school for the children of the well-to-do in which humane pedagogy was the order of the day; then he established a free school for the poor, from which grew his famous orphanage. Nor was Francke only concerned with the education, rather than the exploitation, of children; by means of his "Cansteinsche Bibelanstalt" he produced low-priced Bibles for the poor.

Pietism still lacked an authentic genius of the pen, however; this genius it found in Gottfried Arnold. Arnold, like Spener and Francke, was a Lutheran minister – he had been trained at Wittenberg itself – and like his predecessors, he managed to stay all his life within the church, a remarkable accomplishment when one considers the nature of his major work, and the gigantic mass of polemical writings aroused by it. In the *Unparteyische Kirchen- und Ketzerhistorie (Impartial History of Churches and Heretics*, 1699-1702), the villains are the clergy of the organized churches, Catholic or Protestant, the heroes are those simple seekers after truth whom formal Christianity condemns as "heretics." Arnold stated the pietistic case with a brilliance (and a concommittant exaggeration), which moved Christian Thomasius to call it "the best and most useful book which we have had *in hoc scribendi genere*." Literary historians also remember Arnold for another accomplishment; together with the "Reformed pietists," Neander and Tersteegen, and (later on) Zinzendorf, Arnold is a principal representative of the pietistic song, the effects of which can be detected in German literature as late as Novalis' *Geistliche Lieder*. In Arnold's songs one sees the best and the worst of what pietism gave to letters. Deeply interested in the personal experience, especially that of conversion, pietism furnished later baroque literature with a dimension it had lacked. For all its emotionalism, the baroque lyric before pietism expressed emotion in set, albeit brilliant, formulae. Pietism – which also produced important autobiographical works by Spener, Francke, and, in Goethe's day, Jung-Stilling – taught men a new and more personal vocabulary: it is the tension between baroque formalism and pietistic individualism that makes the lyrics of Johann Christian Günther so fascinating. Yet something sickly lay in the pietistic song, too: the tendency to confuse the religious and the erotic experience. Greiffenberg expressed her love of God in intellectual terms, Friedrich Spee wrote of the "Gespons Jesu," the "bride of Christ," with such pastoral grace that the reader is seldom offended; but Arnold and his colleagues engage in spiritual dalliances that are disquieting, to say the least. In "The Soul Refreshes Itself With Jesus," Arnold writes:

> Thus sweet do the paramours play at their games
> And fan in their playing the heavenly flames.
> The one makes the other one's pleasure but grow,
> And both do of naught but of loving's deed know.

Religious ecstasies, from whatever time and nation, easily admit psychological interpretation as something inspired more by the libido than by God; and in the confessions of the pietists, frequently simple folk and quite incapable of putting a veneer on their spiritual adventures, one can come across the most startling traffic between flesh and soul. Arnold, in the *Kirchen- und Ketzer-historie*, includes the autobiographical sketch by Anna Vetter, a stonemason's wife. Blessed with seven children in ten years of unhappy marriage, Anna came down with an illness which she attributed to the incantations of a neighbor woman. "In this my illness my husband once came home very early from the castle and got into bed with me and forced me to do his will, and I became pregnant with a daughter, against my wish and desire, for I was weak and sick.... When I was ten days pregnant with this child, I was taken up into Heaven and beheld indescribable joy. Oh joy! Oh splendor! Oh eternity! Oh beauty!" Her visions include "a mighty four-square oaken cudgel" which she "must carry about everywhere," a "mighty pregnant woman," and a rape committed by the stonemason on the hapless Anna while she lies in chains. The visionary is a woman of strong passions who, with apparent suddenness but actually after long preparation, has transferred her affections from her clumsy yet potent husband to Jesus Christ. As a matter of fact, Anna makes her new marriage retroactive: she has a vision of her wedding day (with the stonemason), and among the guests there appears a stranger, asking: "'Where is the woman who can dance so well?'.... So I know surely that Jesus Christ came to me even on my wedding day."

Anna Vetter suffered from the itch that seems to have raged with special violence in the baroque age; others, who likewise gave literary expression to their feelings, kept love of the flesh and love of Christ somewhat better separated than she did. Eroticism, quite naturally, is at work in the literary production of all ages; the man and the woman of the baroque, however, felt the Old Adam with a violence which, if not unique in itself, at least received an expression of incomparable directness. Baroque eroticism can be obscene, to be sure, but its obscenity is almost always graceful; it has nothing to equal the ugly lustings of Wittenweiler's Triefnas' and Ruerenzumph, and it but rarely engages in the scatology of "Grobianism" and the Shrovetide plays. It has occasionally been called perverse, but whatever perverseness it demonstrated is the result of excessive strength rather than impotence; the baroque has no Stanislaw Przybyszewski, no Hans Henny Jahnn.

The direct violence of baroque passion is part and parcel of the time. The baroque hero stands like a rock against a sea of troubles or of Turks, the baroque religionist seeks to come face-to-face with God, the baroque lover feels a desire which climbs higher, in his elegantly explicit speech, than any mast. The baroque lover may very easily grow sick from the fevers of his love, but he does not mope about his fate; if his unambiguous pleas are not answered, he will try his luck elsewhere. The Minnesingers or Werther or Adolphe would have seemed incomprehensible, or silly, to the baroque man:

> Yet if her heart without a counter-love would be,
> To what shall I be pledged by Sylvia, my sweet?

asks Assmann von Abschatz, deserting his frigid love. Cardenio, in Gryphius' pseudo-tragedy, *Cardenio und Celinde*, loves Olympia, but refuses to marry her upon learning that Lysander has forced his way into her bed-chamber. Olympia weds the nocturnal intruder, and Cardenio, in a pet, takes up with Celinde, whose earlier lover, Marcellus, he kills. Then, tiring of Celinde, he again lusts after Olympia – and all conflicts are resolved by magic and some handy conversions to a chaster way of life. Cardenio, if he is a Werther at all, is a Werther of lust, not sentimental love. Now and then, people die of unrequited love in baroque literature: Zesen's Rosemund is a case in point; but Rosemund, after all, is a high-strung Venetian lady, and one cannot be sure that her Markhold will not find consolation with a beauty who, like the successor to David Schirmer's deceased Marnia, has inherited all the sweet equipment of the former love.

At the beginning of the seventeenth century, Aegidius Albertinus, the moralizing secretary of Maximilian of Bavaria, paid Venus a handsome tribute in his warning against her: "The most excellent net with which the Devil catches souls is a lustful woman. The ancients, that they might depict the great power of love, painted her with a flower in her right hand and a dolphin in her left; the flower, to be sure, she had plucked from the earth and she had drawn the fish out of the water: hereby it is indicated that love extends to all the places of the whole world, that it rules on land as well as on the sea, and that no one is safe from its arrows." Albertinus' praiseful warning was repeated a thousand times by the poets of the baroque; they knew from experience that what the crabbed Dutchman said was true. Grimmelshausen, whose works offer the fullest picture of the actualities of baroque life, reveals on almost every page that lust, after religion, was the chief moving force in the baroque man. His Simplicius, in his contemplative Lippstadt days, has six mistresses at once; in Paris he is kidnapped and spends eight days as the lover of – if he can judge aright – four French ladies. Lust gnaws at Simplicius throughout the most of his life; even after he is shocked into self-examination by the death of his friend, Herzbruder, he finds himself once more "entangled in the cords of Venus, or, better said, in the fool's rope," and since he can "satisfy [his] bestial desires in no other way," he decides to marry a peasant girl. (His first wife has long since passed away.) The fruit of the marriage is double, or even triple: his bride bears a child who looks like the man-servant, the house-maid brings a child with Simplicius' face into the world, and, on the selfsame night, Simplicius finds a third babe lying on his doorstep. Some months before, he had met a beautiful lady at a spa in the Black Forest, and she had given him "not only free entrance, but also every delight": of this entrance and delight the third infant had been born.

Nevertheless, as he grows old, Simplicius repents of his fleshly sins; the fair lady of the Saurbrunnen does not, for she is the Landstörzerin Courasche, the heroine of the most famous of the *Simplicianische Schriften*, the writings in which Grimmelshausen expands upon his original picaresque narrative. Daniel Defoe's Moll Flanders spends her twilight years in Virginia, prosperous and penitent. Courasche, in the introduction to her tale, tells the reader baldly that "what I lack is repentance." Neither Defoe nor Grimmelshausen is a clumsy psychologist, and the attitudes of their heroines, grown old, are completely congruous with their respective pasts. Moll, at bottom, has been more sinned against than sinning, the victim of sophisticated lechers and poverty, while Courasche but once in her life, under extraordinary circumstances, finds her "otherwise unquenchable fleshly appetites" put to rest. Even trickery and deceit, to which she devotes much of her almost superhuman energy, do not fascinate her as does that "Gaukelfuhr," from which, so far as one knows, she never leaves off.

Not only rogues and camp followers suffered from Cupid's itch; the whole age could say with Donne: "All rest my powers defy;/ Until I labor, I in labor lie." Even an honorable churchman like Friedrich Lucae, who turned his passion straightway into honorable channels, wrote after he had first seen a certain maiden: "My singing blood and excited heart seemed to me to be a sign that the spirit of love must have some special intent with me, since never in my life had I borne such lustful affection to any maiden as I did to this one." And another honorable churchman, Johann Rist, composed songs about Daphnis with an authentic Catullian ring ("Come let yourself a thousand times, come let yourself a thousand times be by your Daphnis kissed"), songs that had a wide popularity in the baroque, as did the plain-spoken ditties of the *Venus-Gärtlein* and of Caspar Stieler's *Geharnschte Venus*. For important nuptials, Simon Dach, professor of poetry at Königsberg, wrote epithalamia that celebrate fertility in an almost African manner; his less official wedding poems have a second meaning that inevitably gets the better of the first. Cupid strikes the young lover's breast with such force:

> That no more he'll quiet know,
> And must as in leaping go
> And his body make behave
> Like the wave.

Students, like Venereus in Happel's *Akademischer Roman*, are hot on the trail of "douce Volupté," as one might expect; after all, they reason, pleasure was "jadis maîtresse/ Du plus bel esprit de la Grêce," and so why should she not be the mistress of the "beaux esprits" of the German university? Town is not a whit better than gown; the merchant who narrates the second part of Grimmelshausen's *Wunderbarliches Vogelnest* abandons respectability for simple concupiscence. At first, the merchant seems a pitiable figure, for he has discovered that his wife is betraying him with a doctor, but pity is soon dispelled. He catches his wife's maiden cousin as she plays love's messenger, and compels her to give herself to him, a penalty she readily accepts; next he visits a revolting punishment upon his wife (a survival, probably, of the cloacal vengeances which Reformation polemicists liked to devise), but not until he has "sown grass in his garden" with her. Later, in Amsterdam's Jewish colony, the merchant misuses a young girl on the pretext that he is Elijah, come to beget a new Messiah on her. The merchant falls ever deeper in his lusts and in his company, ending as a common soldier; other satyrs of his class managed, by hypocrisy, to serve both Mercury and Venus to the full extent of their powers. Johann Balthasar Schupp won the hatred both of Hamburg's patricians and of a good many pastors by claiming, in *Corinne, die ehrbare Hure (Corinna, the Honest Whore*, 1660), that the well-to-do business men of the town had brought Corinna her chief trade and were, indeed, responsible for her appalling demise. Yet, how could the good burghers of the Jungfernstieg defend themselves against the plague of the century, a plague so awful that it made the musician Jan Rebhu, in Johann Beer's *Der simplizianische Weltkucker (The Simplician World-Spyglass*, 1677-1679), want to submit himself to a most drastic operation. Otherwise, the musician thought, he would have no energies left for his art.

In the baroque, the mighty rulers of the earth must perform on a grander scale the acts of ordinary men, and so it is no wonder that the heroes of the courtly novels of Buchholtz, Lohenstein, Anton Ulrich, and Zigler und Klipphausen, perform Zeus-like achievements in the marriage bed, and, indeed, father new Herculean figures. The grandest moment in any courtly novel of the baroque is the state wedding – a ceremony for which the nuptials of Leopold I with Margareta of Austria (1666), with Claudia Felicitas of the Tyrol (1673), and the somewhat hardier Eleonora Magdalena of Pfalz-Neuburg (1676), provided the inspiration and the model. So enamoured was the baroque mind with the royal match that the union of a single couple was not enough: Zigler's *Banise* ends with the joining of six Oriental bluebloods in matimony, and Anton Ulrich's *Durchläuchtige Syrerin Aramena (Illustrious Syrian Aramena*, 1669-1673) piles Pelion on Ossa with marriages between thirty-four royal personages. These marriages, although imaginary, satisfied some very real psychic needs of the reader. A royal ceremony offered an unique opportunity for pomp and circumstance; royal marriage usually meant peaceful union of nations if not the individuals involved; a royal husband, incomparable in love as elsewhere, might be thought to accomplish superhuman feats as the canopy's *putti* cheered him on. Even the baroque appetite for religion was subtly fed by means of the popular identification between Hercules and Christ. Lohenstein takes pains to point out that Hermann and Thusnelda are going to produce a Hercules; urging the sun to hasten forth with the wedding day, he cries:

> Oh sun, our wish relieve!
> Since for our festival the night has grown too mean,
> Since Hermann is this hour what Jupiter has been,
> And since Thusnelda now will Hercules conceive.

The good pastor Buchholtz, in *Herkules und Valiska* (1659-1660), goes so far as to commit a *parusia ad absurdum*: the child of the hero and heroine – who are, respectively, a German prince and a Bohemian princess – is born at Jerusalem and named Herkuliskus.

Hermann and his fellow princes are, do not forget, giants of virtue as well as of procreative strength, and never do the members of this insurpassable, indeed, this divine race use their passions for aught but the begetting of new monarchs, equally splendid, equally great-hearted. Yet the baroque, with its urge to create a complete picture of the world, must also have monarchs who demonstrate their royal supremacy in extra-marital lust. The high-born satyr is never presented as a German prince; just as the German authors of the nineteenth century were wont to make their immoral women Italians or Bohemians or Jewesses, so the baroque poet made his erethic potentate a Persian, a Turk, a Nubian, a Roman. No baroque poet believed that royal immorality on the heroic scale was an accomplishment peculiar to Mohammed's lands or to classical antiquity. The prodigies of Denmark's Christian IV were well-known throughout the German North, and the popularity of Augustus the Strong rested in large part upon Saxon wonderment at his inexhaustibility; but it was neither literary custom nor good literary business (in an age of the Maecenas) to look too closely at the Don Juan in the nearby palace. The most that a writer might dare undertake was the scandalous *nouvelle à clef*, like that tale of illicit love which Anton Ulrich embedded in the gigantic body of his *Römische Octavia* (in the later editions of 1711 and 1712). Other courtly novelists, less well-protected by birth, wrote *romans à clef* which, for the most part, could only bring smiles of moral self-satisfaction to princes who found themselves therein depicted; Anton Ulrich, in the story of Prince Aquilia's love for Soltane and his murder by Soltane's husband, Cotys, retold one of the most celebrated royal mysteries of the baroque age. Princess Sophie of Hannover, feeling herself desperately neglected by her husband, Georg Ludwig (later George I of England), fell in love with a dashing office, Philipp von Königsmarck. The two were planning flight together when, on the night of July 1, 1694, poor gallant Königsmarck disappeared without a trace. Sophie, after her divorce from Georg Ludwig, was confined for the rest of her life in Castle Ahlden. The romantic story (and, no doubt, its more secret and more sordid details) had become known to Anton Ulrich not merely by gossip or popular outcry; it was to him that the lovers had planned to flee.

Anton Ulrich, a duke, could write what Leibniz termed a secret history of the courts of Europe; other, less well-born authors could not. Instead, they built horrific edifices upon the reports of the enormities committed by Oriental potentates, who possessed, of course, a power more absolute than that of any European monarch. To German eyes, califs and shahs were capable of every heinous deed, but even at their most bestial moments – in German tragedy, at least – they never laid the purple aside. Gryphius, apparently respecting majesty in all its forms, including the Persian, did not turn Chach Abas (in *Catharina von Georgien*) into a villain of darkest hue. Abas, although "enflamed with unchaste love" for the Christian Catharina, makes her a most chaste proposal of marriage, according to his Mohammedan lights, and asks: "Does one think virtue's not in virtuous marriage praised?". Catharina offers violent objections to the plan: "But is Your Majesty to other wives not wed?", to which Abas, with barbarian magnanimity, replies: "They, goddess, as your maids shall 'neath your rule be led." But there is no reasoning with Catharina; she remains adamant: "The Christian law does join but two within this bond." Abas, hoping in vain to break her spirit, martyrs her; her constancy, on the contrary, makes his spirit snap, and, when last Abas is seen, he has fallen into a repentance that takes even stronger expression than his passion did:

> Oh princess, princess! Oh, we are aflame!
> Fire! Fire! Fire! Fire! Fire! within this heart does smite!
> We do melt and we do smolder, burned in
>   sulphur-candle's light!

Obviously, Abas is prone to emotional storms worthy, in their drum-and-trumpet quality, of his position, but he does not attain the last extremes of royal satyriasis; these are reserved for Lohenstein's Ibrahim Sultan, the hero of a display of priapean fireworks written to celebrate the marriage of Leopold and Claudia Felicitas. Leopold (the final chorus points out) partakes of virtuous love, but Ibrahim's forte is basest lustfulness, a lustfulness which, however, Lohenstein describes with a great deal of admiration. As *Ibrahim Sultan* opens, Ibrahim is hot after Sisigambis, the widow of his departed brother, Amurath. The lady makes it clear to her importunate brother-in-law that, in her opinion, her withered charms should no longer attract him; he rejoins that she was the object even of his juvenile affections:

> When Amurath was prince, and I was still a child,
> My brother's mouth indeed upon your breast grew wild,
> But you already built your temples in my heart.

His passions have benefited by their long period of gestation:

> The elephant does thus so long a lifetime get
> Since it for ten whole years within the womb is set.

Fortunately, Sisigambis has a knife at hand with which to defend her widow's honor, and Ibrahim's monstrous lust is then directed, by his court procuress, toward a prey with charms very unlike those of Sisigambis: Ambre, the Mufti's nubile daughter. Ambre, as virtuous as she is appetizing, refuses to heed his cajolery, and Ibrahim issues an order of the sort one expects from sultans:

>   Quick, Achmet, take her hence
> And have her stripped to buff and cast into our bed:
> If love's dart cannot be by kindness brought to head,
> Let force the whetstone play.

As two choruses, of women and of maids, argue the respective merits of pleasure and virginity (the scene is "a warm bath"), little Ambre is raped; she kills herself, and eventually Ibrahim is brought to a terrible and well-deserved end.

Not all monsters of lust are men: the baroque has a high-born equivalent of its camp follower Courasche and its burgheresses Celinde and Corinna (for this hapless doxy was by birth a member of the middle class from which she drew her trade). As a matter of fact, if one could name a champion among the vicious folk of baroque literature, the champion would be a woman, Lohenstein's Agrippina (in the drama of that name). The words which Agrippina directs to her son, the Emperor Nero, heave with incestuous passion:

> My light, come, feel the itch these marble breasts to take
> And suck out oil, as once you milk from them did wake.
> Discover if they more than sop for babes encase:
> Because these mountains are high Ida's judgment place,
> Where wit and majesty by beauty are enslaved.

Such talk is too much for Nero, and he has his mother murdered; but before the play ends, he has fallen into remorse at the matricide. Nero regrets Agrippina's death because he is beset by a spirit company composed of the Furies, of Alcmaeon, and of Orestes; the reader is inclined to regret Agrippina's passing because of the wonderfully ornate verse which Lohenstein put into her depraved mouth.

Agrippina's confessions are not isolated stylistic phenomena in Lohenstein's works; his other royal ladies of mighty appetite, Cleopatra and Sophonisbe, are entrusted with the grandest speeches conceived for any figure in baroque drama. Lohenstein's heroines (like Grillparzer's later on) perhaps stood closer to their creator's heart than did their male opposites: the latter are monsters of lust (like Ibrahim Sultan) or of jealousy (like Soliman in *Ibrahim Bassa*), changeable (like Nero in the Roman plays, Antonius in *Cleopatra*, and Masanissa in *Sophonisbe*), or coldly wise (like Augustus in *Cleopatra*). On the other hand, Lohenstein's women are enthusiastic victims of their own conviction or passion: be they virtuous, like Ambre and Epicharis (a Roman lady tortured to death by Nero in the drama that bears her name), or vicious, like Cleopatra and Agrippina, or madly in love, like Sophonisbe, they possess that fiery constancy of purpose and that vigor of execution which the baroque so greatly admired. Sophonisbe receives a tribute intended for all her sex when she – not her bridegroom, Masanissa – is allowed to speak the famous lines opening the bridal scene in Lohenstein's Carthaginian play; lines, too, that have implicit in themselves the vitality which beautifies baroque passion and makes baroque erotic poetry an almost unique kind of literary expression:

> Is this the golden night which puts the day to shame?
> In which Diana's horn the dew as pearls does lay?
> Fond Heaven decorates this night with thousand lamps...

In English literature the name of Sophonisbe has become forever associated with James Thomson's ill-found line, "Oh, Sophonisba, Sophonisba, Oh!" In German literature, Sophonisbe should stand for the best expression of the baroque's dynamic eroticism.

Save for some heroines of the heroic-gallant novel, like Grimmelshausen's anaemic Lympida (in *Proximus und Lympida*), the women of baroque literature belong to a lively tribe, saints and sinners alike, and one cannot help imagining all of them – for the saints, Catharina, Ambre, and Epicharis, were handsome women too – in the shape of Ruben's Brabant Venuses, Hélène and Susanna Fourment. In reality, too, the baroque age had a genius for producing real women who were, in the spirit and in the flesh, the equals of their literary sisters. A Queen Christina may have been too mannish to qualify for membership in the gifted company (although she managed to bewitch such unlike lovers as Klas Tott and Cardinal Azzolini), a Sophie Charlotte of Prussia, the "philosophical queen" and Leibniz's friend, seems to have had a bulbous nose; but there were others who fulfilled every requirement, of beauty, intelligence, and determination. Leonora Christina Ulfeld loved her husband with such fire that she spent more than two decades in prison as a punishment for her love, and, during those years in Copenhagen's Blue Tower, wrote the *Jammersminde*, the Danish baroque's masterpiece. Marie de' Medicis conquered the heart of Henri IV, and was herself conquered only by Richelieu, who struggled with her for the rule of France. Aurora von Königsmarck (the sister of the vanished Philipp) became the mistress of Augustus the Strong, was a talented poetess, and failed only in her attempts to seduce the virginal lion of Sweden, Charles XII. Sophie, electoral princess of Hannover, patroness of Leibniz, mother of George I of England, beloved of her brother-in-law, the ambiguous George William, became the authoress of memoirs that are not only an important source book for the baroque, but in themselves a "brag" (in the seventeenth century sense of the word) giving expression to the defiance which inspired many a lady of the time.

Courtesan, woman of letters, regent, they had the admiration of their male contemporaries, and the admiration extended, in one way or another, to less illustrious women as well. The attitude of the baroque man to the other sex is difficult even for twentieth century readers to understand; it was still more difficult for our

Victorian or Wilhelmine grandfathers, who found it indecent. The never ending concern with lust might have conceivably led to sheerest animalism, but it did not. The baroque was a courtly age, and pleasure, no doubt, was heightened by the introductory compliment, by the mythical allusion. Even Grimmelshausen's merchant gives his wife's cousin some highfalutin praise before he sets about his evil work. And the woman was supposed to react to the compliment and to feel a passion sufficient unto the man's; both partners practiced "Lustbrauch," to use Hofmannswaldau's term, in equal measure. It may seem that the baroque man engages in erotic mechanics, and certainly his view of his mistress's charms is constructional: he praises each part of her in turn. Nonetheless, as he investigates her, she represents a new aesthetic experience, or series of experiences; she is a new continent, as Donne says: "Oh my America, my new-found land!/ My kingdom safeliest when with one man mann'd." The baroque man is curious; like Hofmannswaldau, he peeks at Lesbia's most intimate charms through a chink in the door. The baroque man is a collecter; like Assman von Abschatz (or Assmann's model, Adimari), he finds amusement in mistresses of various ages or possessing various physical flaws. But he is neither as nasty as a Peeping Tom nor as cynical as a Don Juan who has made his "catalogo." What he does, is performed with the grace that the worthy prey demands – a prey, of course, that may also be huntswoman.

Women may have a wit surpassing that of men. Moscherosch in "Praise of Woman," the third vision of Philander von Sittewald, gives expression to an idea that must have struck the Swedish marauders who were, according to legend, hunted down by the enraged peasant women of the Bregenz Forest: "What thoughts, however, the dear maiden had, I shall let none save maids decide; for a man can never know nor understand it – such secrets are still concealed to men's eyes." Moscherosch is being poetical; Master Johannes Diez, a soldier-of-fortune, puts it more directly as he recounts the most awful of his adventures. After having survived, among other things, the storming of Ofen and a whaling expedition, he married a wicked and clever woman of Halle, and "Right after the wedding the storm began." Women were not only admired as Sphinxes and feared as Xanthippes; they were praised for their practical bent of mind as well. Peter Dass, telling of his trip among the Lapps in *Nordlands Trompet*, has special commendation for the way womenfolk use their mouths in the preparation of household articles:

> Yet this does entrap me in wonderment's snare:
> That women can thus with their jawbone prepare,
> And naught else, such a fine piece of handwork.

In Germany's less savage clime, women were praised for other skills. Women, men's sexual partners, were likewise made their partners in witty chatter; as one might expect, the talkative sex outstripped men here, too, and Georg Philipp Harsdörffer gave his conversational compendium the title, *Frauenzimmer-Gesprächspiele (Ladies' Conversation-Games)*. In this guide for those who would speak both wisely and well, the roles are divided evenly between men and women: two noble maidens and a wise matron compose the team for the distaff side, an old courtier, a cultured officer, and a widely traveled scholar represent men. Women were not emancipated, in the modern sense, but they were taken seriously; they could (one is surprised to hear the sober Andreas Gryphius say it) bear within themselves the whole harvest of life's good things:

> Eugenia, you give strange tulip-bloom to me,
> Rose, jasmin, marjoram, the flower of granate-tree,
> Each tribe of violets, narcissus, emperor's crown;

and the wise but still lovely woman, she who had both fought in "Cupid's wars" and studied Harsdörffer's conversational work, was the finest treasure of all, a true cornucopia:

> no one may dare suppress
> Nor fail to praise enough the autumn's joyful boot;
> For through such tasty figs it can our taste caress,
> Through such gay crop, that it without the faintest bruit
> Outstrips the others: two this truth will glad confess.

The baroque man loved woman best at her harvest-tide and, in like manner, he loved nature best in its golden days, when it was fullest of delights. The minnesinger and the romantic excelled in the spring song, for these are literary periods, as it were, of the young; the baroque poet, whose ideal was a vigorous maturity, made his masterpieces in the autumn strain. However, "autumn" is a misleading term if we think of a gentle Stifterian "Nachsommer" or a death-consecrated melancholy, in Lenau's or Trakl's vein. The baroque autumn was a time when a bounteous nature filled the woods with game, the fields with grain, the vineyards with the grape. It was a time when baroque man, who loved to splash his lace cuffs in the sauce dish, could eat his fill (and it is worth noting that, in an age when hunger could breed cannibalism, the poet and his prince not infrequently died of a stroke, a fat man's doom). The baroque man loved and trusted nature, cataloging her delights – as Sigmund von Birken has his Floridan do – with all the care of a baroque lover listing the charms of his mistress. Nature could even make Gryphius, himself one day to be the victim of apoplexy, cry out: "Come, friends, and let us to the banquet start." The night was usually treated by the baroque man with a good deal of caution (Gryphius, in the sonnet just quoted, enhances the charms of noon with a reference to awful night's temporary banishment), but the night, too, could become a time of pleasure when it was graced by the fruits of day, when the strings played and the goblet – in Klaj's poem – made the rounds.

The night terrified the baroque man if it appeared as Stygian blackness, as the abode of demons and their Prince; it did not terrify him when the stars or the moon shone, since these heavenly illuminations signaled that God, in Whom man put his single and unswerving trust, was on guard. Nature, by day or by night, was the present proof of God's kindness to man; the latter realized very well that his existence depended upon the Former's kindness. Man implored that kindness and was thankful whenever he received it:

> Among our needy spirits share
> Your bountiful and precious ware;
> You did to us the life-spark give,
> Give then what we must have to live.

The prayer was answered; in his *Alcaic Ode*, Matthäus Apelles von Löwenstern recites the manners of God's aid:

> He holds his banquet ample and everywhere,
> He feeds all men at once with a father's air.
> He late and early rain does make,
> Thus with his blessings us all to slake.

When nature misbehaved, when there were tempests on land and storms at sea (the latter was apparently the most terrifying natural phenomenon to the German of the seventeenth century), these catastrophes were the work not of God but of Satan's rebellious spirit, attempting in vain to wreck the order established by Heaven. Amusingly, the baroque man was less terrified by the storm on land than were his successors in *Sturm und Drang* and Romanticism (compare the storm scenes in *Werther* and in *Maler Nolten*), although the hysterical folk of the eighteenth and nineteenth centuries were protected, one would suppose, by Benjamin Franklin's lightning rod. However, an unshakable faith in God is a considerably better cushion for the nerves than faith in the invention of a mere Philadelphian. Schottelius, in his *Thunder Song*, seems to have regarded the tempest as a theatrical entertainment arranged by a thoughtful Providence for Its appreciative subjects, a divine – and a free – equivalent of fireworks, of which the baroque was very fond.

The wintertime, which the medieval poets, in their badly heated castles, had dreaded – which had, indeed, a bad poetic reputation all the way back to Hesiod, with his complaints at the Boeotian snows – got a good press from the German baroque. Johann Wilhelm Simler and Johann Dach, in their winter songs, might register the obligatory complaint at the snow, the cold, and the bare branches, but Simler could see a good chance for the pleasures of the hunt and of the table:

> We slaughter now
> Fat swine and sow,
> And seat ourselves to sausage,

while Rist, a more sensitive poet, is aware of the beauties of the snow-covered Holstein landscape;

> The meadows all with frost are burned,
> The fields some metal's shine reveal,
> The flowers into ice are turned,
> The rivers stand as hard as steel.

God has seen to it that even the winter, that worst of seasons, is full of delights for stomach and soul. An ill-tempered complaint at bad weather (which, in an agrarian society, could cause something far more serious than mere discomfort) is rare in the German baroque; there is no German poem like that unique flower of a poverty-stricken baroque literature, Lars Wivallius' scolding of God for having allowed a cold, dry spring: *Klagewijsa öfwer thenna torra och kalla wåhr*. Wivallius, it might be added, was a rogue, wanderer, and impostor, who, as a result of his sins, was imprisoned in Finland for seven years, a career and a fate which must have given him rather less confidence in the Almighty's goodness than that held by the German poets, a group which, for all its vicissitudes, maintained a strong hold on respectability.

Nature, to the German poets, had been created by God to serve man. As Simplicius asked the Prince of the Mummelsee "to what end the kind Creator created so many wonderful lakes, since they are of no good to any man," his question revealed the common attitude of his time. Each thing in nature had some use for man; else God would not have included it. The Prince of the Mummelsee did not disappoint his visitor; his reply concerning the lake's purpose has a clarity of structure and a wealth of detail that show the Prince to be a skillful apologist and the bearer of a message the baroque man took delight in hearing. Such a well-intentioned and wise God offered, in nature, a consolation to men exposed by their fellows (those rebels against order and usefulness) to an often sadistic whimsicality. Some officers are supposed to have remonstrated with General Tilly as his troops ravaged Magdeburg; the commander replied to these scrupulous souls with: "Come back in an hour's time, and then I'll see what's to be done; the soldier must have something for his peril and his toil." The reply horrified the baroque mind more by its disregard for the final good of things than by the brutality it revealed; it seemed that Satan spoke against the nice order Heaven had established. Nature served as a constant reminder that if man was cruelly wasteful, God was not. Nature was a sanctuary, and the poet desired to see it only at its kindest.

The favorite landscape of the baroque is not the mountain, whose grandeur Albrecht von Haller was to discover just at the end of the baroque age; the mountain could inspire but it could not console. Nor is it the plain; the plain, uninteresting and indefensible, lacks the protective and charming curve of the hill. The German landscape painters of the baroque, Matthäus Merian, Adam Elsheimer, Michael Willmann, preferred to paint rolling or gently mountainous country, which they clothed in a serene ideality; the heroic landscape, as practiced during the late eighteenth century by a Joseph Anton Koch, had little popularity in this age of heroes. For the baroque, the hero must dominate the landscape, while in the budding romantic age (see Koch's *Hercules at the Crossroads*) he is dominated by his surroundings. Martin Opitz, the rule-maker of seventeenth century German poetry, has left some of the best literary examples of what the baroque man liked his nature to be. At the beginning of *Schäfferey von der Nimfen Hercinie (Pastoral of the Nymph Hercinia*, 1630), Opitz delineates the dream landscape of his contemporaries: "There lies... beneath the graceful Giant Mountains a valley, whose vasty range resembles a half circle." The landscape is gentle, but it does not lack grandeur; it is safe, but it does not lack the "window to infinity" which the baroque liked to put in the cupolas of its churches and the wall-hedges of its gardens: the path to God had to be left open. The stroller could easily move through such a landscape, enjoying the golden mediocrity of the scene while engaging in a sport that gave a golden mediocrity of movement; extremist in the realm of the spirit and of love and of war, the baroque man was Horatian in his sanctuary. "Walking has this attribute, that it keeps to the mean, and brings not too much nor too little movement with it... The movement warms the body, awakens the tender humors, drives away the crude vapors as they arise, and releases the intellect from each burden of care through gracious contemplation of the wide field," says Harsdörffer, showing once again how nature is the servant of man. As the stroller goes along, he has the chance to take full pleasure in the various delights the "wide field" contains, again cataloging them as the lover would: here is a region of poetic endeavor where the poets of the Nürnberg school surpassed all the others. The stroller may come upon a Franconian "fons Bandusiae," which he describes with all the virtuosity at his disposal, since he is attempting to give expression to the virtuosity of God, or he may discover frogs "waxing and co-axing" in their ponds, or, like Greiffenberg making an excursion to the banks of the neighboring Ybbs, he may read in the "bloom-book" and find greater pleasure in "grassy emeralds" and "diamond dew" than in "Turkish tapestry." The baroque man knew, or dreamt of, a lovely world, and, although the baroque is supposed to stand outside the main stream of German letters, the great literary landscape-painters of the nineteenth century, Eichendorff and Stifter, specialized in a fruit-laden, green and gold world – a world "dulci digne mero non sine floribus" – very like that of Opitz and von Birken. The Silesian Eichendorff and the Austrian Stifter had, of course, grown up in South German lands where the baroque still existed, in architecture, in painting, and, perhaps, in frame of mind.

The Horatian concept of nature is sophisticated; one doubts that the Sabine farmer took his agricultural work too seriously. Vergil, though probably quite as polished as his good friend, looked at nature with eyes having the calm and skillful gaze of the patriarch and the practical farmer; the *Georgics*, with their sunny days and their concern for the good things of life, had a natural appeal to the seventeenth century country gentleman as well as to the poet. Wolfgang von Hohberg, thinking to give Vergil that encyclopaedic aspect so popular in the literature of the late baroque, produced a *Georgica curiosa oder Adeliges Land- und Feldleben*, in which the exiled poet told gentleman farmers all they needed to know to become a master "super arvorum cultu pecorumque... et super arboribus." Two generations before Hohberg brought out the *Georgica curiosa* (1682), Opitz had discovered a region possessing the simplicity and the richness of life portrayed in Vergil's agricultural manual, and he described the blessed land in *Zlatna*, a lengthy poem whose subtitle, "Concerning peace of spirit," states precisely what baroque man would have nature give him. In 1622-23, Opitz – like his contemporaries, an indefatigable traveler – taught at the gymnasium in the Transylvanian town of Weissenburg, and was excited to find himself in Trajan's old Roman colony of Dacia. The local peasantry (not, one should add, the solid "Saxon" burghers whose children Opitz instructed) both spoke like ancient Roman husbandmen and lived like them:

> Now Italy has kept but small its tongue of old,
> And Spain and Gallish land the same weak measure hold.
> So little like unto the Romans are these three,
> So close do Wallachish and Latin seem to me.

> There hides much noble blood in peasant huts today
> Which still its ancient use and its forefather's way
> Has not put all aside.

Opitz's burgeoning Transylvania was the classical landscape of the baroque mind, classical in answering the baroque need for orderly abundance, classical in its demonstration of what the baroque loved in antiquity: just as it preferred Imperial Rome to the Republic (and certainly to anything authentically Greek, a culture for which it had no understanding at all), so it preferred a Dacia antiqua, heavy with grain, to a Sicilian idyl.

Not that the German baroque had a shortage of shepherd poetry: the *Eclogues* were as well known as the *Georgics*. Germany, like every other western nation, had become infected with the Theocritan madness that, emerging from Italy during the Renaissance, in Sannazaro's *Arcadia*, Tasso's *Aminta*, and Guarini's *Pastor Fido*, spread like a hardy weed to Spain, France, England, and even more barbarous lands. Opitz, by his translations of Philip Sidney's *Arcadia* and Rinucinni's little shepherd opera, *Daphne* (which, set to music by Heinrich Schütz, is often called the first German opera), had helped the rustic company of Damon and Corydon enter German meadows, where it was welcomed by the pious Spee, the roisterer Stieler, the virtuosi Birken, Klaj, and Zesen, and by Gryphius himself, who tempered his ditty to the oaten flute in *Geliebte Dornrose*. The "bella età dell'oro,/ Quand' era cibo il latte" ("lovely age of gold./ When milk was nourishment"), whose coming Guarini had predicted, did indeed dawn in Germany, and scarcely a poet remained uninfluenced by it. Even that tough ex-soldier, Grimmelshausen, ventured into the sister field of the imitation Greek novel, becoming a follower of Heliodorus, if not Longus, with the stillborn *Dietwald und Amelinde*; the ex-actor Johann Martin set his warnings of hell-fire and brimstone to a *musica boscareccia;* and Simon Dach, in fog-bound Königsberg, celebrated "the most worthy and praiseworthy, the faithful shepherd of the crown of Poland," Vladislav IV, in a political bucolic, *Cleomedes*. Nonetheless, the shepherd pipes never rang quite true in the German baroque. Some poets, like Johann Hermann Schein, succumbed to the temptation of the playful diminuitive:

> Oh greening forestlet!
> Oh myrtle-thicketlet!
> Oh cooling fountainlet!
> And crystal rivulet!

Some used the pastoral jug to hold excellent but unsuitable wines: Spee's spiritual eclogues and Birken's shepherd laments are cases in point. No true fusion between stuff and form came to pass in the shepherd poetry of the German baroque; Germany produced no *Lycidas* or *Comus* in the seventeenth century, just as it did not produce a Milton. As a matter of fact, when comparing the German use of classical myth and classical reference with the English or the Italian employment of the company of the gods, one is compelled to conclude that the German poets were far less at home with the Renaissance inheritance: perhaps because of the failure of the Renaissance to take deep root in Germany, perhaps, too, because of the German baroque urge toward the monumental and the practical, toward the emperor and the georgic. Exceptions exist: Paul Fleming, the most "Elizabethan" of the German baroque poets, wrote an unforgettable sonnet to Hecate as moon-goddess, Casper Stieler's *Geharnschte Venus* is a rough but vigorous German answer to Griffen, Drayton, and Lodge, and Lohenstein's *Triumph of Venus* is as colorfully grand as the opening pages of *The Golden Ass;* but "Venus and Adonis sitting by her" were, on the whole, uncomfortable guests in the Hercynian Forest. Even great poets, like van den Vondel, came a cropper when they sallied into the mythological realm; Vondel's antique embellishments upon the slaughter at Magdeburg make painful reading:

> Now, tresses rent and tears made disappear
> War's cloud, when Roman sword and Sabine spear
> Had, raging, met in stern and bitter fight.
> Where Venus weeps, the stormy floods turn bright.

A similar recourse to an inappropriate mythology is not unusual in the German baroque, but here, happily, the creations of classical phantasy appear for the most part as incidental decoration in the poem, like a Boreas or a Favonius puffing out his cheeks at the corner of a baroque map. One suspects that the failure of the German muse to absorb classical myth during the baroque age is a blessing in disguise; it meant that a Goethe, later on, did not have to struggle with quite the same traditional ballast of classical allusion as did, say, the English Romantics. The almost incredible naturalness of Goethe's lyrics may have been helped into being by the German baroque's orientation, in its thought about antiquity, toward the hard-won delights of Vergil's farm and the colossal stonework of Imperial Rome.

The baroque lord, decorating his lands, tried hard to combine the golden practicality of the Vergilian estate with the splendor of the Vergilian capital. One can trace modern Europe's intellectual history through its parks and gardens as well as through its books; every reader of *Werther* recalls that hero's lonely communing with nature in the wild "English" garden of the late Count M., Karl

Theodor's park at Schwetzingen reveals the artificial Frenchness of spirit against which Werther's contemporaries rebelled, a visit to any of the surviving baroque parks of Germany and Austria – be it an emperor's, like Schönbrunn, or a general's, like the Belvedere complex, a churchman's, like Pommersfelden, or a border magnate's, like Schileithen – will tell the observant promenader a good deal about the ways of baroque thought. The park, like all of nature, has been put at the service of man; delighted, the park's owner has set out to aid God in His intentions, turning the park into a sanctuary which one can enter for solace and profit. The park is conceived as a room. It is enclosed by a hedge or a wall, just as the life of man is enclosed by God's will, and within the precincts of the hedge are found what a right-thinking sociologist would call guideposts for living, symbols that instruct even as they please. The visitor will be delighted by the "anmutige Abwechslung," the charming variety which he finds between the park's different sections. He will look at full-bosomed statues, smell the fragrance of the orangery, rest in the pavilion; but at the same time he will learn from the well-stocked fish pond that beauty has its nutritional uses, the splash of water in the fountain will remind him that time is never still, the "window to infinity," cut into the garden wall or even painted there, will suggest that while the park is enclosed and man is limited, God is infinite, and the labyrinth, through which the visitor wanders, will show him how the soul is led into painful straits from which it must, by its courage alone, find its way. (Thus the labyrinth serves much the same purpose as the wilderness which Gryphius and Greiffenberg constructed as a coulisse to some of their poems: even the desert places of earth have a use as man's testing place.) And when, at last, the visitor to the baroque park has escaped from the labyrinth, he may ascend the little hill at the park's farther end, there to observe the prosperity and the perils through which he has passed. Leaning on the gloriette's balustrade, he beholds, in small, the "fair and well-cultivated land" of the baroque dream.

The baroque man did not allow nature to overawe him, nor, if he had the proper faith in God and in himself, could the worst extravagances of human cruelty cow him. Although – except for the pietistically influenced – not what a denizen of the present psychological age would call self-analytic, the baroque man was terribly interested in himself: in learning how to maintain his courage in the face of odds, in learning how to appear, and how to be, worthy of his humanity and of his station in the world. He had a plethora of aids toward the achievement of these ends: he had his religious conviction or, failing that, his stoic outlook, he had plays and poems for inspiration to constancy, he had the enormously instructive courtly novel from which both prince and commoner might draw, he had lexicons to tell him what to say and what to do. He learned behavior from Julius Bernhard von Rohr's late baroque *Einleitung in die Ceremonial-Wissenschaft der Privat-Personen (Introduction to the Ceremonial Science of Private Persons)* or, earlier, from the the simpler pages of the anonymous *Anleiting zur Höflichkeit (Primer of Politeness)*; he was instructed in the nobler content of ceremony and custom by Justus Georg Schottel's *Ethica, die Sittenkunst (Ethics, the Art of Manners)*. He learned how to write poetry from Opitz's classic *Buch von der deutschen Poeterei (Book of German Poetry)*, or from August Buchner's *Anleitung zur deutschen Poeterei (Primer of German Poetry)*, or from that liveliest and most useful of all the German poetics, Philipp von Zesen's *Hoch-Deutscher Helikon oder Grund-richtige Anleitung zur hoch-deutschen Dicht- und Reim-Kunst (High German Helicon or Utterly Correct Primer of the Art of High German Poetry and Rhyme)*; Christian Gueintz's *Deutsche Rechtschreibung (German Orthography)* taught him to regulate his spelling, which may have taken a curious turn after too close a reading of Zesen. He polished his speech and style on the criticisms of his fellows in the language societies, but he loved to belong as well to clubs with a less serious purpose. Unlike the romantic Hölderlin, making the woods mournful with his lonely flute, he preferred to practice his music in the company of others, and joined the *collegium musicum* of his town. In his dress he favored the showy over the quiet, thinking to assert his personality in this way too; and just as the designer of the baroque park filled his flowerbeds with tulips, beautiful, brilliant, and puffed, so the baroque tailor was called upon to design clothes in the ornate and puffy style, clothes that were dyed with the new "bastard shades" the baroque had discovered, "body-color," "glitter-tone," bleumourant, olive-green, pearl. The baroque man imported foreign fashions, just as he imported foreign words (of which the language societies then had to purge him), and these presumably bad habits gave the chauvinistic literary criticism of the nineteenth century occasion to dispose of the baroque with some handy quotations from Logau and Moscherosch about the infamous "A-la-Mode-Wesen."

There is no denying that charges of falseness and artificiality may be placed against the baroque man, and that he will be found guilty by the most lenient jury. But he was no hypocrite; in essential matters he was less given to illusions, one suspects, than the scholars of Wilhelmine Germany who affected such scorn for him and his age. He was not unlike a certain misunderstood Englishman of the baroque century, Oliver Cromwell, whom David Hume, armored in rationalistic superiority, called "a mixture of so much absurdity with so much penetration." Today, now that the baroque has passed from literary oblivion into the hands of searchers for academic new-land, one is compelled to the opinion that the baroque's penetration far outweighed its absurdity. The baroque man had a clearer vision of life's final things than his descendants did, or do; he sought to accept them, rather than hiding them or forgetting about them. Knowing that death existed, he adorned his monuments, and his poetry, with a charnal-house's contents. The skeleton did not appear on the tomb alone, where its presence is hardly surprising; it pursued the lover as he beheld the picture where the fair face, seen from a second angle, becomes a skull (a kind of *trompe-l'oeil* in which the baroque took great delight), it accompanied the avid scholar to his books (witness Thaddäus Stammel's grisly statues in the library at Cloister Admont). Death never came to the baroque man as consoler and friend, but as the pale killer anxious to find new prey. Andreas Schlüter, the North German Lutheran, seems to have realized the horror of death with an acuteness equal to that of his Catholic colleagues: in his sarcophagus for Sophie Charlotte, the wife of the Great Elector, he presented death with a grisly detail that should have prompted art-patrons of another, more optimistic age to fits of outrage; yet Schlüter's Death, with frayed lips and leprous nose, helped the baroque man to face what he thought to be the truth of things. However sure he might be of eventual elevation into a wondrous Asam heaven, he knew all too well the tribulations he must endure before beginning the flight; Christian IV did not speak those awful words, "Døden, Doktor, Døden," to Otto Sperling for the mere dramatic effect. Schlüter's dying warriors on the Berlin armory, Permoser's tortured Christ, that wretched Tartar attributed to Johann Georg Weckemann, give plastic form to the despond of Bunyan's Christian. The parting with life was hard, the torment of that parting unspeakably bitter. The baroque drama's fascination with death by torture but reflects the baroque fear of the pains of death.

Death had to be faced, the baroque man knew, and with it war, pestilence, and the perilous journey, be it on earth or in the soul. Even the ordinary day had its dangers, and, having arrived safely at its end, the baroque man must perforce remember that he had come a step nearer to the final test and torment. The baroque, for all its sense of the real and the monumental, was mightily troubled by the variety and the changeability of life; one might deduce that its urge to massiveness and practicality grows of its desire to defy the awful dictum which Bidermann, in *Cenodoxus*, set up over the portal of the baroque: "Vita enim hominum/ Nil est nisi somnium." Perhaps the baroque wish to undertake the perilous voyage falls under the same rubric of the defiant act; in the strange lands of the earth or the soul, the baroque man could face down fear in, as it were, its classical purity, of his own free will and without distractions, conditions not pertaining for the good burgher who found Croats pillaging his home. When Hofmannswaldau describes the journeys he would make for love's sake:

> Shall I in Lybia the lions' fortress tread?
> Shall I in Etna's snow the blaze put to my hand?
> Shall naked I and bare attempt New Zemlya's strand?
> Shall I then multiply the Black Sea's withered dead?,

when Grimmelshausen's Simplicius voyages to Korea, Japan, and Constantinople, or when Zigler und Klipphausen conducts his readers to blood-stained Pegu, these trips not only satiate the baroque curiosity about far-off places; they reflect the baroque man's desire to place himself, albeit in the imagination, in death's despite. The Scotch and Irish officers who followed the Imperial flag at Lützen , the Italians (like Hofmannswaldau's Serini) who took part in the Austrian army's Turkish campaigns, the Germans who went with Charles on the road to Poltava, were not all of them booty-hungry adventurers. Gold lured them, naturally enough; but in addition they were nagged on by a serpent like the one that had sent the conquistadores out to the New World a century and more before: they wanted to confront danger. However, where the conquistador had foreseen an ultimate triumph over insurmountable odds, the baroque adventurer could not free himself from the image of Hercules self-immolated, of Samson pulling down Dagon's temple "Upon the heads of all who sat beneath." Lacking faith in the permanence of earthly fortune and earthly things, the adventurer could only believe that he – like Wallenstein and Gustav Adolf, like the early dead Bernhard of Weimar, like Pappenheim, slain as he rode to save a minor garrison at Maastricht – must end in defeat. And, could he forget the treachery and the chance that had brought proud generals to a fall, he must still conclude, in accordance with his realistic thanatopsis, that man's life ended in darkness, however splendid paradise might be. For all his bluster and self-assertion, he would have well understood what Isaac Watts meant in his comforting hymn:

> Time, like an ever-rolling stream,
>   Bears all its sons away;
> They fly, forgotten as a dream
>   Dies at the opening day.

Therefore, in defiance of time's flight and death's surety, the baroque man undertook, in imagination or reality, the perilous journey. Opitz went to Rumania, Finkelthaus found his way to Brazil, Paul

Fleming and Adam Olearius made their expedition to Russia and Persia, Sibylla Merian, the daughter of Matthäus Merian and a noted illustrator in her own right, made a trip to wildest Surinam, Johann Weikhard von Valvasor, the classical geographer of Carniola, halfway realized Lohenstein's prophecy that Africa's beaches would lie beneath the Austrian flag: he traveled extensively in the land of Sophonisbe. Of these journeys, Fleming's is, without question, the most important for literary history; unhappily, nothing is known about Finkelthaus's adventures in the New World. Fleming's sonnets from Moscow and Samarkand belong to the great tradition of adventure poetry arising out of the Age of Discovery; they are the German equivalent of Camoens' *Lusiads* or Alonso de Ercilla's *La Araucana*. Admittedly, they lack the scope of these Romance epics (Fleming did not live long enough to attempt any larger poetic form), but they are perhaps more revelatory about seventeenth century man than the works of Camoens and Ercilla are about the culture which spawned Portuguese seamen and Spanish soldiers. Fleming was an apt student of the literary customs of his day; he knew how to lace his muse into the tight corsets of the baroque's conceits, antitheses, farfetched similes, and *pointes*, and one would guess that, for the most part, her figure was improved by the lacing. But, contrary to baroque rule, he was not inspired so much by God or love or war as by the supremely exciting adventure. God, war, and death defeat the baroque man, and love turns to defeat with age; in the adventure, the baroque man, egoist that he was, could assert himself not only in defiance but in triumph. The fact that Germany lacked a New World may account in part for the dark strain that runs through her baroque poetry. The Englishman, the Frenchman, the Spaniard owned a perpetual prospect of the happy lands beyond the seas which the German did not; and, possibly, the exuberance of Austrian art and architecture during the early decades of the eighteenth century may have been influenced, spiritually as well as materially, by the breakthrough to the Southeast. Not Germany, but Austria, with its Balkan New World, produced a program of Elizabethan self-confidence like Philipp Wilhelm Hörnigk's argument for a Hapsburg empire dominating the heart of Europe, *Oesterreich über alles, wenn es nur will (Austria Supreme, If It But Will,* 1684). Sadly enough, the exuberance was not allowed to find literary expression. Hörnigk's book depends upon economic arguments rather than artistic expression, Hörnigk himself, an emigré from Darmstadt, had grown up unfettered by the restraints placed upon the Austrian man-of-letters. Germany, despite the efforts of many of its sons, kept the freedom of spirit necessary for a golden age of literature, but lacked the other conditions essential to such a blooming. Austria acquired those conditions, but the Hapsburgs had long since put the Austrian mind into a not unpleasant prison.

Almost every German poet who lived in the shadow cast by the Thirty Years' War said, at one time or another, "cupio dissolvi." Even Günther, born half a century after the conclusion of the ruinous conflict, suffered from that melancholy which runs like a thread of darkness through the most joyful creations of the German baroque; like the majority of his fellow baroque authors, he was from Silesia, which, of all the German lands, had been kept in the most harrowing condition of intellectual tension by the war and its aftermath – a productive tension, to be sure, but not a situation likely to foster optimism. Only Fleming and the older Weckherlin (who was thirty-four when the war began) succeeded in presenting the magnificent egocentricity of the baroque without falling sooner or later into the anguish, or worse, the disgust at life which made the proud ruler, Anton Ulrich, write his ode to death: "It is enough. Be now my dying done." Fleming, calling himself "young, keen, and unconcerned" (strange words from a German poet of the baroque), composed the noblest and most hopeful line in the century's annals:

> Yet do not be afraid, yet give no post forlorn,

and then was carried away by disease at the very threshold of his career.

Abraham a Santa Clara

DER MOND

Oefters muss des Mondes Schein,
Für die Menschen, schamrot sein,
(Monet rubicunda pudoris)

Es sind so Sonn als Mond des Himmels schönste Fackeln:
Die erste glänzt am Tag, die andre bei der Nacht.
Von jener muss das Feld voll Korn und Ähren wackeln,
Da dieser unsre Flut mit Fischen fruchtbar macht.
Die Sonne gleicht dem Gold, der Mond hat Silberschein;
Von beiden zieht die Welt den grössten Nutzen ein.

Drum sollt man Nacht und Tag dem grossen Schöpfer dienen –
Für Lunae Silberglanz, und für der Sonnen Gold.
Allein was tut man hier? Man schnarcht, wann sie erschienen;
Man bleibt dem kühnen Werk der Finsternüsse hold;
Man deckt die Laster zu mit schwarzem Flor der Nacht.
Das ist es, was den Mond so gar oft schamrot macht.

Hans Assmann von Abschatz

DAS SCHÖNE KIND

Unreiffer Schönheit Blüt und frühes Morgen-Licht,
Mit Tocken mehr gewohnt zu spielen als mit Liebe,
Wenn ich mich wegen dein in stetem Seufftzen übe,
So lacht die tumme Welt und gläubt mein Leiden nicht.
Doch, wie im grünen schon die junge Rose sticht,
Wie man die Blume lobt aus ihrer Knospen Triebe;
So werd ich auch gewahr, wie gern ich ruhig bliebe,
Dass, wo die Flamm entsteht, auch bald die Hitz ausbricht.
Mein Kind, ein neuer Stein schlägt offt am ehsten Glutt:
Ein kleiner Funcke darff in frischen Zunder sincken
So fängt er, wo man nicht bald Gegenwehre thut:
Zur Frühzeit siehet man die Venus heller blincken:
Den Mittags-Glantz besiegt der Morgenröthe Zier:
Dem heissen Sommer geht der bunte Lentz weit für.

Abraham a Santa Clara

The Moon

Frequently the moonlight's flame
Must for humans blush with shame.
(Monet rubicunda pudoris)

The sun and moon are both the heavens' fairest flares.
The first shines in the day, the second in the night.
Now from the first the field both ear and wheat-grain bears,
The second makes our streams with schools of fish alight.
The sun is like to gold, the moon has silver-sheen,
From both of them the world does greatest profit glean.

The great Creator's word men day and night should hear –
For Luna's silver-shine, and for the golden sun.
What do men do? They snore, when either will appear,
And to the work stay true that darknesses have done.
Their vices men conceal with ebon crepe of night:
It's this which often gives the moon its blushing light.

Hans Assmann von Abschatz

The Beautiful Child

Oh unripe beauty's bloom and early morning-light,
Accustomed more with dolls than with sweet love to play,
When I for sake of you an endless sigh essay,
The foolish world but laughs and disbelieves my plight.
Yet, as among the green the young rose comes to sight,
As blossoms earn our praise which but the bud display,
So must I also see, though I would quiet stay,
That if a flame awakes, then heat pursues it tight.
My child, the quickest glow is struck from virgin flint,
A little spark may swift in ready tinder sink
And catch, if none attempts its passage soon to stint.
At borning, Venus' star can all the brighter blink,
The rosy grace of dawn must midday's glare defeat,
The merry spring takes rank before the summer's heat.

Hans Assmann von Abschatz

Die schöne Kleine

Du Mittel-Kreiss der Seel, ein eng-umschräncktes Feld,
Mir aber ausgesetzt zum Ruh-Punct meiner Sinnen,
Die nur auff dich allein die Neigung richten können,
Wie sich iedweder Strich vom Rand ins Mittel hält.
Klein ist der Angel-Stern, die Richt-Schnur aller Welt;
Klein ist des Schützen Ziel, dadurch er muss gewinnen;
Klein ist das Bienen-Volck; iedennoch wird man innen,
Wie süss ihr Honig und wie scharff ihr Stachel fällt.
O Auszug alles gutts, du bist ja billich klein,
Weil auch in tieffer See und in der Berge Gründen
Die Muschel-Kinder zart, Demanten Zwerge sein:
Begriff von aller Lust, die auff der Welt zu finden,
Den Himmels-Bau entwirfft der kleinen Kugel Riss;
Mir ist dies kleine Schoss ein irrdisch Paradiss.

Hans Assmann von Abschatz

Die schöne Blatternde

Ihr Perlen, die ihr seyd vom Eiter-Thau empfangen,
Von innerlicher Hitz' erhöht und ausgekocht!
Ihr feuchten Sternen, wer von Milch die Strasse sucht,
Die sonst am Himmel glänzt, sind sie auff diesen Wangen.
Cupido hat allhier ein Stückwerck angefangen,
Das zarte Fell bedeckt, das Ros' und Purpur pocht,
Wie wenn der Wolcken Schleyr zu Trost erdurster Frucht
Im heissen Sommer wird der Sonnen vorgehangen.
Ihr Buhler seyd getrost, und legt den Kummer hin,
Dass ihrer Liljen Pracht die Fäulniss wird verletzen:
Sie werden freudiger auff diesen Regen blühn.
Pflegt die gescheide Welt der Steine Schmuck zu schätzen,
Das zarte Muschel-Kind aus tieffer See zu ziehn,
Hier zeuget die Natur Opal, Perl' und Rubin.

Hans Assmann von Abschatz

The Lady, Fair and Small

Mid-circle of the soul, a narrow-bordered field,
You resting-point to which my senses take repair:
Since but to you alone they can their yearning bear,
As every stroke goes straight from edge to heart of shield.
Small is the polar star, which does earth's plumb-line yield,
Small is the markman's goal, where he wins triumph's share,
Small is the folk of bees, and yet we are aware
How sweet their honey is, how sharp a sting they wield.
Oh excerpt of good things, you are quite fairly small,
For in the fathomed sea and in the mountain's ground
The conch's tender babes and diamond midgets crawl.
Oh essence of all joy that in the world is found!
To sketch the heavens does a little globe suffice:
This little lap's to me an earthly paradise.

Hans Assmann von Abschatz

The Pimpled Beauty

Oh pearls, you which are bred and spawned from pussy dew,
And which an inward heat has caused to bake and swell!
You sodden stars: whoe'er may seek the milky route,
Which else the sky adorns, finds on these cheeks its view.
Here Cupid has essayed a work in needles' lieu,
And hid the skin which rose and crimson did excel,
As when the veil of clouds, the aid of thirsty fruit,
Is hung in summer's heat, the sunlight to subdue.
You lovers, be consoled, and let no care remain
That rottenness will bring her lilies' pride dismay.
More joyfully they'll bloom for having sipped this rain.
The clever world is wont stones' splendor to assay,
The tender mussel's child from ocean depths to loose:
Here nature opal, pearl, and ruby may produce.

Hans Assmann von Abschatz

Die Schöne mit hohem Rücken

Wie ists? Verirrte sich die kluge Meister-Hand?
Schlieff irgend die Natur, die alles prägt und heget,
Ward sie durch Zorn, ward sie durch Eyfersucht beweget,
Dass sie dich ohne Schuld versetzt in solchem Stand?
Als sie dein Angesicht gantz überirrdisch fand,
So hat sie eine Last dem Rücken auffgeleget:
Weil deiner Augen Paar des Himmels Feuer träget,
So zeigt das Hintertheil der Erde finstres Land.
Ach ja, sie irrte sich durch des Verhängniss Trieb:
Denn sie die Liebe nackt und fliegend bilden wolte,
Nur dass ihr zu viel Stoff zu Flügeln überblieb:
Und, hat sie nicht gefehlt, so sag ich, dass es solte
Des Atlas Bildniss seyn, den Männern darzuthun:
Dass auch der Welt-Kreiss könnt auff einer Frauen ruhn.

Hans Assmann von Absschatz

Die schöne Hinckende

Muss dieses Wunder-Bild, der Abgott vieler Hertzen,
Auff ungewissem Grund ungleicher Pfeiler stehn?
Was Pracht und Witz erhebt, macht Demuth noch so schön
Was will uns denn an ihr derselben Bildniss schmertzen?
Pflegt nicht die Königin der göldenen Himmels-Kertzen
Auch wechsels-weise sich zu sencken, zu erhöhn?
Der schönen Venus Wirth, Vulcan, muss hinckend gehn:
Man sieht sein schönes Feur mit falschen Springen schertzen.
Vielleicht wird sie dadurch, Verliebte, minder kühn;
Und wär auch dieses nicht, so hilfft doch solcher Mangel,
Dass sie euch nicht so bald kan aus den Augen fliehn.
Das kleinste Theil der Welt sieht die zwey Himmelsangel
In gleichem Stande ruhn; je mehr sich einer neigt,
Jemehr sein Gegentheil dort in die Höhe steigt.

Hans Assmann von Abschatz

The Beauty with the Hunchback

What's this? Was there a lapse of clever master hand?
Had nature dropped asleep, who must all stamp and nurse?
Could jealousy or rage turn nature so perverse
That she your innocence to such condition banned?
When she your countenance (far more than earthly) scanned,
She laid upon your back a burden and a curse:
Because your eyelight's brace the starry fires rehearse,
The rearward parts display our planet's gloomy land.
In truth, she tripped herself by some desire of fate:
For she had wished to form Love nude and flying free,
And found that for the wings she'd cut too large a plait.
And, if she has not erred, I say that it must be
An Atlas-image which for men makes manifest
That even the globe of earth could on a woman rest.

Hans Assmann von Abschatz

The Beauty Who Limps

An idol much beloved, must then this wonder-mien
Rest on the treacherous ground of unlike pillars' pair?
What wit and grace enhance, her meekness makes more fair.
Why should we taste of pain in gazing at this scene?
For does not, change-about, the gold sky-candles' queen
Make it her wont a path twixt fall and rise to share?
And Vulcan, Venus' spouse, a limping gait must bear:
One sees his handsome fire in clumsy leaps careen.
Perhaps she's for this cause, oh lovers, grown less bold;
And though this were not true, still, such a fault must aid
In making her less swift to flee your vision's hold.
The world's least part can tell when in some equal grade
The skies' twain hinges rest: the more the one descends,
The more his comrade there his coursing upward wends.

Hans Assmann von Abschatz

Die schöne Gross-Nase

In einer See voll Milch und Blutt der frischen Wangen
Ist deiner Nase Thurm zum Pharus ausgestellt.
Damit der Hoffnung Schiff am Felsen nicht zerschellt,
Glänzt ein gedoppelt Licht von oben ausgehangen.
Recht, was dem Himmel schmeckt, muss in die Höhe prangen.
Cupido, der dein Aug als seinen Bogen hält,
Hat ihm so starcken Pfeil mit Fleisse zugestellt,
Dass er uns desto mehr ins Hertze könne langen.
O Nase, werth dem Stirn-Gebürge beyzuwohnen,
Du kanst in dem Gesicht, das aller Hügel rein,
Der Klugheit Wetzstein und der Schönheit Brücke seyn.
Wem deine stoltze Zier in Augen ist ein Dorn,
Der schmäh den Adler auch, das grosse Nasenhorn,
Den Naso, den Nasic, und alle Nasamonen.

Hans Assmann von Abschatz

Die schöne Schwangere

Vor führtestu ein Hertz allein in deinem Leibe/
Und blühtest Rosen-gleich in Anmutts-voller Zier;
Izt trägstu deren zwey/ und macht Verdruss bey dir/
Dass deine Röthe nicht in altem Stande bleibe.
Nicht klage/ dass die Frucht der Blütte Glantz vertreibe:
Geht nicht der volle Mond dem halben Lichte für/
Und wär er noch so blass? zeigt sich ein Mangel hier/
So dencke/ dass man ihn der Schuld der Zeit zuschreibe.
Dir steht wohl an und frey/ was andern ist verwehrt.
Das schwange Schiff im See trägt Last/ doch unbeschwert/
Dieweil es an dem Port sich zu entladen sucht.
Ulysses keusche Frau beschloss ihr langes Weben/
Dass sie nach gleicher Kost der bitter-süssen Frucht/
Was Händ und Füsse hat/ der Nachwelt konte geben.

Hans Assmann von Abschatz

The Beauty of Great Nose

Within your fresh cheeks' sea, where milk and blood do flow,
The tower of your nose for lighthouse-duty's starred.
That not upon some cliff hope's ship to wreck be jarred,
Upon its pinnacle a double-light does show.
What Heaven fills with joy into the sky must grow.
And Cupid, who your eye must as his bow regard,
Has to it with design attached a bolt so hard
That it with greater ease into our heart can go.
Oh nose, which worthy bounds the forehead's mountain yoke,
You can within that face, which of all hills is free,
Both wisdom's whetting stone and bridge of beauty be.
If any man does deem your ornament a thorn,
Let him the eagle too and mighty rhino scorn,
And Naso, Nasica, and all Nasoma-folk.[2]

Hans Assmann von Abschatz

The Lady, Fair and Pregnant

Before, a single heart within your breast held sway
And like the roses you in blooming grace had grown.
But now you bear two hearts, and in annoyance moan
That your red cheeks do not in old condition stay.
Yet weep not, if the fruit its blossom drives away:
Is not a half-way light worse than the moon full-blown,
Though pale this moon may be? If some fault here is shown,
Consider that to time we must the credit lay.
Much you may freely do which others may not dare,
Careless the heavy ships at sea their burdens bear,
While to some port they seek to take their laden route.
Ulysses' virtuous wife at length her loom did leave
That, after she had known that same sweet-bitter fruit,
Posterity could a gift with hand and foot receive.

Heinrich Albert

MUSICALISCHE KÜRBS-HÜTTE
   (Ein Kürbis spricht:)

Mit der Zeit ich kommen bin/
Fall' auch mit der Zeit dahin!

Mensch/ hierinnen sind wir gleich/
Du magst Schön seyn/ Jung und Reich:
Unser Pracht kan nicht bestehn/
Beyde müssen wir vergehn.

Nun ich jung noch bin und grüne/
o/ so hält man mich im Wehrt!
Bin ich welck und nicht mehr diene/
Wer ist dann der mein begehrt?

Mensch/ ich kan es leichtlich gläuben
Dass du wünscht/ ich möchte bleiben;
Nicht dein Will'/ auch meiner nicht/
Gottes Wille nur geschicht.

Wenn der rauhe Herbst nun kömpt/
Fall' ich ab/ und muss verderben.
Wenn dein Ziel dir ist bestimmt/
Armer Mensch/ so mustu sterben.

Sieh mich an/
Und dencke dran:
Ich muss fort
Von diesem Ort!
Mit dir helt auch
Gott solchen Brauch.

Dem Herbst verlangt nach mir/
Mich zu verderben;
Dem Tod'/ O Mensch/ nach dir/
Auch Du must sterben!

Heinrich Albert

Musical Pumpkin-Hut [3]
(A Pumpkin Speaks)

I with time to life ascend,
And with time do come to end.

Man, in this we are the same:
You wealth, beauty, youth can claim,
Yet our splendor must grow sere,
We must twin-like disappear.

Now that I'm still young and green,
Men do high my worth admire!
When I spent and withered seem,
Who will know for me desire?

Man, I easy can believe
That you'd wish I would not leave;
Not your will, nor mine, has won.
Heaven's will alone is done.

When the cruel fall holds sway,
I must sick and ruined lie.
When an ending stops your way,
Wretched man, then you must die.

See me aright,
And weigh the sight:
That I am bound
To leave this ground.
God has with you
Such usage too.

That he my end might gain
Does autumn sigh;
Man, death would you obtain,
You too must die!

Wer wird nach kurtzen Tagen
    Mich beklagen/
  Wenn ich verwelckt nun bin?
Auch Dir wirds widerfahren
    Nach wenig Jahren/
  Wenn Dich der Tod nimpt hin.

Die Zeit und wir vergehn!
Was wir hie sehen stehn
In diesem grünen Garten/
Verwelckt in kurtzer Zeit/
Weil schon des Herbstes Neid
Scheint drauff zu warten.

Ich/ und meine Blätter/ wissen
Dass wir dann erst fallen müssen
Wenn der rauhe Herbst nun kömpt:
Aber Du/ Mensch/ weist ja nicht
Ob's nicht heute noch geschicht
Dass dir Gott das Leben nimpt?

Ob ich gleich muss bald von hier/
Kriegstu dennoch Frucht von mir;
Wenn man dich/ Mensch/ wird begraben/
Was wirst Du für Früchte haben?

O ich habe schon vernommen
Dass mein Feind/ der Herbst/ wird kommen/
Dessen Raub ich werden sol!
Lieber Mensch/ gehab dich wol!

Who, when brief days are spent,
        Will lament
    How blighted I have grown?
  Though death will make you die
        Ere few years fly,
    My fate will be your own.

  Time goes, we disappear!
  What we see standing here
  Behind this garden-gate
  In little time does fade,
  Since autumn's envious shade
  Already seems to wait.

  I and all my leaves do know
  That we then to earth must go
  When the cruel fall holds sway.
  Man, you ne'er a pledge have won
  That God, ere the day be done,
  Will not take your life away.

  Though but brief I can remain,
  You will fruits from me obtain.
  When you, man, are borne to earth,
  To what fruits will you give birth?

  Now the news is brought to me
  That fall comes, my enemy,
  And will me as quarry fell:
  Oh, dear human, fare you well.

Johann Georg Albini

ENGLISCHE ANREDUNG AN DIE SEELE

Liebste Braut du Schöne/
Bürgerin der Ewigkeiten/
 Freundinn Gottes steh doch auff!
  Steh doch auff!
Dein Bräutgam läst dich holen/
Die Lufft brent voll Violen/

Der sanffte Westwind webt auss seinem blauen Grunde/
 Jtzunder ist die Stunde/
Da der Silber-Weisse-Wagen/
Dich soll von der Erde tragen/
 Steh auff O Liebster Schatz!
 Steh auff dort ist der Platz!
Wo die Rubinen bluten/
 Wo die grünen Mandel Ruthen
  In voller blüthe stehn.
O Seele steh doch auff/ nim ein das Reich der Freuden/
 Das weisse Kleid von Seiden/
 Das wird dir zugebracht/
Auff! sage doch der Welt nur immer gute Nacht!

Unbekannter Dichter

ALLEGORISCH SONNET

Amanda liebstes kind, du brustlatz kalter hertzen,
 Der liebe feuerzeug, goldschachtel edler zier,
 Der seuffzer blasebalg, des traurens lösch-papier,
Sandbüchse meiner pein, und baum-öl meiner schmertzen,
Du speise meiner lust, du flamme meiner kertzen,
 Nachtstülchen meiner ruh, der poesie clystier,
 Des mundes alecant, der augen lust-revier,
Der complementen sitz, du meisterin zu schertzen,
 Der tugend quodlibet, calender meiner zeit,
 Du andachts-fackelchen, du quell der frölichkeit,
Du tieffer abgrund du voll tausend guter morgen,
 Der zungen honigseim, des hertzens marcipan,
 Und wie man sonsten dich mein kind beschreiben kan.
Lichtputze meiner noth, und flederwisch der sorgen.

Johann Georg Albini

ANGELIC ADDRESS TO THE SOUL

Beauty, dearest bride,
Dweller of eternity,
  Mistress of the Lord, arise!
          Now arise!
Your groom bids you return,
The winds with violets burn,

The gentle zephyr stirs from out its azure sphere.
  Now is that moment here
  When the white and silver wain
  Takes you from the earth again.
      Awake, oh dearest love!
      Your dwelling is above!
  There where the rubies bleed,
  And where the greening almond-reed
    In fullest blossom stands.
Oh spirit, now arise! The realm of joy receive,
  White cloths of silver weave:
    All this is brought to you.
Arise! And bid the world forever sweet adieu.

Anonymous

ALLEGORICAL SONNET

Amanda, dearest child, you cold heart's stomacher,
  Gold-chest of charms, and box where loving's tinder lies,
  A blotting pad for woe, a bellows of cruel sighs,
Sand-strewer to despair, sweet oil to sufferer.
My candle's very flame, my joy's provisioner,
  The Muses' enema, night-jar that sleep defies,
  The lips' dark alicant, lust-pasture to my eyes,
Abode of compliments, and jests' sweet fashioner.
  You virtue's quiddity, my time's ephemeris,
  Devotion's midget torch, and fountainhead of bliss,
You yawning chasm filled with thousand mornings fair,
  Pure honey of the tongue, and marchpane of the heart,
  And whate'er else, my child, that may your grace impart,
You snuffer of lament and feather-broom of care.

Anton Ulrich,
Herzog von Braunschweig-Wolfenbüttel

STERBLIED

Es ist genug! Mein matter Sinn
Sehnt sich dahin, wo meine Väter schlafen.
Ich hab es endlich guten Fug,
Es ist genug! Ich muss mir Rast verschaffen.

Ich bin ermüdt, ich hab geführt
Die Tages Bürd: Es muss einst Abend werden.
Erlös mich, Herr, spann aus den Pflug,
Es ist genug! Nimm von mir die Beschwerden.

Die grosse Last hat mich gedrückt,
Ja schier erstickt so viele lange Jahre.
Ach lass mich finden, was ich such.
Es ist genug! Mit solcher Kreuzes-Ware.

Nun gute Nacht, ihr meine Freund,
Ihr meine Feind, ihr Guten und ihr Bösen!
Euch folg die Treu, euch folg der Trug.
Es ist genug! Mein Gott will mich auflösen.

So nimm nun, Herr, hin meine Seel,
Die ich befehl in deine Händ und Pflege.
Schreib sie ein in dein Lebens Buch,
Es ist genug! Dass ich mich schlafen lege.

Nicht besser soll es mir ergehn,
Als wie geschehn den Vätern, die erworben
Durch ihren Tod des Lebens Ruch.
Es ist genug! Es sei also gestorben!

Anton Ulrich,
Herzog von Braunschweig-Wolfenbüttel

Dying Song

It is enough! My feeble sense
Yearns to that place my fathers slumber in.
At last I have good legacy;
It is enough! I must my sabbath win.

For I am tired; I long have borne
The charge of day; sometime must darkness fall.
Unspan the plow, Lord, set me free;
It is enough! Take from me trouble's thrall.

This mighty weight has pressed me down,
Yea, near has throttled me these many years:
Oh, what I seek, that let me see;
It is enough! Put end to cross and tears.

And now good night, my faithful friends,
And you, my foes, you good men and you ill!
May you have troth, you treachery;
It is enough! My Lord will make me still.

So take then, Lord, my soul away,
Which I commend into Your hands and keep.
Into Your life-book enter me;
It is enough! That I may go to sleep.

No better shall it fare with me
Than with my fathers, who themselves have won
By very death life's remedy;
It is enough! Be now my dying done!

Gottfried Arnold

Gedoppelt Licht

O Glanz der Herrlichkeit, du unsre Sonne,
Der du der Lichter Brunn und Ursprung bist:
Schick uns dein Feur aus deines Reiches Wonne,
Bis unser Geist in Eins vollkommen ist.
Entzünd uns mehr zugleich in einer Kraft,
Erhalte uns in deinem Liebeleben:
Was uns dein Sinn für Lieb und Frieden schafft,
Das sei nur zum gemeinen Nutz gegeben.
Dein Evangelium sei uns gemein
Und müsse sich auf andre so erstrecken,
Dass ihrer mehr in dir recht eines sein,
Bis dein Erkenntnis wird die Erd bedecken.
Ach zeuch uns ganz in dein verborgen Licht,
Da wir vor deinem Thron als Fackel stehen:
Wenn einem ja bisweilen Licht gebricht,
So lass von dir den neuen Strahl ausgehen.
Kein wankend Mondenlicht, kein Irrungsstern,
Kein Schatten, keine Nacht darf uns verdunkeln:
Wir wollen hier und ewig dort so gern
Zu deinem Ruhm nur stehen, brennen, funkeln,
So wird das doppelt helle Licht verdunkeln nicht!

August Ausgpurger

Arte & Marte

Wie mancher schöner Geist/ wie mancher kluger Sinn/
  Muss durch das Unglücks-Joch gedrücket unterliegen?
  Er schwinget offtermals die Federn/ auffzufliegen
  Zum hohen Helicon/ da Er möcht nehmen hin
Das grüne Lorberreiss/ den endlichen Gewinn/
  Muss aber alsobald sich wieder unterbiegen/
  Und siehet keinen Weg/ wie dass er könte kriegen
Den Lohn/ den Tugend giebt/ die Arbeit-Trösterin.
Drumb nimmt Er offtermals den blancken Stahl zur Hand/
  Und geht Bellonen nach/ für welcher flieht das Land
Der schewe Bawersmann. Und wer wolt diss versprechen?
Es liegt in gleicher Waag die Ehr' erlangt durchs Schwerd/
  Als durch geschickte Kunst; und ist im höchsten werth/
  Wenn Stahl nicht Tugend kan/ noch Tugend Stahl zerbrechen.

Gottfried Arnold

Doubled Light

Oh You our sun, oh our magnificence,
Who are of lights both origin and source:
From out Your empire's bliss Your fire send hence
Until our soul in oneness takes true course.
Ignite at once in single strength our hand
And us within Your loving life preserve:
What love and peace we garner from Your hand,
Let them but to a common profit serve.
Then make Your gospel our community
And over others thus itself unfold,
So that their host in You true One may be,
Until Your knowledge all the earth does hold.
Oh draw us whole into Your hidden light,
Since we as torches stand before Your throne:
If it should chance that someone's light know blight,
Then let from You the novel beam be sown.
No fickle light of moon, no false-starred glare,
No night, no shade makes us to darkness turn:
Both here we will and will eternal there
For Your renown but stand and spark and burn:
Thus will the doubly burning light not drown in night!

August Augspurger

Arte & Marte

How many a noble soul, how many a clever mind
  Must by misfortune's yoke be bowed down in despair?
  The spirit beats his wings to test if they will bear
  Him up to Helicon, where he would seek and find
The final branch, the goal with laurel branch entwined,
  But instantly he must from this attempt forbear;
  No highway can he spy where he might come to share
  The pay that virtue gives, who's to the toiler kind.
Therefore he oftentimes the shining steel does seize,
  And walks Bellona's [4] path, before whose coming flees
  The timid husbandman. And who might this gainsay?
There lies in equal weight the honor won by sword
  And that of skillful art, and has its best reward,
  When virtue slays not steel nor steel can virtue slay.

Johann von Besser

Beschreibung der Schlacht bey Fehrberlin,

in welcher Seine Churfl. Durchl. gantz unverhofft aus Francken
zurück kommende, die Schwedische Armee mit der blossen Cavallerie
angegriffen hatte den 18. Jun. 1675.

Der Adler, der zum Schirm des Reiches ausgezogen,
Kam, wie ein schneller Blitz, verdeckt zurück geflogen;
Und sass der Löwen-Brut so schleunig auf der Haut,
Dass sie ihn fast noch ehr gefühlet, als geschaut.
Den man bissher am Rhein, die Reichs-Macht zu erhalten,
Als einen Fabius behutsam sehen walten;
Wiess nun, dass er für sich auch ein Marcellus sey:
Der nur mit einem Klump geschwinder Reuterey
Den überraschten Feind biss auf das Haupt geschlagen:
Sein blosses Volck zu Ross bracht Er, den Kampf zu wagen.
Krieg, Kranckheit, Schmertz und Gram, sein todter Carl Aemil,
Und was für Unglück mehr Ihn eben itzt befiel,
Kont aller Hertzen zwar mit Furcht und Leid erschüttern;
Ihn aber muste diss nur so viel mehr erbittern.
Er kam von Francken her, wie sporen-streichs gerannt;
Und als er Ratenau voll seiner Feinde fand:
Must Dörfling, Dönhof, Götz es bey der Nacht ersteigen,
Und sich dem Wangelin im besten Schlaffe zeigen.
Wie sonsten, wenn des Nachts ein plötzlicher Rumor
Sich in der Stadt erhebt, der Feind sey in dem Thor,
Der durch die Gassen schon mit hellem Hauffen dringet;
Dann idermann erwacht, und aus dem Bette springet:
Vor Schrecken aber doch nur hin und wieder läufft,
Und mit der Aengstigung mehr die Verwirrung häufft;
Voll Zweifels was zu thun, was erstlich zu beginnen:
So wenig konte sich auch Wangelin besinnen.
Die er noch fern geschätzt, und nicht gedacht zu sehn;
Sah er, umb sich herumb, mit blossen Schwerdtern stehn:
Wie zwar vermeinete, doch cörperliche Schatten,
Die würcklich seinen Tod in ihren Händen hatten.
Man grief ihn; und im Plotz, ward dessen Regiment,
Das ihn zu retten lief, auf ewig abgetrennt,
Und, wie man es ertapt, in seinem Blut begraben.
Wir eilten ferner fort, den andern nachzutraben.
Hingegen wie ein Wolff, wenn er in einem Stall,
Des Hirten Ankunfft merckt, noch vor dem Uberfall
Mit angezognem Schweiff versucht davon zu wischen:

Johann von Besser

DESCRIPTION OF THE BATTLE AT FEHRBELLIN

in which His Majesty, the Electoral Prince, returning all unexpectedly from Franconia, had attacked the Swedish Army with his mere cavalry, on the 18th of June, 1675 [5].

The eagle who had gone to be our empire's shield,
Came flying back, a bolt both hasty and concealed,
And dug his claws so quick into the lion's pelt,
That it scarce saw the bird, ere it his talons felt.
The man, who on the Rhine, the empire to preserve,
We'd seen until today like careful Fabius [6] serve —
He demonstrated now he could Marcellus [7] be:
Who with a single band of swift-hoofed cavalry
The puzzled enemy a mortal blow did smite:
His merest mounted men he brought to dare the fight.
War, sickness, pain, and woe, his Carl Emil's decease [8],
And whate'er else must now his list of cares increase,
Could every heart indeed with fear and grief turn sore,
Yet in his case could but incense him all the more.
He from Franconia did hell-for-leather go;
When he found Rathenow [9] all swollen with the foe,
It Dörfling, Dönhof, Götz [9] must in the darkness scale,
And Wangelin [9], who lay in deepest sleep, assail:
As elsewise, when at night a sudden rumor's spate
Does in the city rise, that foes are at the gate,
And even now their troops along the byways sweep,
Then all the sleepers wake, and from their covers leap,
And yet for very fear but helter-skelter run
And have, with their distress, still more confusion won,
Not knowing what to do, what first to undertake:
Just so could Wangelin small sense of matters make.
Those whom he'd thought still far, nor dreamed to see so near,
He saw with naked swords from every side appear:
Like fancied – to be sure – and yet corporeal shades
Who in reality bore death upon their blades.
They seized him, and at once that regiment was stayed
And cut forever off, which hastened to his aid,
And buried in its blood, as soon as it was caught.
We, trotting further on, the other armies sought.
But yet, even as the wolf, when he within the fold,
Before he strikes, is made by shepherd's tread less bold,
And, tail between his legs, attempts to steal away,

Bemühte Wrangel sich, in unwegsamen Büschen,
Uns zeitig zu entgehn, nach aufgerafftem Stab.
Wir aber schnitten ihn vom Gross des Heeres ab,
An welches alsobald sich Homburg muste hängen;
Biss, da sie sich gesetzt, der Held in vollem Sprengen,
Zunechst bey Fehrberlin auf deren Lager stiess:
Das mit Geschütz verschantzt, sich allen Sieg verhiess.
      O Tag! an dessen Glück die gantze Marck gehangen!
Wer, als nur unser Held, hätt' dess sich unterfangen?
Mit Reutern kleiner Zahl, ermüdet zu dem Streit,
Ein ausgeruthes Heer, stoltz von der alten Zeit,
Das zweymahl stärcker war, im Vortheil anzugreiffen?
Sein Vortrab muste schon den einen Flügel streiffen.
Der Kriegs-Rath widerrieth die allzukühne That;
Er aber blieb darauf: Nur Treffen sey der Rath.
Der Feind ist in der Furcht, sprach Er, und in der Enge:
Was irrt des Höchsten Schutz, und unsern Muth die Menge?
Das Volk verlangt den Kampf. Er redt es kürtzlich an:
Was ihr am Rhein gesucht, findt ihr auf diesem Plan.
Ihr wist, was man verübt: So übt auch nun die Rache:
Ich sterbe heut, mit euch, für die gerechte Sache.
Man trieb im ersten Stutz uns alsobald zurück;
Er hielt den Abfall auf mit seinem blossen Blick.
Sein Hertz verliess Ihn nicht, schien gleich das Glück zu wancken;
Er rief: Ihr Freunde halt, diss ist der Ehren Schrancken:
Und drang selbst in den Streit, wo der am dicksten war.
Man unterschied ihn nicht, als nur durch die Gefahr:
Nur dadurch, was umb Ihn die Stücke nieder schossen;
Womit zugleich sein Geist sich auf sein Heer ergossen.
Nicht anders, wie ein Feur, das bey entstandnem Wind,
Man in die Wälder steckt, erst eintzelweiss beginnt,
Und bald den gantzen Forst in eine Flamme kehret:
So stürzte sich sein Volck, von seinem Grimm bewehret,
Im Wetter des Gefechts, und der Canonen Dampf,
Nun desto hitziger in den erneurten Kampf,
Und mengten sich in eins mit dem so grossen Heere,
Trotz aller ihrer Macht und ihrer Gegenwehre.
Des Feindes Fuss-Volck traf; allein im ersten Strich,
Trat unsre Reuterey es Rottweiss unter sich.
Unendlich drungen ein die Fürstlichen Trabanten;
Die mit den Anhaltschen den Delwig überrannten.
Der tapffre Dörfling bog das Ostrogotsche Horn;
Da ging es umb und umb, von hinten und von vorn:
Man breitete sich aus, auf alle Reih und Glieder;
Schoss, stach, hieb, warf und brach, ohn Unterschied darnieder,

Just so, in pathless woods, Sir Wrangel [10] would essay
A timely flight, when he in haste his camp had left:
We made the army's trunk of Wrangel's head bereft.
Our Homburg to that trunk his weight did swiftly latch,
Till, when they'd stopped their flight, the hero with dispatch
At last near Fehrbellin on their encampment came,
Whose cannoned trenches seemed their victory to proclaim.
      Oh day, whose end will tell the fortunes of the Mark!
Who, save our hero, would upon this quest embark?
With but small cavalry, from all its fighting tired,
To charge a rested corps, by ancient pride inspired
And twice the strength of his, and posted on good ground?
His vanguard even now the Swedish wing has found.
War's wisdom would against the too bold deed advise,
Yet he stayed adamant: "The blow alone is wise.
The foeman is afraid," he said "and sore perplexed.
Have numbers God's defence and Prussian valor vexed?
The troopers' wish is war, and quick their task they're taught:
You'll find upon this field what by the Rhine you sought.
You know what they have done. Do now your vengeance take.
Today I shall meet death with you for justice' sake."
At first attack the foe straightway made us retreat,
Yet he with but a glance could each defection meet.
His heart did not play false, though fortune would resign;
He cried: "You friends, stand firm. Here's honor's borderline!"
He joined himself the fray, where it the hottest burned:
One could not make him out, save by the dangers spurned,
Save by the count of balls which all around him fell;
And thus his spirit began upon his men to tell.
Not other than the fire, which at the rising blast
Is set within the woods, and here and there takes fast,
Then turns the forest soon into a holocaust,
His people plunge, their arms by his quick rage embossed,
Into the combat's gale and through the cannon's reek,
And all the hotter now the fight's renewal seek,
Then 'gainst that mighty force their little squadron smite,
In spite of hard defence and all the Swedish might.
The foe's footsoldiers struck, but quick our horsemen trod
Them at the first affray to death by troop and squad.
The prince's own trabants unceasing made attack,
And with the Anhalt men drove Delwig's legions back.
The Ostrogothic horn [11] then valiant Dörfling bent,
And from the rear, the front, and round and round it went.
Against each rank and file there spread our charging folk,
And, indiscriminate, shot, thrust, hewed, cast, and broke

Was wich und widerstand. Kurtz: der das Land geprest,
Ward todt darauf gestreut; und dessen Überrest
Must' über Hals und Kopf nach seiner Heymath weichen:
Und hinterliess der Marck Geschütz, Gewehr und Leichen.

Whatever flew or fought. The tyrants of our land
Were strewn on it in death, and their surviving band
Was to its native place precipitately fled,
Bequeathing to the Mark its cannon, arms, and dead [12].

Sigmund von Birken

HIRTENGEDICHT

Hier sitz' ich an dem Rand/ in deines Ufers Schatten/
   Du schlanker Pegnitzfluss/ hier nehm' ich meine Rast/
   Hier schau ich deiner Fluht nicht-ungestuemmen Brast/
   Hier seh ich neben dir die frischbegruenten Matten.

Du aber/ Vatterstrom in meinem Mutterland/
   Ist dein Geraeusche dann von Lust so weit entsessen/
   Dass deiner Ufer mich ein fremdes macht vergessen?
   Nein/Ungluekk Ungluekk hat dich mir/mich dir entwandt.

Es schwebet ueber dir ein schweres Himmelhassen/
   Der Weltgemeinde Sturm/ des Krieges Jammerglut.
   Kuertz'/ O du Wolkengott/ des starken Wetters Wut/

Lass ach! die Eger frey durchrauschen ihre Gassen/
   Die manches Thal durchwaescht. Dann soll mir ihre Lust
   Staets eine Wollust seyn/ ein suesser Sinnenmust.

Sigmund von Birken

TRAUR-HIRTEN-SPIEL

Das schöne Himmel-blau lacht von Bogen-schanzen.
Das Welt-aug äuglet ab: die güldne Flittern danzen
und kreutzen durch die Luft. Der Wolken Purpurschein/
erfreut die warme Welt. Nur ich/ muss traurig seyn!

Die Nymfen spieglen sich dort in den klaren Brünnen.
Die Quellen wallen auf/ die jezt entfässelt rinnen/
und schlürfen durch die Au/ der Herden süsser Wein.
Die Felder freuen sich. Nur ich/ muss traurig seyn!

Das Jahr in wochen ligt/ gebieret tausend Freuden.
Der Wälder haube laubt. Die Schäflein wieder weiden.
Die Blume/ stirnt das Gras. Er siht und tritt herein
die liebe Lenzenlust. Nur ich/ muss traurig seyn!

Sigmund von Birken

SHEPHERD-SONG

I sit here at your edge, in your embankment's screen,
   You slender Pegnitz-tide; here I do seek repose,
   Here I see how your flight in hasteless vigor goes,
Here I beside you watch the meadows freshly green.

Oh father-flood which cuts my mother region through,
   Is then your sound from joy at such great distance set
   That on a foreign strand I must your strand forget?
No, mishap you from me did take and me from you.

There hovers over you a heavy Heaven's hate,
   The world-troop's hurricane, the war's hot plunderage.
   Make brief, oh welkin-god, the awful tempest's rage.

Oh let the Eger [13] free its paths negotiate
   And water many dales. Then will its joy for me
   Sweet cider of the sense, and endless pleasure be.

Sigmund von Birken

PLAY OF THE SHEPHERD'S LAMENT

The handsome heaven's blue laughs from its bow's expanse.
The world-eye ogles on: the golden midges dance
And criss-cross through the air. The cloudbank's crimson glow
Makes glad the warming world. But I must sadness know.

The nymphs behold themselves within the limpid well,
And presently unchained, the sources run and swell,
The herds' sweet wine does soft along the pastures flow.
The meadows jubilate. But I must sadness know.

The year in childbed lies, a thousand glees to bear,
The wood's hood greens, and forth the feeding lambs do fare.
The flower crowns the grass. Sweet springtime-joy this show
Discerns and makes its own. But I must sadness know.

Sigmund von Birken

HIRTENGEDICHT

Jener mag fluechtige Froelichkeit finden/
Kraentze von schaetzbaren Bluemelein binden.
Unsere Blumen/ so jedermann frey/
Bringen das Singen zur Schaefer-Schalmey.
      Die froelichen Lieder
      Erfreuen uns wieder.
Wir ruhen voll riechenden Dufftens allhier.

Blumen/ in niemahls-bepflantzeten Garten/
Blumen/ von wilden/ doch lieblichen Arten.
Lentzen-beglaentzend-erneurender Lust
Hurtigen Hirten und Heerden bewust.
      Beschminket die Felder/
      Beschmukket die Waelder.
Wir leben voll loeblicher Liebesbegier.

Flora/ die sonder Bemuehung gebieret/
Unsere Wiesen und Fluesse bezieret/
Schliesset den schrofen truebkiesslichen Sand/
Mahlet die Ufer mit buntlicher Hand.
      Die Pegnitz Najaden
      Sich neben ihr baden/
Wir sehen die nakkicht/ entweichet mit mir!

Sigmund von Birken

Ihr Blätter/ Wetterspiel/ ihr Vortrab frischer Früchte/
Des Zephyrs Buhlgewächs/ ihr leichte Lentzenbruht/
Ihr macht/ dass unsre Ruh im Schatten prächtig ruht/
Wie solten wir dann nicht euch dichten ein gedichte.
Der Zweige Zittern rauscht/ und weidet das Gesichte/
Von euch kömmt/ dass wir oft aufklären Sinn und Muht.
Nun Flora schütz euch fort für harter Hagels-Wut/
Es mache spätlich euch der Bläste Brast zu nichte.
Du aber/ fettes Gras/ Smaragden nahgesipt/
Du Blumenbunter Rokk der Wöchnerinn der Erden/
Wir zimmern ober dir oft unsrer Sorgen Sarg/
Die Heerden speisest du/ und bist uns nimmer karg;
Wohlan/ du müssest auch spat abgestreiffet werden/
Spat werde deine Zier vom Nordwind abgeknipt.

Sigmund von Birken

SHEPHERD-SONG

All men may hasty-gone happiness find,
Wreaths out of gold-worthy blossoms may bind;
Flowers which everyone picks to his need
Bring us sweet singing to shepherd-boy's reed.
      These high-hearted lays
      Make merry our days.
We rest full of fragrancy's sweet company.

Flowers from gardens that never knew spade,
Flowers in wild and yet lovely parade,
Sparkle-spring's gladness renewing its shine,
Known to the swift-footed shepherds and kine.
      Embellish the field,
      Emblazon the weald.
We live full of laudable love-lechery.

Flora, who fleeing each labor can bear,
Gives stream and meadow adornments to wear,
Closes the cruel, the sad-graveled sand,
Patterns the banks with a many-hued hand.
      The Pegnitz-sprites ride
      The waves at her side.
We see them all naked; come, vanish with me!

Sigmund von Birken

You leaves, you weather-game, you fresh fruit's cavalry,
The Zephyr's mistress-growth, you light brood of the spring,
Who to our rest a bed in restful shadow bring,
Why should we not for you a poem now compose?
The branches' trembling sings, and gives our sight repose,
From you we often learn to clear our hearts and sense.
May Flora give you now 'gainst hailstorm's rage defence,
May you the awful blasts destroy but tardily.
Yet you, you strong-sapped grass, near kin to emerald stone,
You bloom-bright coat that does the young earth-mother hide,
Above you we have built the coffin of our care;
You give the herds to eat, nor do our banquet spare.
Indeed, you should but late be stripped and put aside:
May late your life away by northern winds be blown.

Sigmund von Birken

DES EHRLIEBENDEN FLORIDANS LUSTIGES
HERBST- UND LIEBESLIED

Lustig zu Felde mit Pferden und Wagen,
Holet die Früchte, so Tellus getragen,
Sparet das Feiren, füllet die Scheuren,
Weizen und Roggen und Gersten bringt ein.
Floridan selber will Erntemann sein.

Lustig zu Walde mit Jägern und Hunden,
Bis man ein flüchtiges Hirschlein gefunden,
Suchet mit Winden, Hasen und Hinden,
Habt ihr gefangen, so stellet euch mild,
Floridan küsset vor Freuden sein Wild.

Lustig zum Garten mit Körben und Säcken,
Früchte zu brechen nehmt Leitern und Stecken,
Schüttelt die Zweige bis auf die Neige,
Floridan liebet vor allen die Nuss,
Solche zu brechen ist sonder Verdruss.

Lustig zu Wasser mit Reusen und Netzen,
Karpfen und Hechte die sollen ergetzen
Bellende Magen, hungrige Kragen,
Füllet mit Krebsen den ledigen Bauch,
Floridan angelt nach altem Gebrauch.

Lustig zur Auen mit Büchsen und Stangen,
Enten und Schnepfen und Lerchen zu fangen,
Schärfet den Nagel, schiesset mit Hagel,
Floridan ist es im Beizen geglückt,
Dass er ein liebliches Täublein berückt.

Lustig zun Reben die Trauben zu schneiden,
Presset die rötliche Beere mit Freuden,
Jauchzet und singet, hüpfet und springet,
Preise die Kelter mit fröhlichem Ton,
Floridan schmecket den Lippenwein schon.

Lustig zum Felde, zum Walde, zum Reben,
Lustig zum Garten, zum Wasser daneben,
Lustig zur Auen, lustig zur Frauen,
Lustig zur Tafel und lustig zur Bank,
Lustig im Leben und nimmermehr krank.

Sigmund von Birken

A Merry Autumn- and Love-Song
of Honor-Loving Floridan

Glad to the acres with wagon and four,
Fetch in the harvest which good Tellus bore;
Your slumber keep, make the barns heap.
Let us take barley, wheat, rye, as our own.
Floridan will as the reaper be known.

Glad to the forest with huntsman and hound,
Till we a hasty-foot staglet have found;
With greyhound go, rabbit and doe.
When you've made captives, then mercy essay,
Floridan kisses rejoicing his prey.

Glad to the garden with ladder and stick,
Take sack and basket if fruits you would pick.
Trouble the trees down to their lees.
Floridan's love is the nut before all,
Sheer delight comes with such dainties to fall.

Glad to the water with weir and with net,
Carp-fish and pike-fish to pleasure will set
Stomachs that bark, throats hungered stark.
Fill up with crayfish the belly that sighs,
Floridan fishes in old-fashioned wise.

Glad to the meadow with rifle and stake,
Larks there and wood-cocks and duck-folk to take.
Sharpen the nail, shoot with graped hail.
Floridan well in his hawking has fared,
Since he a passing sweet dovelet has snared.

Glad to the vineyard, to prune there the grape,
Press the red berries that joy may escape,
Rollick and sing, caper and spring,
Honor the wine press with merriment's cry,
Floridan now does the tasting wine try.

Glad to the acres, the forest, the vines,
Glad to the water, the garden's confines,
Glad to our dells, glad to our belles,
Glad to the table and glad to the jill,
Glad in our living and nevermore ill.

Lustig zu schlafen und lustig zu wachen,
Lustig zu tanzen, und lustig zu lachen,
Lustig zu zielen, lustig zu spielen,
Lustig zur Feder und lustig zum Schwert,
Lustig zu Wagen und lustig zu Pferd.

Lustig zu trinken und lustig zu essen,
Lustig vor allen Gott nimmer vergessen,
Lustig im Herzen, lustig zu scherzen,
Lasset uns lustig mit Floridan sein,
Floridan lustig mit Fillis allein.

Barthold Heinrich Brockes

Kirschblüte bei der Nacht

Ich sahe mit betrachtendem Gemüte
Jüngst einen Kirschbaum, welcher blühte,
In kühler Nacht beim Mondenschein;
Ich glaubt', es könne nichts von grössrer Weisse sein.
Es schien, als wär' ein Schnee gefallen;
Ein jeder, auch der kleinste Ast
Trug gleichsam eine rechte Last
Von zierlich weissen runden Ballen.
Es ist kein Schwan so weiss, da nämlich jedes Blatt,
Indem daselbst des Mondes sanftes Licht
Selbst durch die zarten Blätter bricht,
Sogar den Schatten weiss und sonder Schwärze hat.
Unmöglich, dacht ich, kann auf Erden
Was weissers aufgefunden werden.
Indem ich nun bald hin, bald her
Im Schatten dieses Baumes gehe,
Sah ich von ungefähr
Durch alle Blumen in die Höhe
Und ward noch einen weissern Schein,
Der tausendmal so weiss, der tausendmal so klar,
Fast halb darob erstaunt, gewahr.
Der Blüte Schnee schien schwarz zu sein
Bei diesem weissen Glanz. Es fiel mir ins Gesicht
Von einem hellen Stern ein weisses Licht,
Das mir recht in die Seele strahlte.
Wie sehr ich mich an Gott im Irdischen ergetze,
Dacht' ich, hat er dennoch weit grössre Schätze.
Die grösste Schönheit dieser Erden
Kann mit der himmlischen doch nicht verglichen werden.

Glad in our slumber and glad at its flight,
Glad to be dancing and glad at delight,
Glad in our aim, glad in our game,
Glad to the goose quill and glad to the blade,
Glad to the wagon and glad to the jade.

Glad to the banquet and glad to the pot,
Glad before all to a God ne'er forgot,
Glad in our breast, glad in our jest,
Let us with Floridan gladness enthrone,
Floridan's glad with his Fillis alone.

Barthold Heinrich Brockes
Cherry Blossoms at Night

With pondering spirit I did see
Of late a blooming cherry tree,
In cool of night by moonlights' glow:
I thought: men can no greater whiteness know.
It seemed that it with snow were crowned;
For every branch, and e'en the least,
Bore as it were a burden pieced
Of balls together, white and round.
No swan may be so white, since here each leafy blade
(For even through the tender leaves does smite
The moon and pierce them with its light)
Possesses shadows white and shadows without shade.
Impossible, I thought, that earth
Can to some whiter thing give birth.
The while I this and that way went
Beneath the tree's wide shadow, I
Looked up by accident
Through all the blooms toward the sky.
And there did still a whiter glow,
A thousand times as white, a thousand times as clear
To my half-dazzled eyes appear.
Black seemed to be the blossom's snow
Against this white magnificence. There struck my sight
From some bright-burning star so bright a light
That it burned straight into my soul.
However I rejoice at God in earthly things
(I thought), He nonetheless far greater treasures brings:
The greatest beauty of the earth
Bears not comparison with that of heavenly birth.

Barthold Heinrich Brockes

Geteilte Sinnen

Indem ich jüngst im Frost annoch
Vor dick gefrornen Fenstern stand
Und meiner Blumen Balsam roch,
Den ich recht ungemein erquickend lieblich fand,
Und ich zu gleicher Zeit bei diesem süssen Duft
Des warmen Zimmers laue Luft,
Die sanft mir um die Glieder spielte,
Mit nicht geringer Anmut fühlte,
Doch auch zugleich, wie draussen alles weiss
Und sich die Welt mit Reif, mit Schnee und Eis
In silbergleichem Schimmer schmückte,
Durchs dichte Fensterglas erblickte
Und auch zugleich von Wagen und von Karren
Gefrorne Räder pfeifen, knarren
Und vom getretnen Schnee ein lautes Knirschen hörte,
Gedacht' ich bei mir selbst: Wie soll ich dieses fassen?
Kann meine Seele sich denn teilen lassen?
Sie kann zu einer Zeit durch zweier Sinne Thüren
Im Winter und durch zwei im Frühling sich verspüren:
Wo sind denn ihrer Kräfte Grenzen?
Sie ist im Winter halb und halb im Lenzen.

Friedrich Rudolf Ludwig von Canitz

Sinn-Schriften
Auf einige Teutsche Käyser

Carl der Grosse

Diss ist der grosse Carl, Pepins, des Kleinen, Sohn,
   Der, weil sein eignes Reich der Francken ihm zu enge,
   Die Teutschen überwand und ihrer Götzen Menge.
In Welschland fand er auch noch einen neuen Thron,
Da ihm Pabst Leo gab die Käyserliche Kron.

Ludwig der Fromme

Weil Ludwigs Mildigkeit die Kirchen wohl verpflegt,
Wird billig ihm das Lob des Frommen beygelegt.
   Dem Vater folgt er nach in allen seinen Reichen,
   Muss, aber, eh er stirbt, noch seinen Kindern weichen.

Barthold Heinrich Brockes

SEPARATED SENSES

The while I late at frost-time went
Before my thick-iced window pane,
And smelled my flower's balsamed scent,
Which me uncommonly did gladden and sustain,
And, with this fragrance, I could at the same time share
The heated chamber's lukewarm air,
Which soft around my body swayed
And no small loveliness displayed,
And yet I jointly saw, how all without
Was white, and how the world was decked about
With hoarfrost and with ice and snow,
Through tight glass spied, in argent glow,
And heard then, too, the groaning and the squeal
Of barrow and of wagon-wheel,
And from the trodden snow a loud and grinding sound:
I asked myself, how I these things might comprehend,
And if my spirit could itself to doubling lend?
It at one time can through two senses' portals bring
Its winter rations, and through two the foods of spring:
Where does its power's bourn reside?
It half in winter lives, and half in vernal tide.

Friedrich Rudolf Ludwig von Canitz

EPIGRAMS
CONCERNING SOME GERMAN EMPERORS

Charles the Great

The short Lord Pepin's son, this then is Charles the Great:
   Who since his Frankish realm too little space allowed,
   Subdued the German tribes and all their idol's crowd.
In Italy he came once more to royal state:
Pope Leo did to him an emperor's crown donate. [14]

Louis the Pious

Since Louis' charity the churches nourished well,
Men justly do of him with pious praises tell.
   In all his many lands his father he succeeds,
   However, ere he dies, yields to his children's needs. [15]

Lothar

Ein Strich im Teutschen Reich, Austrasien genannt,
   Rom und Italien, zusamt der Käyser-würde,
Ward mir, nach hartem Streit, zum Erbtheil zuerkannt.
   Der Purpur schien zuletzt mir eine solche Bürde,
Dass ich ein Ordens-Kleid im Closter besser fand.

Ludwig der Zweyte

Es war Italien mein erblich Eigenthum,
   Dabey ich aber auch den Käyser-Titel führte,
   Durch Muth und Tapfferkeit, die mancher Feind verspührte,
Und durch Verstand zugleich erwarb ich grossen Ruhm.

Carl der Kahle

Der Himmel lässt sich nicht durch langes Unrecht höhnen:
   Ich trat im Käyserthum dem ältern Bruder vor,
Und nahm das Welsche Reich, biss ich, von dessen Söhnen
   Geschlagen und gejagt, durch Gifft den Geist verlohr.

Otto der Grosse

Der Ungarn wildes Volck, die Böhmen, Dänen, Wenden
Und Welschen zittern schon, wenn sie in meinen Händen
   Das Schwerdt der Rache sehn; die Satzung führ ich ein:
   Dass, wer in Teutschland herrscht, hinfort soll Käyser seyn.

Otto der Zweyte

Ich fand im Teutschen Reich, und sonst, viel Widerwillen,
Doch konnten Tapfferkeit und Glück diss alles stillen;
   Ich war der Frantzen Furcht, der Saracenen Tod,
   Allein der Griechen Krieg bracht mich zuletzt in Noth.

Otto der Dritte

Die Hoheit meines Reichs beschützt ich durch die Waffen,
Man machte mir zu Rom, mit Aufruhr, viel zu schaffen;
   Ein Weib, voll Zorn und List, bracht endlich mich ins Grab,
   Als sie mir Gifft und Tod, durch Handschuh, übergab.

Lothar

A tract of Germany, Austrasia by name,
   And Rome and Italy, combined with emperor's crown,
All, after dulling strife, my heritage became.
   The purple cloth at last so cruelly weighed me down,
That cowl and cloister-walls seemed more to me than fame. [16]

Louis the Second

The realm of Italy was my inheritance,
   And also on my head the emperor's title dwelt;
   By valor and high heart, which many foemen felt,
And by my wisdom I won fame's extravagance. [17]

Charles the Bald

The Heavens will not be made sport by lengthy wrong:
   An elder brother I deprived of emperor's role,
And took the southern realm: till I, by nephews' throng
   Defeated and pursued, through poison lost my soul. [18]

Otto the Great

Bohemians, Danes, and Wends, wild folk of Magyar-land,
And Rome's poor progeny do shake when in my hand
   They see the vengeful sword: that ordinance I found
   That he shall emperor be who rules o'er German ground. [19]

Otto the Second

I found in Germany much hate, nor only there;
Yet bravery and luck these troubles could repair.
   Both death to Saracens I was, and Frenchmen's fear:
   At last the Greekish war to doom my course did steer. [20]

Otto the Third

My empire's sovereignty I guarded by my arms.
In Rome they caused me care with tumults and alarms.
   A woman's rage and craft at last prepared my grave,
   When poison and cruel death she by a gauntlet gave. [21]

Heinrich der Heilige

Die Feinde müssen sich vor meiner Macht verkriechen;
Aus Welschland trieb ich weg den gantzen Schwarm der Griechen;
   Dieweil mein Ehgemahl stets Jungfrau bey mir bleibt,
   Werd ich der Heiligen Verzeichniss einverleibt.

Conrad der Zweyte

Ich sah vor meinem Glück Gewalt und List zerrinnen,
Mir konte weder Slav noch Ungar abgewinnen.
   Nachdem das Teutsche Volck zum Käyser mich gemacht,
   Hab ich Burgundien ihm wieder zugebracht.

Heinrich der Dritte

Der Ungarn Ubermuth, der gar zu hoch gestiegen,
Muss doch der Majestät des Reiches unterliegen,
   Die ich zu meiner Zeit noch unverletzt behielt;
   Ob gleich die Päbste selbst auf ihren Fall gezielt.

Heinrich der Vierdte

Nunmehr verfällt das Reich in Aufruhr, Mord und Brand,
   Und, ob ich gleich mit Ruhm viel Gegen-Käyser dämpfe,
   Und, mehr als sechtzigmahl, in Schlachten glücklich kämpfe,
Behält der Päbste Bann doch endlich Oberhand.
Darauf mir wiederfährt, was kaum die Nachwelt glaubt;
Dass mir mein eigner Sohn so Kron als Ehre raubt.

Henry the Saint

Before my puissance my enemies must flee,
The band entire of Greeks I drove from Italy.
   Because my wedded wife remained with me a maid,
   I am a member of the sainted cavalcade. [22]

Conrad the Second

Before my luck I saw deceit and force dissolve;
No gain from me to Slav nor Magyar did devolve,
   And when the German folk of me an emperor made,
   I once more at its side Burgundian borders laid. [23]

Henry the Third

The Magyar impudence, which far too high had swelled,
Must by the majesty of emperor be felled,
   Which I within my time could keep undamaged still,
   Although the popes themselves had made its fall their will. [24]

Henry the Fourth

In murder, flames, revolt, the Empire now is cast;
   Though splendidly I stilled my anti-emperors,
   And more than sixty times had fortune of my wars,
The papal ban obtained the upper hand at last.
Posterity can scarce give credence to my lot:
My very son by theft my crown and honor got. [25]

Daniel von Czepko

Spiele wohl!
Das Leben ein Schauspiel

Was ist dein Lebenslauf und Tun, o Mensch? Ein Spiel.
Den Inhalt sage mir? Kinds, Weibs und Tods Beschwerde.
Was ist es vor ein Platz, darauf wir spielen? Die Erde.
Wer schlägt und singt dazu? Die Wollust ohne Ziel.

Wer heisst auf das Gerüst uns treten? Selbst die Zeit.
Wer zeigt die Schauer mir? Mensch, das sind bloss die Weisen.
Was ist vor Stellung hier? Stehn, schlafen, wachen, reisen.
Wer teilt Gesichter aus? Allein die Eitelkeit.

Wer macht den Schauplatz auf? Der wunderbare Gott.
Was vor ein Vorhang deckts? Das ewige Versehen.
Wie wird es abgeteilt? Durch Leben, Sterben, Flehen.
Wer führt uns ab, wer zeucht uns Kleider aus? Der Tod.

Wo wird der Schluss erwart't des Spieles? In der Gruft.
Wer spielt am besten mit? Der wohl sein Amt kann führen.
Ist das Spiel vor sich gut? Das Ende muss es zieren.
Wenn ist es aus? O Mensch, wenn dir dein Jesus ruft.

Daniel von Czepko

Angst und Hohn der Liebe Lohn

Nihm die Rose von den Dörnern,
Zeige dann den Frühling an:
Nihm die Aehren mit den Körnern,
Sage, was der Sommer kan.
Nihm der Trauben süssen Preiss,
Sprich darauf, der Herbst ist kommen:
Nihm das Schmeltz Glas von dem Eyss,
Auch der Winter wird genommen.
Nihm der Liebe Quaal und Pein,
Liebe wird nicht Liebe seyn.

Daniel von Czepko

Act Well!
Life is a Play

What is your course of life, your deed, oh man? A play.
Will you the plot recount? Child's, woman's, dying's care.
The place on which we play? Earth does us actors bear.
Who drums and sings for it? Base pleasure's endless sway.

Who bids us tread the boards? Time does this office own.
Who are the spectators? That task but wise men keep.
What then is here performed? Stay, journey, wake, and sleep.
Who passes out the masks? But vanity alone.

Who opens up the house? God is His majesty.
What curtain hides the stage? Eternal accident.
What does its scenes divide? Life, death, and argument.
Who leads us off and takes our costumes? Death is he.

Where will the play's end come? Within the funeral hall.
Who plays it best? The man who well his task has borne.
Is it good of itself? The end must it adorn.
When is it done? Oh man, when Jesus you does call.

Daniel von Czepko

Scorn and Dismay the Lover's Pay

Take the rosebud from the thorn,
Then announce the start of spring;
Take the ear from out the corn,
Say what summertime can bring.
Take what grapes can sweet bestow,
Say then that the fall has sway;
Take from ice its burnished glow,
Winter too you take away.
Take away love's ache and pain,
Love will no more love remain.

Daniel von Czepko

Aus den Monodisticha

1. Anfang   Ende
   im
   Ende   Anfang

Das Ende, das du suchst, das schleuss in Anfang ein,
wilt du auf Erden weis', im Himmel seelig sein.

2. Vorgeführtes Leben

Dein Leben hört nicht auf, wie tieff man dich begräbt,
wenn du in Gott und gott hinwieder in dir lebt.

3. Gott unterm Menschen:
   Mensch unter Gott

Mensch, wie sich Gott in dich, must du in Gott dich kleiden!
Du sollst um seiner Lieb: Er wil um deiner leiden.

4. Nicht in dir

Schau alle Ding in Gott und Gott in allen an!
Du siehst, dass alles sich in ihm vergleichen kann.

5. Keinen vorn andern

Wann du in Einem All, und Einen suchst in allen,
Stehst du, wo Adam stund, eh als er war gefallen.

6. Stapffen der Dreyfaltigkeit

Es bringt dir einen Gott ein iedes Grässlein bey,
Und macht es dazu klar, dass er dreyfaltig sey.

7. Alles eines

Was ausser der Natur das höchste Wesen ist,
Das bist du, wenn du dich ohn Leib und Sinnen siehst.

8. Ruh

Mensch, der Bewegung Quell und Ursprung ist die Ruh;
Sie ist das best. Ihr eilt die gantze Schöpffung zu.

Daniel von Czepko

From the Monodisticha

1. Beginning   End
   in
   End   Beginning

The ending which you seek, make introductory,
Would you on earth be wise, and blest in Heaven be.

2. Life Continued

Your life will not take end, however deep your tomb,
If you a life in God, and God in you, assume.

3. God Within Man:
   Man Within God

Man, just as God in you, be you in God disguised!
You for His love shall be, He for you, martyrized.

4. Not in You

Do now all things in God, God in all things behold:
You'll see that all in Him their likeness can unfold.

5. None before the Others

If you seek one in all and yet all seek in one,
You stand where Adam stood ere Paradise was done.

6. Traces of the Trinity

Each little blade of grass for you will God pervade
And show it clear besides that He threefold is made.

7. All One

What outside nature can the highest being be,
Is you, when you yourself all flesh- and sense-less see.

8. Rest

Oh man, the source and womb of movement lies in rest;
And all creation runs to her, for she is best.

9. Sey vollkommen

Wann das vollkomne kömmt, so geht das Stückwerck hin,
Zutheilt hier, dorte leb und bleib ich, was ich bin.

10. Nihm nichts mit

Hier ist kein Mein noch Dein. Mensch, lass das deine fallen,
Geh ausser dir zu Gott, der alles ist in allen.

11. Wol scheiden, wol einen

Der hat das höchst erlangt auf seiner Himmels Bahn,
Der Gott von Gott durch Gott in sich entscheiden kan.

12. Erforsche dein Gewissen

Was liesest du so viel in frommer Leute Leben?
Schau deines an: es wird dir bessre Lehren geben.

13. Je mehr, ie weniger

Der weiss nicht viel, der mehr als andre wissen wil,
Erkennen, was ihm fehlt, das ist des Weisen Ziel.

14. Weise Armuth.
Arme Weissheit

Der nichts wil, nichts bedarff, nichts hat, nichts sucht, nichts ist,
Denselben Menschen hat die Weisheit auserkiest.

15. Höllisches Feuer

Was ist die Höll? Ich sprech: Es ist der eigne Willen.
Was brennt? Der eigne Nutz, der nimmermehr zu stillen.

9. Be Perfect

Whene'er perfection comes, then piece-work falls away.
I live there, dwelling here, and what I am, I stay.

10. Take Nothing Along

Here is not mine nor yours. Oh man, let yours but fall.
Go, leaving you, to God, Who is all things in all.

11. Separate Well, Unite Well

That man does highest on his way to Heaven go
Who God from God through God within himself can know.

12. Explore Your Conscience

Why do you read so much how pious people live?
Behold your life: it will you better teachings give.

13. The More, the Less

He knows but small who more than others' wit will claim.
Perceiving what he lacks: that is the wise man's aim.

14. Wise Poverty, Poor Wisdom

Who naught wills, needs, nor has, nor is, nor does expect,
That very man has been by wisdom made elect.

15. The Fire of Hell

What then is hell? I say: it is the human will.
What burns? Man's selfishness, which nevermore grows still.

Simon Dach

AN REGINA VOGLERIN, VERWITTIBTE OEDERIN
ZUM NAMENSTAGE

Ihr habt euch ja, Frau Muhm, des Trauerns nun entschlagen,
Lasst ruhen, was schon tod den langen Ruhtag hält,
Und habet eure Seel in Gottes Hand gestellt.
Wohlan! so müsst ihr nun auch nach Ergetzung fragen.

Und seht, das Morgenlicht wird euern Namen tragen.
Entreisst euch recht der Pein, die Sinn und Leben fällt,
Treibt alles Ungemach in eine fremde Welt.
Wir Freunde kommen, euch ein LustMahl anzusagen.

Nehmt von uns allen hin für eure werthe Hand
Ein Zeugnüss unsrer Gunst dies schlecht gewundne Band,
Doch mehr, ein treues Hertz, sucht bald euch loss zu machen.

Seht einst den trüben Herbst, der jetzt auch SonnenSchein
Nach vielem Reben giebt. Der Mensch kan einst der Pein,
Die sich fast stündlich häuft, auch wohl zu Zeiten lachen.

Simon Dach

ÜBER DEN EINGANG DER SCHLOSSBRÜCKE

Du Seule Brandenburgs, du Preussens Sicherheit,
O Fridrich Wilhelm, Trost und Hoffnung vieler Lande,
Sey willkomm deinem Volck hie an des Pregels Rande!
Des Höchsten Ehrendienst ist wegen dein erfreut,

Verspricht Uns undter Dir die alte güldne Zeit;
Gerechtigkeit und Fried in jedem Ort und Stande
Verknüppffen dir sich fest mit einem güldnen Bande
Du machst, dass alles wil genesen weit und breit.

In dem dein Eintzug Uns die Hoffnung aber giebet,
So wirstu billich nie von uns auch gnug geliebet;
O leb Uns werthes Haupt, sey Uns ein Sonnen-schein,

Der nimmer untergeht! schon jetzt mit deiner Jugend
Dringt Fama durch die Welt, du wirst bey solcher Tugend
Nicht hie nur, sondern auch im Himmel Hertzog seyn.

Simon Dach

To Regina Vogler, the Widowed Madam Oeder, on Her Name-Day

   From mourning, Madam Aunt, you are this day released.
Let rest, what in its death does hold long holiday,
And in the hand of God your trusting spirit lay.
Come bravely! Your delights must also be increased.

   And see, your name is borne by dawn-light from the east.
Escape the bonds of pain, which life and sense would slay,
And drive care's company to some strange world away.
We friends are come to tell you of our joyous feast.

   Receive then from us all within your worthy hand,
As witness of our love, this poorly winded band –
And more, our faithful hearts: your freedom soon attempt.

   Behold the gloomy fall, which after days of rain
Now lets the sun appear. Man may at times from pain,
Which almost hourly grows, by laughter be exempt.

Simon Dach

On the Entrance of the Castle Bridge

   You Brandenburg's support and Prussia's guarantee,
Oh Frederick William,[26] whom we for hope's solace thank,
Your people greet you now upon the Pregel's bank!
God's honored hosts rejoice to see your regency,

   And do 'neath you for us an Age of Gold desire.
Both righteousness and peace in every place and rank,
Fast joined with golden bands, must march upon your flank;
You lead us, far and wide, to fresh prosperity.

   Since this your entry's brought to us new hoping-stuff,
You cannot have from us just love or love enough.
Live for us, worthy head, and be our ray of sun

   Which nevermore shall set! Now with your youth, sweet Fame
Goes through the world, and you, who may such virtue claim,
Will have not only earth's, but heaven's dukedom won.

Simon Dach

ÜBER DER SCHLOSS-PFORTE, DA IHR FÜRSTLICHE DURCHL.
AUFF DERO BEYLAGER EINZOGEN, ZU LESEN

    Komm glücklich, wehrter Held, O Bräutgam, eingezogen,
Dein Auss- und Eingangk muss von Gott gesegnet seyn,
Schau, unser ChurFürst selbst begleitet dich herein,
Thu, was der Himmel längst dich hat zu thun bewogen,

    Vollbring dein Liebes-Werck. Mercur kömpft angeflogen,
Und bringt Bericht, der Schluss der Götter in gemein
Sey dissfalls Glück und Heil, nach dem sie wegen dein
Bissher in Gegenwart der Parcen Raht gepflogen.

    O Reichthum, den du kömpst zu hohlen in dein Land,
Dergleichen Hoheit hat die Erde kaum erkant,
Mit der vollkommen sich Loys' Charlotte zieret.

    Wer wird, O Churland, nun wol fassen deinen Pracht,
So bald dein Hertzog Sie wird haben heim gebracht?
Uns aber wird hiedurch ein Tugend-Bild entführet.

C. Eltester

ALS SIE EIN LIED IN DIE DARZU GESPIELTE THEORBE SANG

    Wann schönstes Fräulein sich dein kluger mund bewegt
Und ein beseelter thon durch deine lippen dringet
Der durch ein süsses Lied dem Höchsten Opffer bringet
So wird der himmel selbst zur andacht angeregt.
    Ein etwas das uns auch schier aus uns selber trägt
Ein gantz geheimer zug der unser hertz umringet
Und durch verborgne krafft die Geister selbst bezwinget
Zeigt dass dein hoher Schall was göttlichs in sich hegt.
    Es scheint die engel sind von oben rab gestiegen
Und wollen sich durch dich zu unsrem chor verfügen;
Denn was man überall nur um sich hört und spürt
Und was dein schöner mund recht himmlisch abgesungen
Das ist ein meisterstück von ihren reinen zungen
Wodurch die seele gantz wird aus sich selbst geführt.

Simon Dach

To be Read above the Castle-Gate, when His Princely Highness Rode in to His Marriage Bed [27]

Oh happy hero come, oh enter, worthy groom,
Your goings in and out God's blessing must display;
And see, our glorious prince has come with you this way;
What Heaven long has wished, that task tonight assume.

Fulfill your work of love. Let Mercury presume
To read to us the gods' one-voiced report, and say
It's filled with grace and joy, since they till now did stay
And council learn for you before the Parcae's loom.

Oh riches, which you come within your land to bring!
Like majesty on earth has been a seldom thing,
Yet it Louise Charlotte can perfectly adorn.

Who will, Curland, indeed your splendor apprehend,
Now that your Duke with her his way will homeward wend?
But we are thereby of our virtue's crown forlorn.

C. Eltester

When She Sang a Song to the Theorbo's Accompaniment

   When, fairest maid, there stirs your mouth all filled with sense,
And then there through your lips a tone inspired does sing,
Which by sweet song does bear the Lord His offering,
The heavens are themselves seduced to reverence.
   A something which comes near to bearing us from hence,
A hidden current shows – our heart enamoring,
And e'en through secret force the spirits capturing –
That paradise within your voice has residence.
   It seems the angels are descended from the sky
And make themselves through you our singing-band's ally,
For what men everywhere do round them hear and heed,
And what your lovely mouth in heaven's wise has sung,
That is a masterpiece poured from the angels' tongue,
Which does the very soul from out its being lead.

Gottfried Finkelthaus

Der Soldate

O grosser Gott der grossen Krüge/
Den guten Schluckern wolbekant!
Durch dich und durch die schweren Züge
Wird man ein frischer Held genannt.
Den Krieg ich warlich fürchte sehr/
Die Küch und Keller lob ich mehr.

Die lincke Schulter pflegt zu beben/
Im fall sie Eisen tragen sol/
Viel leichter ists ein Glas zu heben/
Ob solches gleich biss oben voll.
Den Krieg ich warlich fürchte sehr/
Die Küch und Keller lob ich mehr.

Mein scharffer Kneiff ist anzuschneiden
Die feisten Braten abgericht.
Das Schwerd mag rosten in der Scheiden/
In der es keine Scharten kriegt.
Den Krieg ich warlich fürchte sehr/
Die Küch und Keller lob ich mehr.

Ein Rauch von Hünern und Capaunen/
Mir wol (doch mehr das Fleisch) behagt.
Das helle Blitzen der Carthaunen
Macht mich hingegen bald verzagt.
Den Krieg ich warlich fürchte sehr/
Die Küch und Keller lob ich mehr.

Mit dir ists aus/ bistu getroffen:
Früh steh ich auff den andern Tag/
Wenn ich mich heute vollgesoffen/
Und eins so viel noch sauffen mag.
Den Krieg ich warlich fürchte sehr/
Die Küch und Keller lob ich mehr.

Ein Landsknecht selbst nach Schaden ringet/
Und suchet ihm den bittern Todt:
Wo man die Gläser hurtig schwinget/
Da weiss man nicht von Sterbens-Noth.
Den Krieg ich warlich fürchte sehr/
Die Küch und Keller lob ich mehr.

Gottfried Finkelthaus

The Soldier

Oh prideful pot's proud deity,
'Mongst goodly topers goodly famed:
Through you and stern libations we
Are now a hot-spur hero named.
I truly fear the battle's roar.
And praise the keg and kitchen more.

The shoulder of my great left limb
Does shake, if iron it must bear:
It's easier, though it may brim,
To lift a goblet in the air.
I truly fear the battle's roar
And praise the keg and kitchen more.

My razored carving knife is trained
To breach the roasts grown round and thick:
My sword has in its sheath remained
To gather rust but ne'er a nick.
I truly fear the battle's roar
And praise the keg and kitchen more.

The chickens' and the capons' steam
(Their flesh still more) does suit me well:
Whereas the mortars' sudden gleam
Does quick upon my courage tell.
I truly fear the battle's roar
And praise the keg and kitchen more.

If you are struck, then you are still:
I early on the morrow rise,
(Though I today did swill my fill)
And swill again in equal wise.
I truly fear the battle's roar.
And praise the keg and kitchen more.

A trooper strives for injury
And hunts himself a bitter death:
Where men swing glasses hastily
They give no heed to dying's breath.
I truly fear the battle's roar
And praise the keg and kitchen more.

Zum Pancketiren und zum Sauffen
Da stell ich mich zum ersten ein.
Doch wenn man sol zum Sturm anlauffen/
Wil ich der letzte lieber seyn.
Den Krieg ich warlich fürchte sehr/
Die Küch und Keller lob ich mehr.

Ich eben auch in meinen Zügen
Muss führen einen schweren Krieg:
Wenn andre nun zu Boden liegen/
So bleibet mir zuletzt der Sieg.
Den Krieg ich warlich fürchte sehr/
Die Küch und Keller lob ich mehr.

Paul Fleming

Er redet die Stadt Moskaw an, als er ihre
vergüldeten Türme von Fernen sahe
1636 März

Du edle Kaiserin der Städte der Ruthenen,
gross, herlich, schöne, reich; seh' ich auf dich dorthin,
auf dein vergüldtes Haupt, so kömt mir in den Sinn
was Güldners noch als Gold, nach dem ich mich muss sehnen.
Es ist das hohe Haar der schönen Basilenen,
durch welcher Treflichkeit ich eingenommen bin.
Sie, ganz Ich, sie mein All, sie meine Herscherin,
hat bei mir allen Preis der Schönsten unter Schönen.
Ich rühme billich dich, du Hauptstadt deiner Welt,
weil deiner Götlichkeit hier nichts die Wage hält
und du der Auszug bist von Tausenden der Reussen.
Mehr aber rühm' ich dich, weil, was dich himlisch preist,
mich an ein göttlichs Mensch bei dir gedenken heisst,
in welcher Alles ist, was treflich wird geheissen.

As toper and as trencherman
I gladly will the leader be,
But when they form the foray's van,
I'd rather trail the company.
I truly fear the battle's roar
And praise the keg and kitchen more.

I too must wage an awful war
As I consume my cups' repast:
When others topple to the floor,
The victory is mine at last.
I truly fear the battle's roar
And praise the keg and kitchen more.

Paul Fleming

He Addresses the City of Moscow as He Sees Her Guilded Towers from Afar
March, 1636

You noble empress of these towns in Ruthene air,
Great, splendid, lovely, rich: if I my glance address
Toward your guilded head, then through my dreams must press
What is more gold than gold, and magnet of my care.
    It is the high-piled curls that Basilene does wear,
To whose sweet excellence I captive acquiesce:
She all I, she my all, she my commanderess,
Has won from me the name of fairest of the fair.
    Chief city of your world, I bring you proper praise:
To your divinity no city equal weighs,
And you the essence are of Russia's thousand hordes.
    But I shall praise you more, since what makes you divine
Does to a goddess-maid make me my thoughts consign,
A maid who owns all that which excellence affords.

Paul Fleming

AN DIE GROSSE STADT MOSKAW, ALS ER SCHIEDE
1636 Juni 25

  Prinzessin deines Reichs, die Holstein Mume nennt,
du wahre Freundin du, durch welcher Gunst wir wagen,
was Fürsten ward versagt und Kön'gen abgeschlagen,
den Weg nach Aufgang zu, wir haben nun erkennt,
  wie sehr dein freundlichs Herz in unsrer Liebe brennt.
Die Treue wollen wir mit uns nach Osten tragen,
und bei der Wiederkunft in unsern Landen sagen,
das Bündnuss ist gemacht, das keine Zeit zertrennt.
  Des frommen Himmels Gunst, die müsse dich erfreuen,
und alles, was du tust, nach Wundsche dir gedeien,
kein Mars und kein Vulkan dir überlästig sein.
  Nim itzo diss Sonnet. Komm ich mit Glücke wieder,
so will ich deinen Preis erhöhn durch stärkre Lieder,
dass deiner Wolgen Schall auch hören sol mein Rhein.

Paul Fleming

ÜBER DEN ZUSAMMENFLUSS DER WOLGEN UND KAMEN, XX. WERSTE UNTER SAMAREN
1636 August 17

  Schwimmt näher zu uns her und stellt euch furchtsam nicht,
ihr wilden Fürstinnen des öden Permerstrandes.
Kommt Nymphen an den Port, das Ufer dieses Randes
ist püschig, kühl, und frisch, da keine Sonne sticht.
  Kommt, schauet dieses Schiff, von dem ganz Reussen spricht,
auch diss ist eine Zier der ersten meines Landes,
des treuen Holsteins Pfand, der Knoten eines Bandes,
das zwischen mir und ihm in Ewigkeit nicht bricht.
  Und du, o Vater Kam, geuss deinen braunen Fluss
mit völlern Krügen aus, dass unsern föhrnen Fuss
kein blinder Sand halt' auf, kein flacher Grund versäume.
  Die Wolge fleusst vorweg, bestellt die Sicherheit,
beut auf gut Glück und Heil, setzt Wolfart ein und schreit,
dass Anfall, Mord und Raub ihr beides Ufer räume.

Paul Fleming

TO THE GREAT CITY OF MOSCOW, AS HE WAS LEAVING
June 25, 1636

    Oh princess of your land, whom Holstein [28] cousin names,
True mistress you, through whose good offices we dare
That which to kings was barred, denied to princes' prayer:
The way towards the dawn. Our wisdom now acclaims
    How much your friendly heart in our devotion flames.
This faith we will with us toward the Orient bear
And, when we have returned within our lands, declare:
Alliance has been made to flout all future blames.
    May heaven's pious boon your heart with gladness fill,
And all you undertake show fortune at your will.
May Vulcan not, nor Mars, e'er give you cause to grieve.
    This sonnet then accept. Should I with luck return,
Your praise I'll lift on high and stronger stanzas learn
So that my Rhine may too your Volga-sounds perceive.

Paul Fleming

ON THE CONFLUENCE OF THE VOLGA AND THE
KAMA, TWENTY VERSTS BELOW SAMARA
August 17, 1636

    Swim nearer to us here and do not bow to fright,
Wild princesses beside the lonely Permian [29] sand.
Nymphs, follow to our cove. This province's fair strand
Is leafy, cool, and fresh, and there no sun may bite.
    Come, see this ship, which stirs to speech the Muscovite:
This also is a pride of princes in my land
And faithful Holstein's pledge, as of a knotted band,
Which will twixt me and him eternity despite.
    And you, oh father Kam [30], your swarthy flood pour out
In greater measures, that our fir-made foot may flout
The blind and clinging sand, the river's shallow floors;
    Ahead the Volga flows, and safety would prepare,
Calls fortune up and luck, and, shouting, takes good care
That ambush, plunder, death depart from both her shores.

Paul Fleming

Von sich selber

Ich feure gantz und brenne liechter Loh.
Die Trähnen hier sind meiner Flammen Ammen/
Die mich nicht lässt diss stete Leid verthammen;
Ich kenn' es wohl/ was mich kan machen froh/
　Dass ich fortan nicht dürffte weinen so.
Wo aber ists? So müssen nun die Flammen
hier über mir nur schlagen frey zusammen.
Mein Schirm ist weg/ mein Schutz ist anders wo.
　Ist gantz nichts da/ daran ich mich mag kühlen/
In solcher Gluth/ die meine Geister fühlen?
Der Liebes Durst verzehrt mir Marck und Bein.
　Diss Wasser ists/ die Kühlung meiner Hitze.
Das ich zum Trunck' aus beyden Augen schwitze.
Ich zapfe selbst/ und Amor schenckt mir ein.

Paul Fleming

AN DEN MON

Du, die du standhaft bist in deinem Unbestande,
Steig, Hekate, herab; ich singe dir ein Lied,
Ein Lied von meiner Zier, die itzt auch nach dir sieht,
Ob ich schon bin sehr weit von ihr und ihrem Lande.

Komm, Berezynthie, zu dieses Stromes Rande,
An dem ich geh herum, da meine Hoffnung blüht,
Du weisst es Delie, was itzt mit ihr geschieht,
Du weisst es, wie es steht um meine Salibande.

Komm, Phöbe, Tag der Nacht, Diane, Borgelicht,
Wahrsägrin, Liederfreund; komm, Lune, säume nicht!
Die ganze Welt, die schläft. Ich wache, dich zu loben.

Stromfürstin, Jägerfrau, Nachtauge, Horngesicht,
Herab! Itzt fang ich an das süsse Lobgedicht.
Und kömmst du nicht herab, so hör es nur dort oben!

Paul Fleming

Concerning Himself

  I'm all afire and from bright blaze annealed.
These tears are of my love the nursing dame,
Who does not wish that I this grief should tame;
I know full well what can such gladness yield
    That instantly my tears would be congealed.
    But where's it hid? For freely may the flame
Here over me its mastery proclaim.
My guard is gone and elsewhere is my shield.
    And is there naught upon which I may cool
The awful fires which now my senses rule?
Love's thirsts my marrow and my bone destroy.
    This water is the cooling of my fire,
Which I as drink from both my eyes perspire.
I tap myself and Love's my serving boy.

Paul Fleming

To the Moon

You, who inconstancy so constantly can squander,
Great Hecate, descend; to you a song I'll sing
About my pride, whose eyes now to your brilliance cling,
Although I've journeyed far from land and loved one yonder.

Come, Berecynthia,[31] and join me where I ponder
Beside this river's banks, because my hope's in spring;
You know, oh Delian,[23] what now her fate may bring,
You know full well what ways my Salibande may wander.

Come, Phoebe,[33] loan-o'-light, Diana, midnight's day,
Song's friend and prophetess, come, Luna, nor delay.
The whole world is asleep. I wake to sing your praises.

Stream-princess, huntress fair, night-eye, and horn-cut face,
Descend! For I'll begin a song to praise your grace.
And if you'll not descend, then hear in Heav'n my phrases.

Paul Fleming

Über Herrn Martin Opitzen auf Boberfeld sein Ableben

So zeuch auch du denn hin in dein Elyserfeld,
Du Pindar, du Homer, du Maro unsrer Zeiten,
Und untermenge dich mit diesen grossen Leuten,
Die ganz in deinen Geist sich hatten hier verstellt.

Zeuch jenen Helden zu, du jenen gleicher Held,
Der itzt nichts Gleiches hat, du Herzog deutscher Saiten,
O Erbe durch dich selbst der steten Ewigkeiten,
O ewiglicher Schatz und auch Verlust der Welt.

Germanie ist tot, die herrliche, die freie,
Ein Grab verdecket sie und ihre ganze Treue,
Die Mutter, die ist hin. Hier liegt nun auch ihr Sohn,

Ihr Rächer und sein Arm. Lasst, lasst nur alles bleiben,
Ihr, die ihr übrig seid, und macht euch nur darvon.
Die Welt hat wahrlich mehr nichts Würdigs zu beschreiben.

Paul Fleming

An Sich

Sei dennoch unverzagt, gib dennoch unverloren,
Weich keinem Glücke nicht, steh höher als der Neid,
Vergnüge dich an dir und acht es für kein Leid,
Hat sich gleich wider dich Glück, Ort und Zeit verschworen.

Was dich betrübt und labt, halt alles für erkoren,
Nimm dein Verhängnüs an, lass alles unbereut.
Tu was getan muss sein, und eh man dirs gebeut.
Was du noch hoffen kannst, das wird noch stets geboren.

Was klagt, was lobt man doch? Sein Unglück und sein Glücke
Ist ihm ein jeder selbst. Schau alle Sachen an:
Dies alles ist in Dir. Lass deinen eitlen Wahn,
Und eh du förder gehst, so geh in dich zurücke.
Wer sein selbst Meister ist und sich beherrschen kann,
Dem ist die weite Welt und alles untertan.

Paul Fleming

Concerning the Demise of Mr. Martin Opitz of Boberfeld

So pass away then, pass to your Elysian field,
You Homer, Pindar you, you Maro of our age,
And find your place among that mighty parentage,
Which once itself entire had in your soul concealed.

Hero, those heroes join, whose like you have revealed,
You hero without like, you German muse's mage,
Oh heir who through yourself did claim eternal wage,
Oh deathless gold of earth, which yet the earth must yield.

Germania is dead: her pride, her liberty.
One grave does cover her and her whole fealty.
The mother's gone. Here too her son lies presently,

Her venger and his arm. Oh you, who're left by death,
Let all your striving stand, and think but how to flee:
The world has nothing more that's worth description's breath.

Paul Fleming

To Himself

Yet do not be afraid, yet give no post forlorn,
Rise over jealousy, and to each joy assent,
Think it no ill but stay with your own self content,
If fortune, place, and time 'gainst you a league have sworn.

Assume that all has plan, if it do sooth or scorn,
Accept your fate and leave each deed without repent,
What must be done, that do, ere orders speed event.
Whate'er you still can hope, can each day still be born.

Why do men mourn or praise? His fortune, weal or woe,
Is each man to himself. Into each thing inquire –
All this resides in you. Your vain dreams let expire,
And go into yourself, before you farther go:
Who's master of himself and rules his own desire
Has subject unto him the mighty globe entire.

Paul Fleming

Herrn Pauli Flemingi der Med. Doct. Grabschrift

so er ihm selbst gemacht in Hamburg,
den 28. Tag des Märzen 1640 auf seinem Todbette,
drei Tage vor seinem seligen Absterben

Ich war an Kunst und Gut und Stande gross und reich,
Des Glückes lieber Sohn, von Eltern guter Ehren,
Frei, meine, kunnte mich aus meinen Mitteln nähren,
Mein Schall floh überweit, kein Landsmann sang mir gleich.

Von Reisen hochgepreist, für keiner Mühe bleich,
Jung, wachsam, unbesorgt. Man wird mich nennen hören,
Bis dass die letzte Glut dies alles wird verstören.
Dies, deutsche Klarien, dies Ganze dank ich euch.

Verzeiht mir, bin ichs wert, Gott, Vater, Liebste, Freunde,
Ich sag euch gute Nacht und trete willig ab.
Sonst alles ist getan bis an das schwarze Grab.

Was frei dem Tode steht, das tu er seinem Feinde.
Was bin ich viel besorgt, den Othem aufzugeben?
An mir ist minder nichts, das lebet, als mein Leben.

Paul Fleming

Epitaph of Mr. Paul Fleming, Med. Doct.,

which he made for himself in Hamburg,
the 28th day of March, 1640, upon his death-bed,
three days before his blessed passing.

I was both great and rich in art and wealth and name,
Of honored parents born, by fortune elevated,
Was my own man and free, by my own gold was sated,
No comrade sang my like and boundless flew my fame.

For journeys highly praised, before no effort lame,
Young, keen, and unconcerned. My name will still be feted,
Until the final flame all this has dissipated.
This, German Clarii,[34] I through your aid became.

If worthy, pardon me, God, father, friends, and dearest.
I bid you a good night and gladly take my leave.
All else is done till I the darkling grave achieve.

Toward his enemy let death do his severest.
What should I care that I my breath to heaven render?
Naught has less life in me than what I now surrender.

Johann Franck

AUS DER

VATER-UNSER-HARFFEN

1

Vater, ueber Hoeh' und Grund/
Werde herrlich in der Welt.
Mach' uns auch dein Zepter kund.
Hilff das hier dein Wille gelt!
Halt du taeglich bey uns Haus
Und gib reichen Vorrath aus.
    Lohne nicht nach werken ab;
Gleich wie wir nicht ueben Rach'.
In dem Creutz sey unser Stab.
Uns zu helffen sey gefach.
Denn dein Reich/ das droben ist/
Fuerchtet weder Macht noch List.

2

O Gnaden-Ost/ O Seelen-Trost/
O Schoeppfer dieses Rundes.
Geheiligt sey dein Nahmens-Ruff/
Bau hier das Reich des Bundes.
    Dein Goettlich Schluss Werd' ohn Verdruss
Allhier wie dort vollzogen.
Gib taeglich Brodt. Vergib/ dass wir
Voll Unrecht eingesogen.
    Mach' es nicht aus Wenn Sturm und Braus
Uns wil zu Boden treten.
Erloes' aus Geist- und Liebes-Angst.
 Dein' Huelff' erfolgt aufs Bethen.

Johann Franck

From the

"Lord's-Prayer-Harp"

1

Father over depth and height,
Now be master here on earth,
Make us know Your scepter's might,
Aid that here Your will has worth!
Enter daily to our board
And give well what You hold stored.
    Reckon not reward by deed,
Just as we no vengeance take,
Make our staff the cross's creed,
For our aid do ever wake.
Since Your realm, in Heaven's tier,
Neither force nor trick does fear.

2

East wind of grace, soul's balming place,
Creator of this round,
Make blessed now Your name's address,
Build here Your empire's ground.
    Your grand design, without repine,
Make perfect here as there.
Grant daily bread. Forgive that we
Injustice took as fare.
    Let it not end when storms descend
To tread us to the earth.
Free us from fear of flesh and soul;
Your aid from prayer takes birth.

Christoph Fürer von Haimendorf

STREIT DES FLEISCHES WIDER DEN GEIST

Die Regung/ die vor uns/ und nicht von uns gekommen/
die wir mit dem Geblüt in das Gemüt genommen/
   die fast in uns entsprang eh unser Ursprung war/
   und die die Mutter schon vor der Geburt gebahr/
ist in dem Anfang nichts/ als ein geringer Saame/
der wie ein schlauer Dieb recht eingeschlichen kame;
   man fühlet sie nicht gleich/ sie ist so sehr verdeckt/
   wie ein verborgener Funk/ der in der Asche steckt.
Nach kurzer Jahre Lauf verspürt man ihre Hitze/
doch weil sie lieblich ist/ und zum Vergnügen nütze/
   erhält man sie mit Lust in seines Herzens Hauss/
   biss ihre Wirkung bricht in Glut und Flammen aus.
Zuerst ist sie ein Kind/ und uns gefällt ihr Lallen/
wie man mit Kindern sonst hat insgemein Gefallen;
   man scherzet lang damit/ und lernet allzu spat/
   dass sie in kurzer Zeit wächst wie ein Goliath.
Dann wird sie fast zu stark/ und greiffet immer weiter/
da braucht es Riesen-Stärk/ und mehr als Davids Schleuder/
   damit der kleine Mann dem Riesen wiederstund/
   und von der Liebe doch sein Herz nicht schützen kunnt.
Betracht man schon mit Fleiss die schärfeste Gesetze/
und flieht/ so viel man kan/ die eingelegte Netze/
   so trifft man stetig doch auf dieser glatten Bahn
   den Hetzer/ der da reitzt/ und tausend Schlingen an.
Je mehr man wiedersteht/ je mehr steht sie entgegen;
je stärker man sie druckt/ je mehr sie sich will regen;
   sie ist dem Palmbaum gleich/ der/ wann er wird gebeugt/
   nur immer stärker wächst/ und höher aufwerts steigt.
Gott aber kan allein die böse Regung lenken/
dem Herzen seine Ruh/ dem Leib den Frieden/ schenken;
   des Geistes Orgelwerk wird bald vom Fleisch verstimmt/
   wann man nicht Gottes Geist mit zum Gehülfen nimmt.
Drum muss man je nicht leicht ein falsch Register ziehen/
den süssen Ton der Welt mit allem Eifer fliehen
   und nehmen allezeit Gott zum Gehülfen mit/
   im fall der Wollust Fuss auf unsern Blassbalg tritt.
Durch Ihn wird unsre Stimm sich zu dem Himmel fügen/
der Geist stehn aufgericht/ das Fleisch darnieder liegen:
   dann wann des Davids Hand der Psalmen-Harpfe regt/

Christoph Fürer von Haimendorf

BATTLE OF THE FLESH AGAINST THE SPIRIT

The impulse which before and not in us arose,
Which by our very blood to flood our spirit chose,
   Which nigh in us began before we had begun,
   And which our mother bore before we birth had won,
Is naught at starting save a puny seed and thin,
Which like a clever thief came light-foot stealing in.
   One feels her not at once, for she so sly is hid
   Like to a secret spark beneath the ash's lid.
When brief the years have gone, one must perceive her heat,
And yet, since she is fair and to our pleasure meet,
   With joy one welcomes her into his heart's abode,
   Until her potencies in fire and flame explode.
At first she is a child, her babble makes us smile,
As children commonly our happy sense beguile.
   Too long one jests with her, and all too late we know
   That she in briefest time does like Goliath grow.
Then she is near too strong, her grasp e'er widening:
Giant's strength was needful then and more than David's sling,
   So that the little man the giant could withstand
   And yet could not defend his heart 'gainst love's demand.
Though one may avidly the sharpest laws essay
And flee, the best one can, the nets put in his way,
   Yet constantly one meets along this slippery road
   Snares laid a thousand-fold, the baiter with his goad.
The more one would withstand, the more she stands to fight,
The more one presses her, the more her appetite.
   For she is like the palm, which when it's downward bent,
   But all the stronger grows, and higher makes ascent.
However God alone this evil urge can guide
And see that calm in heart and peace in flesh reside.
   The spirit's organ-works does flesh poor-tempered make,
   If one the Holy Ghost does not as helper take.
Thus one must not pull out false diapason's peal,
But rather flee the world's sweet tone with all his zeal,
   And take in every case God as his boy along,
   In case the foot of lust would tread the bellows wrong.
Through aid of Him our voice will reach the vaulted sky,
Our soul will stand erect, our flesh defeated lie.
   For when young David's hand the psalming harp does stir,

  so ist die Wollust todt/ und Goliath erlegt.
Diss Saitenspeil klingt wol in unsers Gottes Ohren/
der Teufel weicht vom Saul/ der Mensch wird neu gebohren;
  die Unruh stehet still/ das Bley ist ausgehenkt/
wann Gott vor eitle Lust die ware Wollust schenkt.

    Paul Gerhardt

  Geh aus, mein Herz, und suche Freud
  In dieser lieben Sommerzeit
  An deines Gottes Gaben:
  Schau an der schönen Gärten Zier,
  Und siehe, wie sie mir und dir
  Sich ausgeschmücket haben.

  Die Bäume stehen voller Laub,
  Das Erdreich decket seinen Staub
  Mit einem grünen Kleide:
  Narzissus und die Tulipan,
  Die ziehen sich viel schöner an
  Als Salomonis Seide.

  Die Lerche schwingt sich in die Luft,
  Das Täublein fleucht aus seiner Kluft
  Und macht sich in die Wälder.
  Die hochbegabte Nachtigall
  Ergetzt und füllt mit ihrem Schall
  Berg, Hügel, Tal und Felder.

  Die Glucke führt ihr Völklein aus,
  Der Storch baut und bewohnt sein Haus,
  Das Schwälblein speist die Jungen.
  Der schnelle Hirsch, das leichte Reh
  Ist froh und kommt aus seiner Höh
  Ins tiefe Gras gesprungen.

  Die Bächlein rauschen in dem Sand
  Und malen sich und ihren Rand
  Mit schattenreichen Myrthen.
  Die Wiesen liegen hart dabei
  Und klingen ganz von Lustgeschrei
  Der Schaf und ihrer Hirten.

Then lust is dead and then Goliath dead with her.
This play of strings does well within God's ears resound:
The devil goes from Saul, and man new birth has found;
   Disquietude stands still, the anchor's lead is cast,
  When God for empty lust true pleasure gives at last.

Paul Gerhardt

Go out in this dear summertide
And seek to find the joys that bide
In Heaven's gifts, oh heart:
Behold the gardens' lovely hue,
And see how they for me and you
Are decked by fairest art.

The trees in fullest leafage rise,
The earth, to give its dust disguise,
Has put a green dress on.
Narcissus and the tulip-bloom
Far finer vestment do assume
Than silks of Solomon.

The lark soars high into the air,
The little dove departs its lair
And takes the woodland's way.
The sweetly gifted nightingale
Fills hill and mountain, field and dale
With song, and makes them gay.

The hen leads out her little troop,
The stork does build and fill his stoop,
Its young the swallow feeds.
The hasty stag, the agile doe
Are glad, and from their heights do go
A-running through the reeds.

The brooklets rustle in the sand
And o'er them and their banks a band
Of shady myrtles keep.
The meadowlands lie close thereby,
Resounding from the happy cry
Of shepherds and their sheep.

Die unverdrossne Bienenschar
Zeucht hin und her, sucht hier und daar
Ihr edle Honigspeise.
Des süssen Weinstocks starker Saft
Kriegt täglich neue Stärk und Kraft
In seinem schwachen Reise.

Der Weizen wächset mit Gewalt,
Darüber jauchzet Jung und Alt
Und rühmt die grosse Güte
Des, der so überflüssig labt
Und mit so manchem Gut begabt
Das menschliche Gemüte.

Ich selbsten kann und mag nicht ruhn,
Des grossen Gottes grosses Tun
Erweckt mir alle Sinnen.
Ich singe mit, wenn alles singt,
Und lasse, was dem Höchsten klingt,
Aus meinem Herze rinnen.

Paul Gerhardt

DER 121. PSALM DAVIDS

Ich erhebe, Herr, zu dir
   meiner beiden Augen Licht;
mein Gesicht ist für und für
   zu den Bergen aufgericht,
zu den Bergen, da herab
ich mein Heil und Hülfe hab.

Meine Hülfe kömmt allein
   von des Schöpfers Händen her,
der so künstlich, hübsch und fein
   Himmel, Erden, Luft und Meer
und was in den allen ist
uns zum besten ausgerüst.

Er nimmt deiner Füsse Tritt,
   o mein Herze, wohl in acht,
wenn du gehest, geht er mit
   und bewahrt dich Tag und Nacht:
Sei getrost, das Höllenheer
wird dir schaden nimmermehr.

The bee-host back and forth has made
Its trips, thus seeking unafraid
Its noble honey-food.
The goodly vine, with juice grown big,
Gets daily in its weakest sprig
Its strength and force renewed.

The wheat grows large with all its might,
And does both young and old delight:
They sing the bounteousness
Of Him Who soothes so generously
And does such countless property
Upon man's spirit press.

Now I can neither rest, nor will:
Great God's great manufactures thrill
Awake my every sense.
I sing along, when all does sing,
And let what shall to Heaven ring
From out my heart commence.

       Paul Gerhardt

The 121st Psalm of David

Now the twin-light of my eyes,
   Oh my Lord, to You I raise;
Lifted up, my vision flies
   To the mountains all my days,
To the mountains, from whose crown
I fetch strength and succor down.

My salvation's sole design
   From the Maker's hands does fare:
He has, artfully and fine,
   Earth and heaven, sea and air
(And whate'er their bounds admit)
Decked out in our benefit.

He with vigilance does guide,
   Oh my heart, your footsteps' way;
Where you go, He at your side
   Goes and keeps you night and day.
Have good cheer: the hellish swarm
Nevermore will do you harm.

Siehe, wie sein Auge wacht,
  wenn du liegest in der Ruh!
Wenn du schläfest, kömmt mit Macht
  auf dein Bett geflogen zu
seiner Engel güldne Schar,
dass sie deiner nehme wahr.

Alles was du bist und hast,
  ist umringt mit seiner Hut.
Deiner Sorgen schwere Last
  nimmt er weg, macht alles gut.
Leib und Seel hält er verdeckt,
wenn dich Sturm und Wetter schreckt.

Wenn der Sonnen Hitze brennt
  und des Leibes Kräfte bricht,
wenn dich Stern und Monde blendt
  mit dem klaren Angesicht,
hat er seine starke Hand
dir zum Schatten vorgewandt.

Nun, er fahre immer fort,
  der getreue, fromme Hirt;
bleibe stets dein Schild und Hort.
  Wenn dein Herz geängstet wird,
wenn die Not wird viel und gross,
schliess er dich in seinen Schoss.

Wenn du sitzest, wenn du stehst,
wenn du redest, wenn du hörst,
wenn du aus dem Hause gehst,
  und zurücke wieder kehrst,
wenn du trittst aus oder ein,
  woll er dein Gefährte sein.

Georg Greflinger

An eine vortreffliche schöne und Tugend begabte Jungfrau

Gelbe Haare/ Güldne Stricke/
Tauben-Augen/ Sonnen-Blicke/
Schönes Mündlein von Corallen/
Zähnlein/ die wie Perlen fallen.

See now, how his wakeful eye
   E'en to your repose is led!
When you slumber, there does fly
   All in armor to your bed
Quick his angels' golden host,
Taking round you sentry-post.

All you are and all you own,
   He will with His guard defend,
And but take care's heavy stone
   From your back, and make you mend.
He holds soul and body warm,
Though you tremble in the storm.

When the sun's hot fevers smite
   And the body's powers break,
When the stars', the moon's clear light
   Would from you your vision take,
He His mighty hand has laid
Round about you like a shade.

May He thus for evermore
   Be the Shepherd, good and true;
May He stay your shield and store.
   When cruel fears your heart pursue,
When despair is mightiest,
May He close you to His breast.

When you stand and when you sit,
   When you listen, when you speak,
When your household's door you quit,
   Then once more its shelter seek,
Whether out or in you wend,
He will be your constant friend.

          Georg Greflinger

To a Splendid, Beautiful, and Virtuous Maiden

Yellow hair, cords golden spun,
Eye of dove and glance of sun,
Lovely mouthlet, coral-made,
Little teeth in pearl cascade.

Lieblichs Zünglein in dem Sprachen
Süsses zörnen/ süsses Lachen/
Schnee- und Lilgen weisse Wangen
Die vol rother Rosen hangen.

Weisses Hälsslein/ gleich den Schwanen/
Aermlein/ die mich recht gemahnen/
Wie ein Schnee/ der frisch gefallen/
Brüstlein wie zween Zuckerballen.

Lebens voller Alabaster/
Grosse Feindin aller Laster/
Frommer Hertzen schöner Spiegel/
Aller Freyheit güldner Zügel.

Aussbund aller schönen Jugend/
Auffenthaltung aller Tugend/
Hof-statt aller edlen Sitten/
Ihr habt mir mein Hertz bestritten.

Georg Greflinger

GEGENSATZ.

AN EINE SEHR HÄSSLICHE JUNGFRAU

Graues Haar vol Läuss und Nisse/
Augen von Scharlack/ vol Flüsse/
Blaues Maul vol kleiner Knochen/
Halb verrost und halb zerbrochen.

Blatter-Zunge/ kranck zu sprachen/
Affischs zörnen/ Narren-lachen/
Runtzel volle magre Wangen/
Die wie gelbe Blätter hangen.

Halss-Haut gleich den Morianen/
Arme/ die mich recht gemahnen/
Wie ein Kind ins Koth gefallen/
Brüste/ wie zween Druckerballen.

Du bist so ein Alabaster/
Als ein wolberegntes Pflaster/
Aller Ungestalt ein Spiegel/
Aller Schönen Steigebügel.

Tonguelet fair with verbiage,
Sweet in laughter, sweet in rage,
Cheeks snow-white and lily all,
Save where roses red do fall.

Throatlet white and like the swan,
Arms which make me think upon
Snow that but an hour has lain,
Sugar-balls your breastlets twain.

Alabaster, fullest blown,
'Gainst all vice you hatred own,
Pious hearts' fair looking glass,
Rein no license dares to pass.

Youth's fair essence, lacking blame,
Resting-place of virtue's fame,
Court with noble ways imbued,
You my heart from me have wooed.

Georg Greflinger

THE OPPOSITE:

TO A VERY UGLY MAIDEN

Grey hair, nit's and louse's home,
Scarlet eyes, whence rivers foam,
Bluish mouth, where bonelets thrust,
Broken half and half in rust.

Pock-tongue, sick with verbiage,
Foolish laughter, monkey's rage,
Meagre cheeks, so winkled all,
That like yellow leaves they fall.

Dewlap like the morion,
Arms which make me think upon
Children that in filth have lain,
Breasts like printers' bundles twain.

Alabaster you are known,
Like a rain-soaked paving stone,
Monster-folk a looking glass,
Stirrup for the fair that pass.

Schimpff der Jungfern und der Jugend/
Unhuld aller lieben Tugend/
Einöd aller plumpen Sitten/
Lästu' dich zum freyen bitten?

Georg Greflinger

AUF DIE ZURÜCKREISE

Gute Nacht, ihr teutschen Städte,
Gute Nacht, mein Vatterland!
Dass ich meinen Körper rette
Vor den Waffen, vor dem Brand
Und vor andern deinen Plagen,
Kann ich dir kein andres sagen.

Ob nun zwar der Vatter-Erden,
Welches fast natürlich scheint,
Schwerlich kann vergessen werden,
Und was sonst ein lieber Freund,
Ist es mir doch eine Freude,
Dass ich einmal von dir scheide.

Brandstadt, Blutfeld, Sitz der Straffen,
Aller Rauber Dummel-Plan,
Wehland, Zeughaus böser Waffen,
Wohl, wer dich entfliehen kann!
Es ist mir die höchste Freude,
Dass ich einmal von dir scheide.

Sei gegrüsset, edles Preussen,
Sei gegrüsset, Balter-Strand,
Wo das Zanken und das Beissen,,
Etwas minder ist bekannt,
Wo die Recht- und Friedens-Herzen
Lieblich miteinander scherzen;

Wo sich meine Seele findet,
Wo sich meine Freude hält,
Wo mein Feuer, was mich bindet,
Wo mein höchstes, meine Welt,
Wo mein All, mein Ich, mein Leben,
Der ich mehr als mir ergeben.

Mock to youth and maidens' blame,
All dear virtues' loathsome shame,
Wilderness of habits crude,
Would you let yourself be wooed?

Georg Greflinger

CONCERNING HIS RETURN [35]

German cities, fare you well,
Oh my fatherland, good night!
Since I'd save me from the spell
Wove by weapons, wove by blight,
Wove by all your other woe,
I no other parting know.

Though our fathers' earthly plot
(As would surely natural seem)
Scarce by me can be forgot,
Nor my friends of sweet esteem:
Yet my fate takes joyful cast
That I part from you at last.

Burn-town, blood-field, doom's demesne,
Every robber's riding-ground,
Woe-land, cruel arms' magazine:
Blest is he who flight has found!
True, my fate takes joyful cast
That I part from you at last.

Now, oh noble Prussia, hail,
Hail to you, oh Baltic strand,
Where in lesser grade prevail
Discord and the biting brand,
Where hearts wrought of right and peace
Sweet their mutual joy increase.

Where my soul its double finds,
Where my pleasures all reside,
Where does dwell the fire that binds,
Where my world, my highest pride,
Self and life and all must be
Whom I love still more than me.

Fuge, fuge, Wind von Westen,
Lass die Segel schwanger gehn,
Deine Kraft dient uns am besten,
Soll ich was zurückestehn;
Geh voran, sag meiner Floren,
Seladon sei von den Toren.

Catharina Regina von Greiffenberg

GÖTTLICHER ANFANGS-HÜLFE ERBITTUNG

Gott/ der du allen das/ was du selbst nicht hast/ gibest!
Du bist des ganz befreit/ was du den andern bist.
Mein und der ganzen Welt Uranfang vor dir ist/
Weil die mitteilend Kraft du uns erschaffend übest.

In deiner Vorsicht Buch du alles Weltsein schriebest.
Dein Überschwänglichkeit mit Wohltun war gerüst/
Dass sie so göttlich-reich uns schenket jede Frist.
Ob alles kam aus dir/ du alles dennoch bliebest.

Sonst alles/ als nur dich selbst nicht/ anfahends Ding/
Sei mit/ in/ und bei mir/ wann ich das Buch anhebe.
Dein Anfang-Schirmungsgeist ob diesem Redwerk schwebe.

Der gebe, dass ich rein von deinen Wundern sing,.
Mein Gott/ ich fah itzt an/ dich ohne End zu preisen:
Lass, wohl anfahend, mich dich unanfänglich weisen.

Catharina Regina von Greiffenberg

ÜBER GOTTES UNBEGREIFLICHE REGIERUNG
SEINER KIRCHEN UND GLAUBIGEN

Wer kann deinen Sinn ersinnen/ unersinnter Gottheits-Schluss?

Dein' Unendlichkeit verschwemmt alle Fünklein der Gedanken.
Dir ist gleich mein Urteil-Licht/ wie dem Meer ein kleiner Fanken.
All mein Gründen ist gegründet im ungrundbarn Gnadenfluss.

Blow then, blow, wind from the west,
Make the canvas swell with child,
Your stern vigor serves us best,
Should I, mayhap, serve more mild?
Tell my Flora, hastening on:
At the gate is Seladon.

Catharina Regina von Greiffenberg

PLEA FOR HEAVEN'S INITIAL HELP

Oh God, You do not own what You to men dispense!
What You to others are, from that You whole are freed.
The world's prime start and mine was by Your act decreed,
Since You, creating us, did share Your eminence.

The wending of the world You've writ in providence.
With goodness was adorned Your all-exceeding deed,
That it, divinely rich, might us each hour concede,
And You were All, though All must yet from You commence.

Oh starting thing which can each start but Yours assure,
With, in, and by me be when I begin this book.
Your spirit (start and shield) upon this speech-work look,

And grant that I may sing of all Your wonders pure.
My God, I start to lift Your praise unceasingly:
Well-starting, let me prove You without start to be.

Catharina Regina von Greiffenberg

ON GOD'S INCOMPREHENSIBLE RULE OF HIS CHURCHES
AND HIS FAITHFUL

Who can dare to sense Your sense out, sense-closed thought of Him
                                                        Supreme?
All the flickerings of our thought drown in Your infinity;
And my judgment-light's to you like the puddle to the sea.
All my grounds have found their groundings in this groundless
                                                    grace's stream,

Da ich/ dir die Ehre gebend/ mir auch Hoffung geben muss.
Weil dein' Allmacht ohne End'/ ist auch dieser ohne Schranken:
Weil die Grundfest nimmermehr/ kann auch das Gebäu nicht wanken:
Denn dein' Ehr' erhält die Spitzen/ auf der Gnad besteht der Fuss.

Ach wie kann/ was Gottes Hand bauet/ hält und schützet/ fallen?
Kann auch seiner Allhülf steuren/ einigs Erden-Widerspiel?
Aller weltlich' Widerstand muss mit Schand zurucke prallen/

Oder kunst-verkehrt selbst dienen zu dem Gott-erwählten Ziel.
Fass dir tausend Herz/ mein Herz! deine Sache trefflich stehet/
Durch viel tausend Widerstand in ihr rechtes Ziel doch gehet.

Catharina Regina von Greiffenberg

AUF CHRISTUS MENSCH-WERDIGE WUNDER-TAT

Der selbselbste Lebens-Saft wird mit Milch getränket.
Der die weite Welt besiegt/
In der engen Krippen liegt.
Wunder! aller Himmel Herr sich der Erden schenket.

Der selbst ist das höchste Gut/ sich ins Elend senket.
Die Bewegung wird gewiegt:
Von der selbst der Himmel kriegt
Seines Laufes Ordnungs-Pflicht/ und nach ihr sich lenket.

Hirten! lasst den Himmel stehn/
Und uns in den Stall hingehn!
Kam euch jemals auch zu Ohren

Solch ein Sonder-Wunderwerk/
Dass die Schwachheit hat die Stärk'
Und ein Stern die Sonn geboren?

Since I, giving You all honor may myself in hope redeem.
Your omnipotence lacks end, as the grace-stream boundary.
Since the ground-work cannot shake, so the building rises free:
For on grace the foot is founded, and Your honor holds the beam.

Can that fall which heavenly hands build, hold upright, and protect?
Can His universal-aid not some earth-dislike control?
All the world's hostility must these walls in shame deflect,

Or, art-turned, itself must serve for the God-appointed goal.
Take a thousand hearts, my heart! Happy stands your present case,
Which through many thousand bars goes unfailing to its place.

Catharina Regina von Greiffenberg

UPON CHRIST'S WONDER-DEED: BECOMING MAN

This essential essence now has with milk been laced.
Who the world with victory met
In the narrow crib will fret.
Wonder! Heaven's Lord the earth with Himself has graced,

Has Himself, the highest good, deep in exile placed.
Movement's source is cradling set
From whom even the sky must get
Orders for its dutied course, have its channel traced.

Shepherds! Give us company
To the stall, let Heaven be!
Came there ever to your ears

Such a special wonder-deed
That a star the sun could breed,
And that weakness strength could bear?

Catharina Regina von Greiffenberg

AUF DIE ÜBERNATÜRLICHE MEERWANDELUNG DES HERRN

Was ists/ dass ohne Müh' der Herr im Meer so gehet?
Weicht dann das nasse Glas/ die schnelle Welle/ nicht?
Nein! sie ist Demant-hart/ zu tragen den, verpflicht/
Der samt der Erd sie trägt/ so lang die Welt bestehet.

Wie, dass kein Wirbelwind herwehend ihn umdrehet!
Er macht den Wind geschwind verschwinden/ wann er spricht.
Ein Wort ihm alsobald sein rasends Blasen bricht.
Ist doch sein Mund der Grund/ draus erstlicher gewehet.

Welch eine Tiefe/ seht/ jetzt auf der Tiefe schwebt!
Die unerschaffliche/ auf dieser, die erschaffen/
Die, zu verschlingen auch die erste/ schon anhebt,

Weil ihre Macht sie macht vor ihrer gänzlich schlaffen.
Es ist das ganze Meer ein Tröpflein seiner Witz:
Wie leicht vertrocknet es der Gottheit heller Blitz.

Catharina Regina von Greiffenberg

DAS VI. WORT: ES IST VOLLBRACHT

Es ist der Feind erlegt/ der Höll ihr Macht geraubet,
Der Schlangen Haupt zerknirscht/ Gesetz und Schrift erfüllt/
Gewissens Anklag ist/ auch Gottes Zorn/ gestillt/
Mit diesem Heldenstreich das Höllenreich betaubet/

Den Armen Seelen auch der Himmelstrost erlaubet.
Umsonst der höllisch Drach nun auf die Frommen brüllt:
In meinem Sieges-Fahn sie herrlich sind verhüllt.
Höll'/ Teufel/ Sünd' und Tod/ schadt nicht dem, der fest glaubet.

Das ganz Erlösungswerk ist völlig nun vollbracht,
Das Opfer/ so ich bin/ auf ewig schon geschlachtet.
Ich hab' es alles wohl/ allein/ und gar gemacht:

Wer weiter opfern will/ mein Völligkeit verachtet.
Nun alles ist durch mich/ was euch erlöst/ verricht:
Drum lasst eur Selb-Verdienst/ seid mir allein verpflicht!

Catharina Regina von Greiffenberg

Concerning the Supernatural Walk of Christ upon the Sea

How can the Master move so careless on the main?
Fails not the slippery glass? Can hasty wave hold fast?
No! It is pledged to bear That One (it diamond-cast)
Who bears it and the earth as long as worlds remain.

Why is he not whirled round by some wild hurricane?
He with His single word can break the raking blast;
He speaks: the wailing gale is quickly pale and past,
His very breast's the chest in which that wind had lain.

See what a depth is now come hovering on the deep,
A depth, unmakable on that which has been made,
Already starts the depths within the depths to sweep,

Since it may turn the depths before its depth afraid.
The sea entire is but a droplet of His wit:
The godhead's brilliant bolt can make a drought of it.

Catharina Regina von Greiffenberg

The VI. Word: It is Finished

The foe's laid low and hell for its lost power grieves;
The serpent's head is crushed, and proved are law and writ.
The conscience from its nag, God from His wrath has quit.
Of life this hero's deed the hellish realm bereaves.

From Heaven the wretched soul salvation's balm receives.
In vain the dragon roars at good men from its pit:
My flag of victory has made them favorite.
Hell, devil, death, and sin harm not him who believes.

The whole redemption work is perfect now and done.
The victim (I am He) forever has been slain:
And I have wrought it all and wrought it all alone.

Who still would sacrifice, calls My perfection vain.
But your redemption I have through Myself fulfilled:
Thus pledge to Me alone and hold your self-praise stilled.

Catharina Regina von Greiffenberg

Auf die fröhlich- und herrliche Auferstehung Christi

Engel! blaset die Trompeten! Seraphinen/ singt und klingt/
Jubil-Jubil-Jubilieret/ hoch erfreuter Himmel-Chor!
Sonn und Sterne/ glänzt und danzet eurem Triumphierer vor!
Berg' und Hügel/ Fels und Türne/ auch in frohen Jauchzen springt!

Ihr für alls beglückte Menschen/ weil es euch zu Heil gelingt/
Lobet/ preiset/ ehret/ danket und erhebet hoch empor
Den/ der sich und euch erhebet aus des Tods ins Himmels Chor.
Dann die paradeisisch Unschuld sein' Erstehung euch mitbringt.

Sollte wohl die Sündenmacht dessen Allmacht überstreben/
Der die selbst' Unendlichkeit? Nein, sie muss sich ganz ergeben:
Sein Verdienstes-Meer kann löschen/ nicht nur Fünklein/ ganze Feur.

Ach der lang verlangt' Erlöser tötet alle Ungeheur.
Was will Welt/ Tod/ Teufel/ Höll einem Christen abgewinnen?
Die sind ganz verstört/ verheert: Dieser herrscht im Himmel drinnen.

Catharina Regina von Greiffenberg

Gott Lobende Frühlingslust

Himmel voll Zimbel/ voll Lauten und Geigen/
Bisem- und Amber'-erfüllete Luft/
Rosen- und Lilgen-verlieblichter Tuft!
Wollest/ den Höchsten zu loben/ nit schweigen!

Himmel an wolle die Süssheit aufsteigen/
Herrlich Gott ehrend aus tiefester Kluft.
Seine Genaden und Wunder ausruft/
Wie sie sich mächtig und prächtig erzeigen.

Leset/ in weisslichen Blättern der Blüh/
Göttlicher Allmacht ungleichliche Werke.
Sehet/ in Traidern/ die himmlische Stärke/

Die das Blüh-Härlein bewahret ohn Müh.
Göttliche Wunder in allem man siehet/
Wann man den Vorhang der Faulheit aufziehet.

Catharina Regina von Greiffenberg

Concerning the Joyous and Splendid Resurrection of Christ

Angels, sound upon your trumpets! Seraph-armies, sing and ring!
Oh you rapturous band of Heaven, jubil-, jubil-, jubilate!
Sun and stars, before your Victor dancing, glancing celebrate!
Hill and mountains, cliff and towers, in your joyful triumph spring!

Race of man, by this salvation blest before each other thing,
Praise and worship, thank and honor, high aloft Him elevate,
Who within His person lifted you from death to Heaven's estate.
For to you His resurrection will a sinless Eden bring.

Should then his omnipotence 'gainst some sinful potence fall,
He Who is Eternity? No, for sin itself must fall:
Plunged into His sea of virtue sparks are quenched and mighty fire.

Oh, the long desired Redeemer makes the monster-band expire.
What gain of the Christian soul have the world, death, devil, hell?
It will reign in Heaven's manse; rack and ruin their empire fell.

Catharina Regina von Greiffenberg

Spring-Joy Praising God

Sky full of cymbals, of fiddles and lutes,
Air that the musk and the ambergris fill,
Rose-scent and lily-breath lovelier still,
Cease not your praise of the Lord's attributes!

Sweetness, ascend on the heavenly routes,
Giving God honor from earth's deepest kill.
Cry out his grace, his miraculous will,
Showing how mighty, how bright are their fruits.

Read in the white-tinted leaves of the bloom
Godly omnipotence-works without peer.
See strength divine in the corn and the ear,

Easily guarding the bloom's tiny plume.
Heavenly wonders in all things one finds,
If he but raises his slothfulness' blinds.

Catharina Regina von Greiffenberg

VERLANGEN NACH DER HERRLICHEN EWIGKEIT

Schwing dich/ meine Seel'/ in Himmel/ aus der eitlen Zeitlichkeit!
Schwing dich hin/ woher du kommst/ wo du auch wirst wieder bleiben.
Wollst mit süsser Denke-Lust deine Weil dieweil vertreiben,
Bis du wirst ergetzt/ versetzet in die Zeit-befreite Zeit.

Ach ich mein die Ewig-Ewig-Ewig-Ewig-Ewigkeit/
In die der belebend Tod wird entleibend einverleiben.
Unterdessen woll mein' Hand was von ihrer Hoheit schreiben/
Von der nie gefühlten Fülle/ ihrer Erz-Herz-süssen Freud.

Kraft und Saft der Ewigkeit/ die aus und mit dir entsprungen/
Der du unursprünglich lebtest und dahero ewig bist!
Leg' die künftig Wunder-Wonn' in den Mund und auf die Zungen,

Dass ich klärlich herrlich schreibe/ wie dein Will ohn' Ziel dort ist/
Uns mit dir/ dem höchsten Gut/ zu vereinen unverdrungen.
Komme wieder/ komm hernieder/ zum Gericht gerüster Christ!

Catharina Regina von Greiffenberg

AUF DIE VERFOLGTE, DOCH UNUNTERDRÜCKLICHE TUGEND

Es ist die grösste Ehr, unüberwindlich sein
Und sich auf herculisch dem Unglück widersetzen.
Am Widerstandes Stahl muss Keckheits-Schwert sich wetzen
Damit es schärfer wird und krieg' den Heldenschein.

Der Loorbeer widersteht dem Feur und Donnerstein.
Die Tugend lässet sich von Bosheit nicht verletzen:
Was? Die pflegt sie vielmehr zu Wundern anzuhetzen.
Die Not und Unglück ist der Tugend Wunderschrein.

Was zieret Cyrus Sieg? Die Widerstandes-Waffen.
Es kriegt durch Kriegen nur Philippus Sohn die Welt.
Den Zepter Cäsar auch erst nach dem Streit erhält.

Nicht faulen Siegern nur ist Kron und Thron beschaffen.
Drum biet der Not die Spitz und lass dich nichts abwenden:
Es schwebt schon über dir die Kron in Gottes Händen.

Catharina Regina von Greiffenberg

Desire for Splendid Eternity

Into Heaven soar, my spirit, from the empty temporal dress!
Hasten thither, whence you came, where you once again will stay.
Will you with sweet itch of thought all your while here wile away,
Till enraptured you are captured into timeless timeliness?

Oh, I mean the ever-, ever-, ever-, everlastingness,
Where live death embodies you, although he your body slay.
Meanwhile shall my hand with pen something of its height essay,
Of the fullness, chaste to feeling, of its arch-heart's happiness.

Strength and sap of timelessness, which is from and with You made,
Who are timeless, since You've taken to no origin resort!
Let in mouth and onto tongue future wonder-weal be laid,

That I clearly, that I sheerly of Your end-less wish report:
Us with You (the highest good) to unite all unafraid.
Come once more, oh come before us, Christ accoutered for Your
    court!

Catharina Regina von Greiffenberg

Concerning Persecuted, Yet Indomitable Virtue

    To be unconquerable indeed is pride divine,
    And, aping Hercules, to strike ill-luck asunder.
    From opposition's steel a sword must boldness plunder:
    That it may sharper grow and win the hero's sign.

    The laurel-branch withstands both hail and fiery shine,
    And virtue will not take a hurt from evil's thunder:
    What? Rather she is spurned by ill to some new wonder.
    Misfortune and despair are virtue's wonder-shrine.

    How's Cyrus' triumph graced?[36] By arms of opposition.
    And Philip's son the world with naught save war has won.
    The sceptre Caesar earns but when the strife is done.

    Nor may dull victors make sole claim to crowned condition.
    So bare the point to woe and hold your purpose steady:
    Above you in God's hands the crown does hover ready.

Catharina Regina von Greiffenberg

Brünstiges Weissheit Verlangen

   Herr gib mir die/ durch die/ die Welt und ich erbaut/
die du selb selbsten bist die schönest' aller schönen/
die Seel-erhellend pflegt mit Ehrenglantz zukrönen;
die sich schwingt in ein Herz/ das deinem ist vertraut/
   die auf die/ so auf dich vertrauend schauen/ schaut;
nach der die Sinn' in mir sich hirschengierig sehnen/
mit Lust von aller Lust sich/ ihr zu dienst/ entwähnen!
Die Weissheit meyne ich/ die keusche Hertzen-Braut.
   Wann es mir schon mit ihr auf Danielisch gieng/
sie wär mir Zucker lust auch in dess Löwen Rachen.
Ich wolt/ der Sternen Herr/ im Herzen freyheit lachen/
   Wann auch der höchst' auf mich Leibeigenschafft verhienge.
der schöne Seelen schatz pflegt überall zu funklen.
Kein' unglücks Nacht noch Macht/ ja nichts/ kan sie verdunklen.

Catharina Regina von Greiffenberg

Eiferige Lobes vermahnung

   Ach lobe/ lobe/ lob'/ ohn unterlass und ziel/
den/ den zu loben du/ O meine Seel/ gebohren!
zu diesen Engel-werk bist du von Gott erkohren/
dass du ihm dienen solst im wunderpreisungs spiel.
   Das kleine scherflein ihm von jenem Weib gefiel:
dein' einfalt klinget wol in seinen Demut-Ohren.
Er geht sanfftmütig um mit den zubrochnen Rohren.
Wie schwach und bebend' auch/ beliebt ihm doch dein kiel
   Rühm/ weil du Othem hast; dieweil du ihn entfangen/
allein zu diesem ziel. dess Lebens unwehrt ist/
aus dessen Mund so viel nicht Lob/ als lufft gegangen.
   Weil du der Gottes Güt ein wunderspiegel bist/
so lass den Strahl zu ruck in deine Sonn gelangen.
weil du dazu/ so sey es auch von dir/ erkiest!

Catharina Regina von Greiffenberg

Fiery Longing for Wisdom

    Lord, give me her, who did both world and me provide,
Who is Your very self, the fairest of the fair,
Who, spirit-lighting's, wont the crown of fame to share,
Who flies into a heart which in Yours may confide,
    Whose eyes on those, who look to You in trust, reside,
For whom my senses all in stag's wild rutting flare,
And joyful, serving her, themselves of joy strip bare!
It's wisdom that I mean, the heart's unblemished bride.
    If once I Daniel's fate had in her company,
In lion's jaws she would a sugared joy impart.
A lord of stars, I'd laugh with freedom in my heart,
    Although the highest Lord sold me to slavery.
The fair soul's treasure shows on every side its spark:
Nor troubled night nor might nor aught can turn it dark.

Catharina Regina von Greiffenberg

Zealous Admonition to Praise

    Oh praise Him, praise Him, praise without an end or aim
Him for Whose praise, my soul, your birth was granted you.
For God does you elect this angel-work to do,
That you shall serve Him in the wonder-praising's game.
    That widow's tiny mite to Him a joy became,
Your plainsong His meek-ears will bring sweet revenue.
How soft He does His way midst broken reeds pursue.[37]
Your quill-pen gives Him joy though it be weak and lame.
    Adore, since you have breath: you have been given it
But to this end alone. That man no life does earn
Whose mouth will more of air than of His praise transmit.
    Since you as wonder-glass of Heaven's goodness burn,
Then backwards let the beam into your sun-ball hit;
Since you are chosen for this, then make your choice return.

Catharina Regina von Greiffenberg

UBER GOTTES GNÄDIGE VORSORGE

    Ach hoher Gott/ vor dem die Sternen gleich dem Staube/
die Sonn' ein Senffkorn ist/ der Mond ein Körnlein Sand/
der ganze Erden Ball ein Pflaumen auf der Hand.
verwunderns voll hierob/ ich mich schier ganz betaube.
    Wann deine Haubtobacht'/ auf mich ein nichts/ ich glaube/
ja! reich erfahrner spür'/ im Tausendschickungs-Stand:
so scheints/ auf mich allein sey all dein Fleiss gewandt.
nur dieses Wunders Art zu preissen mir erlaube.
    Ich bin ein nichts/ aus nichts: durch deine Gnad so viel/
dass deiner Güte Mäng' ich ein eintreffends Ziel.
der Menschen bösser Sinn möcht diss vor Hoffart achten.
    Doch ists der Demutgrund/ Gott/ deine Werk betrachten.
Ich bin/ wie ich gesagt/ ein Nichts: mein Alles du.
hat (Wunder!) Allheit dann in Nichtes ihre Ruh?

Catharina Regina von Greiffenberg

AUF MEINEN VORSATZ/ DIE HEILIGE SCHRIFFT ZULESEN

    Auf deinem Namen will/ O Herr/ ich mich begeben
hin in das tieffe Meer Gott-eingegebner Schrifft/
wo man mit Geistes-Mast und Glaubens-Segeln schifft;
da uns der Himmels-Port vor Augen pflegt zuschweben.
    Die Augen der Vernunfft/ wann man da auf will heben
Corall- und Perlen-Schätz/ wann man hinab vertiefft/
muss man verbinden/ dass Unglaubens Salz nicht trifft:
dass Christus Blut-Corall im Hertzen möge leben/
    O Geist/ mein Steuermann! Herr Christ/ mein Nordestern!
lenk' und erleucht mich stäts/ dass sich mein Zünglein wende/
mit deinem Blut geschmiert/ nach dir/ ob ich noch fern/
    und an dem Hafen bald der Seeligkeit anlände.
In diesem Demant Meer/ das deinen Thron umgibt/
ergez' ich mich/ biss dir/ dich mir zu weisen/ liebt.

Catharina Regina von Greiffenberg

Concerning God's Gracious Care

    Oh lofty God, to Whom the stars are like the dust,
The sun a mustard-seed, the moon a grain of sand,
The whole ball of the earth a plum within Your hand:
Astonished at this sight, in stupor I am thrust.
    Although your chiefest heed for me is naught (I trust,
Indeed, more wise, I trace in infinite fate's demand),
It seems 'gainst me alone You've sent Your tireless band:
Grant that I now towards praise these wondrous ways adjust.
    I am a naught from naught: but so much through Your grace
That for Your goodness' wealth I am a striking place.
The evil minds of men might title this conceit,
    Yet to regard Your work is meekness' final feat.
I am, as I have said, a nothing: You my All.
Can allness nothingness (oh wonder!) refuge call?

Catharina Regina von Greiffenberg

Concerning My Resolution to Read Holy Scripture

    In Your name, oh my Lord, I shall my vessel drive
Upon the seas profound of God-inspired writ,
Where spirit's mast and sails of faith are requisite,
Where in our sight the port of Heaven soars alive.
    When coral's wealth and pearl's have lured the soul to dive,
Across our reason's eyes we must a bandage fit
Lest by the skeptic salt their clarity be smit:
That Jesus' coral red within my heart may thrive,
    Oh helmsman, Holy Ghost! Sir Christ, my northern star!
Lead, light me ever that my compass' arm may wend,
Anointed by Your blood, to You (though I be far),
    That at the blessed bay I soon my voyage may end.
Within these diamond seas which now Your throne surround,
I shall rejoice till You a course for me have found.

Catharina Regina von Greiffenberg

Auf die Thränen

Du treuer Augensafft! wann ich schier gar verschmachte/
in Ohnmacht sink dahin/ so spritzstu ins Gesicht.
Du bist bey mir/ wann ich bin bey mir selber nicht.
Sonst alle Labnuss ich/ nur deine nicht/ verachte.
    Du Brunn der wahren Lieb'! in dir/ ich Gott betrachte/
ja neben mir erblick' in seinem gnaden-Liecht.
Ich senk/ ertränk in dir die Noht/ die mich anficht/
du Herzgrund-Rotes Meer/ den Sündhund dir auch schlachte.
    Die Tugend-Thetis/ so bewohnet deinen grund/
wann Unglück mich verfolgt und ich in dich mich stürze/
nimmt in ihr Königreich mich auff/ mir zuflucht gunnt.
    Du trauer-saure flut/ mein Leben mir verkürze!
ihr Thränen/trennet mich von diesem Jammer Ort!
als Perlen/ Diamant werdt ihr mich zieren dort.

Catharina Regina von Greiffenberg

Gott-lobende Frühlings-Lust

Jauchzet/ Bäume/ Vögel singet! danzet/ Blumen/ Felder lacht!

springt/ ihr Brünnlein! Bächlein rauscht! spielet ihr gelinden Winde!

walle/ Lust-bewegtes Träid! Flüsse fliest geschwinde!
opffert Lob-Geruch dem Schöpffer/ der euch frisch und neu gemacht!
    jedes Blühlein sey ein Schale/ drauff Lob-Opffer ihm gebracht/
jedes Gräslein eine Seul/ da sein Namens-Ehr man finde.
an die neu-belaubten Aestlein/ Gottes Gnaden-Ruhm man binde!
dass/ so weit sein Güt sich strecket/ werd' auch seiner Ehr gedacht.

    Du vor alles/ Menschen Volck/ seiner Güte Einfluss Ziele!
aller Lieblichkeit Geniesser; Abgrund/ wo der Wunderfluss
endet und zu gut verwendet seinen Lieb-vergulten Guss.
    Gott mit Hertz/ Hand/ Sinn und Stimm/ lobe/ preisse/ dicht' und
                                                                     spiele.
Lass/ vor Lieb' und Lobes-Gier/ Muht und Blut zu Kohlen werden/
lege Lob und Dank darauff: Gott zum süssen Rauch auf Erden.

Catharina Regina von Greiffenberg

On Tears

Oh faithful eye-born wine! When I near pass away
And into darkness sink, my countenance you wet;
You've not forgotten me, when I myself forget.
Each other cooling drink, save yours, I glad gainsay.
   You fountain of true love! In you I God survey,
And have Him next to me within His grace- light met.
In you I dip, I drown the griefs which me beset:
Oh Red Sea of heart's ground, the hound of sinning slay!
The virtue-Thetis [38] who below is said to live,
When I, pursued by woe, into your waves must leap,
Will in her empire me a place of refuge give.
   Abbreviate my life, oh sorrow-sourish deep!
Oh teardrops, sever me from this abode of care!
As pearls and diamonds you will adorn me there.

Catharina Regina von Greiffenberg

Spring-Joy Praising God

Trees, exult! sing, birds! dance, flowers! Let the fields be laughter taught!
Leap, you fountains! Rustle, brooks! Gentle winds, play out your game!
Wander, wind-enchanted wheat! River, sweet your speed proclaim!
Offer incense to the Maker Who you fresh and new has wrought!
   Let each blossom be a salver where some sacrifice is brought!
Make of all the grassy blades pillars for His honored name!
Bind upon the new-leaved branchesHeaven's generous-handed fame,
That, where'er His goodness reaches, men will know His honor's thought!
   Mankind! You before all others come beneath His kindness' sway!
Customer of every beauty, chasm where the wonder-flood
Will His love-begilded torrent end and channel to the good!
   With your heart, hand, sense, and voice, praise God, raise Him, sing, and play!
Let for love and praising's lust soul and blood to charcoal turn!
On it pile your praise and thanks, that sweet-smoked for God they burn.

Catharina Regina von Greiffenberg

AUF DIE FRUCHTBRINGENDE HERBST-ZEIT

Freud'-erfüller/ Früchte-bringer/ vielbeglückter Jahres-Koch/
Grünung-Blüh und Zeitung-Ziel/ Werkbeseeltes Lustverlangen!
lange Hoffnung/ ist in dir in die That-Erweisung gangen.
Ohne dich/ wird nur beschauet/ aber nichts genossen noch.
  Du Vollkommenheit der Zeiten! mache bald vollkommen doch/
was von Blüh' und Wachstums-Krafft halbes Leben schon empfangen.
Deine Würkung kan allein mit der Werk-Vollziehung prangen.
Wehrter Zeiten-Schatz! ach bringe jenes blühen auch so hoch/

  schütt' aus deinem reichen Horn hochverhoffte Freuden Früchte.
Lieblich süsser Mund-Ergetzer! lab' auch unsern Geist zugleich:
so erhebt mit jenen er deiner Früchte Ruhm-Gerüchte.
  zeitig die verlangten Zeiten/ in dem Oberherrschungs-Reich.
Lass die Anlas-Kerne schwarz/ Schickungs-Aepffel safftig werden:
dass man Gottes Gnaden-Frücht froh geniest und isst auf Erden.

Hans Jacob Christoffel von Grimmelshausen

Komm Trost der Nacht, o Nachtigal,
Lass deine Stimm mit Freudenschall,
Auffs lieblichste erklingen;
Komm, komm, und lob den Schöpffer dein,
Weil andre Vöglein schlaffen seyn,
Und nicht mehr mögen singen!
  Lass dein Stimmlein,
    Laut erschallen, dan vor allen
    Kanstu loben
Gott im Himmel hoch dort oben.

Obschon ist hin der Sonnenschein,
Und wir im Finstern müssen seyn,
So können wir doch singen;
Von Gottes Güt und seiner Macht,
Weil uns kan hindern keine Macht,
Sein Lob zu vollenbringen.
  Drum dein Stimmlein,
    Lass erschallen, dan vor allen
    Kanstu loben
Gott im Himmel hoch dort oben.

Catharina Regina von Greiffenberg

Concerning the Fruit-bringing Autumn-season

   Glee-fulfiller, fruit-producer, cook who glad the year can feed,
Greening's bloom, time's terminus, wish-for-pleasure worker-weaved!
Long desiring has in you proof by means of act achieved.
From your lack would contemplation, not experience, proceed.
   You perfection of the ages, perfect make all that in deed
Which from bloom and burgeon-might half a life ere now received.
Only by your wonder-work can work's ending be conceived.
Worthy treasure of time's passage! Now thus high that blooming lead,
   Shake from out your copious horn highly hoped rejoicing's fruit.
Sweet and lovely mouth-delighter! Make our spirit too expand,
That it raise up with the others this your harvest's famous bruit.
   Bring to time the times desired in the super-sovereign-land.
Let the causal-kernels black, let fate-apples juicy grow:
That the gracious fruit of God we on earth glad eat and know.

Hans Jacob Christoffel von Grimmelshausen

   Come, balm of night, oh nightingale,
And let your voice with joyful tale
Ring out in fairest ways.
Come, come, your Maker's praise essay,
Since other birds in slumber stay,
Nor will their voices raise.
    Let your faint lay
      Loudly call, since you 'fore all
        Can glorify
God Who reigns in Heaven on high.

   Although the sun has gone away
And we must in the darkness stay,
Yet we our voice can raise:
Of God's benevolence and might,
Since there can hinder us no might
In making full His praise.
    Bid your faint lay
      Thus to call, since you 'fore all
        Can glorify
God Who reigns in Heaven on high.

Echo, der wilde Widerhall
Will seyn bey diesem Freudenschall,
Und lässet sich auch hören;
Verweist uns alle Müdigkeit,
Der wir ergeben allezeit,
Lehrt uns den Schlaff bethören.
   Drum dein Stimmlein,
      Lass erschallen, dan vor allen
         Kanstu loben
Gott im Himmel hoch dort oben.

Die Sterne, so am Himmel stehn,
Sich lassen zum Lob Gottes sehn,
Und Ehre ihm beweisen,
Die Eul auch die nicht singen kan,
Zeigt doch mit ihrem Heulen an,
Dass sie Gott auch thu preisen.
   Drum dein Stimmlien,
      Lass erschallen, dan vor allen
         Kanstu loben
Gott im Himmel hoch dort oben.

Nur her, mein liebstes Vögelein,
Wir wollen nicht die fäulste seyn,
Und schlaffend ligen bleiben,
Vielmehr biss dass die Morgenröth,
Erfreuet diese Wälder öd,
In Gottes Lob vertreiben.
Lass dein Stimmlein,
      Laut erschallen, dan vor allen
         Kanstu loben
Gott im Himmel hoch dort oben.

Johann Grob

EPIGRAMME

1. Von dem Bertramen

Bertram liebet nur die nacht, diese kan ihm freude bringen,
Denn da stellt er gastung, pflegen zu spielen und zu springen,
Kömt der tag so geht er schlaaffen, denn er macht ihm nur verdrus;
Was bedünkt euch, ist dan Bertram nicht ein kind der finsternus.

Echo, the wild response's sound,
This joyful pealing will compound,
Nor will her silence keep:
She chides us for our weariness
To which we'd fain ourselves address,
And tells us tricks 'gainst sleep.
   Bid your faint lay
      Thus to call, since you 'fore all
         Can glorify
God Who reigns in Heaven on high.

The stars which stand along the skies
Will by their light God eulogize,
And Him will honor show.
The owl, which knows not how to sing
Would by its hoot a warrant bring
That it God's praise does know.
   Bid your faint lay
      Thus to call, since you 'fore all
         Can glorify
God who reigns in Heaven on high.

My sweetest bird, come but this way,
For we will not the sluggard play,
And sleep the night to end,
But rather till the ruddy dawn
Rejoicing through these woods has gone,
In praise the darkness spend.
   Let your faint lay
      Loudly call, since you 'fore all
         Can glorify
God who reigns in Heaven on high.

Johann Grob

Epigrams

1. Concerning Bertram

Bertram loves the night alone; only night can bring him joy;
Then he holds his feasts, and puts games and gambols to employ.
With the day he hastes to slumber, since the day but makes him wild.
Now what think you? Is not Bertram to be called the darkness' child?

2. Amsterdam

O kaufplaz aller welt, o pracht der tapfren Staaten,
Wie herrlich blühest du mit eitel zier berahten,
Du gleichest einer braut, o grosses Amsterdam,
Gar recht, Mercurius, der ist dein bräutigam.

3. Die Schweiz

Es bringt kein hoher berg, noch enger pass zu wegen,
Dass meine leute noch der stolzen freiheit pflegen,
Kein schneller wasserstrom, kein unergründter see:
O nein, die einigkeit macht dass ich noch besteh'.

4. Samuel Pufendorf

Schweden hätt' im Deutschen krieg' ohne manchen Deutschen degen
Nimmer sich so weit gebracht, sonder wäre vor erlegen:
Drum ist billich, dass es Schweden gleichfals für ein' ehre helt,
Wan auch eines Deutschen feder seine tahten schön erzehlt.

5. General Werdmüller

Die dapfre Kriegeskunst, so Frankreich mir gewiesen,
Dalmatien bewert, und Deutschland letzt gepriesen,
Die bracht nur in der Schweiz mir wenig ruhm und huld:
Was mag der fehler sein? Man gab mir fremde schuld.

6. Auf einen kurzweiligen Ostindienfahrer

Dass dir nach Batavia mit zu fahren nicht gegrauet,
Dass du Siam, Indostan, und auch Sina selbst beschauet,
Und gesund bist wieder kommen, diss ist gleichwohl eine taht,
Welche bei uns Oberdeutschen billich preis und ehre hat.
Du erzehlest wunderding' aus Japan und Coromandel,
Von der Indianer pracht, glauben, kleidung, tuhn und handel:
Doch ist eines so von allen uns füraus verwundert macht,
Namlich dass du einen Affen nur allein herausgebracht.

7. Prag

Der Böhmen mutterstatt beschliesst in weiten mauern
Studenten, Edelleut', Hebreer, Burger, Bauern,
Soldaten, Betelvolk, und Pfaffen allerhand,
Ist Schuhle, Hof, Spital, Burg, Kloster, Statt, und Land.

2. Amsterdam

Oh brave Estates' delight! Oh market of the world!
How splendidly have you your purest bloom unfurled.
Oh mighty Amsterdam, you're very like a bride –
Indeed, since Mercury's the bridegroom at your side.[39]

3. Switzerland

No lofty mountain peak, no narrow pass can claim
That they my people helped to keep proud freedom's fame,
No hasty water-course, and no unfathomed lake:
No, my existence I from unity do take.

4. Samuel Pufendorf [40]

Lacking all its German blades, Sweden in the German war
Would these many years have been conquered and not conqueror.
Thus it's fair when Sweden likewise must it for an honor hold
That a pen of German author goodly of its deeds has told.

5. General Werdmüller [41]

That valiant art of war which France within me raised,
Dalmatia proved, and last the German nation praised,
Brought but in Switzerland to me small grace and fame:
Now where may be the fault? Men gave me foreign blame.

6. Concerning an Amusing Traveler from the East Indies

That to raise Batavia you no spark of fear did know,
That to Siam, Hindustan, e'en to China you could go,
And have homeward come all healthy: this adventure is indeed
Such as midst us Upper Germans fair does praise and honor breed.
Of the Coromandel Coast, of Japan you wonders tell,
Of the Indians' wealth and dress, how they pray and buy and sell.
Yet one thing before all others does arouse us to surprise:
That you brought from all your journeys but a monkey home as prize.

7. Prague

Bohemia's mother-town in its wide walls includes
Students, aristocrats, Jews, burghers, peasant-broods,
And soldiers, mendicants, jack-priests of every sort:
It's pesthouse, fortress, town, land, cloister, school, and court.

Andreas Gryphius

UEBER SEINE SONNTAG- UND FEIERTAGS-SONNETTE

In meiner ersten blüth', ach! unter grimmen schmertzen,
    Bestürtzt durchs scharffe schwerdt und ungeheuren brand,
    Durch liebster freunde tod und elend, als das land,
Indem ich auffgieng, fiel, als toller feinde schertzen,
Als läster-zungen spott mir rasend drang zu hertzen,
    Schrieb ich diss, was du siehst, mit noch zu zarter hand,
    Zwar kindern als ein kind, doch reiner andacht pfand.
Tritt leser nicht zu hart auf blumen erstes mertzen!
    Hier donnert, ich bekenn, mein rauer Abas nicht,
    Nicht Leo, der die seel auf dem altar ausbricht;
Der märtrer helden-muth ist anderswo zu lesen.
    Ihr, die ihr nichts mit lust als fremde fehler zehlt,
    Bemüth euch ferner nicht! Ich sag' es, was mir fehlt,
Dass meine kindheit nicht gelehrt, doch fromm gewesen.

Andreas Gryphius

AN GOTT DEN HEILIGEN GEIST

O feuer wahrer lieb! O brunn der guten gaben!
    O meister aller kunst! O höchste heiligkeit!
    O dreymal grosser Gott! O lust, die alles leid
Vertreibt! O keusche taub! O furcht der höllen raben!
Die, eh das wüste meer mit bergen rings umgraben,
    Ehr lufft und erden ward, eh das gestirnte kleid
    Dem himmel angelegt, vor anbegin der zeit,
Die zwey, die gantz dir gleich, von sich gelassen haben!
    O weisheit ohne mass! O reiner seelen gast!
    O theure gnaden-quell'! O trost in herber last!
O regen, der in angst mit segen uns befeuchtet!
    Ach lass ein tröpflein nur von deinem lebens-thau
    Erfrischen meinen geist! Hilff, dass ich doch nur schau'
Ein füncklein deiner glut! so bin ich gantz erleuchtet.

Andreas Gryphius

Concerning His Sunday and Holiday Sonnets

Surrounded by cruel pains, in my first blossoming,[42]
    Dismayed by holocausts and by the sharp-edged brand,
    By best friends' misery and murder – when the land,
The while I grew, did fall, when mad foe's harrying,
When jibes of blaspheme-tongue wild through my heart did ring:
    I wrote this, which you see, with still too tender hand,
    A child for children, yet at piety's command.
Tread, reader, not too hard on blooms of early spring.
    Here does not, I confess, my rampant Abas roar,[43]
    Nor Leo, who his soul lost on the altar floor.[44]
The martyr's hero-heart is elsewhere to be read.
    Oh you who naught with joy save others' failings list,
    Have care no more, for I shall tell you what I missed:
My childhood piously, not learnedly, was led.

Andreas Gryphius

To God the Holy Ghost

Oh true love's fire! Oh fount, that all good gifts provided!
    Oh master of all art! Oh highest holiness!
    Oh thrice great God! Oh joy, that each pain can suppress!
Oh virgin dove! that has with fear Hell's ravens derided!
That, ere the wild sea's shape with mountains was decided,
    Ere earth and air were made, and ere the starry dress,
    Before the start of time, in Heaven could egress:
These Two, Your very likes, had from Yourself divided!
    Oh untouched spirit's guest! Oh wisdom without end!
    Oh precious source of grace! Oh bitter burden's friend!
Oh rain, which us in fear with blessing's moisture brightened!
    Oh let a single drop from this your living dew
    Refresh my spirit! Aid, that I may only view
A small spark of your blaze! Then I am all enlightened.

Andreas Gryphius

ÜBER DIE GEBURT JESU

Nacht, mehr denn lichte nacht! nacht, lichter als der tag!
    Nacht, heller als die sonn'! in der das licht geboren,
Das Gott, der licht in licht wohnhafftig, ihm erkohren!
    O nacht, die alle nacht und tage trotzen mag!
    O freudenreiche nacht, in welcher ach und klag
Und finsternis, und was sich auf die welt verschworen,
Und furcht und höllen-angst und schrecken war verlohren!
    Der himmel bricht; doch fällt nunmehr kein donnerschlag.
Der zeit und nächte schuff, ist diese nacht ankommen
Und hat das recht der zeit und fleisch an sich genommen
    Und unser fleisch und zeit der ewigkeit vermacht.
Die jammer trübe nacht, die schwartze nacht der sünden,
Des grabes dunckelheit muss durch die nacht verschwinden.
    Nacht, lichter als der tag! nacht, mehr denn lichte nacht!

Andreas Gryphius

MENSCHLICHES ELENDE

Was sind wir menschen doch! ein wohnhaus grimmer schmertzen,
    Ein ball des falschen glücks, ein irrlicht dieser zeit,
    Ein schauplatz herber angst, besetzt mit scharffem leid,
Ein bald verschmeltzter schnee und abgebrannte kertzen.
Diss leben fleucht davon wie ein geschwätz und schertzen.
    Die vor uns abgelegt des schwachen leibes kleid
    Und in das todten-buch der grossen sterbligkeit
Längst eingeschrieben sind, sind uns aus sinn und hertzen.
    Gleich wie ein eitel traum leicht aus der acht hinfällt
    Und wie ein strom verscheusst, den keine macht auffhält,
So muss auch unser nahm, lob, ehr und ruhm verschwinden.
    Was itzund athem holt, muss mit der lufft entfliehn,
    Was nach uns kommen wird, wird uns ins grab nachziehn.
Was sag ich? wir vergehn, wie rauch von starcken winden.

Andreas Gryphius

On the Birth of Jesus

Night, lighter than the day! Night, more than brilliant night,
   Night, brighter than the sun, in which the light's erected
That God, light dwelt in light, has for that light elected:
   Oh night, which to all nights, all days may give despite.
   Oh night, replete with joys, in which lament and fright
And gloom and what against the world a plot effected,
And fear and agony and terror were rejected.
   The heavens break, but now no thunderbolt may smite.
Who made time and the nights has on this night descended
And rights of time and flesh unto Himself extended,
   To timelessness our flesh and time has signed away.
   The night grown dull with woe, the night in sin defeated,
The darkness of the grave must by the night be cheated.
   Night, more than brilliant night! Night, lighter than the day!

Andreas Gryphius

Human Misery

What are we men indeed? Grim torment's habitation,
   A toy of fickle luck, wisp in time's wilderness,
   A scene of bitter fear and filled with keen distress,
And tapers burned to stubs, snow's quick evaporation.
This life does flee away like jest or conversation;
   Those who before us laid aside the body's dress
   And in the domesday-book of monster mortalness
Old entry found, have left our mind's and heart's sensation.
   Just as an empty dream from notice lighty flees,
   And as a stream is lost whose course no might may cease,
So must our honor, fame, our praise and name be ended.
   What presently draws breath, must perish with the air,
   What after us will come, someday our grave will share.
What do I say? We pass as smoke on strong winds wended.

Andreas Gryphius

Thränen des Vaterlandes, anno 1636

Wir sind doch nunmehr gantz, ja mehr denn gantz verheeret.
   Der frechen völcker schaar, die rasende posaun,
   Das vom blut fette schwerdt, die donnernde carthaun
Hat aller schweiss und fleiss und vorrath auffgezehret.
Die thürme stehn in glut, die kirch ist umgekehret,
   Das rathaus liegt im graus, die starcken zind zerhaun,
   Die jungfern sind geschänd't, und wo wir hin nur schaun,
Ist feuer, pest und tod, der hertz und geist durchfähret.
   Hier durch die schantz und stadt rinnt allzeit frisches blut.
   Dreymal sind schon sechs jahr, als unser ströme flut
Von leichen fast verstopfft, sich langsam fort gedrungen.
   Doch schweig ich noch von dem, was ärger als der tod,
   Was grimmer denn die pest und glut und hungersnoth.
Dass auch der seelen-schatz so vielen abgezwungen.

Andreas Gryphius

An einen unschuldigen leidenden

Ein brand-pfall und ein rad, pech, folter, bley und zangen,
   Strick, messer, hacken, beil, ein holtzstoss und ein schwerdt
   Und siedend öl und bley, ein spiss, ein glüend pferd
Sind den'n nicht schrecklich, die, was schrecklich, nicht begangen.
Wer um die tugend leid't, um recht-thun wird gefangen,
   Und wenn es noth, sein blut, doch ohne schuld, gewehrt,
   Dem wird für kurtze pein unendlich preis beschert.
Er wird den ehren-krantz, der nicht verwelckt, erlangen.
   Er lebt, in dem er stirbt; er steigt, in dem er fällt;
   Er pocht, was tödlich ist, und trotzt die grosse welt
Und küsst die ewigkeit, die er ihm anvertrauet.
   Hat nicht der höchste selbst sein höchstes wunderwerck
   Auf Salems schädelberg vollbracht in höchster stärck?
Der ist kein rechter Christ, dem für dem creutze grauet.

Andreas Gryphius

Tears of the Fatherland, anno 1636

Entire, more than entire have we been devastated!
   The maddened clarion, the bold invaders' horde,
   The mortar thunder-voiced, the blood-annointed sword
Have all men's sweat and work and store annihilated.
The towers stand in flames, the church is violated,
   The strong are massacred, a ruin our council board,
   Our maidens raped, and where my eyes have scarce explored
Fire, pestilence, and death my heart have dominated.
   Here through the moat and town runs always new-let blood,
   And for three-times-six years our very rivers' flood
With corpses choked has pressed ahead in tedious measure;
   I shall not speak of that which is still worse than death,
   And crueller than the plague and torch and hunger's breath:
From many has been forced even the spirit's treasure.

Andreas Gryphius

To an Innocent Sufferer

A burning-stake, a wheel, tar, rack, and lead, and tong,
   Rope, knife, hook, oil, and lead, all boiling o'er the glede,
   Stacked wood, an axe, a sword, a spear, a glowing steed:
Cannot fill men with fear who've done no fearful wrong.
Who torment bears for good, for right the prisoner's thong,
   And without guilt does spill his blood, if there be need:
   Upon his short-lived pain will endless praise succeed.
To him will honor's wreath, which grows not sere, belong.
   He climbs the while he falls, he lives the while he dies,
   He beards mortality, the mighty world defies,
And loves eternity, which he his own has made.
   Did not the Highest Lord His highest wonder-will
   In highest strength complete on Salem's skull-topped hill? [45]
True Christians at the Cross blanch not, nor are afraid.

Andreas Gryphius

AN DIE STERNEN

Ihr lichter, die ich nicht auf erden satt kan schauen,
   Ihr fackeln, die ihr nacht und schwartze wolcken trennt,
   Als diamante spielt und ohn auffhören brennt;
Ihr blumen, die ihr schmückt des grossen himmels auen;
Ihr wächter, die, als gott die welt auff-wolte-bauen,
   Sein wort, die weisheit selbst, mit rechten namen nennt,
   Die Gott allein recht misst, die Gott allein recht kennt,
(Wir blinden sterblichen! was wollen wir uns trauen!)
   Ihr bürgen meiner lust! wie manche schöne nacht
   Hab ich, in dem ich euch betrachtete, gewacht?
Herolden dieser zeit! wenn wird es doch geschehen,
   Dass ich, der eurer nicht allhier vergessen kan,
   Euch, derer liebe mir steckt hertz und geister an,
Von andern sorgen frey werd unter mir besehen?

Andreas Gryphius

AN EUGENIEN

Gleich als ein wandersmann, dafern die trübe nacht
   Mit dicker finsternis lufft, erd und see verdecket,
   Betrübt irr't hin und her und mit viel furcht erschrecket,
Nicht weiss, wohin er geht, noch was er lässt und macht,
So eben ists mit mir; doch wenn der mond erwacht
   Und seiner strahlen kertz im wolckenhaus anstecket,
   Bald find't er weg und rath: so wird mein geist erwecket,
Nun mich der neue trost aus eurem brieff anlacht.
Doch, warum heisst ihr mich diss schöne pfand verbrennen?
   Wolt ihr in meiner nacht mich bey der glut' erkennen?
   Diss, meines hertzens feu'r ,entdeckt ja, wer ich sey.
Sol, schönste! diss papier nur meine brust berühren,
So wird es alsobald in aschen sich verlieren,
   Wo von der flamm' es nicht wird durch mein weinen frey.

Andreas Gryphius

To the Stars

You lights, for which on earth my sight's thirst ne'er is stilled,
   You torches, which the night and ebon clouds entame,
   Which glow like diamonds and without ceasing flame,
You flowers, which the fields of mighty Heaven gild,
You watchmen, who when God the orb of earth would build,
   His word, high wisdom, did by proper title name,
   You stars whose way and bounds great God alone can claim:
(Blind mortals! How can we to trust ourselves be willed?)
   You pledges of my joy! How many a wondrous night
   Have I held vigil while I pondered on your light?
Oh heralds of this time! When will it be my fare,
   That I, who here below can never you forget,
   You stars, whose love my heart and soul to fire does set,
Shall see you under me, all freed from alien care?

Andreas Gryphius

To Eugenia

Just as a wanderer, when gloomy night does make
   With heavy dark its way o'er earth and sea and air,
   And this way errs and that, tormented with much care,
Not knowing where he goes, what path to leave or take:
Just so it is with me: yet if the moon awake
   And in its cloudy house ignite its candle's flare,
   He path and plan finds: thus my soul from sleep does fare,
Since, laughing, my new balm does from your letter break.
And, still, why order me to set this prize alight?
   Would you think by the glow to spy me in my night?
   This flame born of my heart can tell who I may be.
Should, fairest, I but touch this paper to my heart,
It in that moment would to ashes take depart,
   Unless it from its flame come by my weeping free.

Andreas Gryphius

AN SICH SELBST

Mir grauet vor mir selbst; mir zittern alle glieder,
   Wenn ich die lipp' und nas' und beider augen klufft,
   Die blind vom wachen sind, des athems schwere lufft
Betracht' und die nun schon erstorbnen augen-lieder.
Die zunge, schwartz vom brand, fällt mit den worten nieder
   Und lallt, ich weiss nicht was; die müde seele rufft
   Dem grossen tröster zu, das fleisch reucht nach der grufft,
Die ärtzte lassen mich, die schmertzen kommen wieder.
   Mein cörper ist nicht mehr als adern, fell, und bein.
   Das sitzen ist mein tod, das liegen meine pein.
Die schenckel haben selbst nun träger wol vonnöthen.
   Was ist der hohe ruhm und jugend, ehr und kunst?
   Wenn diese stunde kommt, wird alles rauch und dunst,
Und eine noth muss uns mit allem vorsatz tödten.

Andreas Gryphius

AN DIE WELT

Mein offt bestürmtes schiff, der grimmen winde spiel,
   Der frechen wellen ball, das schier die flut getrennet,
Das wie ein schneller pfeil nach seinem ziele rennet,
   Kommt vor der zeit an port, den meine seele wil.
   Offt, wenn uns schwartze nacht im mittag überfiel,
Hat der geschwinde blitz die segel schier verbrennet.
Wie offt hab ich den wind und nord' und sud verkennet!
   Wie schadhafft ist der mast, steur, ruder, schwerdt und kiel!
Steig aus du müder geist! steig aus! wir sind am lande.
Was graut dir für dem port? itzt wirst du aller bande
   Und angst und herber pein und schwerer schmertzen los.
Ade, verfluchte welt? du see voll rauer stürme!
Glück zu mein vaterland! das stete ruh' im schirme
   Und schutz und frieden hält, du ewig-lichtes schloss!

Andreas Gryphius

To Himself

I sicken of myself, my members all are shaking,
   When I my lip and nose, my breathing's heavy wave,
   My lids already numb, and next my two eyes' cave
Will contemplate, which last are blind from too long waking.
My tongue, with fever black and sense of words forsaking,
   Babbles I know not what, my spent soul can but crave
   The great consoler's aid, my flesh smells of the grave.
The doctors leave me now, whom pains again are taking.
   My body is no more than skin and bone and vein;
   To sit my certain death, and yet to lie my pain,
My thighs themselves are come into the need of bearers.
   Of what do lofty fame, youth, honor, art consist?
   When this hour has approached, all turns to smoke and mist,
One curse with all design must slay us through its terrors.

Andreas Gryphius

To the World

My often storm-wracked ship, the cruel winds' delight,
   The bold waves' ball, which floods had in a moment parted,
Yet like a rapid bolt toward its target darted,
   Comes early to that port my spirit had in sight.
   When often at midday there fell on us the night,
A flame within our sails the lightning all but started.
How often have I wind and north and south mischarted!
   How are the sprit and mast, helm, plank, and keel grown slight!
Descend, exhausted soul, descend, for we have landed.
Now are all burdening ties, anxiety, remanded,
   Cruel torment, grievous pain. Why shudder at this port?
Farewell, you brutal sea, farewell, you world infernal!
I greet you, fatherland, which keeps repose eternal
   In sure defence and peace, you ever lighted fort!

Andreas Gryphius

Morgen sonnet

Die ewig-helle schar wil nun ihr licht verschliessen;
   Diane steht erblasst; die morgenröthe lacht
   Den grauen himmel an; der sanffte wind erwacht
Und reitzt das federvolck, den neuen tag zu grüssen.
Das leben dieser welt eilt schon die welt zu küssen
   Und steckt sein haupt empor; man sieht der strahlen pracht
   Nun blinckern auf der see. O dreymal höchste macht!
Erleuchte den, der sich itzt beugt vor deinen füssen!
   Vertreib die dicke nacht, die meine seel umgibt,
   Die schmertzen finsternis, die hertz und geist betrübt!
Erquicke mein gemüth und stärcke mein vertrauen!
   Gib, dass ich diesen tag in deinem dienst allein
   Zubring! und wenn mein end' und jener tag bricht ein,
Dass ich dich, meine sonn! mein licht! mög ewig schauen!

Andreas Gryphius

Mittag

Auf freunde! lasst uns zu der taffel eilen,
   Indem die sonn ins himmels mittel hält
   Und der von hitz und arbeit matten welt
Sucht ihren weg und unsern tag zu theilen!
Der blumen zier wird von den flammen pfeilen
   Zu hart versehrt, das ausgedörte feld
   Wündscht nach dem thau', der schnitter nach dem zelt;
Kein vogel klagt von seinen liebes-seilen.
   Itzt herrscht das licht; der schwartze schatten fleucht
   In eine höl, in welche sich verkreucht,
Den schand und furcht sich zu verbergen zwinget.
   Man kan dem glantz des tages ja entgehn,
   Doch nicht dem licht, das, wo wir immer stehn,
Uns sieht und richt und höll' und grufft durchdringet.

Andreas Gryphius

Morning Sonnet

The ever-shining host its light will now secrete,
   Diana pallid stands, the rosy dawn does smile
   At graying skies, and soft the waking winds beguile
The feathered company the coming day to meet.
The tenants of this world that world with kisses greet
   And skyward stretch their heads. The sun's great beams compile
   Their glory on the sea. Oh triune might, beguile
All brilliantly that man who kneels before your feet.
   Drive off the massy night, which black my soul surrounds,
   The darkness wrought of fear, which heart and mind empounds.
Now make my spirit fresh and my reliance bold.
   Oh grant that I this day but in your service spend,
   And when the last day comes and brings my mortal end,
That you, my light, my sun, I may fore'er behold.

Andreas Gryphius

Midday

Come, friends, and let us to the banquet start,
   The sun has halfway passed the firmament,
   And, for a world 'neath heat and labor bent,
Does seek her passage and our day to part!
The flower's bloom is by the sunny dart
   Too cruelly seized, the fields, with thirsting spent,
   Wish for the dew, the reaper for his tent.
No bird cries presently his passion's smart.
   Now light does reign; the ebon shadow flies
   Into a cave, where secretly it lies,
Compelled by shame and fear here shy to dwell.
   Indeed one can escape the shine of day,
   Yet not that light which, wheresoe'er we stay,
Does see and judge us, piercing grave and hell.

Andreas Gryphius

Abend

Der schnelle tag ist hin; die nacht schwingt ihre fahn
  Und führt die sternen auf. Der menschen müde scharen
Verlassen feld und werck; wo thier und vögel waren,
  Traurt itzt die einsamkeit. Wie ist die zeit verthan!
Der port naht mehr und mehr sich zu der glieder kahn.
Gleich wie diss licht verfiel, so wird in wenig jahren
Ich, du, und was man hat, und was man sieht, hinfahren.
  Diss leben kömmt mir vor als eine renne-bahn.
Lass, höchster Gott! mich doch nicht auf dem lauffplatz gleiten!
Lass mich nicht ach, nicht pracht, nicht lust, nicht angst verleiten!
  Dein ewig-heller glantz sey vor und neben mir!
Lass, wenn der müde leib entschläfft, die seele wachen,
Und wenn der letzte tag wird mit mir abend machen,
  So reiss mich aus dem thal der finsternis zu dir!

Andreas Gryphius

Mitternacht

Schrecken und stille und dunckeles grausen, finstere kälte bedecket das land.
  Itzt schläfft, was arbeit und schmertzen ermüdet; diss sind der traurigen einsamkeit stunden.
Nunmehr ist, was durch die lüffte sich reget, nunmehr sind menschen und thiere verschwunden.
  Ob zwar die immerdar schimmernde lichter der ewig schitternden sternen entbrant,
Suchet ein fleissiger sinn noch zu wachen, der durch bemühung der künstlichen hand
Ihm die auch nach uns ankommende seelen, ihm, die anitzt sich hier finden, verbunden?
Wetzet ein blutiger mörder die klinge? wil er unschuldiger hertzen verwunden?
  Sorget ein ehren-begehrend gemüthe, wie zu erlangen ein höherer stand?

Andreas Gryphius

EVENING

The rapid day is gone; her banner swings the night,
   And leads the stars aloft. Men's wearied hosts have wended
Away from field and work; where beast and bird attended,
   Now solitude laments. How vain has been time's flight!
The vessel of our limbs draws nearer to the bight.
In but a little while, just as this light descended,
Will I, you, what we have, and what we see be ended.
   E'en as a runner's track seems life within my sight.
Great God, grant me that I in coursing do not blunder!
Nor joy trick me nor fear nor woe nor earthly wonder!
   Let Your unfailing light my comrade be and guide!
When my tired body sleeps, grant that my soul be waking,
And when the final day my eventide is making,
   Then take me from this vale of darkness to Your side!

Andreas Gryphius

MIDNIGHT

Terror and stillness and ebon-hued horror, night in its iciness covers the land.
These are the hours of sad isolation; sleeps sooths the victims of labor and pain.
Vanished are men now, and animals vanished, nor do the troublers of Heaven remain.
Though the eternally shimmering lanterns of the e'er glittering stars fiery stand.
Does an industrious mind keep its vigil, which through the efforts of talented hand,
Allies itself with the souls that succeed us, and with the folk of earth's present domain?
Do bloody murderers sharpen their daggers? Shall by them innocent spirits be slain?
Does an ambitious heart wake in its worry, how higher rank it might think to command?

Sterbliche! Sterbliche! lasset diss dichten! Morgen, ach morgen,
         ach muss man hinziehn!
Ach wir verschwinden gleich als die gespenste, die um die stund
         uns erscheinen und fliehn!
Wenn uns die finstere gruben bedecket, wird, was wir wündschen
         und suchen, zu nichte.
Doch wie der gläntzende morgen eröffnet, was weder monde noch
         fackel bescheint,
So wenn der plötzliche tag wird anbrechen, wird was geredet,
         gewürcket, gemeynt,
Sonder vermänteln eröffnet sich finden vor des erschrecklichen
         Gottes gerichte.

Andreas Gryphius

Einsamkeit

In dieser einsamkeit der mehr denn öden wüsten,
 Gestreckt auf wildes kraut, an die bemooste see,
 Beschau ich jenes thal und dieser felsen höh',
Auf welchen eulen nur und stille vögel nisten.
Hier, fern von dem pallast, weit von des pöbels lüsten,
 Betracht ich, wie der mensch in eitelkeit vergeh',
 Wie auf nicht festem grund' all unser hoffen steh',
Wie die vor abend schmähn, die vor dem tag uns grüssten.
 Die höl', der rauhe wald, der todtenkopff, der stein,
 Den auch die zeit auffrisst, die abgezehrten bein
Entwerffen in dem muth unzehliche gedancken.
 Der mauren alter graus, diss ungebaute land
 Ist schön und fruchtbar mir, der eigentlich erkannt,
Dass alles, ohn ein geist, den Gott selbst hält, muss wancken.

Andreas Gryphius

Auf die letzte nacht seines XXV. jahres.
Den 11 Octobr.
St. Gregor

Komm mitternacht und schleuss diss thränen-reiche jahr,
 Die schmertzen-volle zeit, die mich so tieff verletzet,
 Die dich, mein bruder! hat in jenes reich versetzet,
Und schwester! deine leich gestellet auf die baar.
 Die zeit, die auf mich angst und grimmer seuchen schaar

Mortal men! mortal men! let this be written! Oh, with tomorrow,
                                                  tomorrow, we die!
Oh, we must vanish e'en as the fey spirits, which at this hour sur-
                                                  prise us and fly!
All that we wish for and seek for, is nothing, when by the gloom of
                                              the grave we're concealed;
Yet as the glittering morning lays open what neither moonlight nor
                                                torchlight could find,
So, when that sudden day enters upon us, all that was born of the
                                                tongue, hand, and mind,
Will in the terrible court-room of Heaven, stripped of its cover
                                                stand bare and revealed!

Andreas Gryphius

Solitude

In this deep solitude of wastes more than forlorn,
    At rest on wild-grown grass, beside the mossy sea,
    I gaze upon that vale, these high cliffs' aery
On which the owls alone and silent birds do mourn.
Far from the rabble's joys and from the palace borne,
    I contemplate: how man must pass in vanity
    And how each solid ground our every hope must flee,
How welcomes at the dawn are changed to twilight's scorn.
    The cave, the barbarous wood, the death's head and the stone,
    Which also time devours, the flesh-depleted bone
Have sketched within my soul of thoughts an endless chain.
    The ramparts' ancient wreck, this land without the plow
    Is rich alone to him who has determined now
That all must fail whose soul does not in God remain.

Andreas Gryphius

Concerning the Last Night of His XXV. Year.
The IInd of October.
Saint Gregory

Come, midnight, and put end to this tear-sotted year,
    This time which cut me deep, in which rich pain has thriven,
Which to that distant bourn has you, my brother, given,
    This time which, sister, placed your corpse upon the bier.
    This time which after me fierce sickness' host and fear,

Und trauren und verdruss und schrecken hat verhetzet.
Wer hat noch neulich mich nicht schon vor todt geschätzet,
   Da, als ich mir nicht mehr im siechbett ähnlich war.
Wenn deine treu', o Gott! mich nicht mit trost erquicket,
Als so viel grause noth den blöden geist verstricket,
   So wär ich gantz in angst ertruncken und verschmacht.
Herr! dessen linde faust wischt die bethränten wangen,
Lass doch nach so viel sturm mich linder' zeit anfangen,
   Und heiss die herben jahr vergehn mit dieser nacht!

Andreas Gryphius
Als er aus Rom geschieden

Ade! Begriff der welt! Stadt, der nichts gleich gewesen
   Und nichts zu gleichen ist, in der man alles sieht,
   Was zwischen ost und west und nord und suden blüht,
Was die natur erdacht, was ie ein mensch gelesen.
Du, derer aschen man nur nicht vorhin mit besen
   Auf einen hauffen kehrt, in der man sich bemüht
   Zu suchen, wo dein graus (flieht, trüben jahre! flieht),
Bist nach dem fall erhöht, nach langem ach genesen.
   Ihr wunder der gemähld', ihr prächtigen palläst,
   Ob den die kunst erstarr't, du starck-bewehrte fest',
Du herrlichs Vatican, dem man nichts gleich kan bauen,
   Ihr bücher, gärten, grüfft', ihr bilder, nadeln, stein,
   Ihr, die diss und noch mehr schliesst in die sinnen ein,
Fahrt wol! Man kan euch nicht satt mit zwey augen schauen.

Andreas Gryphius
Das letzte gerichte

Auf todten! auf! die welt verkracht in letztem brande;
   Der sternen heer vergeht; der mond ist dunckel-roth,
   Die sonn' ohn allen schein. Auf! ihr, die grab und koth,
Auf! ihr die erd und see und höllen hielt zu pfande!
Ihr, die ihr lebt, komm't an! der herr, der vor in schande
   Sich richten liess, erscheint. Vor ihm laufft flamm' und noth,
Bey ihm steht majestät, nach ihm folgt blitz und tod,
   Um ihn, mehr Cherubim als sand an Pontus strande.
Wie lieblich spricht er an, die seine recht' erkohren!
Wie schrecklich donnert er auf diese, die verlohren,
   Unwiederrufflich wort: kommt freunde! feinde flieht!
Der himmel schleusst sich auf! O Gott! welch frölich scheiden!
Die erden reisst entzwey! Welch weh, welch schrecklich lied!
   Weh, weh dem, der verdamm't! wol dem, der Jesum sieht!

And horror, woe, chagrin, so tirelessly has driven.
Who has not recently thought me for dying shriven,
　　When I upon my bed unlike me did appear?
Had not Your faith, oh God, bestowed on me refreshment,
When my shy spirit fell in horrid woe's enmeshment,
　　Then I had wholly drowned and perished in dismay.
Oh Lord, Whose peaceful hand has dried each tear-damped feature,
Grant after storm a time of peace to Your beseecher,
　　And bid the bitter years with this night pass away!

Andreas Gryphius
When He Departed From Rome[46]

You town incomparable! You heart of earth, adieu!
　　With which naught's to compare, in which men all things see
　　Whose bloom 'twixt east and west and north and south may be,
What nature's e'er conceived, what men from books e'er drew.
Oh you, whose ashes once (nor only then) men threw
　　With brooms to rubbish-heap, where they industriously
　　Now search midst your remains (flee, dismal decades, flee!):
You're from long sickness healed, from falling raised anew.
　　You prideful palaces, you painter's miracle,
　　At which art falls benumbed, you fort defiance-full,
You splendid Vatican, whose like men cannot build,
　　You pictures, brooches, gems, you gardens, books, and tombs,
　　You, who all this and more send to our senses' rooms:
Farewell! Two eyes can ne'er be with your vision filled.

Andreas Gryphius
The Final Judgment

Rise, rise, you dead! The world bursts in its final flame;
　　The star's host disappears; the moon is murky red,
　　The sun stripped of its glow. Rise! leave your muddy bed,
Rise! you who earth and sea and hell had as their game!
You living, hasten hence! The Lord, who let in shame
　　Himself be judged, appears. 'Fore Him course flame and dread,
With Him is Majesty, next death and lightning tread,
　　Round Him more Cherubim than Pontus' sands can claim.
How sweet He speaks to those who once His laws did chose,
How cruel he cries at those who did His customs lose
　　Words irrevocable: "Come, friend!" "Flee, enemy!"
The Heavens open! God, how glad is this farewell!
The earth yawns wide! What woe, what hideous melody!
　　Bane, bane, to those who're damned! Blest those who Jesus see!

Andreas Gryphius

Die Hölle

Ach und weh!
    Mord! zetter! jammer! angst! creutz! marter! würme!
                                              plagen!
  Pech! folter! hencker! flamm! stanck! geister! kälte!
                                            zagen!
      Ach vergeh
        Tieff und höh'!
Meer! hügel! berge! fels! wer kan die pein ertragen!
Schluck abgrund! ach schluck ein, die nichts denn ewig
                                          klagen!
      Je und eh!
Schreckliche geister der dunkelen hölen! ihr, die ihr martert und
                                      marter erduldet!
Kann denn der ewigen ewigkeit feuer nimmermehr büssen diss,
                                    was ihr verschuldet?
O grausam angst! stets sterben, sonder sterben!
Diss ist flamme der grimmigen rache, die der erhitzete zorn an-
                                        geblasen!
Hier ist der fluch der unendlichen straffen; hier ist das immerdar
                                        wachsende rasen;
  O mensch! verdirb, um hier nicht zu verderben!

Andreas Gryphius

Andencken eines auf der See ausgestandenen gefährlichen Sturms

    O Gott! was rauhe noth! Wie schaumt die schwartze see
    Und sprützt ihr grünes saltz! Wie reisst der zorn die wellen
    Durch nebel-volle lufft! Wie heult das wüste bellen
    Der tollen stürm uns an! Die klippe kracht von weh;
    Wir fliegen durch die nacht und stürzen von der höh
    In den getrennten grund! Die offten stösse fällen
    Den halb-zuknickten mast; die schwache seiten prellen
    Auf die gespitzte klipp. O himmel! ich vergeh.
    Der dicke querbaum bricht und schlägt den umgang ein;
    Das seegel flattert fort; der schiffer steht allein
    Und kan noch boots-mann mehr, noch seil, noch ruder zwingen.
    Wir missen glas, compass und tag und stern und nacht;
    Todt war ich vor dem todt. Doch herr! du hasts gemacht,
    Dass ich dir lebend und errettet lob kan singen.

Andreas Gryphius

Hell

Rage and roar!
  Help! Murder! Woe! Distress! Cross! Torment! Worms!
                                                   Despair!
Pitch! Hangman! Terror! Rack! Flame! Ghosts! Cold! Fetid
                                                      air!
      Be no more!
        Peak and floor!
Sea! Hillocks! Mountains! Cliffs! Who can the torment bear?
Drink, oh abyss, devour those who but howl their
                                                  care
        Evermore!
Terrible spirits of ebony caverns! oh you who torture, yet suffer
                                                       the same!
What you have done, can it ne'er be atoned for by this eternal
                                              eternity's flame?
  Oh hideous fear! E'er dying, yet ne'er dead!
This is the fire of inevitable vengeance, on which the hot breath of
                                                   anger does blow!
Here are the punishments done without ending, here is the raging
                                              which ever does grow!
  Oh men! Bleed here, that there you'll not be bled!

Andreas Gryphius

Remembrance of a Perilous Storm, Endured upon the Sea [47]

Oh God, what hard despair! How does the black sea spray
Its emerald salt, and boil! How do the billows steer
For rage through fog-filled air! How wild a roar we hear
Of rabid hurricanes! The reef cries in dismay;
We fly along the night, and from the peak we sway
Into the gaping pit! The frequent blows do sheer
The half-broke mast clean off; the weakened bulwarks veer
Against the pointed reef! Oh God, my senses stray!
The heavy cross-beam breaks and through the gallery's blown;
The sail is whipped away, the skipper stands alone,
Nor rudder, mate, nor rope, can to his will compel.
We compass lack and day and star and night and glass;
Dead I was ere my death. Yet, Lord, it came to pass
Through You, that I alive and saved your praise can tell.

Andreas Gryphius

AUF EINEN IN DER HEILIGEN PFINGST-NACHT ENTSTANDENEN BRAND

Der höll'sche trauer-geist, erhitzt von rach und toben,
Riss mitten in der nacht aus seines kerckers nacht
Und wolt in asch und rauch, durch grauser flammen macht,
Umstürtzen, was sich kaum aus seinem graus erhoben.
Die funcken schwungen sich, der wiederglantz von oben
Erschröckte gass und wall, weil dach und pfost erkracht;
Doch ward sein grimm gedämpfft, weil du vor uns gewacht,
Du freuden-geist! den wir als Gottes flamme loben.
Du feuer! das den pusch entzündet, nicht verzehrt,
Hast des verderbers gluth allmächtig abgewehret,
Gleich wie der lichte blitz den schwachen brand erstecket.
Der feind trug unrein feur auf deinen lob-altar.
O quelle reiner lust! du löschest die gefahr;
Wir schlieffen, du hast uns bestürtzt in freud erwecket.

Andreas Gryphius

UBER NICOLAI COPERNICI BILD

Du dreymal weiser geist! du mehr denn grosser mann!
Dem nicht die nacht der zeit, dem nicht der blinde wahn,
Dem nicht der herbe neid die sinnen hat gebunden,
Die sinnen, die den lauff der erden neu gefunden;
Der du der alten träum und dünckel widerlegt
Und recht uns dargethan, was lebt und was sich regt:
Schau! itzund blüht dein ruhm, den als auf einem wagen
Der kreiss, auf dem wir sind, muss um die sonnen tragen!
Wann diss, was irrdisch ist, wird mit der zeit vergehn,
Soll dein lob unbewegt mit seiner sonnen stehn.

Andreas Gryphius

Concerning a Fire Which Arose in the Holy Night of Pentecost

Hell's gloomy spirit, wild with rage and vengeful blame,
Broke in the heart of night from out his dungeon's night,
And would in ash and smoke, through fire's horrific might,
Fresh into ruin turn what fresh from ruin came.
The sparks swung wide; from Heaven a counter-blaze took aim,
And frightened street and wall, since roof 'gainst beam did smite.
Yet since You guarded us, You damped his raging blight,
You joyful spirit which we praise as God's own flame.
You fire! Which caught the bush and yet it did not eat,
Omnipotently stayed the foul corrupter's heat,
Just as the shining bolt the weakling flame does choke.
Upon Your altar-place the foe put filthy fire,
But you the peril quenched, oh fount of pure desire!
Us baffled sleepers then You 'midst delight awoke.

Andreas Gryphius

Concerning Nicolaus Copernicus' Picture

You spirit three times wise! you more than mighty man!
Of whom not night of time, nor blind illusion's ban,
Nor sullen envy could the senses seize and bind,
The senses which anew the course of earth did find;
You who the ancients' dreams and arrogance disproved,
And rightly showed to us the things that lived and moved:
Behold! your fame blooms now: the orb, on which we are,
Must bear it round the sun as if upon a car.
If all that is of earth with time will pass away,
Your fame, immovable, will with its sun hold sway.

Christian Gryphius

UNGEREIMTES SONETT

Ob gleich Cloridalis auf ihre Marmorkugeln,
Die wie ein jeder sagt, der Himmel selbst gewölbt,
Und auf ihr Angesicht, das Sternen gleichet, trotzt,
Ob schon, wie sie vermeint, des Paris goldner Apfel

Vor sie allein gemacht, ob gleich viel altes Silber
In ihrem Kasten ruht, doch ists ein eitler Wurf,
Den sie nach mir getan; ich bin gleichwie ein Fels,
Und lieb ein kluges Buch mehr als der Venus Gürtel.

Die Liebe reimet sich so wenig mit Minerven,
Als eine Sterbekunst zu Karten und zu Würfeln,
Das Brautbett in die Gruft, Schalmeien zu der Orgel,

Ein Mägdchen und ein Greis, als Pferde zu den Eseln,
Als Messing zum Smaragd, als Rosen zu den Disteln,
Als diese Verse selbst, ja fast noch weniger.

Christian Gryphius

AUF EINEN ANGENEHMEN HUND

Galantel, welch ein Glück! hat seine Frau erfreuet,
  Galantel, welchem sich kein Sirius vergleicht,
  Galantel, der den Preiss der Trefligkeit erreicht,
Galantel, dem die Gunst der Sternen viel verleihet,
Galantel, den man izt mit Majoran bestreuet,
  Galantel, der den Schwantz oft an den Teppicht streicht,
  Galantel, welcher nicht dem grösten Mopsus weicht,
Galantel, dessen Zahn ein geiler Buhler scheuet.

  Wo, Phöbe, werther Hund, die Augen auf dir hat,
  So kränckt deinen Fuss kein schnelles Wagen-Rad,
Doch hütte dich vor dem, den wir den Pluto heissen:
  Du kommst, so schön du bist, den Katzen ziemlich bey,
  Drum möchte dermaleinst dich in der Raserey
Der Cerberus sein Hund statt einer Katz' erbeissen.

Christian Gryphius

Unrhymed Sonnet

Although Cloridalis boasts of her spheres of marble,
Which, as all men declare, the very gods have arched,
And of her face which bears the likeness of the stars,
Although, as she believes, Sir Paris' golden apple

For her alone is wrought, although much ancient silver
Lies stored within her cask, yet it's a cast in vain
That she has made for me; for I am like a stone
And love a clever book far more than Venus' girdle.

Love can be made to rhyme as little with Minerva
As can the art of death to cards and dice be fitted,
As bridle bed to grave and oboes to the organ,

As maiden and old man, as horses rhyme with donkeys,
As brass with emerald, as roses rhyme with thistles,
As do these lines themselves; indeed they rhyme still less.

Christian Gryphius

Concerning a Pleasant Dog

Galantel (what a joy!) has pleased his mistress fair,
   Galantel, to whose like no Sirius attains,
   Galantel, who the prize of very splendor gains,
Galantel, whom the stars have taken in their care,
Galantel, who finds strewn with marjoram his hair,
   Galantel, who with tail explores the rug's terrains,
   Galantel, who the glance of monster pug sustains,
Galantel, whose sharp tooth hot paramours can scare.

   When on you, worthy dog, you Phoebe's [48] eye-light feel,
     Your foot will take no harm from hasty wagon-wheel;
Yet guard yourself against that one we Pluto call:
     You come, so fair you are, too near unto cat's stage,
     And so you might some day before the awful rage
Of Cerberus's dog in place of feline fall.

Christian Gryphius

WIENERISCHES SIEGES-LIED (1683)

Deine Beständigkeit/ tapferes Wien/
Sol gleichwie die Cedern stäts wachsen und blühn/
    Dein Helden-Mutt
      Trozt Schwerd und Glutt/
Und tritt mit frohem Fuss auf Stambols Brutt.

Krone van Oesterreich/ herrliche Stad/
Du Perle des Isters/ du Deutscher Agat/
    Dein Lorber-Hayn
      Giebt einen Schein/
Dem kein Gestirn leicht wird gewachsen seyn.

Strahle noch ferner/ o Sonne der Welt/
Der niemals der Monden den Gegen-Stand hält.
    Was raast der Hund?
      Sein Spott ist kund/
Denn deine Käyser-Kron schimpft seinen Bund.

Lernt/ ihr Beschnittenen/ dass euch nichts schützt/
Wenn Gottes Gerechtigkeit über euch blizt.
    Denn wenn sein Schwerd
      Den Feind verzehrt/
Stürzt fast im Augenblick so Mann als Pferd.

Johann Christan Günther

AN SEINE MAGDALIS

Das Glücke muss vorwahr mich als sein Schooskind lieben,
  Und das Verhängnüss mich zu quälen müde seyn,
  Weil du, getreues Kind, mir nach so mancher Pein
Dein unverfälschtes Herz zum Eigenthum verschrieben.
Mein Schif, das Wind und Meer an manchen Fels getrieben,
  Lauft den Vergnügungsport mit vollen Seegeln ein,
  Und meine Hoffnung kann sich schon im Geiste freun,
Nachdem dein freyes Ja den Zweifel aufgerieben.
  Versiegle nun den Bund durch einen feuchten Kuss,
Bis dich des Priesters Hand mir völlig überreiche,
  Und glaube, dass mich selbst der Himmel strafen muss,
Wofern mein Wanckelmuth dein Bild in mir verstreiche.
  Drum liebe nur getrost, denn die Beständigkeit
    Würckt mir den Hochzeitrock und auch das Leichenkleid.

Christian Gryphius

A VIENNESE SONG OF TRIUMPH (1683)

Doughty Vienna, your stern constancy
Shall burgeon and bloom like the high cedar tree;
    Your stout command
    Braves fire and brand
And treads with happy foot on Stambul's band.

Pearl of the Ister [49] and Austria's crown,
You Germany's agate, you glorious town:
    Your laurel-glade
    Brilliance has made,
Whose light defies the very stars' scalade.

Sun of the nations, send further your flame,
Which crescent moons never do equal nor tame:
    Does the dog rage?
    Jeers are his wage:
For Emperor's crown defies his brigandage.

Circumcised rascals, learn that you stand bare
When Heaven's just lightning takes course through the air:
    For when its blow
    Devours the foe,
Then straight to death must steed and rider go.

Johann Christian Günther

TO HIS MAGDALIS

Good fortune must indeed have me as favorite,
    And evil fate, grown tired must from its sport refrain,
    Since you, my faithful child, arrived at end of pain,
Have made my property your heart uncounterfeit.
My ship, which wind and sea would to the rocks commit,
    Runs for the port of joy with all its sails a-strain;
    And jubilating hope can in my spirit reign,
Which your free-given yes has of its doubtings quit.
    Seal moist the covenant, now readied, with your kiss,
Until the clergy's hand has given you complete,
    And think that heaven itself will play my nemesis,
If my inconstancy your image will delete.
    Thus love me unafraid for, in me, faithfulness
    Has sewn the wedding-coat and cut the coffin-dress.

Johann Christian Günther

ALS SIE AN SEINER TREU ZWEIFELTE

Mein Kind, was zweifelstu an meiner Redligkeit,
  Die ihres gleichen doch in deiner Brust verspüret?
Wo meiner Adern Blut nur einen Tropfen führet,
  Der sich nicht tausendmahl vor dich zu sterben freut,
  So wüntsch ich ihm den Fluch, den Ebals Felsen dräut,
Und Kain's Fuss erfährt; der Stern, so mich regieret,
Und dessen Trieb in mir die reine Glut gebiehret,
  Folgt nicht wie ein Planet dem Wechsel dieser Zeit.
Mein Sinnbild ist ein Ring, der Denckspruch: Sonder Ende.
  Denn wer nicht ewig liebt, der liebet nimmermehr;
  Mein Engel, giebstu nun dem Argwohn kein Gehör,
So lege mir dein Herz in die getreuen Hände.
  Ich sichre, diesen Schaz wird deinem Saladin
  Kein Räuber, kein Verlust, auch nicht der Tod entziehn.

Johann Christian Günther

ABSCHIEDSARIA

Schweig du doch nur, du Hälfte meiner Brust;
  Denn was du weinst, ist Blut aus meinem Herzen;
Ich taumle so und hab' an nichts mehr Lust
  Als an der Angst und den getreuen Schmerzen,
Womit der Stern, der unsre Liebe trennt,
              Die Augen brennt.

Die Zärtligkeit der innerlichen Qual
  Erlaubt mir kaum, ein ganzes Wort zu machen.
Was dem geschieht, um welchen Keil und Strahl
  Bei heisser Luft in weitem Felde krachen,
Geschieht auch mir durch dieses Donnerwort:
              Nun muss ich fort.

Ach harter Schluss, der unsre Musen zwingt,
  Des Fleisses Ruhm in fremder Luft zu gründen,
Und der auch mich mit Furcht und Angst umringt!
  Welch Pflaster kan den tiefen Riss verbinden,
Den tiefen Riss, der mich und dich zuletzt
              In Kummer setzt?

Johann Christian Günther

As She Doubted His Faithfulness

My child, why must you find my honesty untrue,
  Which yet has thought to find within your breast its twin;
If in my body's blood a single drop has been
  Which not a thousand times would gladly die for you,
  On that drop I shall place the curse that Cain's foot knew
And Ebal [70] cast; the star whose way I wander in,
From which the virgin flame in me takes origin,
  Does not in planet's wise the change of time pursue.
My symbol is a ring, its motto: "without end."
  Who knows not endless love can know no love at all;
  My angel, be you deaf to base suspicion's call,
Then to my faithful hands your heart you may commend.
  For from your Saladin this sweet reward to tear
  No robber and no loss, nor even death would dare.

Johann Christian Günther

Departure-Aria

Oh, be but still, you half-part of my breast!
  For what you weep is blood tapped from my heart.
I stumble and for nothing else have zest
  Than for my fear and for that faithful smart
Wherewith the star, which our love's end conspires,
              My eye-light fires.

The tenderness of torment's inner ways
  Scarce gives me leave a single word to yield;
What him befalls, who's stunned by bolt and blaze
  In sultry weather on the open field,
Befalls me through this thunder-word's cruel blow:
              Now I must go.

Hard end, by which our Muses' quire is bound
  To build our labor's fame in foreign air,
And which does me with fear and woe surround:
  What bandage can the gaping wound repair,
The gaping wound, which you and me at last
              In woe makes fast.

Der Abschiedskuss verschliest mein Paradies,
　　Aus welchem mich Zeit und Verhängnüss treiben;
So viel bisher dein Antliz Sonnen wies,
　　So mancher Blitz jezt wird mein Schröcken bleiben.
Der Zweifel wacht und spricht von deiner Treu:
　　　　　　　Sie ist vorbey.

Verzeih mir doch den Argwohn gegen dich,
　　Wer brünstig liebt, dem macht die Furcht stets bange.
Der Menschen Herz verändert wunderlich,
　　Wer weis, wie bald mein Geist die Post empfange,
Dass die, so mich in Gegenwart geküst,
　　　　　　　Entfernt vergisst!

Gedenck einmal, wie schön wir vor gelebt,
　　Und wie geheim wir unsre Lust genossen.
Da hat kein Neid der Reizung widerstrebt,
　　Womit du mich an Hals und Brust geschlossen,
Da sah uns auch bey selbst erwüntschter Ruh
　　　　　　　Kein Wächter zu.

Genung! Ich muss; die Marterglocke schlägt!
　　Hier liegt mein Herz, da nimm es aus dem Munde
Und heb es auf, die Früchte, so es trägt,
　　Sind Ruh und Trost bei mancher bösen Stunde,
Und lis, so oft dein Gram die Leute flieht,
　　　　　　　Mein Abschiedslied.

Wohin ich geh, begleitet mich dein Bild,
　　Kein fremder Zug wird mir den Schaz entreissen;
Es macht mich treu und ist ein Hofnungsschild,
　　Wenn Neid und Noth Verfolgungssteine schmeissen,
Bis dass die Hand, die uns hier Dörner flicht,
　　　　　　　Die Myrthen bricht.

Erinnre dich zum öftern meiner Huld
　　Und nähre sie mit süssem Angedencken;
Du wirst betrübt, diess ist des Abschieds Schuld,
　　So muss ich dich zum ersten Mahle kräncken,
Und fordert mich der erste Gang von hier,
　　　　　　　So sterb ich dir.

Ich sterbe dir, und soll ein fremder Sand
　　Den oft durch dich ergözten Leib bedecken,
So gönne mir das lezte Liebespfand
　　Und las ein Kreuz mit dieser Grabschrift stecken:
Wo ist ein Mensch der treulich lieben kann?
　　　　　　　Hier liegt der Mann.

The parting kiss my Paradise shuts tight,
   From which both time and fate have driven me,
So many suns your face till now did light,
   So many a bolt will now my terror be.
Doubt grows apace, and of your faith takes store:
                Faith is no more.

And yet forgive the way my surmise goes.
   Who loves with fire, for fear is easy prey.
The heart of man strange transformation knows.
   Who'll tell when my soul's messenger will say:
That she, who me with present kisses pets,
                Far off forgets.

Reflect again, how fair we once did live,
   And how with secret joy we once were blest.
No envy then that charm made fugitive
   With which you gathered me to throat and breast.
Nor did our self-desired repose fall prize
                To sentry's eyes.

Enough! I go, the death-bell breaks the air.
   Here lies my heart, it from my mouth remove
And keep it safe: the fruits, which it will bear,
   In evil hours will rest and comfort prove;
And read, whene'er your grief would flee the throng,
                My farewell-song.

Where'er I go, your image follows too,
   A treasure proof 'gainst every foreign blast;
It is a shield of hope, and makes me true,
   When need and envy nagging cobbles cast,
Until the hand, which here our thorn-wreath makes,
                The myrtle breaks.

Think often how my love did you exalt,
   And feed it with sweet memory's dessert;
Now you are saddened: this is parting's fault,
   That I must for the first time do you hurt.
When from this place my infant steps I try,
                For you I die.

I die for you, and if some foreign sand
   That body hides which you oft pleasure gave,
Then put our love's last pledge within my hand,
   And let a cross, thus written, grace my grave:
Where is a man, who true love does revere?
                That man lies here.

Johann Christian Günther

Trostaria

Endlich bleibt nicht ewig aus,
Endlich wird der Trost erscheinen;
　Endlich grünt der Hofnungsstrauss,
Endlich hört man auf zu weinen,
　Endlich bricht der Thränenkrug,
　Endlich spricht der Tod: Genug!

Endlich wird aus Wasser Wein,
Endlich kommt die rechte Stunde,
　Endlich fällt der Kercker ein,
Endlich heilt die tiefe Wunde.
　Endlich macht die Sclaverey
　Den gefangnen Joseph frey.

Endlich, endlich kan der Neid,
Endlich auch Herodes sterben;
　Endlich Davids Hirtenkleid
Seinen Saum in Purpur färben.
　Endlich macht die Zeit den Saul
　Zur Verfolgung schwach und faul.

Endlich nimmt der Lebenslauf
Unsers Elends auch ein Ende;
　Endlich steht ein Heiland auf,
Der das Joch der Knechtschaft wende;
　Endlich machen vierzig Jahr
　Die Verheissung zeitig wahr.

Endlich blüht die Aloe,
Endlich trägt der Palmbaum Früchte;
　Endlich schwindet Furcht und Weh,
Endlich wird der Schmerz zu nichte;
　Endlich sieht man Freudenthal;
　Endlich, Endlich kommt einmahl.

Johann Christian Günther

Consolation-Aria

Finally stays no more away,
Finally balm its pledge will keep,
　Finally burgeons hope's bouquet,
Finally men will cease to weep,
　Finally will the tear-jug break,
　Finally death its share forsake.

Finally water turns to wine,
Finally will the right hour peal,
　Finally falls the vault's confine,
Finally gaping wounds will heal,
　Finally will that slavery
　Turn imprisoned Joseph free.

Finally can e'en jealousness,
Finally can e'en Herod end,
　Finally David's shepherd-dress
Can its hem to purple lend.
　Finally Saul, by time made weak,
　Will no more his quarry seek.

Finally will the life-long sum
Of our woes an ending take,
　Finally will that Savior come
Who our serfdom's yoke can break,
　Finally forty years' accrue
　Timely makes the promise true.

Finally will the aloe bloom,
Finally will the palm bear fruit,
　Finally fear must pass, and gloom,
Finally pain is destitute,
　Finally joy's demesne we see,
　Finally will some morrow be.

C. H.
An eine liebens-würdige Schlesierin

Ich will den Rübenzahl aus Schlesien verjagen;
Ich will dir seinen schatz zum leibgedinge weihn:
Ich will sein zauber-schloss bis auf den grund zerstreun:
Ich will den zoten-berg von seiner stelle tragen:
Ich will mich gar bis auf den riesen-knoppe wagen:
Ich will ins gantze land von deiner schönheit schreyn:
Ich will, wo du's verlangst, ein glaubens-eifrer seyn,
Und da des Schwenckfelds schwarm bis auf das haupt erschlagen,
Ich will den Oder-Strohm in andre gänge bringen:
Ich will zu deiner lust sein Ufer schöner baun:
Ich will den Oderwald der erde gleiche haun:
Ich will viel Arien zu deinem lobe singen:
Wenn ich nur kan dadurch dir den gefallen thun,
Dass du mich lässt davor auf deinem schose ruhn.

Johann Christian Hallmann
Der Unüberwindliche Leopoldus

Ein Thron/ wo Rath und That wie Diamanten gläntzen/
   Und Gottes Auge selbst als Wächter ihn beschützt/
Den muss die gantze Welt mit Palm und Lorbern kräntzen/
   Ob gleich Verrätherey und Ehrsucht auff ihn blitzt.
O Tapfrer Leopold! Du Wunder aller Wunder/
   Mein Geist erstarret fast! Mein Auge wird entzückt/
Wann ich besehen wil den grossen Liebes-Zunder/
   Womit der Fürsten Fürst dein Fürstlich Hertz erquickt.
Durch wolbedachten Rath und Helden gleiche Thaten
   Hastu des Zepters Gold/ der Länder Heil vermehrt!
Der Weichsel und dem Leu ward durch dich wol gerathen;
   Man weiss/ wie Bossphors Mond stets deine Sonnen ehrt.
Iberus Perle kan die Engel dir verbinden/
   Weil deine Majestät der Juden List verjagt;
Dich kan kein schlaues Gifft/ kein Meineid überwinden:
   Die Tugend is dein Schild/ das Glücke deine Magd.
Der fällt in's Unglücks Nacht/ der deinen Glantz wil dämpfen/
   Und wer dich tastest an/ trägt Beil und Strick davon.
Wie sol O Leopold, dich doch ein Feind bekämpfen/
   Weil selbst der Himmel kämpft vor deine Kron' und Thron?
Du kanst den Erdkreiss mehr als Alexander zwingen/
   Denn Zorn und Gnade stehn mit dir in einem Bund:
Ja weil die Engel selbst dir ein Triumphslied singen/
   So muss ich Sterblicher verschliessen meinen Mund!

C.H.
To a Lovable Silesian Girl

I will old Rübezahl from his Silesia scare,[51]
I will decree his gold to be your jointure's wage,
I will his magic-keep to its foundations raze,
I will the Zobtenberg [53] out of its socket tear.
I will my life upon the Riesenkoppe [52] dare,
I will for all the land proclaim your beauty's praise,
I will, if you desire, assume some pious craze,
And then to Schwenckfeld's band [54] deal out a deadly share.
I will the Oder's stream in other channels bring,
I will for your delight make lovelier its shore,
I will the Oder-wood to earth's embrace restore,
I will a throng of airs in your laudation sing:
If I can through these things so far your pleasure win
That for them you will let me to your heart come in.

Johann Christian Hallmann
Leopold the Invincible [55]

A throne where creed and deed like diamond-lights shine down,
   Which Heaven's very eye as sentinel defends:
Him must the world entire with palm and laurel crown,
   Though treason, in its lust for might, on him descends.
Oh marvel, marvel-born! Oh valiant Leopold!
   My spirit's next to death! My eyes enraptured start!
When I but loving's fuse and touchwood will behold,
   With which the Princes' Prince restores your princely heart.
Through well-considered words and deeds that heroes fit
   You have the scepter's gold, the nation's weal increased!
The Lion, the Vistula,[56] learned from your wisdom wit;
   Your sun has honor from the crescent of the East.[57]
The Spanish pearl can you with angel-hosts unite,
   Since by your majesty you made the sly Jew yield;[58]
All proof 'gainst perjury and cunning poison's blight,
   Your serving-maid is luck, and virtue is your shield.
Whoever dims your praise, misfortune's night must know,
   Whoever you assails, calls axe and noose his own.
How then, oh Leopold, might you be faced by foe,
   Since even Heaven fights to save your crown and throne?
Twice Alexander, you constrain this planet's ring,
   For grace and anger are with you of single will:
Yes, since the angel-bands to you a paeon sing,
   So must I, mortal man, bid then my mouth be still.

Martin Hanke

VON DER LETZTEN ZEIT

Was ist ein Tag, ein Jahr, die Zeit von hundert Jahren,
In welcher aus der Welt viel tausend Seelen fahren?
Ein Spiel, das vielen kurz und vielen lang muss sein –
O Mensch, nimm alle Zeit genau in Augenschein!

Ein Tag kommt, dessen Macht die Jahre wird verschlingen,
Ein Jahr kommt, dessen Lauf nicht mehr wird Tage bringen.
O wunderbares Jahr! O wunderbarer Tag!
In welchem aufersteht, was in den Gräbern lag.

Wer soll nicht alle Tag an dieses Jahr gedenken,
Das aller Zeiten Stand wird in zwei Teil verschränken,
Wo stete Trauernacht, wo stetes Freudenlicht,
Des Himmels Wollust strahlt, der Hölle Marter sticht.

Ihr freches Lastervolk, ach lasset alle Tage
Zu beiden Ohren ein des letzten Tages Klage:
Nun muss die ganze Welt vor ihrem Richter stehn,
Der keiner Sünde Zeit lässt ungestraft hingehn.

Wollt ihr, o Sterblichen! nicht mit der Zeit verderben,
So legt die Zeit wohl an im Leben und im Sterben;
Der ist klug, der wird fromm, wer stets denkt an die Zeit,
Wenn ihn ein Augenblick setzt in die Ewigkeit.

Georg Philipp Harsdörffer

DIE LILJENNYMPHE

Gott hat mein Kleid gesticket ohn mein Sorgen,
Mit Silber mich beglücket spat und morgen:
Die Lilje, szeptergleich gestaltet,
Hoch über alle Blumen waltet, mit Pracht beschmücket.

Der weise König Salomon den Liljen weicht,
Sein hoher Thron und Königskron sich mir nicht gleicht:
Weil ihn der Weiber Lust verführet,
Ist er nicht wie ich bin gezieret, weiss, rein und schön.

Der in erhabnen Würden lebt und ist befleckt,
In dessen Herz und Munde schwebt, was ihn ersteckt.
Die aber reine Geister haben,
In denen sind des Höchsten Gaben bald aufgeweckt.

Martin Hanke

Concerning the Final Time

What is a day, a year, the time of hundred years,
In which a myriad of spirits disappears?
A game, where some must long, some brief must seek the prize –
Oh man, you must all time most closely scrutinize!

A day will come, whose might will make the years its feed,
A year will come, whose course no further days will breed.
Oh supernatural year! Oh supernatural day!
When all will rise who long beneath the gravestones lay.

Who shall not every day that year then contemplate
Which will in double part divide all time's estate.
Where constant funeral-dark, where constant joyful light
Will shine with Heaven's bliss and with Hell's torment smite.

Oh let each day, you folk all vile and impudent,
At both your eardrums beat the final day's lament:
The whole world must before its judge stand presently.
Who lets no time of sin pass with impunity.

Would you, oh mortal men, not be with time undone,
See that your time does well in life and dying run.
He's wise, who pious turns, nor does that time forget,
When into timelessness he's by an instant set.

Georg Philipp Harsdörffer

The Lily-Nymph

God did my dress without my care adorn,
With silver blest me late and at the morn:
The lily, cast in scepters' form,
High over all the blossoms reigns, with great glory crowned.

The wise king Solomon must from the lilies flee.
Nor his high throne nor kingly crown can equal me.
Since women's lust did him seduce,
He has no splendor like to mine, lovely, fair, and white.

Who dwells in noble office and yet bears a stain,
His throttling cord within his heart and mouth is lain.
But those who spirits pure possess,
In them there soon does wake from sleep the Almighty's gain.

Georg Philipp Harsdörffer

AUS DEN GESPRÄCHSPIELEN:

Schau wie wundersam die Natur sich weiset!
   Wie sie Wurtzel aus manchem Stamm forttreibet/
   welcher ungepflegt sonsten wild verbleibet/
und das Bauervolk in den Wäldern speiset:
Wann die Gartenkunst Aeste ritzt und reiset/
   und dem Erdenkorb' artig einverleibet/
   deren Fäserlein zarter Saft bekleibet/
wird geschlachtere Frucht darvon gepreiset.
   Oft des Fleisses Spuhr auch zu impfen pfleget/
   wann ein starken Ast man herunter säget/
dass die Reiserlein bessre Nahrung ziehen.
   So die Teutsche Sprach' unbemerkt verwildert/
   die gesamter Fleiss reiflich-zart gemildert/
wann Fruchtbringende sich hierbey bemühen.

Georg Philipp Harsdörffer

ALCAISCHE ODE
BESCHREIBEND DIE KÜNSTLICHEN
UND UNKÜNSTLICHEN MUSIC-INSTRUMENTEN
IN VORGESETZTEM KUPFERTITEL

Ein jeder steckt ihm selbest erwehltes Ziel:
Der liebet etwan künstliche Musicspiel'/
   erlustigt sich mit Orglen und Trompeten/
   schlurffenden Zinken und grossen Flöten.

Posaunen/ Geigen/ Lauten und anders mehr/
beliebet vielen neben der Music-Lehr.
   Ein minderer Geist liebt auszuschweiffen/
   Bauren und Burgeren aufzupfeiffen.

Die Citter/ Leyer/ das schallende Jäger Hifft
im Feld und in den Dörfferen Freude stifft/
   Schalmayen/ Triangel/ Maultrommel
   liebet der Pövel im Zechgemommel.

Ein jeder lobt das Seine so viel er wil;
Unkunst' und Künste/ Saiten und Sinne-Spiel':
   ich denk' ihr keinen zu befeden/
   höret mich/ höret von Spielen reden!

Georg Philipp Harsdörffer

FROM THE CONVERSATION-GAMES

See how wondrously nature's ways are leading!
   How from many a trunk she is conceiving
   Roots which otherwise, wild and careless weaving,
Would the peasant folk of the woods give feeding.
When (by gardener's art) branches slit and bleeding
   Are submitted to earth-baskets' nice receiving,
   Branches to whose threads tender juice is cleaving:
Finer fruits will come honored from this seeding.
   Oft has industry such a graft created,
     When the saws to earth mighty boughs have fated,
That the tiny twigs draw their ration double.
     Thus the German tongue, in neglect grown wilder,
     All our industry tender-ripe makes milder,
If fruit-bringing men [59] give themselves the trouble.

Georg Philipp Harsdörffer

ALCAIC ODE
DESCRIBING THE ARTIFICAL
AND NATURAL MUSICAL-INSTRUMENTS
IN THE ABOVE ENGRAVING

All men self-chosen targets may well essay;
One loves perchance some fanciful music's play,
   Takes joy in organs, trumpets' loud disputes,
   Shuffling cornetts,[60] and in monster flutes.

Trombones and fiddles, lutes and still more of same
Are dear to many, joined to wise music's game.
   A less noble soul loves revelry,
   Piping for burgess and peasantry.

Of lyre, of cither, of echoing huntsman's horn
Is joy for field and villagers ever born:
   Jew's harp and triangle and shawm
   All are the roistering mob's imaum.

Each man can praise his own, all the ways he may,
Un-art and arts and strings and the senses' play,
   I think with none of them to feud:
   Hear me then to the art's games allude!

August Adolf von Haugwitz

An seine Bücher

Diss ist der traute Sitz den ich mir auserwehlt/
Was acht ich Sorgen-Last/ was acht ich Unglücks-Wetter/
Hier diese stumme Zunfft ist meiner Seelen Retter/
   Hier such und find ich das/ was andern Leuten fehlt/
   Hier stirbt und schwindet das/ was meinen Geist sonst qvält/
Hier hab ich trotz der Welt und ihrer blinden Spötter
Nechst Gott dem grösten/ selbst der Sinnen wahre Götter
   Den'n sich mein Hertz und Geist auff ewig anvermählt.
Hier hab ich meinen Sitz/ hier hab ich meine Reise/
Hier hab ich meinen Tranck/ hier hab ich meine Speise/
   Hier hab ich meinen Schatz und theuren Edelstein/
Hier hab ich meinen Ruhm/ mein Reichthum und mein Prangen
Hier hab ich/ was ich wil/ und was ich kan verlangen/
   Ach! dass doch nicht auch hier mein letztes Grab soll seyn.

August Adolf von Haugwitz

An seiner Freundin übelgetroffenes Bildnüss

Und darff der Pinsel sich wohl dieses unterfangen!
   Wer soll es? soll es Sie? Sie meine Schöne seyn?
   Sie solls/ und ists doch nicht/ die Farbe trifft nicht ein/
Die Augen sind zu starr/ es können ihre Wangen
Mit noch weit schön'rer Zier als dieses Mahlwerck prangen/
   Die Lippen sind zu blass/ der Stirne heller Schein
Sieht allzu dunckel aus/ nur bloss der Demant-Stein/
Der hier diss kleine Blat/ worauff sie steht/ umbfangen/
   Ists so alleine Ihr und zwar dem Hertzen gleicht/
   Das weder Ihm an Glantz noch an der Härte weicht/
Das andre ist gantz falsch. Was wilst du mich denn äffen
   Du frecher Pinsel du mit deiner falschen Kunst!
   Du tuschst/ entwurffst /und mahlst /und müh'st dich nur umbsonst/
Der Sie in Hertzen trägt/ der nur der kan Sie treffen.

August Adolf von Haugwitz

To His Books

This is my cozy seat where I have chosen stead.
Why should I worry-load or mishap-weather mind;
The saviors of my soul are of this voiceless kind.
  Here I may seek and take what other men has fled.
  Here dies and disappears what filled my soul with dread.
Here I, despite the world's dull-sighted mockers, find
The true gods of the wit, who stand but God behind,
  And to whom for all time my heart and mind are wed.
Here I my journey have and here I have my seat;
Here I too have my drink, and here I have my meat;
  Here I my treasures have and precious jewelry;
Here I have all my wealth, my splendor, and my fame;
Here I have what I will, and what I still can claim.
  Oh, would that in this place my final grave might be!

August Adolf von Haugwitz

To the Ill-struck Portrait of His Mistress

And may the brush indeed such forgery propound?
  Who is it? Is it she? Is here my beauty shone?
  It is and yet is not: here fails the color's tone,
The eyes are not alive; her cheeks can be renowned
With better ornament than in mere paint is found.
  The lips are done too pale; the forehead's brilliant zone
  Has far too dark a look; and but the diamond stone,
(Which shall this little sheet, on which she stands, surround),
  Resembles her and is indeed most like her heart,
  Which in bright renitence can play the diamond's part.
The rest is wholly false. Why will you me deceive,
  You brush in bluster dipped and all your art's chicane?
  You dabble, sketch, and paint, and tire yourself in vain:
Who bears Her in his heart alone can Her achieve.

Johann Heermann

IN KRIEGES- UND VERFOLGUNGSGEFAHR

Gross ist, o grosser Gott, die Not, so uns betroffen:
Das Unrecht haben wir wie Wasser eingesoffen;
Doch das ist unser Trost: Du bist voll Gütigkeit,
Du nimmst die Strafe hin, wann uns die Sünd ist leid.

Wir liegen hier für dir, betrauren unsre Sünden:
Ach, lass uns Gnade doch vor deinen Augen finden!
Treib ab die Kriegsgefahr durch deine starke Hand,
Gib uns den lieben Fried, schütz unser Vaterland.

Erhalte deine Kirch in diesen letzten Zeiten,
Da Teufel, Höll und Welt sie plagt auf allen Seiten.
Dein ist die Sach, o Gott, drum wach und mach dich auf,
Schlag eine Wagenburg um deinen kleinen Hauf,

Der sich auf dich verlässt, der sich dir ganz ergibet,
Der dich im Herzen trägt, der dich von Herzen liebet,
Der dein Wort höher acht' denn alles Gut und Geld
Und was die Welt sonst mehr für ihre Freude hält.

Lass sehen jedermann, lass jedermann erfahren,
Du eben seist der Gott, der sein Volk kann bewahren,
Der Hilfe senden kann, wann niemand Hilfe weiss:
Dafür wird alles Volk dir singen Lob und Preis.

Theobald Höck

VON DER WELT HOFFART UND BOSSHEIT

   Lachen möcht eins doch ders recht wolt bedencken
Wür billicher stets wainen und sich krencken/
Und zu Todt sich lencken/
Wenn er es recht kund sehen/
Wie alle ding so ungleich jetzund stehen.

Johann Heermann

In Peril of War and Persecution

Great is the woe, great God, which now on us does break:
And we our thirst with wrong, as though 'twere water, slake.
Yet this our balsam is: You are benevolent;
When we our sin abjure, You ban our punishment.

Here at Your feet we lie, and do our sin despise:
Oh, let us win the gift of grace within Your eyes!
Drive off the risk of war through your puissant hand,
Give us our cherished peace, defend our fatherland.

Preserve your faithful church within this final hour,
Though devil, hell, and world it from all sides devour.
Yours is the cause, oh God; thus wake and take Your blade:
Put round Your tiny band a wagoned barricade,

The band which calls You strength and all to You is true,
Which loves You from its heart, and there does carry You,
Which higher holds Your word than gold and property,
And whate'er else the world may think felicity.

Let everyone detect, let everyone be told:
You are that very God, Who safe His folk can hold,
Who succor sends when none on earth can succor bring:
Thus all the peoples will to You their paeons sing.

Theobald Höck

Of the World's Pridefulness and Spite

Laugh as man will: if he would think aright
'Twere better, would he weep and mourn his plight,
And death to him invite,
Could he but clear descry
How all things presently unequal lie.

Nichts mehrers ist auff Erden undern Leuthen/
Dann nur ungleichheit/ list/ untrew und neiden/
Und unrecht leyden/
Der Stärcker wil den Schwachen
Vertilgen/ damit er sich nur gross kan machen.

O Menschliches leben wie mancher gfar so tücke/
Bist underworffen schier all Augenblicke/
Das untrew Glücke/
Sich täglich stets verkehret/
Wie kurtz dein Frewd und Lieb auff Erden wehret.

O Welt wie ist dein pracht Reichthumb und gwalde
So gar zergengklich und gleich Todes gestalde/
So manigfalde/
Gleich wie der Wind und Pfeilen/
Also das Leben/ die Lieb und zeit hin eylen.

O Glück wie wanderstu herumb auff Erden/
Heut König morgen kanst ein Bettler werden/
Bleibest hewr wie fernden/
Nichts ist dein aigen darneben/
Was hilffts dich dann/ du kanst nit ewig leben.

Warumb bistu so stoltz im Geist ersoffen/
Und hast nit gnug biss dich der Todt hat troffen/
Ohn alles verhoffen/
Wilt künfftiges erben und haben/
Und kanst das gegenwertig doch nit tragen.

Die gröste witz das beste recht die beide/
In die gröste Thorheit und Unbilligkeite/
Ohn Rew und Laide/
Zu Hoff man jetzt verkehret/
Wer schwetzen kan der wird auffs höchst geehret.

O Welt/ O Zeit/ O Glück/ O Lieb/ O Todte/
Wie bringt dein Pfeil uns offt in angst und nothe/
Fragen nach keim spotte/
Was wollen wir denn drauss machen/
Wir müssen sterben wir wainen oder lachen.

'Midst men on earth no other thing has use
Than inequality, trick, envy, ruse,
And hard abuse.
The stronger will the weak
Wipe out, so that he alone can greatness seek.

Oh human career, what device and jeopardy
Keep you each moment slave to their decree;
Luck faithlessly
Does daily shift its worth.
How brief do last your joy and love on earth.

Oh world, how is your glory, might and gold
So transitory, and like death in its mold:
As manifold
As arrows and the breeze:
Thus does our time and our life and loving cease.

Oh fortune, how you through this planet stray!
Tomorrow's beggar is a king today.
Though this year you stay,
Nothing is yours for your keep:
What gain is in it? You at last must sleep.

Now why are you so proud in spirit drowned,
And are not full, till in a sudden bound
By death you're found?
You someday intend to be heir,
And yet cannot this present ending bear.

The finest right and keen wit's best resource
Into the greatest wrong and dullest course
(Without remorse)
At court men now have turned:
There chatterers have highest honor earned.

Oh world, oh time, oh luck, oh love, oh end:
How oft your bolt does us to terror send:
We no more pretend.
Whatever we think to try,
We still, however we laugh or weep, must die.

Christian Hofmann von Hofmannswaldau

Er liebt vergebens

Ich finde keinen Rat, die Liebe wächst alleine
Und wenig neben mir, es sei denn meine Not,
Die Brunst bestricket mich, warum nicht auch der Tod?
Frisst jene Mark und Fleisch, so fresse der die Beine.
Was aber hilft mein Wunsch, was hilfts mich, dass ich weine?
Der Tod hört nicht viel mehr, als sonst der Liebesgott,
Wo sollte meine Qual und meines Lebens Spott
Nun besser sein bedeckt als unter einem Steine?
Und bin ich endlich tot, vergraben und verscharrt,
So schwatzt die Grabschrift noch, dass dieser Mensch genarrt,
Und sagt: Hier liegt ein Narr und lässt nicht wenig Erben.
Ach! dass den schwarzen Leib das erste Wasserbad,
So mir die Mutter gab, nicht bald ersäufet hat,
So dürft ich jetzt allhier nicht wie ein Narr verderben.

Christian Hofmann von Hofmannswaldau

Vergänglichkeit der Schönheit

Es wird der bleiche Tod mit seiner kalten Hand
Dir endlich mit der Zeit um deine Brüste streichen,
Der liebliche Corall der Lippen wird verbleichen;
Der Schultern warmer Schnee wird werden kalter Sand,

Der Augen süsser Blitz, die Kräfte deiner Hand,
Für welchen solches fällt, die werden zeitlich weichen.
Das Haar, das itzund kann des Goldes Glanz erreichen,
Tilgt endlich Tag und Jahr als ein gemeines Band.

Der wohlgesetzte Fuss, die lieblichen Gebärden,
Die werden teils zu Staub, teils nichts und nichtig werden,
Denn opfert keiner mehr der Gottheit deiner Pracht.

Diss und noch mehr als diss muss endlich untergehen.
Dein Herze kann allein zu aller Zeit bestehen,
Dieweil es die Natur aus Diamant gemacht.

Christian Hofmann von Hofmannswaldau

He Loves In Vain

Love grows alone (though I my brain for council harrow),
And little's at my side unless it be despair.
If lust entangles me, why not a deathly snare?
Let death have then my bones, if lust eats flesh and marrow.
But death heeds me no more than does the god with arrow:
What profit that I weep? What profit my desire?
Where should my parody of life, my pain require
A better hiding place then 'neath the stony barrow.
And when I'm finally dead and buried and decayed,
My epitaph will boast that I a fool was made,
And say: "Here lies a fool, who many leaves successor."
Oh! if that newborn bath which me my mother gave
Had drowned my blackened self straightway into the grave,
I were not presently but foolish ruin's possessor.

Christian Hofmann von Hofmannswaldau

Beauty's Transitoriness

Then pallid death at last will with his icy hand,
Where time hides in the palm, your lovely breasts contain;
The coral of your lips will from its beauty wane,
Your shoulder's warmth of snow will change to icy sand.

Sweet lightning of your eyes, the powers of your hand,
That do such conquests make, will but brief hours remain.
Your locks, which presently the glance of gold attain,
The day and year at last will ruin in common band.

Your well-placed foot will then, your movements in their grace,
To naught and nothing part, and part to dust give place.
Before your splendor's god no offering more is laid.

This and still more than this at last must pass away.
Your heart alone has strength its constant self to stay,
Since nature this same heart of diamond has made.

Christian Hofmann von Hofmannswaldau

Beschreibung vollkommener Schönheit

    Ein haar, so kühnlich trotz der Berenice spricht,
Ein mund, der rosen führt und perlen in sich heget,
Ein zünglein, so ein gifft vor tausend hertzen träget,
    Zwo brüste, wo rubin durch alabaster bricht.
    Ein hals, der schwanen-schnee weit weit zurücke sticht.
Zwey wangen, wo die pracht der Flora sich beweget,
Ein blick, der blitze führt und männer niederleget,
    Zwey armen, derer krafft offt leuen hingericht,
Ein hertz, aus welchem nichts als mein verderben quillet,
    Ein wort, so himmlisch ist, und mich verdammen kan,
    Zwey hände, derer grimm mich in den bann gethan,
Und durch ein süsses gifft die seele selbst umhüllet,
    Ein zierrath, wie es scheint, im paradiess gemacht,
    Hat mich um meinen witz und meine freyheit bracht.

Christian Hofmann von Hofmannswaldau

Er ist gehorsam

Soll ich in Lybien die löwen-läger stören?
    Soll ich in Aetnae schlund entzünden meine hand?
    Soll ich dir nackt und bloss ins neuen Zembels strand?
Soll ich der schwartzen see verdorrte leichen mehren?
Soll ich das Lutherthum in den mosqueen lehren?
    Soll ich, wenn Eurus tobt, durch der Egypter sand?
    Soll ich zu deiner lust erfinden neues land?
Soll ich auf Peters stul Calvin und Bezen ehren?
    Soll ich bey Zanziba die jungen drachen fangen?
    Soll ich das gelbe gifft verschlingen von den schlangen?
Dein wille ist mein zweck, ich bin gehorsams voll,
    Es höret, geht und folgt dir ohre, fuss und willen,
    Was mir dein mund befiehlt, mit freuden zu erfüllen,
Nur muthe mir nicht zu, dass ich dich hassen soll.

Christian Hofmann von Hofmannswaldau

DESCRIPTION OF PERFECT BEAUTY

A hair which boldly speaks in Bernice's [61] despite,
A mouth which starts with rose and pearls within it hides,
A tonguelet where a bane for thousand hearts resides,
   Two breasts where ruby breaks through alabaster's white,
   A throat which snow of swans has put to distant flight,
Two cheeks within whose veins the pomp of Flora glides,
A glance which conquers men and lightning's weapon guides,
   Two arms whose power has oft wild lions slain in fight,
A heart from which alone my ruination flows,
   A word which both can damn and yet from Heaven stem,
   Two hands, whose awful rage can me to death condemn
And through sweet bane a cloak about the spirit throws:
   An ornament, it seems, born out of Paradise,
   Has made me both my sense and freedom sacrifice.

Christian Hofmann von Hofmannswaldau

HE IS OBEDIENT

Shall I in Lybia the lions' fortress tread?
   Shall I in Etna's snow the blaze put to my hand?
   Shall naked I and bare attempt New Zemlya's strand?
Shall I then multiply the Black Sea's withered dead?
Shall I, within the mosques the faith of Luther spread?
   Shall I, when Eurus [62] storms, pass through Egyptian sand?
   Shall I to meet your wish discover some new land?
Shall I on Peter's throne crown Calvin's, Beza's [63] head?
   Shall I in Zanziba [64] the yearling dragons chain?
   Shall I ingurgitate the serpents' yellow bane?
I am obedient; your will is but my fate.
   My ear, my heart, my will hark, hasten, and pursue
   Whatever your mouth commands with fullest joy to do.
But do not ask of me that I my love must hate.

Christian Hofmann von Hofmannswaldau

GRABSCHRIFFT GRAFENS SERINI/
WELCHER/ DEM VORGEBEN NACH/
AUF DER JAGT VON EINEM WILDEN SCHWEIN
SOLL SEYN GETÖTET WORDEN

   Mein auge war ein blitz, mein arm ein donnerschlag,
Mein säbel war bemüht, den monden bleich zu färben,
Aus meinem hertzen quall der Türcken ihr verderben,
   Wenn um mein Tzacatur das feld voll leichen lag:
Das blut-vergiessen war mein rother feyertag.
Doch liess der himmel mich nicht das gelück erwerben;
Auff eines Bassen brust, mit blut bespritzt, zu sterben.
   Ach dass doch nicht Serin wie Simson sterben mag!
So muss der mensch ein spiel des sternen-himmels bleiben.
   Bald ist er stern, bald stein, bald gold, bald trüber sand,
   Bald lockt, bald drücket ihn des zufalls harte hand.
Ach könt ich diesen reim um meine grabstätt schreiben:
   Der niemahls sich gebückt vor seines feindes fahn,
   Den schlägt des feindes feind, ein wilder schweines-zahn.

Christian Hofmann von Hofmannswaldau

SONETT
ER SCHAUET DER LESBIE DURCH EIN LOCH ZU

   Es dachte Lesbie, sie sässe ganz allein,
Indem sie wohl verwahrt die fenster und die thüren;
Doch liess sich Sylvius den geilen fürwitz führen,
   Und schaute durch ein loch in ihr gemach hinein.
   Auf ihrem lincken knie lag ihr das rechte bein,
Die hand war höchst bemüht, den schuch ihr zuzuschnüren,
Er schaute, wie der moss zinnober weiss zu zieren,
   Und wo Cupido will mit lust gewieget seyn.
Es ruffte Sylvius: wie zierlich sind die waden
Mit warmen schnee bedeckt, mit helffenbein beladen!
   Er sahe selbst den ort, wo seine hoffnung stund.
Es lachte Sylvius, sie sprach: du bist verlohren,
Zum schmertzen bist du dir, und mir zur pein erkoren:
   Denn deine hoffnung hat ja gar zu schlechten grund.

Christian Hofmann von Hofmannswaldau

Epitaph of Count Serini,[65]
WHO, ACCORDING TO THE REPORT
WAS KILLED BY A WILD BOAR
WHILE HUNTING

    Like lightning did my eye, my arm like thunder play,
A paleness on the moon my saber strove to cast,
Destruction for the Turks sprang of my heart's wild blast,
    When round my band the field all full of corpses lay.
    Blood-letting was to me a ruddy holiday,
Yet Heaven would not let me make my fortune fast:
Upon some Bassa's breast, blood-stained to breathe my last –
    Oh, that Serini could not end in Samson's way.
Thus man must needs remain the starry heavens' jibe:
    Now he is star, now stone, now gold, now wretched sand,
    Now he is charmed, now crushed by chance's fearful hand.
Oh, if upon my grave I could this rhyme inscribe:
    "He who ne'er bowed his head to flag of hostile shore,
    Found death from foeman's foe, the tusk of savage boar."

Christian Hofmann von Hofmannswaldau

Sonnet
He Observes Lesbia through a Hole

    It seemed to Lesbia that she all lonely stayed
Since she so tight had put the doors and windows to,
Yet Sylvius could not his clever lust subdue,
    And through a little hole her chamber he surveyed.
    Upon her knee (the left) her leg (the right) she laid,
Her hand was all engaged to buckle up her shoe,
He saw how dainty moss around vermilion grew,
    He saw where Cupid would with joy his head have laid.
Then Sylvius exclaimed: how lovely are these thighs,
Where warming snow is piled and where sweet ivory lies!
    He saw indeed the place towards which his hope was bound;
He laughed aloud – she said: "Now you are surely lost.
What pains you have yourself and me what torments cost.
    In truth your confidence has but a faulty ground."

Ernst Christoph Homburg
Was ist die Liebe

Ein Feuer sonder Feuer, ein lebendiger Tod,
Ein Zorn, doch ohne Gall, ein angenehme Not,
Ein Klagen ausser Angst, ein überwundner Sieg,
Ein unbeherzter Mut, ein freudenvoller Krieg;
Ein federleichtes Joch, ein nimmerkrankes Leid,
Ein zweifelhafter Trost und süsse Bitterkeit,
Ein unverhofftes Gift und kluge Narretei,
Ja, kürzlich: Lieben ist nur blosse Phantasei.

Henrich Hudemann
Von der Zeit

Gleich wie des Neptuns Frewd/ dass blawe Wasser fliesset
Mit schnellem stillen Lauff/ welchs jederman geniesset/
  Dass wirs vermercken kaum; Also die edle Zeit/
  Darin wir leben all/ auch mit Geschwindigkeit
Hinläuffet/ wann wir nicht jhr köstligkeit recht achten/
Und unsers Leben End gebürlich thun betrachten;
  Die ungewisse Stund dess Todts verborgen ist/
  Welch doch zu ihrer Zeit uns treffen wird gewiss/
Auff dass mit frechem Muth wir uns nicht hoch erheben/
Sondern zu aller Frist im anvertrawten Stand
  Verüben/ wass gereicht zum eigenem Wolstand/
  „Und auch gemeinen Nutz: dann die wohl/ und recht leben/
  „Die immerdar mit des Gewissen Sauberkeit
  „Zu leben lenger/ und zu sterben seyn bereit.

Christian Friedrich Hunold
Auf die unmässige Hunde Liebe

Wie? sind die Hunde mehr/ als Menschen dein Ergetzen?
Sind sie in der Vernunft dir etwan gleich zu schätzen?
  Was vor Vergnügung hat doch ihr Gespräch in sich?
  Erbauen sie dein Hertz und unterrichten dich?
Verdienen sie ihr Brod? O Armer/ sie verzehren
Dich und dein Capital. Doch wilst du sie ernehren.
  Dieweil nun/ wie man sagt/ sich gleich und gleich gesellt/
  Was wunders/ dass dein Hertz so viel von Hunden hält:
Du bist dem Leben nach nicht in der Menschen Orden/
Und biss auf die Gestalt bereits zum Thier geworden.

Ernst Christoph Homburg
What Is Love?

A fire without a fire, a death that life does share,
A rage, yet lacking gall, a pleasurable despair,
A wail born not of fear, a conquered victory,
A courage of faint heart, a war's felicity,
A yoke hewn feather-light, a never-sick distress,
A doubtful comforting, and a sweet bitterness,
An unexpected bane, and folly of the wise:
Yes, briefly, love does but the merest dreams comprise.

Henrich Hudemann
Concerning Time

Just as old Neptune's joy, the azure waters, flow
Their quick and quiet course (which we with pleasure know
   Yet scarcely give our heed): thus noble time does flee,
   In which we all must dwell, with like rapidity
Departing: Should we not its value contemplate
And with becoming thought life's end anticipate?
   The dubious hour of death before us lies concealed,
   Yet certain at its time will be to us revealed,
In order that we'll not with saucy spirit swell,
   But rather each new day our souls to God commit,
   And practive what pertains to our own benefit,
And to the common good: for they live just and well
   Who always are prepared in conscience' purity
   To live still more and yet prepared from life to flee.

Christian Friedrich Hunold
Concerning the Immoderate Love of Dogs

How now? Are mongrels more than men in your esteem?
Can they in reason's realm perchance your equal seem?
   What sort of pleasure then may in their converse lie?
   Do they your wit increase, your spirit edify?
And do they earn their bread? Oh wretch, they gobble up
You and your capital. Yet you do give them sup.
   Since now like-feathered birds so oft together fly,
   What wonder that your heart the canine holds so high.
Nor do you by your life in human order fall:
In all but in your form you have turned animal.

Caspar Kirchner

FRAWENLOB H. MICHAEL BARTSCHEN
UND
FRAWEN HELENE BURKHARDIN
ZU EHREN ENTWORFFEN

Euch ruff ich erstlich an jhr dreymahl drey Göttinnen,
  Macht auff, dass ewer Brunn, und Flügelspferde Fluss
  Abfliessen her zu mir in mein gemüthe mus.
Regieret meinen Geist, regieret meine Sinnen,
  Dass ich wie ich gern wolt und solt je mehr und mehr,
  Erhebe weit und breit dess Frawenzimmers Ehr,
Wolan so strecke dich, o Feder wohlbekandt,
Und mache dich an den so hoch geehrten standt,
Damit jhr Lob und Ruhm, so weit mög umbher fliegen,
  So weit die Sonne laufft durchs grosse Himmelshauss,
  Beweise, dass sie mit vollkommenheit durchauss,
Zwar wider den gebrauch, den Männern selbst obliegen.

Johann Klaj

AUF! güldenes Leben! glückliche Nacht!
Die Sonne hat sich zu Bette gemacht.
Ihr Gäste! Halt' feste die Früchte der Reben,
Ein jeder sei wieder zu trinken bedacht.
Nun heisset geschnittene Gläser hergeben.
Wie? Trauret ihr, wann die Fröhlichkeit wacht?
Auf güldenes Leben!

Der silberne Monde schimmert mit Macht,
Er führet auf die beflammete Wacht.
Die Zinken die winken, die Saiten die beben,
Man höret der Musik lieblichen Pracht.
Auf lasset die Becher fein reihenweis heben.
Dem Bräutigam haben wir dieses gebracht.
Auf güldenes Leben!

Caspar Kirchner

A Praise of Woman Composed in Honor of
Master Michael Bartsch
and
Mistress Helene Burkhard

I call you, goddesses, who number three by three,
    Unlock your fountain's stream, the winged horse's source,
    And let it, flowing down, take to my heart its course.
Oh, govern well my soul, my senses' company,
    That they (as is my wish and task for evermore)
    To sing that maiden's fame both far and wide will soar.
Come and perform your task, you goose-quill of good name,
    And see to it that you a lofty station claim
Which will allow her praise to hasten through the sky,
    E'en as the sun does through the heavens' house progress,
    And bear the proofs that she in utter perfectness
(Indeed, defying use) a maid o'er men may lie.

Johann Klaj

Oh golden life, waken! Fortunate night!
The sun's orb to bed has taken its flight!
You guests! Shall the best of the vine spill or shake?
Again to the cup each his promise must plight.
Now let the carved goblets their cupboards forsake!
What! Can you be saddened at merriment's sight!
Oh golden life, wake!

The moon in its silver shimmers with might,
Leading aloft the hot stars in their light.
The zinks as they wink and the strings as they quake
For sweet music's splendors our ears do excite.
Fair, row after row, we our beakers do take,
And now to the bridegroom this paeon recite!
Oh golden life, wake!

Johann Klaj
Die Soldaten Luzifers singen

Luzifer, wann deine Waffen rasseln
In dem blankgeharnschten Heer,
Wann die heisern Kälberfelle prasseln,
Dann erstaunet Land und Meer,
Wenn die lautbar-hellen Feldtrommeten
Uns verjagen Todesnöten.

Wann der helle Küriss und die Schilde
Halten inner dampfbestaubt,
Wann die milden Reiter werden wilde,
Wenn das Pferd stolzdramplend schnaubt,
Wenn ein Wald voll Piquen, voller Lanzen
Dich und uns nun wird ümschanzen,

Wollen wir als dapfre Männer stehen
Und verschiessen Lot und Kraut,
Um ein Haar nicht aus den Gliedern gehen,
Den, der fürchtet seiner Haut,
Wollen wir bestrickt mit Luntenstricken
Unsern Feinden überschicken.

Himmelherze, Schild des heitern Himmels,
Warüm schwärzest du dein Haupt?
Es wird wegen diese Lustgetümmels
Unser Haupt mit Laub ümlaubt,
Wann sich unser Panzer nur erschüttert,
Ross und Mann und alles zittert.

Johann Klaj
Spazierlust

Hellglänzendes Silber, mit welchem sich gatten
der astigen Linden weitstreifende Schatten,
    deine sanftkühlend-geruhige Lust
        ist jedem bewusst!
Wie sollten kunst-ahmende Pinsel bemalen
die Blätter, die schirmen vor brennenden Strahlen?
    Keiner der Stämme, so grünlich beziert,
        die Ordnung verführt.
Es lispeln und wispeln die schlüpfrige Brunnen,
von ihnen ist diese Begrünung gerunnen.
    Sie schauren, betrauren und fürchten bereit
        die schneeichte Zeit.

Johann Klaj
The Soldiers of Lucifer Sing

Lucifer, when all your weapons clank
In the shining-armored band,
When hoarse skins roar 'gainst the drummer's flank,
Then stand gaping sea and land,
When the bugle's bright and piercing bray
Drives our fears of death away,

When the glittering breastplate and the shield
Steaming bear their inner side,
When to rage the gentle riders yield,
When steeds snort and stamp in pride,
When the lance-woods, pike-woods burst the ground
You and us now to surround:

We shall then as doughty men stand firm,
Shoot our powder 'way and lead,
Nor a hair's breadth from the column squirm:
He who trembles for his head,
We shall tight with lanyards trussed about
Carry to the foe's redoubt.

Shield of Heaven serene and Heaven-heart,
Why do you smear black your face?
We, to fete this joyful jousting-art,
Shall with leaves our head enlace.
When our arms but tiny movement take,
Every steed and man must shake.

Johann Klaj
Stroll-Joy

Oh bright-glancing Silver, who marriage has made
With branch-blessed linden's wide-wandering shade,
    Your gentle-cooling, your calm delight's fall
        Is known to us all.
How should then the art-aping brushes dare paint
The leaves which defend us from sun's hot constraint?
    None of the tree-trunks, so greenly adorned,
        Has order suborned.
They lisp and whisper, these slippery wells:
From them all this greening, this growing all swells.
    They shake, waking solemn, and already fear
        The snow's time of year.

Christian Anton Philipp Knorr von Rosenroth

ABENDS-ANDACHT

Der Sonnen Untergang/ des Himmels Abend-Roth/
Das schwartze Kleid der Nacht/ der Schlaff/ der halbe Tod;
   Entkleidung/ Müdigkeit und Hoffnung auffzustehen/
   Diss alles reitzet mich/ O Gott vor dich zu gehen.

Die Sonne geht: nicht du! O meiner Seelen Licht/
O Wärm! O Lebens-Trieb! O Freud! entweiche nicht.
   Lass deines Sohnes Sonn' am Himmel meiner Erde/
   Dass seines Lebens Tag in mir nie dunckel werde!

Der Seelen Abend-Roth das Bild der Heucheley/
Da zwar viel bunter Schein/ und sonst doch nichts dabey/
   Als Nacht und Finsternis der Straffen wie der Sünden;
   Das lass/ O Heuchler-Feind/ sich doch in mir nicht finden.

Die Nacht/ der Höllen Art/ dess Satans Herschens-Zeit/
Der Träum' und Larven Spiel; das Bild der Traurigkeit/
   Der Sünden Conterfet/ die Blindheit im Gemüthe/
   Treib ferne von mir weg durch steten Tag der Güte.

Und bleibt gleich noch in uns der alte Seelen-Schlaf/
Der durch der Schlangen Gifft in Adam uns betraff:
   So lass das Lebens-Wort doch mich stets auferwecken/
   Wenn andre mit der Welt noch immer Mohn-Safft lecken.

Den bunten Rock der Welt; dess alten Adams Schuh/
Dess Fleisches Camisol als unbequem zur Ruh/
   Die hab ich abgelegt/ die lass ich auch mit Freuden
   Und Christi Grabe-Tuch soll mich zu Bette kleiden.

Auch fühlt die Seele zwar dess Leibes Müdigkeit
In ihrem Wette-Lauff' und langem Christen-Streit/
   Und sehnt durch Christum sich nach ihres Tages Ende/
   Doch gibt sie sich und diss allein in deine Hände.

Ist dieses denn für sie der Erden letzte Nacht
So hat sie ja genug in Nächten zugebracht/
   In Faulheit/ Traum und Schlaff': und hofft die Ertz-Trompete
   Der dort versproch'nen Zeit und jene Morgen-Röthe.

Diss ist mein Andachts-Feur/ mein Hertz ist dein Altar/
Ich bin das Opffer selbst/ hier brenn ich gantz und gar:
   Wenn Sonn'/ und Abendroth/ Nacht/ Schlaff/ Kleid/ Glied/ vergehen/
   So lass mein feurig Hertz dort wie die Sonne stehen.

Christian Anton Philipp Knorr von Rosenroth

Evening Devotions

The passing of the sun, the sky's red even-breath,
The black dress of the night, and sleep, that half-way death,
   Undressing, lassitude, the hope again to rise:
   All this does urge me, God, to pass before Your eyes.

The sun goes, yet not You! Oh You, my spirit's light!
Oh warmth! Oh surge of life! Oh joy! Take not to flight.
   Grant that Your Son's sun stand upon my planet's sky
   That His life's day in me shall never fail or die.

The spirit's sunset has hypocrisy's design,
Since it is nothing more than much and garish shine.
   Like night and darkness do both sins and torments go:
   Oh let them not in me be found, You shammer's foe!

The night, the ways of hell, the time of Satan's reign,
The game of dreams and masks, the portraiture of pain,
   The counterfeit of sins, the blindness of the heart:
   Through constant goodness' day make these from me depart.

And though there stay in us that slumber of the soul,
Which through the serpent's tongue on us through Adam stole:
   Grant that the word of life forever make me quick,
   If others with the world still poppy-juices lick.

The bright coat of the world, the body's clinging vest,
Old Adam's very shoe as comfortless for rest:
   These I have put aside, these I have gladly fled,
   And Jesus' winding sheet shall clothe me for my bed.

Indeed the spirit feels how cruel the flesh is spent
In its long running-meet and Christian argument;
   It through Christ's person yearns toward its daylight's end,
   Yet it but to Your hand would self and day commend.

Be this the final night which it on earth will keep,
Then it has spent enough, in sloth and dream and sleep,
   Of nights indeed, and hopes to hear the brazen horn
   Of that our promised time and see that dawning born.

My heart Your altar is; this is my pious fire,
I am the sacrifice, here I shall burn entire.
   If sun and evening's red, night, sleep, dress, limbs must go,
   Then let my fiery heart like yonder sun-orb glow.

Christoph Köler

AN DIE BIENEN

Ihr sinnenreiches volck, ihr Bienen, die ihr welet
Durch lehre der Natur den König unter euch,
Der wol regiren sol das wächsen Königreich,
Die ihr den grünen Klee und blümelein bestelet,

Bestelt das regement, das nichts an klugheit fehlet,
Macht honigseim, das ihr im winter zehrt,
Und ewren zoll und schoss dem Bienmann hin gewehrt, –
Poeten ewer sinn und witz wird zugezehlet

Durch gabe der Natur: Apollo hat die kron
Und Zepter über uns auf seinem Helicon.
Wir gehn in Griechenland nach rosen und Violen,

Wir fliegen auch nach Rom umb gute blümelein
Und ziehen aus den safft, biss wir satt worden sein.
Dann lassen wir bey uns die leser honig holen.

Johann Ulrich von König

AUF IHRO KÖNIGL. MAJESTÄT
DER REGIERENDEN KÖNIGIN VON UNGARN UND BÖHMEN
KRÖNUNGS-FEST ZU PRAG

Zu hart geängstigtes nunmehr erlöstes Prag,
  Wie billig feyerst du den heut erlebten Tag,
An welchem dir ein Heil von neuem wiederfahren,
Das ich in dir ersah bereits vor zwanzig Jahren.
  Die Krone, die damals der Eltern Haupt geschmückt,
  Wird auf der Tochter Stirn' itzt ebenfals erblickt,
Die, nach so viel Verdruss, ihr desto schöner sitzet,
Als, nach der Finsterniss, die Sonne heller blitzet.
  Wie viel verliehret ihr, ihr die ihr nicht gesehn,
  Theresien allhier zu ihrer Krönung gehn!
Erdichtet euch ein Bild von solchen Vorzugsgaben,
Die alles, was nur gross, in sich besonders haben;
  Ein Bild, auf dem Verstand, Rath, Einsicht, tapfrer Muth
  Standhafftigkeit, Geburt und Herrschkunst zweyfach ruht;
Ein Bild, wo Sitten, Zucht, Kunst, Sprachen, Wissenschafften
Und alle Tugenden fest aneinander hafften,

Christoph Köler

TO THE BEES

You nation rich in sense, you bees who have deputed
A king among yourselves, as learnt from Nature's guide,
A skillful ruler of the waxy countryside,
Who've robbed the clover green, the flowers persecuted,

Arranged a government of wisdom constituted,
Made honey-drink from which you feast at winter-tide,
And to the bee-man still your tax and toll provide:
To bards your secret sense and meaning well are suited

Through Nature's generousness: a crown Apollo's won
And scepter over us upon his Helicon.
We travel into Greece for violets and roses,

To Rome we too may fly for flowers when we will,
And suck the juices out till we have had our fill:
Then let the readers fetch the sweets our comb disposes.

Johann Ulrich von König

UPON THE CORONATION FESTIVAL OF HER ROYAL MAJESTY, THE RULING QUEEN OF HUNGARY AND BOHEMIA, AT PRAGUE

Prague, presently redeemed and once so hardly tried,
You justly celebrate this coronation-tide.[66]
The day that happiness once more upon you falls,
Which twenty years ago I spied within your walls.
   The crown, which at that time adorned the parents' head,
Upon the daughter's brow is now beheld instead.
It after so much woe her all the better suits,
As, after gloom, the sun its rays the brighter shoots.
   How much you forfeit now, you folk who have not seen
Theresa go this day to take the crown of queen;
A picture for yourself of such deserts compose,
Which every grandeur will especially enclose;
   A picture where twofold rest judgment, bravery,
   Wit, council, ruler's art, and birth and constancy,
A picture, where the arts, tongues, science, breeding, grace
And all the virtues lie in mutual embrace,

Ein Bild, worinn sich selbst die Schönheit abgemahlt,
Dem Majestät und Huld aus beyden Augen strahlt,
Das, Amazonen gleich, sich in den Sattel schwinget,
Wie ein Orackel spricht, und wie ein Engel singet.
Erdenkt ein Männer Herz in einer Weiberbrust,
Und alles, was euch noch vollkommenes bewusst,
Sucht alles diss zugleich in eines zu verbinden!
In ihr, in ihr allein, könnt ihrs beysammen finden.
O Schicksal, eile dann, und mache wieder gleich
Was noch nicht einig ist im Erzhauss Oesterreich!
Gieb bey dem Zepter ihr den Oelzweig in die Hände,
Dass Fried und Einigkeit umarmt sich zu ihr wende,
Ihr Wink verjage ganz der Zwietracht Ueberrest,
Es sey der Krönungstag auch ein Versöhnungsfest!
So kan Theresien kein Ruhm kein Glück mehr fehlen,
So herrscht sie allerwerts in allen edlen Seelen;
So sieht ein jeder sie nun für ein Wunder an,
Weil keiner, der sie sieht, bey sich entscheiden kan,
Wie sie, recht nacht Verdienst, benennet müsse werden,
Ob Heldin? Königin? ob Göttin hier auf Erden?

Quirinus Kuhlmann

Der Wechsel menschlicher Sachen

Auf Nacht, Dunst, Schlacht,
   Frost, Wind, See, Hitz, Süd, Ost, West,
   Nord, Sonn, Feur, und Plagen
Folgt Tag, Glanz, Blut, Schnee,
   Still, Land, Blitz, Wärm, Hitz, Lust,
   Kält, Licht, Brand und Not:
Auf Leid, Pein, Schmach, Angst,
   Krieg, Ach, Kreuz, Streit, Hohn,
   Schmerz, Qual, Tück, Schimpf als Spott
Will Freud, Zier, Ehr, Trost,
   Sieg, Rat, Nutz, Fried, Lohn, Scherz,
   Ruh, Glück, Glimpf stets tagen.

Der Mond, Glunst, Rauch, Gems,
   Fisch, Gold, Perl, Baum, Flamm, Storch,
   Frosch, Lamm, Ochs und Magen
Liebt Schein, Stroh, Dampf,
   Berg, Flut, Glut, Schaum, Frucht, Asch,
   Dach, Teich, Feld, Wies und Brot:

And where sweet loveliness has loveliness portrayed,
  Whose glance has majesty and graciousness displayed,
That, like an Amazon, into the saddle swings,
Speaks like an oracle, and like an angel sings.
  Conceive a manly heart in woman's bosom sown,
  And every perfect thing which else to you is known,
Try all of this at once in single sheaf to bind:
In her, in her alone you can this union find.
  Oh Providence, take haste, and seek to unify
  In Austria's high house what things still separate lie.
Make then the olive branch at one with scepters' wand
That peace and unity may turn to her in bond,
  That discord's scant remains her nod may drive away,
  And mediation's feast may crown her crowning day.
Thus can Theresa lack no happiness nor fame,
Thus in all noble souls rules everywhere her name.
  To think her wondrous is the general habitude,
  Since none, beholding her, can in his heart conclude
How she must be addressed, according to just worth:
As queen? As heroine? As goddess here on earth?

Quirinus Kulhmann

The Change of Human Things

On night, fog, fight,
  Frost, wind, sea, heat, south, east, west,
  North, sun, fire, ill deed,
Come day, shine, blood, snow,
  Calm, land, bolt, warmth, heat, joy,
  Cold, light, blaze, and dread.
To wound, rack, shame, fear,
  War, groan, cross, strife, scorn,
  Ache, gripe, trick, mocking prod
Will joy, grace, rank, balm,
  Palm, wit, use, peace, praise, jest,
  Rest, cheer, luck succeed.

Chamois, moon, spark, smoke, fish,
  Gold, pearl, tree, flame, stork,
  Frog, lamb, ox, craw's need
Love peak, light, straw,
  Steam, flood, glow, foam, fruit, ash,
  Roof, pond, field, pasture, bread:

Der Schütz, Mensch, Fleiss, Müh, Kunst, Spiel,
   Schiff, Mund, Prinz, Rach,
   Sorg, Geiz, Treu und Gott
Suchts Ziel, Schlaf, Preis, Lob,
   Gunst, Zank, Port, Kuss, Thron, Mord,
   Sarg, Geld, Hold, Danksagen.

Was gut, stark, schwer, recht,
   lang, gross, weiss, eins, ja, Luft, Feur,
   hoch, weit genennt,
Pflegt bös, schwach, leicht,
   krumm, breit, klein, schwarz, drei, nein,
   Erd, Flut, tief, nah zu meiden.
Auch Mut, lieb, klug, Witz,
   Geist, Seel, Freund, Lust, Zier, Ruhm, Fried,
   Scherz, Lob muss scheiden,
Wo Furcht, Hass, Trug, Wein,
   Fleisch, Leib, Feind, Weh, Schmach, Angst,
   Streit, Schmerz, Hohn schon rennt.

Alles wechselt; alles liebet; alles scheinet was
   zu hassen:
Wer nur diesem nach wird denken, muss der Menschen
   Weisheit fassen.

Quirinus Kuhlmann

Aus tiefster Not

Aus tiefster Not schrei, abgemergelt Herz!
Lass mich noch einst die matte Hand aufheben!
Es harnischt mich und panzert recht der Schmerz!
Die Zunge klebt! Angst hat mich rings umgeben!
Mein Gott, mein Gott! Du zentnerst stete Last!
Hör auf, hör auf, eh ich bin ganz verdrücket.
Gib endlich, gib um Jesu Kreuz mir Rast!
Wie lange soll dein Werk sein ganz entschmücket?
Was ist der Mensch, der ewigst wird gepresst?
Halt innen, halt, eh Geist und Seel ausbläst.

The shot, man, work, toil, art, game,
    Ship, mouth, prince, feud,
    Care, faith, miser, God
For mark, sleep, prize, praise,
    Aid, brawl, port, kiss, throne, death,
    Grave, thanks, coin, love plead.

What good, strong, thick, straight,
    Long, great, white, one, yes, air, fire,
    High, far is named,
Thinks bad, weak, thin,
    Bent, broad, small, black, three, no,
    Earth, flood, deep, near to shun.
His heart, love, wit, sense,
    Mind, soul, friend, joy, pride, fame, peace,
    Jest, praise are done,
Whom fear, hate, fraud, wine,
    Flesh, lust, foe, woe, shame, fear,
    Strife, pain, scorn have claimed.

All is changing, all is loving; all things seem some
    things to hate:
He must human wisdom fathom, who this but would
    contemplate.

Quirinus Kulhmann

From Deepest Need

From deepest need cry out, oh hungered heart!
Let me but once again my tired hand raise!
Pain armors me and does good plate impart!
My tongue sticks fast! Fear round about me stays!
My God! my God! You hundred-weighted load!
Desist, desist, ere whole it crushes me!
For Jesus' cross in peace give me abode!
How long shall then your creature naked be?
What's man, 'neath most eternal burden cast?
Stop, stop, ere mind and spirit breath their last.

Beschwerst du mich als deinen ärgsten Feind?
Es hat mich Schmach nach aller Wunsch getroffen.
Sie schaun mehr Lust als sie zu schaun vermeint:
Verloren wird mehr täglich mir mein Hoffen.
Dein Wort scheint nichts als nur ein leerer Traum:
Dein Führen wird ein lauteres Verführen.
Sie zweigen sich gleich einem Eichenbaum:
Du aber lässt mich mehr und mehr verlieren.
Du mästest sie und nimmst mir alles hin:
Verirrest mich, gibst Schaden zum Gewinn.

Christ Gott und Mensch! Schau her, ich bin dein Glied!
Soll Harmung, Frost und Armut mich aufzehren?
Ich liege hier, stimm an dies Trauerlied,
Voll Elend, Ach, und tausender Beschweren!
Voll Kummer, Sorg, und was mein Stand erweckt!
Muss Herzenleid unhörlich in mich fressen!
Bin höchst bedrängt und überall befleckt,
Als hättest du schon deines Knechts vergessen!
Mein Gaumen klebt vor Durst an meine Lipp
Und werde ich lebendig zum Geripp.

Die Jugend fleucht! Verging als wie das Laub!
Ihr Süsses ist mir bitter weggeflossen.
Ich träne hier: Heut etwas, morgen Staub.
Die Tage sind mit Jammern mir entschossen.
Bin ich, mein Gott, zu lauter Schand gemacht?
Sollt ich allein unendlich mich abquälen?
Mein Leben war nur eine Trauernacht:
Es ist zu viel, mein Elend zu erzählen.
Doch traue ich, mein Gott, dir felsenstark:
Hilf gnädigst, eh vertrocknet Blut und Mark!

Quirin Kuhlmann

DER 15. KÜHLPSALM,

Triumffunfzig betittelt über das herrliche Jesusreich, dessen Anfang
das Kühlmannsthum; fortgang das 7. Jahrtausend; Ausgang di
Ewikeit, gesungen den 28. Sept. 1677.

Triumf! Mein Jesus hat! Triumf! sein Reich bekommen!
Triumf! das Paradis! Triumf! ist eingenommen!
Triumf! drum singt mein Geist! Triumf! mit hohem schall!
Triumf! der sig verbleibt! Triumf! mein widerhall!

Do you oppress me as Your basest foe?
Disgrace to suit each taste does strike me sore.
(Men know more joy than they had thought to know.)
Each day my hoping vanishes the more.
Your word seems to be naught but empty dream,
Pathfinder, you a path of error choose.
(Men's branches like unto the oaktree's seem.)
But yet the more and more you let me lose.
You fatten them and take my all away:
For gain you give me hurt, lead me astray.

Christ, God and Man! I am your arm, look hence!
Shall want and frost and sorrow me consume?
I lie here and my song of woe commence,
Of misery, a thousand kinds of doom!
Pain, care, and all the rest my work must bear,
I must to heart-wound endless food allot,
I'm cruelly grieved and tainted everywhere,
As though You had Your vassal all forgot.
From thirst my palate to my tongue is caught,
And living I to skeleton am brought.

Youth flees away! Just as the leafage must!
Its sweetness bitterly from me is gone.
I weep here: present's something, morrow's dust.
My days have with loud mourning darted on.
Am I made, oh my God, for sheerest bane?
Should I alone in endless torment dwell?
My life was but a single night of pain,
My wretchedness did grow too great to tell.
Yet stone-strong, God, I on Your aid rely:
Help graciously, ere blood and marrow dry!

Quirinus Kuhlmann

The 15th Kühl-Psalm

Triumphal Pentecost entitled: Concerning the Splendid Realm of Jesus, Whose Beginning is Kuhlmann-dom; Whose Progression is the Seventh Millenium; Whose Exit is Eternity; Sung on the 28th of September, 1677.

Triumph! My Jesus has! Triumph! His empire gained!
Triumph! and Paradise! Triumph! at last attained!
Triumph! thus sings my soul! Triumph! in Jubilee!
Triumph! my echo is! Triumph! His victory!

Triumf! wir sehen schon! Triumf! di Heilgen eilen!
Triumf! die Braut des Lamms! Triumf! beginnt zu pfeilen!
Triumf! in voller Lib! Triumf! in voller Pracht!
Triumf! weil Jesus si! Triumf! so herrlich macht!

Triumf! Ein Feur entzünd! Triumf! mir Leib und Glider!
Triumf! Ich stimme an! Triumf! di Hochzeitlider!
Triumf! zu ehren Gott! Triumf! und Gottes Sohn!
Triumf! dem Heilgen Geist! Triumf! im Himmels Thron!

Triumf! di Engel sind! Triumf! im triumffiren!
Triumf! weil widerbracht! Triumf! mit groessern ziren!
Triumf! dem Jesuel! Triumf! der Koenigstuhl!
Triumf! weil Lucifer! Triumf! im Schwefelpfuhl!

Triumf! das heilge Licht! Triumf! hat sich belichtet!
Triumf! di heilige Stadt! Triumf! ist angerichtet!
Triumf! Gott wird gesehn! Triumf! zur unser Sonn!
Triumf! wir sind verfüllt! Triumf! mit lauter wonn!

Triumf! der Erdkristall! Triumf! traegt heilge Früchte!
Triumf! unsehbar sind! Triumf! di Lichtgesichte!
Triumf! O Freudenfreud! Triumf! so gar behend!
Triumf! Triumf! Triumf! Triumf! der sonder
End.

Laurentius von Schnüffis

DIE ACHTE MIRANTISCHE WALD-SCHALLMEY

Höre/ mein Teutschland/ ich muss dir was sagen/
Schmertzlich beyneben dein Elend beklagen/
Massen nunmehro du/ schwanger mit Thoren/
Selber dein eignes Verderben gebohren;
  Raisen/ und Kleider
  Machen/ ach leyder!
Dass du den rühmlichen Namen verlohren.

Kurtz zuvor hat man dich höchlich geprisen/
Allerdings Göttliche Ehren bewisen/
Weilen du dapffer/ treu/ redlich/ fürsichtig/
In den Geschäfften gehandlet aufrichtig:
  Aber/ ach leyder!
  Raisen/ und Kleider
Machen/ dass alles diss eitel/ und nichtig.

Triumph! we see forthwith! Triumph! the saints make haste!
Triumph! and full of love! Triumph! and splendor chaste!
Triumph! she hastens too! Triumph! the lamb's sweet bride!
Triumph! since Jesus her! Triumph! has glorified!

Triumph! set me afire! Triumph! in flesh and limbs!
Triumph! I shall entone! Triumph! the bridal hymns!
Triumph! to honor God! Triumph! His Son, His Own!
Triumph! and Holy Ghost! Triumph! on Heaven's throne!

Triumph! the angels now! Triumph! triumphant are!
Triumph! since there's returned! Triumph! and fairer far!
Triumph! to Jesus Lord! Triumph! the royal chair!
Triumph! since Lucifer! Triumph! knows sulphur's snare!

Triumph! the holy light! Triumph! itself has lit!
Triumph! the holy town! Triumph! will welcome it!
Triumph! God is elect! Triumph! to be our sun!
Triumph! by very bliss! Triumph! we are undone!

Triumph! earth's crystal orb! Triumph! bears holy fruit!
Triumph! the sights of light! Triumph! our sight confute!
Triumph! oh joy of joys! Triumph! that swift ascends!
Triumph! Triumph! Triumph! Triumph! that never
                  Ends!

Laurentius von Schnüffis

The Eighth Mirantian Forest-Shawm

Hear, oh my Germany, what I must say,
Sadly lamenting your present dismay,
Since in your belly you folly do bear,
Whence your own ruin will presently fare.
          Journeys and dress
          Cause (oh distress!)
That you your honorable name do forswear.

Ere a brief time men did highly you praise,
Even to heavenly honors did raise,
Since you, brave, honest, true, careful of thought,
Led your affairs in the way that you ought.
          But (oh distress)!
          Journeys and dress
Cause this to turn to a void, to a naught.

Gäntzlich hingegen bist worden verächtlich/
Anderen Völckern aufwartend gantz knechtlich/
Dessen ist Ursach dein närrisches raisen/
Deinem Glück schädliches Welt-herumb kraisen:
    Raisen/ und Kleider
    Machen/ ach leyder!
Deine Nachkömmling zu Bettlern/ und Waisen.

Welche nicht raisen/ die last du nichts gelten/
Müssen Thor-Hüter sich lassen nur schelten:
Suchest zu werden in Ländern geehret/
Alles dahero man dorten verzehret:
    Raisen/ und Kleider
    Machen/ ach leyder!
Dass man vil ärmer/ als Irus, heimkehret.

Weilen die Teutsche in Ländern umbstreichen/
Thorecht sie ihre Missgönner bereichen:
Bringen denselben/ ihr Thorheit zu straffen/
Selber die Mittel zu feindlichen Waffen:
    Weit herumb kraisen/
    Länder durchraisen/
Machen die Teutsche bey ihrem Glück schlaffen.

Kehrt man nach Hause/ so findt man nur Schulden/
Welche auf ewig sich müssen gedulden:
Schelten die Einfalt demütiger Alten:
Wöllen sich immer nur prächtiger halten:
    Raisen/ und Kleider
    Machen / ach leyder!
Dass sie versetzte Herrschaften verwalten.

Legen den Bauren auf grosse Beschwerden;
Edelleuth wöllen Freyherren stracks werden/
Dise den Grafen sich stellen entgegen
Ohne geringen Einkommens erwegen:
    Raisen/ and Kleider
    Machen/ ach leyder!
Dass sie mehr schuldig offt/ als sie vermögen.

Weilen dann höhere Würden/ und Titel
Nöthig erforderen grössere Mittel/
Müssen sie solche mit andrer Verderben
Listig durch allerhand Räncke erwerben:
    Raisen/ and Kleider
    Machen/ ach leyder!
Dass sie die Billigkeit völlig absterben.

Now you do wholly in manner of knave
For other nations play toady and slave
This from your idiot trips does descend,
World-girding journeys that fortune offend:
           Journeys and dress
           Cause (oh distress!)
That your sons beggars and orphans will end.

Those who'll not travel you worthless do call,
Naming them porters who're chained to their hall.
You seek abroad greater honor to earn,
Where men in truth but a wasting can learn.
           Journeys and dress
           Cause (oh distress!)
That men still poorer than Irus [67] return.

While German travelers fare far and wide,
Foolish they aid those who Germans deride,
Bringing them (thus their own folly to reap)
Even the means hostile weapons to keep.
           That they wide wend
           To the earth's end
Causes the Germans 'midst fortune to sleep.

Come again homeward, they find naught but debt
Which must forever to patience be set:
As they the ancients' shy plainness berate,
They will e'er fatter their splendor inflate.
           Journeys and dress
           Cause (oh distress!)
That they must manage a mortgaged estate.

They on the peasants great burdens do lay,
Knights will turn barons and brook no delay,
And these new barons the counts will oppose,
All in forgetting how thin their gold flows.
           Journeys and dress
           Cause (oh distress!)
That a man owns not so much as he owes.

Since higher title, more elegant charge,
Has as requirement a purse still more large.
They must such profits, to other men's bane,
Craftily through varied intrigues attain.
           Journeys and dress
           Cause (oh distress!)
That they their honor's quick death do unchain.

Welche vorhero Verkäuffer gewesen/
Müssen jez kauffen Wein/ Haber/ und Vesen:
Welche Schuld-freye Herrschaften besessen/
Jezund der Gläuberen Schulden-Brodt essen:
        Raisen/ und Kleider
        Machen/ ach leyder!
Dass sie die Schulden zu zahlen vergessen.

Welche vor disem gar ehrbar bekleidet/
Werden vor Gauglern schwerlich entscheidet:
Prangen mit ihren befederten Köpffen/
Dass sie gleich scheinen den bunten Widhöpfen:
        Raisen/ und Kleider
        Machen/ ach leyder!
Dass sie ihr Gütlein ehzeitig erschöpfen.

Dises doch alles noch wäre verschmertzlich/
Ob es bey Frembden schon schmächlich/ und schertzlich:
Aber es ligen noch andere Schlangen
Hinder den Hecken/ gefährlich zu fangen:
        Raisen/ und Kleider
        Machen/ ach leyder!
Dass sie offt Vatterlands-Feinden anhangen.

Werdet/ ihr Teutsche/ dann endlich gescheider/
Euer Traur-Kleider nicht eigne Leib-Schneider:
Machet die Kinder/ zur Weisheit gebohren/
Selber nicht widrumb durch raisen zu Thoren/
        Dass ihr nicht minder
        Glücke/ als Kinder
Närrisch beweinet/ wann alles verlohren.

Gottfried Wilhelm Leibniz

Auf die Nachahmer der Franzosen

Wenn der Franzosen Schaum die teutschen Häupter ehren
Und unsre Nation das Joch zu tragen lehren
Von denen, die ihr Land auch selbsten unwerth acht,
Wenn, was in Frankreich alt, bei uns die Mode macht,
Wenn ihre Grillen uns Gesetze geben sollen,
Wenn wir die Kleider selbst aus Frankreich holen wollen,
Wenn auf der Teutschen Kopf muss stehn ein fremder Hut,
Wenn man fast nichts bei uns mehr ohne Larve thut,
Wir Andrer Affen seyn, und sie uns äffen müssen,

Those who beforehand as buyers did dwell,
Now must their spelt-wheat, and wine and oats sell.
Those who had debt-free domains at their feet,
Now do the debt-bread of creditors eat.
          Journeys and dress
          Cause (oh distress!)
That they their debts have forgotten to meet.

Those who went decently costumed of old,
Now can from juggler-folk scarcely be told.
They with their feathered heads boastfully swing,
Seeming a twin to the pied hoopoe's wing.
          Journeys and dress
          Cause (oh distress!)
That they their gold to an early end bring.

All this were nonetheless still to be borne,
Though it in strangers rouse mocking and scorn;
But there still lie other orders of snake
Under the hedge, and are risky to take.
          Journeys and dress
          Cause (oh distress!)
That they oft friends of our enemies make.

If you, oh German, at last will turn wise,
Nor be the tailor of your weeping-guise,
Then try your children in wisdom to rear,
Nor let their senses through trips disappear:
          That you no less
          Child than success
Mourn, when all's lost, with an idiot tear.

Gottfried Wilhelm Leibniz

CONCERNING THE IMITATORS OF THE FRENCH

If German princes grant esteem to Frenchy scum
And teach our countrymen to go beneath the thumb
Of those, who e'en are thought a shame in their abode,
If what is old in France with us becomes the mode,
If their caprices stand as parent to our law,
If we our very clothes from France are willed to draw,
If on the German head a foreign hat must sit,
If we without a mask but little dare commit,
(We strangers' apes), and they do make these apes absurd,

Wenn keiner wird gehört, er muss französisch wissen,
In Frankreich aber man aus uns ein Sprichwort macht,
Und lobt das teutsche Geld, wenn man des Teutschen lacht,
Wenn manche Höfe sich der teutschen Sprache schämen,
Franzosen an den Tisch und gar zu Rathe nehmen,
Bis die Franzosen selbst uns kommen auf den Leib,
Und eine lange Pein lohnt kurzen Zeitvertreib;
Was ist es Wunder dann, dass auf der teutschen Erden
Die Unterthanen auch zuletzt französisch werden!
Bei Herren wird der Schad am allergrössten seyn.
Der Bürger lernet Franzsch weit leichter als Latein.

G. List

Auf die liederlichen Vers-Verderber

Ihr ungestimmten flöten
Verhungerter poeten!
Pfeifft vor ein maas verdorbnes bier
Der welt verwegne possen für.
Geht ohngefehr dem dorff ein richter ab,
Wie foltert ihr den kopff durch tieffes sinnen,
Und seyd bemüht bey dessen grab
Durch einen reim ein tag-lohn zu gewinnen.
Vor kleines geld verkaufft man grosse lügen,
Die stein und eisen überwiegen.
Schlaf aus, du träumender poet!
Suchst du die todten aufzuwecken,
So must du selbst nach geist und leben schmecken.

Matthäus Apelles von Löwenstern

Alkaische Ode

Nu preiset alle Gottes Barmherzigkeit,
Lob ihn mit Schalle, werteste Christenheit,
Er lässt dich freundlich zu sich laden,
Freue dich, Israel, seiner Gnaden.

Der Herr regieret uber die ganze Welt,
Was sich nur rühret, ihme zu Füssen fällt.
Viel tausend Engel um ihn schweben,
Psalter und Harfen ihm Ehre geben.

If none, unless he speaks in Frenchman's tongue, be heard,
Though they of us in France have certain proverbs wrought
And mock at German ways while German money's sought,
If many courts indeed our German speech abhore,
Have Frenchmen grace their board and e'en their council floor,
Until the French themselves descend on us with sword,
And lengthy suffering is short-lived joy's reward:
How shall men be surprised that here in Germandom
The multitude at last will also French become!
The harm will by all odds for masters be the worst:
The burgher's easier in French than Latin versed.

G. List

CONCERNING THE LEWD CORRUPTERS OF VERSE

    You discord-blowing flutes
Of starveling verse-recruits
Will pipe, to get a sourish beer,
Bold jests for all the world to hear!
And should some village lose its magistrate,
Through deep reflection you your head do pain,
And struggle as he lies in state,
In hopes that you by rhyme a wage will gain.
For little gold men mighty lies essay,
Which stone and iron do outweigh.
You dreaming poet, sleep your fill!
If you would call the dead to life,
You must yourself with spark and wit be rife!

Matthäus Apelles von Löwenstern

ALCAIC ODE

Now let all men with praise of God's mercy come,
Praise Him with trumpets, worthiest Christendom.
Glad He does lead you to His way,
Israel, be of His goodness gay.

The Lord rules o'er each part of this earthly ball,
Whate'er but stirs, before Him does humble fall,
Great bands of angels round him soar,
Psalter and harp make His glory more.

Wohlauf ihr Heiden, lasset das Trauren sein.
Zur grünen Weiden stellet euch willig ein.
Da lässt er uns sein Wort verkünden,
Machet uns ledig von allen Sünden.

Er gibet Speise reichlich und überall;
Nach Vaters Weise sättigt er allzumal.
Er schaffet früh- und spaten Regen,
Füllet uns alle mit seinem Segen.

Drum preis und ehre seine Barmherzigkeit;
Sein Lob vermehre, werteste Christenheit.
Uns soll hinfort kein Unfall schaden.
Freue dich, Israel, seiner Gnaden.

Friedrich von Logau

Epigramme

1. Die unartige Zeit
Die Alten konten frölich singen
Von tapffern, deutschen Heldens-Dingen,
Die ihre Väter aussgeübet.
Wo Gott noch uns ie Kinder gibet,
Die werden unsrer Zeit Beginnen
Beheulen, nicht besingen können.

2. Trunckenheit
Wer vielleichte soll ertrincken,
Darff ins Wasser nicht versincken,
Alldieweil ein Deutscher Mann
Auch im Glas ersauffen kan.

3. Der Ärtzte Glücke
Ein Artzt ist gar ein glücklich Mann.
Was er berühmtes hat gethan,
Das kan die Zeit selbst sagen an;
Sein Irrthum wird nicht viel gezehlet;
Dann wo er etwa hat gefehlet,
Das wird in Erde tief verhölet.

Come then, you heathens, put your laments aside,
And willing on his emerald fields reside.
He will us there His word proclaim,
Making us blameless of sinning's blame.

He holds His banquet ample and everywhere,
He feeds all men at once with a father's air.
He late and early rain does make,
Thus with His blessings us all to slake.

Then pay his mercy praise and encomium,
Increase His honor, worthiest Christendom.
Henceforth no ill shall us dismay:
Israel, be of His goodness gay!

Friedrich von Logau

Epigrams

1. Our Naughty Time
The ancients happily could sing
Of German's brave adventuring,
The deeds that were their fathers' will.
If God will grant us children still,
These, seeing what our time has bred,
Will sing no more but howl instead.

2. Drunkenness
He who thinks perchance to drown
Need not in the depths go down,
Since truehearted Germans may
In their goblets pass away.

3. The Physicians' Fortune
A doctor's fortunate indeed:
Where'er his brilliant skills succeed,
Time does itself his glory plead.
Of his mistakes but little's heard,
For where he may perchance have erred,
His error's in the tomb interred.

4\. Die Geburt ist der Tod; der Tod ist die Geburt
Der Tod ist nicht der Tod; der Tod ist die Geburt.
Durch diese kam ich kaum, so must ich wieder fort.
Der Tod ist nicht der Tod; er ist das rechte Leben,
Drauss ich mich mehr nicht darff in Ewigkeit begeben.

5\. Frantzösische Kleidung
Diener tragen in gemein ihrer Herren Lieverey;
Solls dann seyn, dass Franckreich Herr, Deutschland aber Diener sey?
Freyes Deutschland schäm dich doch dieser schnöden Knechterey!

6\. Glauben
Luthrisch, Päbstisch und Calvinisch, diese Glauben alle drey
Sind vorhanden; doch ist Zweiffel, wo das Christenthum dann sey.

7\. Beute aussm deutschen Kriege
Was gabe der deutsche Krieg für Beute?
Viel Grafen, Herren, Edelleute.
Das deutsche Blut ist edler worden,
Weil so geschwächt der Bauer-Orden.

8\. Weiber-Herrschung
Haus, Dorff, Stadt, Land und Reich wird Wolfahrt bald gelosen,
Wo Männer tragen Röck, und Weiber tragen Hosen.

9\. Wasser und Wein
Es kan, wer Wasser trinckt, kein gut Getichte schreiben;
Wer Wein trinckt, kriegt die Gicht und muss erschrecklich schreyen;
Es sey nun, wie ihm wil; eh mag das tichten bleiben,
Eh dass ich soll so tief in Gichten hin gedeyen.

10\. Ein Frosch
Die Stimm ist gross, der Mann ist klein;
Was nahe nichts, hat ferne Schein.

11\. Seele und Leib
Seel ist ein Gefangner; Leib ist ein Gefängnüss;
Wer den Leib verzärtelt, gibt der Seele Drängnüss.

12\. Narren und Kluge
Narren herrschen über Kluge; ihre Händel, ihre Sachen,
Die die Narren arg verwirren, müssen Kluge richtig machen.

13\. Alter Adelstand
Weiland war dess Adels Brauch in dem Felde durch das Blut,
Nicht im Acker durch den Schweiss, zu erwerben Ehr und Gut.

4. Birth is Death, Death is Birth
Death is not death, for death is but the borning day.
Through death I've hardly come, and I must pass away.
Death is not death, for death is but life's verity,
From which I may not go for all eternity.

5. French Dress
As a rule all servants dress in their masters' livery;
Can it be that France is lord, and the servant Germany?
German freedom, go in shame at this base servility.

6. Faith
Lutheran, Popish, Calvinistic, all of these confessions three
Stand before us, yet we wonder where then Christendom may be.

7. Booty from the German War [68]
What booty gave the German war?
Why, nobles, counts, and lords the more.
Our German blood has changed to blue
Because the peasants are made few.

8. Women's Rule
House, village, city, land, and empire harvest hurt
When women trousers wear, and husbands wear the skirt.

9. Water and Wine
Whoever water drinks, writes wretched poetry;
Who lives on wine gets gout, and screams for very pain;
But nonetheless I'd let my rhyming sooner be,
Than that I would at last the joys of gouting gain.

10. A Frog
The voice is large, the man is small;
What far is much, near's not at all.

11. Soul and Body
Soul is a prisoner, and body is its jail;
Who spoils the flesh, his soul's sweet freedom would curtail.

12. Fools and Wise Men
Fools have power over wise men: each transaction, each affair,
Which the fools so badly muddle, wise men's wit must needs repair.

13. The Old Nobility
Once noble custom was: by blood on battle-ground
And not by sweat on soil, its gold and fame to found.

14. Die Freyheit
Wo dieses Freyheit ist: frey thun nach aller Lust,
So sind ein freyes Volck die Säu in ihrem Wust.

15. Göttliche Rache
Gottes Mühlen mahlen langsam, mahlen aber trefflich klein;
Ob auss Langmuth er sich seumet, bringt mit Schärff er alles ein.

16. Ein Glaube und kein Glaube
Deutschland soll von dreyen Glauben nunmehr nur behalten einen;
Christus meint, wann er wird kummen, dürfft er alsdann finden keinen.

17. Mächtige Diener
Den grossen Elephant führt offt ein kleiner Mohr,
Und grossen Herren auch schreibt offt ein Bauer vor.

18. Die deutsche Sprache
Kan die deutsche Sprache schnauben, schnarchen, poltern, donnern,
    krachen,
Kan sie doch auch spielen, schertzen, liebeln, gütteln, kürmeln,
    lachen.

Daniel Caspar von Lohenstein

SONETTE AUS ARMINIUS

I.

Komm Sonne/ Brunn des Lichts/ zu unsern Hochzeit-Freuden!
Bring' uns den güldnen Tag; und gieb nicht nach: dass wir
Und unser Fackeln-Glantz kommt deinen Stralen für!
Was hemmet deinen Lauff? kanstu/ O Riese/ leiden:
Dass Zwerg-Gestirne dir so Preiss als Lust abschneiden?
Weil der gestirnte Bär/ der faule Schwan und Stier/
Der blasse Mohnde sich aus Eyversucht von dir
Nicht lassen dringen weg/ den Tag die Nachte neiden?
Treib so viel schneller um dein Rad/ O Angelstern/
Als du's zu langsam triebst zu Liebe Jupitern/
Wie er Alciden zeigt'. Erzwinge diss Verlangen/
O Sonne/ weil die Nacht zu schlecht ist für diss Fest/
Seit Hermann eben diss/ was Jupiter gewest/
Und einen Hercules Thussnelde soll empfangen.

14. Freedom
Where this is freedom: free to follow each desire,
Then men are sows set free, delighting in their mire.

15. Divine Revenge
Heaven's mills are grinding slowly, but they grind exceeding small;
Though from patience they be tardy, still they stern do capture all.

16. One Faith and No Faith
Germany of three confessions now shall keep a single one.
Christ must think that, when returning, he most likely will find none.

17. Powerful Servants
Oft mighty elephants by little Moors are led,
Oft mighty lords must do what some small peasant's said.

18. The German Language
Can the German language crack and snore and rumble, thunder, snort?
Then it too can jest and love and cuddle, babble, coo, and sport.

Daniel Caspar von Lohenstein

SONNETS FROM ARMINIUS [69]

I

Light-spring, oh sun, in light our wedding joys immure.
Bring us the golden day, and do not fail, lest we
(Our torches' shine) may take your beams' ascendancy:
What has restrained your course? Can you, oh giant, endure
That midget-stars your fame and joy as well obscure?
Since now the starry bear, the swan so lazily,
The steer, the pallid moon, for very jealousy
Will not depart your side, shall night the day abjure?
So much the quicker now, oh arch-star, turn your wheel,
As once for Jupiter you did that speed repeal
When he Alcides made. Oh sun, your wish relieve,
Since for our festival the night has grown too mean,
Since Herman is this hour what Jupiter has been,
And since Thusnelda now will Hercules conceive.

Daniel Caspar von Lohenstein

II

Hier liegt der weiseste der Sterblichen begraben/
Der grosse Socrates. Diss glaubt ganz Griechenland/
Streut Blumen auff sein Grab/ und Weyrauch in den Brand/
Weil ein solch Zeugnüss ihm die Götter selber gaben.
Gott/ den die Griechen nie vorhin erkennet haben/
Den kein Verstand begreifft/ war ihm allein bekand.
Denn ihm war ein gut Geist vom Himmel zugesand/
Im Leben ihn zu lehr'n/ im Sterben ihn zu laben.
Athen/ das ihn bracht' um/ beseelt nun seinen Ruhm/
Vergöttert seinen Geist durch dieses Heiligthum/
Verdammt den Urtels-Spruch/ der ihn zwang zu erblassen;
Und machet sich hierdurch von Schmach und Unrecht frey.
Denn wer will nicht gestehn/ dass irren menschlich sey/
Was über-menschliches den alten Irrthum hassen?

Daniel Caspar von Lohenstein

III

Allhier ist Spartacus der edle Knecht geblieben/
Der seiner Fessel Stahl brach als ein Löw entzwey/
Und hundert tausend sprach von ihren Halsherrn frey.
Rom zehlt die Todten kaum die er hat aufgerieben/
Durch derer Blut er ihm den Frey-Brieff selbst geschrieben.
Die güldne Freyheit legt ihm selbst diss Zeugniss bey:
Dass gar nichts knechtisches an ihm gewesen sey.
Ja Feind und Adel muss den Helden-Sclaven lieben.
War sein zerfleischter Leib gleich hier nicht zu erkennen;
So wird sein Nahme doch unendlich kennbar seyn.
Rom gräbt zugleich sein Lob in dieses Siegs-Mal ein/
Das man nun erst kan Frau und Freygelass'ne nennen.
Denn hätte nicht der Todt ihn untern Fuss gebracht,
So hätt' er endlich Rom noch gar zur Magd gemacht.

Daniel Caspar von Lohenstein

II

The wisest of all men lies buried on this spot,
The mighty Socrates. All Greece this fact will own
And has the grave with blooms, the flame with incense sown,
Since from the very gods he such a witness got.
True God, of Whom the Greeks before this time knew not,
And Whom no wit perceives, appeared to him alone:
From Heaven a spirit came by whose help he has known
Instruction during life, at death a kinder lot.
Athens, his murderer, encourages his fame,
And through this holy place his godhead will acclaim,
Condemning that decree which forced him to depart;
It thus inequity and shame seeks to allay:
For who will not confess: to do wrong is man's way,
To hate the ancient wrong demands an angel's heart.

Daniel Caspar von Lohenstein

III

Here lies the noble flesh of Spartacus the knave
Who like a lion broke his fetters' steel array,
Who hundred-thousands taught to put their lords away.
Rome scarce can count the dead for whom he dug the grave,
And through whose blood to Rome he freeman's patent gave.
E'en golden freedom will this statement's truth display:
That nothing of the knave within his nature lay.
Nobility and foe must love the hero-slave.
Were his maimed body here not presently to see,
Life nonetheless would cling forever to his name.
Into this monument Rome has inscribed his fame,
Rome, which but now one may call mistress and set free:
For had he not by death been brought beneath the loam,
He would at last have made a serving-girl of Rome.

Daniel Caspar von Lohenstein

Nacht-Gedancken über einen Traum

GOtt ewig guter GOtt! ich falle dir zu Füssen/
Halb stum/ halb todt/ nun ich des Traumes Bild verliehr/
Ach GOtt was stellst du denn mir im Gesichte für?
Ich irre lange Zeit mit Schertze/ Tantz und Küssen
Durch Lust-Gemächer durch doch als solch Lust-Genüssen/
Zum höchsten Gipffel kam/ so stürtzt mich die Begier
In einen Pful/ wo Schlang und Natter nagt an mir:
Biss nach viel Qual ich ward an ersten Ort gerissen.
Ach GOtt! ich fühle mich die Lust-Gemächer sind
Der Wollust Irrebahn; der Pful ist das Gewissen/
Das durch bewust der Schuld von Würmen wird zerbissen/
Und gleichwohl kehr ich um und renne so gar blind
Ins erste Sünden-Garn. GOtt zäume mein Beginnen/
Wo du nich hilffst/ werd ich der Höllen nicht entrinnen.

Daniel Caspar von Lohenstein

Die Augen

Lasst Archimeden viel von seinen Spiegeln sagen,
Da durch geschliffen Glas der heissen Sonne Rad
Der Römer Schiff und Mast in Brand gestecket hat,
Die in der Doris Schoss für Syracuse lagen:
Den Ruhm verdienet mehr der güldnen Sonne Wagen,
Als Archimedens Kunst und seines Spiegels Blatt.
Denn dies sein Meisterstück hat nur an Dingen statt,
Mit denen jede Glut pflegt leichtlich anzuschlagen.
In deinen Augen steckt mehr Nachdruck, Schwefel, Tag,
Als hohler Gläser Kunst der Sonnen-Strahl vermag,
Ja ihr geschwinder Blitz hat viel mehr Macht zu brennen:
Sie zünden übers Meer entfernte Seelen an
Und Herzen, denen sich kein Eis vergleichen kann.
Soll man die Augen nun nicht Brenne-Spiegel nennen?

Daniel Caspar von Lohenstein

Night-Thoughts Concerning a Dream

God, ever gracious God! Here I myself debase,
Half mute, half dead, when now the dreamer's world grows small.
Oh God, what did you then into my vision call?
With jest and dance and kiss I made an endless chase
Through pleasure-palaces, yet when I would embrace
These pleasures' highest peak, my lusting let me fall
Into a pit where snakes and gnawing adders crawl;
Until, long-tortured, I must meet my starting place.
Oh God! I think those rooms of joy where I'd begun
Were lust's deceiving path; the conscience is the pit,
Which, pondering its guilt, by worms is cruelly bit;
And yet I turn my course, and like a blind man run
Into sin's starting net. Dear God, my yearnings stay;
Without your help I shall not come from Hell away.

Daniel Caspar von Lohenstein

Her Eyes

Let Archimedes loud his glasses' glory roar,
Since hot Apollo's wheel, through polished mirror passed,
Did make a holocaust of Roman ship and mast
That lay in Doris' [70] arms off Syracusa's shore.
The sun's gold chariot deserves these praises more
Than Archimedes' art, his pane in crystal cast:
For this his masterwork but to such things holds fast,
In which each glow is wont all easily to bore.
Within your eyes there do more strength, light, sulphur dwell
Than sunbeams from the art of hollow glass compel.
Indeed, their hasty bolt owns much more force of flame:
Their fire across the seas has distant spirits won,
And hearts, with which no ice can bear comparison.
Now shall men not these eyes their burning-glasses name?

Ludwig, Fürst zu Anhalt-Koethen

KLING-GEDICHTE
AUF DIE FRUCHTBRINGENDE GESELSCHAFT
DAS GEMAEHLDE IST
EIN INDIANISCHER NUS- ODER PALMENBAUM:
DAS WORT:
ALLES ZU NUTZEN

Komt/ lernt vom Palmenbaum' ihr/ die ihr euch begeben
   In die Geselschaft wolt/ wie ihr es stellet an/
   Das euch Fruchtbringend' heisz' und halt' ein jedermann/
Ihr muesset seiner frucht in allem folgen eben.

Fast alles/ was bedarf der Mensch in seinem Leben/
   Bringt vor der baum/ draus man Nehnadeln machen kan/
   Garn/ Seile/ Stricke/ Schiff'/ auch Mast und Segel dran/
Wein/ Ehsig/ Brantewein/ oehl seine fruechte geben/

   Brot/ Zucker/ Butter/ Milch/ Keesz': aus der Rinde wird
   Ein Becher/ Leffel/ Topff: ein blat von ihm formirt
Dachschindeln/ Matten auch von ihm geflochten werden.

In iedem Monat' Er vor neüe fruechte bringt:
   Wol dem/ der/ gleich wie er darnach nur strebt und ringt/
   Das er in allem Frucht und Nutzen bring' auf Erden.

Zacharias Lund

AN DIE LIEBSTE

   Diss Kräntzlein schick ich dir voll schöner Blumen Pracht/
     Zu deines Häuptes Zier mit meiner Hand gemacht:
Magst gelbe Veilgen hier/ hier weisse Lilien sehen/
Dort rothe Rosen auch als noch voll Thawes stehn:
   Doch was kömpt diss Geschenck bey deiner Würdigkeit?
     Zerbrichs/ als dir gefellt/ bist selbst voll Zierligkeit:
Das Häupt ist Veilgen voll/ voll Lilien die Wangen/
Das Zuckermündlein ist mit Rosen rings umbfangen.

Ludwig, Fürst zu Anhalt-Koethen

SONNET
CONCERNING THE FRUITFUL SOCIETY [71]
WHOSE VIGNETTE IS
AN INDIAN NUTTREE OR PALMTREE
ITS MOTTO
ALL THINGS USEFUL

Come, from the palmtree learn, oh you who would aspire
    To join our company, how this you may begin.
    That every man will think you of the fruitful kin,
Into the palmtree's fruits you closely must inquire.

For almost everything that men for life require
    The palmtree gives: it is the needle's origin,
    From it men yarn, rope, cord, mast, sail, and vessel win.
Wine, brandy, vinegar, and oil its fruits can sire.

    Bread, sugar, butter, milk, cheese: from its rind we take
    A cup, a spoon, a jug: a leaf of it will make
    Roof-shingles; weavers too from it may mats produce.

Each month upon the palm fresh harvests do arrive.
Oh blessed is the man, howe'er he toil and strive,
Who may in everything bring us both fruit and use.

Zacharias Lund

TO HIS DEAREST ONE

I send this wreath to you filled with fair blooms's renown,
    All woven by my hand to make your head a crown.
You yellow violets here, and here white lilies view,
And there red roses stand as though still wet with dew.
    Yet can this gift presume to share your merit's place?
    Destroy it as you will, for you yourself are grace.
Your head's of violets, your cheeks do lilies bear,
Your sugar-mouth's besieged by roses everywhere.

Paul Melissus

Sonett
Jörgen von Averli und Adelheiten von Grauwart

Was im Weltkreise rund allenthalb lebt und schwebet,
    Wehrhafft erhalten wirdt durch gleich eintrechtigkeit,
    Dann Gott vorkommen hat alle Zwyspaltigkeit
    Dass inn all seim Geschöpff keins widers ander strebet.
Zwar jglicher Natur ihr eigenschafft anklebet,
    Irrdisch und Himmlisch ding helt seine Richtigkeit.
    Diss alles wirckt die Lieb durch jhr Einhelligkeit,
    Und macht, dass in seim Standt nichts widersinns sich hebet.
Lieb ist ein Bidergeist, auss Fewr und Lufft vereint,
    Ders Hertz mit Girdt entzündt, den mut mit Luste kühlet,
    Da eins Gemüths und Willn ein par Ehvolck sich meint,
Solch jnre Brunst und Hitz mit frischer labung fület,
Dem Edlen Averli Adelheit die Hertzliebe.
Die Seel Menschlicher Seel ist Flammbrünstige Liebe.

Johann Michael Moscherosch

Aus den
Gesichten Philanders von Sittewald

    Ich lob die Poln in ihrer Zier,
    Sie bleibn bei der Alten Monir,
    Bekleiden sich nach Landes-brauch
    Wie Türck und Moscowitter auch.

    Aber Ihr in dem Teutschen Land
    In Kleidung haltet kein bestand,
    Daran man euch mit wahrem grund
    Wie andre Völcker kennen kund.

    Sondern Ihr seit recht wie die Affen,
    Nach Wälschen und Frantzosen gaffen,
    So wohl nach Böhmen und dergleichen,
    Die Ihrer Lande Grentz erreichen.

    Was die an Rüstung, Ross und Wagen
    Gebrauchen und am Leibe tragen,
    Dass müssen Jungfraw, Mann und Knaben
    Auch allenthalben umb sich haben.

Paul Melissus

SONNET
TO JÖRGEN VON AVERLI AND ADELHEIT VON GRAUWART

What in the world's wide round dwells fast or hovering
    Most truly is preserved through equal unity;
    For God has wished to shun each incongruity,
    That of his creatures none may war 'gainst others bring.
Indeed, a specialty does to each nature cling,
    Each thing of earth and sky does keep its equity.
    This all is brought about by loving's harmony,
    Which sees that in each class no heresy may spring.
Love is a goodly sprite, combined of earth and fire,
    Which heats the heart with lust, and lustful makes it cool.
    When couples think they have one will and one desire,
They place their lust and heat 'neath sweet refreshment's rule.
Thus lovely Adelheit pets Averli's desire:
The soul of human soul is loving's lustful fire.

Johann Michael Moscherosch

FROM THE
GESICHTE PHILANDERS VON SITTEWALD

    The Poles in their estate I praise:
    They stay with modes of former days;
    And to their country's dress they plight
    Their faith, like Turk and Muscovite.

    But you who dwell in Germany
    Have in your clothes no constancy,
    That men, with honest cause, might know
    Where you, like other nations, go.

    But rather you, e'en as the ape,
    At French and foreign fashions gape,
    And Czech and other customs seize
    Whose lands bound on your boundaries.

    What they in armor, coach and pair,
    May use, or on their body wear,
    That thing must maiden, man, and boy
    Have ever near him to his joy.

Mit welcher Tracht und losen Dingen
Sie sich nur umb die Heller bringen.
Und machen, wie mans wohl erfind,
Dass alles Gelt im Land verschwind.

Ja wann sie noch bei einem blieben,
Und nicht so offter Wechsel trieben
In Röcken, Wambsen, Stiffel, Hut,
So gieng es hien, und wär noch gut.

Aber, eh dann man sich umbsicht,
So wird was Newes auffgericht,
Darauff so fallen sie in gemein,
Wie solt ihr dann vermüglich sein?

Bedenckt doch diss in allem Stand,
Ihr liebe Leut im Teutschen-Land,
Auff dass ihr nicht von ewrer Haab
Durch a la mode nemmet ab.

Heinrich Mühlpfort

Sechstinne
Wett-streit der haare, augen, wangen, lippen, hals und brüste

Haare
Wer sagt, dass unser ruhm nicht güldne fessel schencket,
Wenn sie ein linder west um beyde brüste schwencket,
Entkerckert frey und loss? hier wird ein geist umschräncket
Mit steter dienstbarkeit, der vor sich weggelencket
Von band und ketten hat. Ein wenig nectar träncket
der haare liebes-reitz, der nur auf lust gedencket.

Augen
Wo unser flammen quell nicht heisse strahlen schencket,
Und den entbrannten blitz in hertz und seele schwencket,
So wird kein sterblich mensch mit huld und gunst umschräncket,
Hat unser leit-stern nicht der liebe glut gelencket,
So wird sie gantz und gar in thränen-gluth ertränket;
Wer ist der iemals liebt, und unser nicht gedencket?

For what attire, what feckless bent,
They cast away their smallest cent,
And fix it that, as men have found,
All treasure's fled from German ground!

Yes, if they with one style would stay
And not change fashion every day,
In coat and jerkin, boot and hat,
There'd be but small to quibble at.

But ere we've time to turn our head
To some new thing their fancy's fled
On which they as one man do fall:
How can you prosper thus at all?

You folk who breath our German air,
Of every class and kind, take care,
That you not steal what you possess
By wearing a-la-modish dress.

Heinrich Mühlpfort

SESTINA

Contest of the Hair, Eyes, Cheeks, Lips, Throat and Breasts

The Hair

Who dares to say our fame bears not gold fetters round,
When soft west winds do make them round this bosom bound,
Set from their dungeon free? Here servitudes surround
A soul forever which no irons could impound
Nor shackles ere this time. In little nectar's drowned
These locks' love-charm, that has but thoughts of pleasure found.

The Eyes

Where our flames' spring spreads not its fiery beams around,
Nor makes it lightning's glow through heart and spirit bound,
There will no grace nor good a mortal man surround;
Should we not for love's heat a leading-star propound,
Then love were utterly in tearful torrents drowned.
Who's ever loved and yet has not our mystery found?

Wangen

Uns hat Cupido glut, die rose blut geschencket,
Die lilie schnee, der sich um beyde zirckel schwencket,
Hier stehet helffenbein mit purpur rings umschräncket
Und manch verliebter mund steht bloss auf uns gelencket,
Wen nicht die lilien-milch und rosen-öle tränket,
Der ist ein marmolstein, der nie an lust gedencket.

Lippen

Den köcher voller pfeil hat Venus uns geschencket,
Und ist es wunderns werth, dass unsre glut sich schwencket
Bis an das sternen-dach! Hier liegt ein brand versencket,
Der ewig zunder giebt, der mit rubin umschräncket,
Die feuchte süssigkeit, wenn mund am munde hencket,
Und die vergnügte seel mit zimmet-säfften tränket.

Hals

Seht meine perlen an, die Venus selbst getränket
In ihrem liebes-schooss: Seht was sie mir geschencket,
Als um der mutter hals Cupido sich geschwencket,
Und seine süsse pein ins helffenbein versencket;
Hier lieget schnee und glut im gleichen kreiss geschwencket,
Ich bin der thurm, an dem der liebe rüst-zeug hencket.

Brüste

Diess schwesterliche paar, das voll von flammen hencket,
Von aussen vieler hertz mit liebes-öle tränket,
Inwendig aber feur als wie ein Aetna schencket,
Da doch das schnee-gebürg sich von dem athem schwencket,
Und wieder von dem west der seuffzer nieder sencket,
Hält alle lust und lieb in seinem platz verschräncket.

Nachklang der Sechstinne

Der haare schönes gold, der augen lichter brand,
Der wangen paradiess, der Lippen himmel-wein,
Hat mit des halses zier, ohn allen zwang, bekannt,
Dass auf den brüsten soll der liebe ruhstatt seyn.

The Cheeks

Us Cupid gives his flame, the rose its blood sends round,
The lily snow, which does the comrade circles bound.
Here stands fair ivory that crimson shades surround,
And many smitten mouths us as sole aim propound;
Who's not by lily-milk and oil of roses drowned,
Is merely marble-stone, and never lust has found.

The Lips

This quiver Venus gave to bear her bolts around.
Is it a wonder then that our wild fevers bound
Unto the starry roof? Men here that brand can sound
Which gives eternal spark, which ruby-gems surround,
The lovely damp that comes when mouth with mouth is crowned,
And saps of cinnamon the sated soul have drowned.

The Throat

Now scrutinize my pearls, which very Venus drowned
Within her loving lap. When Cupid scampered round
His mother's throat, she gave me that which her had bound
— That time his sweet disease did deep her ivory sound.
Here snow and ardor lie in self-same region bound.
I am the tower which by loving's tools is crowned.

The Breasts

This sister-pair that hangs, and with flame's store is crowned,
And many hearts without in loving's oil has drowned,
Within does Etna's fire bear hidden in its round.
But when a breath does make these snowy mountains bound,
And once more from the west the sighing choirs resound,
The pair does every joy and every lust surround.

Envoy of the Sestina

The ringlets' handsome gold, the eye-flames, brightly lit,
The cheeks' sweet paradise, the lips, whence wine is pressed,
Do with the throat's delight (all unconstrained) admit
That on the bosom love shall have its place for rest.

Joachim Neander

Der Muntere
Matth. 24 : 44

O Sünder dencke wohl; du lauff'st zur Ewigkeit;
Nimm deine Zeit in acht; sey immerdar bereit
   Der grosse Menschen-Sohn steht fertig vor der Thür/
   Der Hertzenkündiger/ der Richter bricht herfür!

O tolle sicherheit! verfluchter sündenschlaff!
Wach auff du/ der du schläff'st/ erschrecke doch/ und schaff
   Mit Zittern und mit Furcht/ mit bebendem Gemüht
   Der Seelen Seeligkeit/ den edlen Schatz behüt.

Die Macht der Finsterniss wird nunmehr kaum geseh'n/
Das böse Stündlein komm't/ wer will? wer kan besteh'n?
   Verzehrend ist das Feur/ es bricht aus Zion an
   Der Glantz des Menschen Sohns/ den niemand leiden kan.

Was kan ein Strohalm doch bey dieser heissen Gluht?
Was kan ein sandigt Grund bey ungestümer Fluht?
   Wo will der Stoppel hin/ bey solchem Wirbelwind?
   Ein Federleichtes Blat/ zerfleugt/ verweht geschwind.

Wach auff dann/ meine Seel/ in Jesu suche Ruh/
Wann Gluht und Fluht und Wind/ wird stürmen auff dich zu/
   Fleuch mit der Turteltaub in jene Ritzen hin
   Zum Fels der Ewigkeit/ da bistu sicher in.

Mein Nechster/ sey du auch bereit/ ich warne dich;
Ich bitte dich/ bedenck's/ eh' dann der Todes Stich
   Die seel vom Leibe reist; die Stund ist unbekandt/
   Gott komt/ wann du nicht meyn'st/ erforsche deinen Standt.

Benjamin Neukirch

Auf die Krönung Friedrichs I., Königes in Preussen
1701

   Was Cäsar abgezielt, ward von August vollzogen;
   Was Friedrich Wilhelm wünscht, hat Friederich gethan:
   Er legt ein neues Reich wie dort Augustus an.
   Doch hierin hat er noch den Römer überwogen,
   Dass er in Ruh' betritt, was jener blutig schaute,
   Dass er dem Sohne pflanzt, was jener Fremden baute.

Joachim Neander

The Man Who Wakes
Matthew 22 : 44 [72]

Oh sinner, think: you run toward eternity:
Be watchful evermore; your time treat carefully.
  The mighty Son of Man stands ready at the door,
  The judge does come who can each human heart explore.

Oh addled surety! Accursed sleep of sin!
Awake, whoe'er may sleep! Be frightened and begin,
  With trembling and with fear, with heart by shaking scarred,
  Your blissfulness of soul, that noble trove, to guard.

The power of darkness now does almost disappear;
Who will, who can endure, when that hard hour is near?
  Devouring is the fire that breaks from Zion's land,
  The flaming Son of Man, whom no one can withstand.

What can a straw avail before this fiery glow,
Or sandy ground before the torrent's hasty flow?
  Where in such hurricane may fragile stubble hide?
  Leaves feather-light are whipped to bits and cast aside.

Awake then, oh my soul, in Jesus seek repose,
When glow and flow and wind deal out their tempest-blows.
  Fly with the turtle to that stony niche away,
  Cracked in eternity, where you secure will stay.

I warn you, neighbor, be in equal wise prepared;
I beg you, ponder it, before death's prick has snared
  The spirit from the flesh. The hour is all unknown:
  God unexpected comes to see what heart you own.

Benjamin Neukirch

Concerning the Coronation of Frederick I,
King in Prussia
1701

What once was Caesar's aim, Augustus made complete,
What Frederick William wished, is by King Frederick done: [73]
He, like Augustus once, a new empire's begun.
Yet he's surpassed herein the mighty Roman's feat:
The Roman ruled by blood, but he by peace commands,
He sows but for his son, [74] the Roman for strange hands.

Benjamin Neukirch

Auf das Bündnis des Königs in Frankreich mit den Türken

Die Welt verwundert sich, warum der Saracen
An Frankreich Bündnis sucht und Frankreich es beliebet,
Noch mehr, dass Ludewig ihm selber Lehren giebet,
Wie er den Christen recht soll in die Flanken gehn.
Verwundert euch nur nicht und lebet ohne Sorgen;
Ihr wisst, dass Ludewig will eine Sonne sein;
Die Türken sind der Mond, drum trifft es billig ein:
Ein Monde muss sein Licht ja von der Sonne borgen.

Georg Neumarck

Sonnet

Als ich zu Lübekk im 1643sten Jahre den 12. April zu Schiffe/
üm nach Königsberg auff die Universitet zu reisen/ gieng.

Neptunus sol zwar seyn ein Gott der stoltzen Wellen
   Und Eolus der Wind' im fall dasselb' ist war
   Was uns zusagen pflegt die kluge Tichterschar;
Und gleichwol können sie noch niemals nicht erhellen

Dass sie besänfftigen der Winde starkes Bellen.
   Hier gilt Neptunus nichts auch Eolus kein Haar!
   Wenn wir armselige gerahten in Gefahr/
So muss uns Gott allein in solchen Unglüksfällen

   Erretten aus der Noht/ wenn der nicht bey uns ist/
   So hilfft kein Ankerseil/ des Schiffers Kunst und List
Wie gross sie auch mag seyn/ kan nichts allhier verfangen.
   Drüm hilff du treuer Gott/ denn du bist Herr der See/
   Dass ich frisch und gesund ohn alles Ach und Weh'
An den gewünschten Port des Pregels an- mag -langen.

Benjamin Neukirch

Concerning the Alliance of the King of France with the Turks

The world asks in amaze, why then the Saracen
With France alliance seeks, and France does deem it fair;[75]
Still more: that Louis will with him instruction share,
And teach him to harass the flanks of Christian men.
Oh be no more amazed, and let your cares be done:
You know that Louis claims himself the sun to be,
The Turks are called the moon, thus fairly we agree:
The moon its light, of course, must borrow from the sun.

Georg Neumarck

Sonnet

When I went on board ship in Lübeck, on April 12 of the 1643rd year, in order to journey to Königsberg to the university

Neptune is called the god whom prideful waves adore,
   And Eolus the winds, in case the tale is true
   That poets like to tell and their wise retinue;
Yet they have never proved how these gods can restore

Peace to the hurricane and calm its mighty roar.
   To Neptune may no worth, nor Eolus, accrue!
   When dangers of the sea us wretched men pursue,
Then must the Lord alone transport us safe to shore

   In such calamities. If it is not His will,
Then can no anchor-rope, nor seaman's art and skill,
However great they be, deliverance contrive.
   Then help, you faithful God, Who are the ocean's lord,
   That hale and hearty I, dumb of despairing word,
Within the cherished goal, the Pregel's port arrive.

Magnus Daniel Omeis

WENN DU ETWAS LIEBLICHES HÖREST

Kann hier ein süsser Klang mich fast aus mir entrücken,
Wie wird mich dort einmal der Engel Ton entzücken,
Mein Gott, da man vor dir das Dreimal-Heilig singt
Und wo dein Preis und Lob in Ewigkeit erklingt?

Mein Geist wird voller Geist, wann er hört süssen Klang.
O Gott, von dir entspringt der lieblichste Gesang!
Ach, lasse Ton und Weis in deiner Furcht erschallen,
Dass, wie er mir gefällt, er dir auch mög gefallen.

Martin Opitz

AN DISS BUCH

So wiltu dennoch jetzt auss meinen Händen scheiden
Du kleines Buch und auch mit andern seyn veracht?
Gewiss du weissest nicht wie hönisch man jetzt lacht/
Wie schwerlich sey der Welt Spitzfindigkeit zu meiden.
 Es muss ein jeglich Ding der Menschen Urtheil leiden/
Und/ ob es tauglich sey/ steht nicht in seiner Macht;
Der meiste Theil ist doch auff schmähen nur bedacht/
Und denckt was er nicht kan/ dasselbe muss' er neiden.
 Noch dennoch/ dass du nicht so offt' und viel von mir
Auffs neue dulden dürffst dass ich dich nehme für/
Muss ich dir loss zu seyn und auss zu gehn erleuben.
 So ziehe nun nur hin/ weils ja dir so gefellt/
Und nimb dein Urtheil an/ zieh' hin/ zieh' in die Welt;
Du hettest aber wol zu Hause können bleiben.

Martin Opitz

Ich wil diss halbe mich/ was wir den Cörper nennen/
Diss mein geringstes Theil/ verzehren durch die Glut/
Wil wie Alcmenen Sohn mit unverwandtem Muth'
Hier diese meine Last/ den schöden Leib/ verbrennen/
 Den Himmel auff zu gehn: mein Geist beginnt zu rennen
Auff etwas bessers zu. diss Fleisch/ die Hand voll Blut/
Muss aussgetauschet seyn vor ein viel besser Gut/

Magnus Daniel Omeis

Whenever You Hear Something Sweet

If here sweet notes can bring me near to ecstasy,
How blissful I shall hear the angels' melody,
My God, when they for You Your thrice blest praises sing,
And through eternity Your grace and glory ring.

My soul turns full of soul, when it a sweet sound hears.
The sweetest song of all, oh God, from You appears.
Oh, in Your awfulness let key and tune resound,
That, where I pleasure find, Your pleasure too be found.

Martin Opitz

To This Book

  So you will presently my loving hands abjure,
You little book, and thus with others be despised?
Indeed, men's mockery you have not realized,
And how against the world's sharp cavils to be sure.
  Each thing and everything must men's decree endure:
And nothing's sure that it will properly be prized.
The major part of men in scorn has specialized,
And thinks its feebleness with envy best to cure,
  But since you'll not allow that ever and anew
I take you from the shelf and look your pages through,
Then I must set you free and let you wanton roam.
  Depart now from this place, since you will have it so,
Attempt, attempt the world, and to your judgment go;
And yet you could have stayed as well within your home.

Martin Opitz

I'll lay this halfway me, which we the body name,
My least momentous part, beneath the fire's hot blade,
And, like Alcmene's son, with courage undismayed,
This burden and base form I'll cast into the flame, [76]
  That I to Heaven may climb: toward a better aim
My soul begins to haste, and I this flesh must trade,
This clutch of blood against a ware far better made,

Dass sterbliche Vernunfft und Fleisch und Blut nicht kennen/
   Mein Liecht entzünde mich mit deiner Augen Brunst/
Auff dass ich dieser Haut/ des finstern Leibes Dunst/
Des Kerckers voller Wust und Grauens/ werd entnommen/
   Und ledig/ frey und loss/ der Schwachheit abgethan/
Weit uber alle Lufft und Himmel fliegen kan
Die Schönheit an zu sehn von der die deine kommen.

Martin Opitz

   Ich gleiche nicht mit dir des weissen Mondens Liecht:
Der Monde fellt und steigt; du bleibst in einem Scheine:
Ja nicht die Sonne selbst: die Sonn' ist gantz gemeine/
Gemein' auch ist ihr Glantz; du bist gemeine nicht.
   Du zwingst durch Zucht den Neid/ wie sehr er auff dich sticht.
Ich mag kein Heuchler seyn/ der bey mir selbst verneine
Dass was ich jetzt gesagt: es gleichet sich dir keine/
Du bist dir ähnlich selbst; ein ander Bild gebricht
   Dass dir dich zeigen kan; du bist dein eigen Glücke/
Dein eigenes Gestirn/ der Schönheit Meisterstücke.
Du hettest sollen seyn wie noch die Tugend war
   Geehret alss ein Gott/ in der Welt ersten Jugend/
So were wol gewiss gewesen deine Tugend
Die Kirch' und Opfferung/ der Weyrauch und Altar.

Martin Opitz

   Du güldne Freyheit du/ mein wündschen und begehren/
Wie wol doch were mir/ im fall ich jederzeit
Mein selber möchte seyn/ und were gantz befreyt
Der Liebe die noch nie sich wollen von mir kehren/
   Wiewol ich offte mich bedacht bin zu erwehren.
Doch/ lieb' ich gleichwol nicht/ so bin ich wie ein Scheit/
Ein Stock/ und rawes Bley. die freye Dienstbarkeit/
Die sichere Gefahr/ das tröstliche Beschweren/
   Ermuntert meinen Geist/ dass er sich höher schwingt
Alss wo der Pöfel kreucht/ und durch die Wolcken dringt/
Geflügelt mit Vernunfft und mutigen Gedancken.
   Drumb geh' es wie es wil/ und muss ich gleich darvon/
So uberschreit' ich doch des Lebens enge Schrancken:
Der Nahme der mir folgt ist meiner Sorgen Lohn.

Whose knowledge mortal thought and flesh and blood disclaim.
    My light, let fire to me from your eyes' passion swell,
So that I from this skin, this gloomy body's smell,
This madhouse-dungeon full of terror may be freed;
    And that, loosed from my bonds, my frailty at end,
I can above the air and every sky ascend,
That beauty to admire from which yours must proceed.

Martin Opitz

    With snowy light of moon I cannot you compare:
The moon must grow and shrink: you in your strength stay one;
Nor with the sun itself; for everywhere's the sun,
And everywhere its shine: you are not everywhere.
    With courtesy you dull the point of envy's stare.
I am no hypocrite, who've instantly undone
What I have barely said: for like to you is none.
You are most like yourself; no image that might share
    You with yourself exists; your own bliss you will be,
Your beauty's masterpiece, your starry company.
You should have lived that time when virtue was revered
    Even as a deity, in Earth's initial youth;
Then would your virtue have as temple (in all truth),
As altar, frankincense, and sacrifice appeared.

Martin Opitz

    You golden freedom, both my wish and my desire,
What happiness were mine, if now I might conclude
Always to be myself, and if I might elude
The love that never yet has wanted to retire,
    Though oft I hoped to find some shield against her fire.
Yet, out of loving I am like a log rough-hewed,
A stick, unpolished lead. This chainless servitude,
This certain peril, and this consolation dire
    Arouse my spirit so that it may higher soar
Above the creeping mob, and through the cloudy floor
Ascend on reason's wings and with courageous thought.
    Then let things take their course: if soon I must away,
I'll overstep no less life's bounds too narrow wrought:
The name which follows me my cares' reward will pay.

Martin Opitz

VOM WOLFFSBRUNNEN BEY HEIDELBERG

Du edele Fonteyn mit Ruh und Lust umbgeben,
Mit Bergen hier und dar, als einer Burg, umbringt,
Printz aller schönen Quell, auss welchem Wasser dringt
Anmütiger dann Milch, und köstlicher dann Reben,
   Da unsers Landes Kron und Haupt mit seinem Leben,
   Der werden Nymf, offt selbst die Zeit in frewd zubringt,
Da jhr manch Vögelein zu ehren lieblich singt,
Da nur ergetzlichkeit und keusche Wollust schweben,
   Vergeblich bistu nicht in diesem grünen Thal,
Von Klippen und Gebirg beschlossen uberal,
Die künstliche Natur hat darumb dich umbfangen
   Mit Felsen und Gebüsch, auff dass man wissen soll
Dass alle Fröligkeit sey Müh und arbeit voll,
Und dass auch nichts so schön, es sey schwer zu erlangen.

Martin Opitz

FOLGEN UNDERSCHIEDLICHE GRABSCHRIFFTEN

1. Eines Hundts

Die Diebe lieff ich an, den Buhlern schwig ich stille,
So ward vollbracht dess Herrn und auch der Frawen wille.

2. Eines Kochs

Wie wird die Welt doch uberal verkehret,
Hie hat ein Koch im grabe seine ruh,
Der mancherley von Speissen richtet zu,
Jetzt haben jhn die Würme roh verzehret.

3. Eines Jägers

In dieser holen Klufft gesuchet hat sein läger,
Ein grausamer Tyrann und Feind der Wilden thier,
Jetzt hat er wiederumb auch seinen Lohn darfür,
Der Todt der war sein Hundt, die Kranckheit war sein Jäger,
So ist der Jäger nun, wie kühn er sey und starck,
Gejaget durch den Todt hier under disen Sarck.

Martin Opitz

Concerning the Wolffsbrunnen near Heidelberg

You noble fountain set in peace and joy's design,
Which mountains here and there do like a keep enring,
Prince of all lovely founts from which these waters spring,
More pleasing still than milk, more precious than the vine,
   Where with his worthy nymph our country's liege benign
   And chieftain often spends the hours' long dallying,
And where the birds' brigade does in her honor sing,
Where only happiness and chaste desire recline:
   You in this greening vale have not been placed in vain;
Enclosed from every side by cliff's and peak's domain,
An artful nature thus has given you a guard
   Of copses and of cliffs, so that we men may know
That all our merriments from pain and labor grow,
That nothing's truly fair lest it to gain be hard.

Martin Opitz

A Series of Various Epitaphs

1. Of a Dog

If thieves, I did attack, if lovers, I lay still,
And thus I did my lord's and did my lady's will.

2. Of a Cook

How strange a turn the world must often make:
Here in the grave a cook his rest does take;
He once prepared all sorts and kinds of meat,
And yet him now the worms uncooked do eat.

3. Of a Huntsman

A savage despot and the wild beast's foe has found
Within this hollow rock a final bivouac:
And now he in his turn for this has been paid back:
For plague his huntsman was, and death did play his hound,
And thus the huntsman now, though he be strong and bold,
By death is hunted here into the coffin's hold.

4. Eines Schmiedes

Ihr Freunde, glaubet allzumahl,
Könt Eisen, Feuer, Flamm, und Stahl
Dess grimmen Todes macht obsiegen,
Ich wolte wohl ietzt hier nit liegen.

5. Eins geilen Weibs

Hier lieget ein sehr schön, doch geiles Weib begraben,
Wünscht jhr nicht, dass sie ruh soll in der Erden haben,
Sie hat dem Himmel gleich zu werden sich geübt,
Und nichts als stetige bewegung mehr gelibt.

6. Eins ertrunckenen

Hier hat der Todt gefürt vor seinen Urtheltisch
Den, welcher in der Flut ist jämerlich versuncken,
Und hat ohn allen durst zu tode sich getruncken,
Die ursach, halt ich, sey, er schwamm, und war kein Fisch.

Joannes Oppelt

DAEDALUS

Mein Leben ist ein öder Labyrinth/
    Ein Irr-Gebäu/ voll Finsternuss und Schröcken/
    Wo Drachen-Zucht/ und Basilisken stecken/
Wo Minotaurus wohnt/ und Abendheuer sind.
Zwar die Vernunfft will Ariadne seyn/
    Beginnet mich auf meiner Reiss zu lencken:
    Ihr Faden kan mich aus den engen Schräncken
Doch gäntzlich führen nicht; Ich bleib geschlossen ein/
Und hoffe nur auf die erseufftzte Zeit/
    Da mir der Tod wird schnelle Flügel bringen/
    Womit ich mög durch Lufft/ und Wolcken dringen/
Von dem bedrängten Hauss/ und Sorgen-Saal befreyt.
Ich werd mit Lust mir singen in der Höh/
    Viel süsser/ als vor Daedalus gesungen/
    Da er sich nun befreyet aufgeschwungen/
Mit Segeln/ die aus Wax/ geflogen über See.

4. Of a Smith

Oh friends, I would your faith require:
Could iron, steel, and flame, and fire
Of bitter death the master be,
I should not lie here presently.

5. Of a Lustful Woman

Here earth does deck a fair, yet lustful woman's breast;
But do not pray that she, entombed, shall have her rest.
For all her life she strove to live in heaven's wise,
And nothing more did love than constant exercise.

6. Of a Drowned Man

Here death before his bar does bring a man to pause,
Who in a cataract all wretchedly did sink,
And, lacking every thirst, to death himself did drink:
He swam and was no fish: this was, I think, the cause.

Joannes Oppelt

DAEDALUS

My life's a labyrinth that I abhore,
    A maze where terror and the darkness hide,
    Where basilisk and dragon-brood reside,
Where perils are, where dwells the Minotaur.
Indeed will reason Ariadne be;[78]
    She starts to guide me on my groping course;
    But thread alone has not the master force
To lead me from these bonds. In slavery
I hope but for the time that sighs would speed,
    When I shall get my rapid wings from death,
    That with them, I'd cut air and cloudy breath,
From grief's abode and burden's ballroom freed.
Then, flying, I shall sing of joy to me,
    A sweeter song than Daedalus once knew
    When he had freed himself at last and flew
With sails sewn out of wax above the sea.

Johannes Plavius

SEY VERSCHWIEGEN

Man lobt beredsamkeit/ man rühmet schöne worte/
  Und warumb lobet man nicht auch die schweige-konst?
  Da doch beredtsamkeit ist ohne sie umbsonst/
Verschwiegenheit erhält der freundschaft beste sorte.
Der jugend schöne zier/ der tugend ehrenpforte/
  Ist die verschwiegenheit/ sie bringet ruhm und gonst?
  Wer nicht wol schweigen kan/ dem ist wol reden donst.
Man achtet seiner nicht/ er bleibt an keinem orte.
  Ein wäschhaftiges maul richtt manches unglück' an/
  Und bringt sich selbst in noth/ ein mund der schweigen kan
Ist vieles lobens werth und keine schlechte gabe.
  Darumb gewehne dich zu schweigen wenn du solt/
  Zu reden wenn du must/ so bleibt dir jeder holdt.
Wol schweigen ist fürwar nicht eine schlechte habe.

Michael Richey

UEBER DAS BILDNISS
SR. KÖNIGL. MAJESTÄT VON SCHWEDEN,
CARLS, DES ZWÖLFTEN

Als Carols Conterfey vor alle Götter kam:
War keiner, der nicht Teil an Seiner Bildung nam.
  Saturn erkannte was, das seiner Hoheit nahe;
  Mars glaubte, dass er hier sich selbst geschildert sahe;
Der Augen Feur-Stral hielt Zeus für seinen Blitz;
Mercur fand sein Gesicht, Apollo seinen Witz.
  Göttinnen hätten selbst ihr Bild zu sehn geglaubet,
  Wenn ihnen Kleid und Schwerdt den Irrtum nur erlaubet.
Jedoch, weil Kleid und Schwerdt von keinem Golde reich,
Sprach Momus: dieses Bild sieht keinem König gleich.
  Gar recht! kein König leb't, der Caroln gleicht, auf Erden;
  Drum darf Sein Bild nur Ihm, nicht andern, ähnlich werden.

Johannes Plavius

BE OF CLOSE COUNCIL

We celebrate fair words and value eloquence,
   But why must we in turn the silent art disdain?
   Since even eloquence without it is in vain,
And silence will receive friendship's best recompense.
Virtue's triumphal arch and youth's sweet excellence
   Is silence, from which art we fame and favor gain.
   His talk is vapor who cannot from talk abstain,
He calls no place his own, he knows no reverence.
   A washerwoman's tongue is much misfortune's cause
   And brings itself to grief; a mouth which knows to pause
In speech, deserves much praise and is no evil bent.
   Therefore instruct yourself to be still when you should,
   To talk but when you must; thus will you harvest good.
Now silence is indeed no evil element.

Michael Richey

CONCERNING THE PORTRAIT OF HIS ROYAL MAJESTY OF SWEDEN, CHARLES XII

When once before the gods there came Charles' counterfeit,
Not one of them disclaimed the part he'd had in it.
   Saturn discovered that which neared his dignity,
   Mars thought that he himself did here depicted see.
Within that fiery eye Lord Zeus his bolt could trace,
Apollo found his wit, and Mercury his face.
   Their pictures here to see had goddesses believed,
   If uniform and sword had let them be deceived.
But yet, since dress and sword were not all hung with gold, [79]
This picture, Momus said, could not a king's be told.
   Quite right! No monarchs live, who Charles's equals are;
   Thus is to him alone his portrait similar.

Martin Rinckart

Das Uhralte: Domine respicere digneris
Rein-Deutsch: Auff Christi Liebes-Augen

Ach sihe mich auch an zur Lebens-Freud und Wonne
Mit dem Genaden-Aug, O meiner Augen-Sonne,
Damit du im Pallast gesehen Petrum an,
Auch da er einen Fehl unnd schweren Fall gethan.

Ach siehe mich auch an, Herr Jesu, mit dem Auge,
Damit du sahest an die, so an statt der Lauge
Auss Augen-Wasser dir ein Liebes-Fussbad setzt,
Unangesehen sie dich schändlich vor verletzt.

Ach siehe mich auch an unnd Furcht unnd Schrecken wende,
Herr Jesu, mit dem Aug an meinem letzten Ende,
Damit du sahest an den Schecher, der da hang,
Unangesehen er schon mit dem Todte rang.

So wil ich bitterlich mit dem Verläugner weynen
Unnd mit der Sünderin dich Hertzen-treulich meynen
Und mit dem Lästerer dort in der Freuden-Schaar
Dich schauen fröhlich an und preisen jmmerdar.

Johann Rist

Auf die Winterszeit

Der Winter hat sich angefangen,
Der Schnee bedeckt das ganze Land,
Der Sommer ist hinweggegangen,
Der Wald hat sich in Reif verwandt.

Die Wiesen sind von Frost versehret,
Die Felder glänzen wie Metall;
Die Blumen sind in Eis verkehret,
Die Flüsse stehn wie harter Stahl.

Wohlan, wir wollen von uns jagen
Durchs Feur das kalte Winterkleid;
Kommt, lasst uns Holz zum Herde tragen
Und Kohlen dran, jetzt ist es Zeit.

Martin Rinckart

The Age-Old: Domine respicere digneris
In Pure German: Concerning God's Loving Eyes

Oh do me but behold, that joy and bliss be won,
With Your grace-bearing eye, oh You, my eyelight's sun:
The eye with which You looked at Peter in the hall,
When he had done great wrong and come to heavy fall.

Oh do me but behold, Lord Jesus, with the eye
With which You looked at her who in the place of lye
Gave You love's foot-bath, and the bowl with tears did fill,
Though she had earlier wreaked You a shameful ill.

Oh do me but behold, and thus my fear forefend,
Lord Jesus, with Your eye when I take final end,
The eye with which You saw the robber at Your side,
Though he already felt cruel death in him abide.

So will I bitterly with the denier weep,
And with the courtesan Your heart's allegiance keep,
And with the blasphemer in bliss's company
See You with joy and sing Your praise eternally.

Johann Rist

Concerning the Wintertide

The winter has begun its sway,
The snow our land entire has won,
The summertime has passed away,
The woods are into hoar-frost gone.

The meadows all with frost are burned,
The fields some metal's shine reveal,
The flowers into ice are turned,
The rivers stand as hard as steel.

Well then, we will from hence pursue
By fire this dress of winter's rime:
Come, let's lay wood and charcoal too
Upon the hearth, for it is time.

Lasst uns den Fürnewein hergeben
Dort unten aus dem grossen Fass!
Das ist das rechte Winterleben:
Ein heisse Stub und kühles Glas.

Wohlan, wir wollen musizieren
Bei warmer Luft und kühlen Wein;
Ein ander mag sein Klagen führen,
Den Mammon nie lässt fröhlich sein.

Wir wollen spielen, scherzen, essen,
Solang uns noch kein Geld gebricht,
Doch auch der Schönsten nicht vergessen,
Denn wer nicht liebt, der lebet nicht.

Wir haben dennoch gnug zu sorgen,
Wann nun das Alter kommt heran;
Es weiss doch keiner, was ihm morgen
Noch vor ein Glück begegnen kann.

Drum will ich ohne Sorgen leben,
Mit meinen Brüdern fröhlich sein.
Nach Ehr und Tugend tu ich streben,
Den Rest befehl ich Gott allein.

Johann Rist

Als die wunderbahre/ oder vielmehr ohnverhoffte Zeitung erschallete/ dass der Hertzog von Friedland zu Eger wehre ermordet worden

Was ist diess Leben doch? Ein Traurspiel ists zu nennen/
Da ist der Anfang gut/ auch wie wirs wünschen können/
   Das Mittel voller Angst/ das End' ist Hertzeleid
  Ja wol der bittre Todt/ O kurtze Fröligkeit!
Diess thut uns Wallenstein in seinem Spiel erweisen/
Der Kayser pflag ihn selbst anfenglich hoch zu preisen
   Als' eine Seul dess Reichs (so nand' ihn Ferdinand)
  Der Teutschen Furcht unnd Zwang/ dess Kaysers rechter Hand.
Bald aber/ wie sein Glaub' unnd Treu fieng an zu wancken
Verkehrte sich das Spiel/ man wandte die Gedancken
   Auff seinen Untergang/ der Tag gebahr die Nacht/
  Das Traurspiel hatt' ein End' unnd er ward umbgebracht.
So tumlet sich das Glück/ so leufft es hin unnd wieder
Den einen macht es gross/ den andren drückt es nieder
   Sein End' ist offt der Todt. O selig ist der Mann
  Der sich der Eitelkeit dess Glücks entschlagen kan.

Make not the seasoned wine delay,
But let it from the great vat pass!
That is the proper winter-way:
A hot room and a cooling glass.

Well then, we will our music make
To heated air and icy wine;
The man may mourn for money's sake
Whom Mammon puts in woe's consign.

But we will play and jest and eat
The while our money stands us stead,
Nor beauty drive from our conceit,
For he who does not love is dead.

We'll soon enough have food for care
When ancient age comes creeping nigh,
And no one knows what special share
Of fate can in tomorrow lie.

Thus careless I shall pass my days,
Rejoicing in my brother's band.
I strive for virtue and for praise,
The rest commending to God's hand.

Johann Rist

When the Marvelous, or, on the Contrary, Unexpected News Sounded Out that the Duke of Friedland Had Been Murdered at Eger

What is this life indeed? It is a tragedy,
Where but the start is good, just as we'd wish it be,
   The middle's filled with fear, the end is pain of heart
   And even bitter death; how swift does joy depart!
This does Lord Wallenstein by his play demonstrate:
The emperor at first did high him celebrate,
   As pillar of the realm (thus called him Ferdinand)
   The Germans' fear and scourge, the emperor's right hand.
But soon, when faith and troth no more so brightly burned,
The play reversed itself, and men their musing turned
   To bring about his fall: the day to night gave birth,
   The tragedy took end, and he was brought to earth.
Thus luck darts back and forth, and wheels about and haws,
The one it glorifies, the other down it draws.
   Its end is often death. Oh how that man is blest,
   Who fortune's vanity can banish from his breast.

Johann Rist

Sie rühmet ihre Beständigkeit

Mein Hertz' ist nicht von Wachs/ mein Hertz ist nicht zugleichen
Den Winden/ die bald Ost bald West herümmer schleichen/
   Es ist nicht wie ein Schiff/ das nach der Wellen Lust
   Bald hie/ bald dort hinläufft; Ach! mier ist nichts bewust

Als nur bestendig seyn. Mein lieben sol bezeugen
Dass es zu seinem Schatz' als ein Magnet sich neigen
   und tapffer halten will. Kein ander wird gedrückt
   In meine keusche Seel' als den ich erst erblickt.

Die Sonne zwar steht auff und geht des Abends nieder/
Der bleiche Mond nimt ab und kommt gefüllet wieder/
   Auff Hitze folget Kält'/ auff Regen Sonnen-schein/
   Auff Traurigkeit die Freud'/ auff schertzen Schmertz und Pein.

Mein Hertz' ist nicht also/ das läst sich nicht erregen/
Das soll kein falscher Sturm in Lieb' und Leid bewegen/
   Ich halte wie ein Felss/ der an den üfern steht
   Bey welchem Wind und Fluth mit Spott fürüber geht.

So lang' ein Thier sich wird mit seines gleichen paaren/
So lang' ein Schiffer wird die Wellen überfahren/
   So lange Sonn' und Mond noch haben ihren Schein
   So lang' O Daphnis solst du mein Hertzliebster seyn.

Robert Roberthin

Frühlingslied

   Er kömmt in seiner Herrlichkeit
   Der holde Lenz hernieder
   Und schenket seine Wonnezeit
   Dem Erdenkreise wieder;

   Er malt die Wolken mit Azur,
   Mit Gold der Wolken Rände,
   Mit Regenbogen Tal und Flur,
   Mit Schmelz die Gartenwände;

Johann Rist

SHE BOASTS OF HER CONSTANCY

My heart is not of wax; nor may it one compare
With winds which east and west go creeping through the air.
   It is not like a ship, which at the wave's desire
   Darts back and forth: Oh, I will to no goal aspire

Save to sheer constancy. My way of love shall prove
That it toward its prize does like a magnet move
   And brave will hold its course. No other may abide
   Within my virtuous soul, save him whom first I spied.

The sun, indeed, ascends, yet seeks its nightly den,
The pale moon loses force, yet, fattened, comes again.
   Cold follows after heat, and sunshine after rain,
   Joy after sadness comes, and after jesting pain.

But thus is not my heart. It adamant shall sit,
Nor shall in weal or woe false storms unsettle it.
   I'll hold fast as a cliff which stands upon the shore:
   Against it wind and tide in foolish rage may roar.

As long as animals but with their like will lie,
As long as seamen will across the billows fly,
   As long as sun and moon may still possess their fire,
   So long, oh Daphnis, shall you be my heart's desire.

Robert Roberthin

SPRING SONG

There comes, clad all in splendid dress
And with sweet regimen,
The spring, who by his tide does bless
The orb of earth again,

He makes the clouds in azure swell
And trims the clouds with gold,
With rainbows paints the field and dell,
With flush the garden's fold.

Er kleidet den entblössten Baum,
Deckt ihn mit einer Krone,
Dass unter seinem Schattenraum
Das Volk der Vögel wohne.

Wie preiset ihrer Lieder Schall
Die Wunder seiner Rechten,
Die Lerch am Tage, Nachtigall
In schauervollen Nächten!

Die Fische scherzen in der Flut,
Die Herden auf der Weide,
Es schwärmt der Bienen junge Brut
Auf der beblümten Heide.

Der Mensch allein, der Schöpfung Haupt,
Vergräbet sich in Sorgen,
Ist immer seiner selbst beraubt,
Lebt immer nur für morgen;

Ihn weckt Auroras güldner Strahl,
Ihm lacht die Flur vergebens,
Er wird, nach selbstgemachter Qual,
Der Henker seines Lebens,

Das ohnehin wie ein Gesicht
Des Morgentraums entfliehet,
Und vor ein schreckliches Gericht
Ihn, den Verbrecher, ziehet.

Jesaias Rompler von Löwenhalt

Zu einer Leich

Als imm 1633.ten jar die böse kranckheit viel leuthe hinweg genommen

Wie eillt die stränge Zeit/ das alter abzukürtzen!
    Es eillt der adler kaum seinen raub so sehr/
    Die segel gehen nicht so flüchtig auff dem mér.
    Drum sollen wir zur fahrt uns unverzüglich schürtzen/

Und unser Schirmungs-lamb mit bitren salsen würtzen:
    Es blast der faule Sud vil brennende geschwehr
    Und anders gifftigs ding mit follen bakken her/
    Als wolt er auff einmal die jung- und alten stürtzen.

He clothes again the naked tree
And tops it with a crown,
That in its shaded bowery
The birds may build their town.

How does their songs' resounding hail
The deeds of his right hand,
The lark by day, the nightingale
In awful night's dark land!

The fish go jesting in the stream,
The cattle as they graze,
Upon the flowered heath a team
Of tender bee-folk plays.

But man alone, creation's head,
Himself in care does hide,
He ever from himself is fled
And dwells at morrow's side.

The meadow smiles at him in vain,
Vain is Aurora's spur,
He turns, from self-created pain,
Own executioner.

And life for all his care flees far
Like phantom dreams at dawn,
Till he before that awful bar,
A criminal, is drawn.

Jesaias Rompler von Löwenhalt

For a Wake

When in the 1633d year the evil sickness took many folk away.

How austere time makes haste the course of age to stay!
    The eagle does not plunge so swift upon his foe,
    Nor do the sails so fleet upon the ocean go.
    Thus we should gird our loins directly for the way,

And our Protector-Lamb in bitter salines lay.
    From cheeks swelled out to burst the south wind, dull and slow,
    Does flaming pestilence and other poisons blow.
    As if it would at once both young and ancient slay.

Ihr sélen! habt die thür des härtzes wol in huth;
    Tunckt Glaubens-isopen in raines Lämbleins-bluth/
    Bestreicht die Pfosten mit! und seyt mit starcken stäben

Des bätens recht gerüstt! so mues des Pharons hand
    Auss der Aegyptens-wält in jens gelobte land
    Uns fridlich lassen gehn/ darinn wir éwig leben.

Jesaias Rompler von Löwenhalt

GAISTLICHE SPIEGELBERAITUNG

Du must ein spiegel seyn/ mein härtz! Es schickt sich eben/
    Dass dich der Glaub erhällt; die Trübsal schleift dich glat;
    Ich unterleg alsdan aus Gottes wort ein blat/
    Bestreich es mit der Lieb/ aufdass es an mag kleben.

Die rám mach ich von holtz/ an dém der Herr sein leben
    Hie für die sünder lies. Ich fass sie: brauch an stat
    Des Geld-grunds/ Gottes-Huld; vergüld mit Tugend-that/
    Dadurch wird disem werck die rechte ziehr gegeben.

Kanst du nun/ liebes härtz! ein solcher spiegel seyn/
    So wird die wahre Sonn (Got selbs) mit seinem schein/
    Wa-hin ich dich nur halt/ sich gegen über finden.

Mit dessen widerschein bländ ich die böst Lust/
    Daraus die Sünd entspringt: ja/ wan der schwartze wuhst/
    (Der Lästerer) selbs komt/ muss er daran erblinden.

Angelus Silesius

(Johann Scheffler)

AUS DEM CHERUBINISCHEN WANDERSMANN

1. Man weiss nicht, was man ist

Ich weiss nicht, was ich bin; ich bin nicht, was ich weiss;
Ein Ding und nicht ein Ding; ein Tüpfchen und ein Kreis.

2. Ich bin wie Gott, und Gott wie ich

Ich bin so gross als Gott, er ist als ich so klein;
Er kann nicht über mich, ich unter ihm nicht sein.

Oh souls, the heart's ingress keep strong within your grip
    And in the pure Lamb's blood conviction's hyssops dip;
    With it your door-posts mark! And with the staves of prayer

Be sturdy armed and well! So must the Pharaoh's hand
    Let us from Egypt's world into the Promised Land
    Go peacefully that we may live eternal there.

Jesaias Rompler von Löwenhalt

SPIRITUAL MIRROR-MAKING

Become a mirror, heart! That faith will you receive,
    Is but propriety: despair you smooth will grind;
    Then I shall lay a sheet of heavenly words behind,
And coat it well with love, that it may better cleave.

The frame will be of wood, on which the Lord did leave
    His life for sinners here; as I this frame-work bind,
    For gold I use God's grace, by virtue's gift refined.
The proper ornament will thus the work achieve.

If you can be, dear heart! a mirror in this wise,
    Then will the true sun's blaze (for God takes sun's disguise)
    Where'er I turn your face, be standing opposite.

With its reflection I can evil's vision break,
    From which our sins arise; and if the swarthy Rake,
    (The Blasphemer) appears, then he'll fall blind from it.

Angelus Silesius

(Johann Scheffler)

FROM THE CHERUBICAL WANDERER

1. One Knows Not What One Is

I know not what I am, and what I know, I'm not:
A thing and not a thing, a circle and a dot.

2. I Am As God And God As I

I am as large as God, and God as small as I;
He cannot over me, nor I beneath Him lie.

3. Leib, Seele, und Gottheit
Die Seel ist ein Kristall, die Gottheit ist ihr Schein;
Der Leib, in dem du lebst, ist ihrer beider Schrein.

4. Ein jedes in dem Seinigen
Der Vogel in der Luft, der Stein ruht auf dem Land;
Im Wasser lebt der Fisch, mein Geist in Gottes Hand.

5. Im Eckstein liegt der Schatz
Was marterst du das Erz? der Eckstein ist's allein,
In dem Gesundheit, Gold, und alle Künste sein.

6. Wer ganz vergöttet ist
Wer ist, als wär er nicht und wär er nie geworden,
Der ist, o Seligkeit, zu lauter Gotte worden.

7. Die geistliche Goldmachung
Ich selbst bin das Metall, der Geist ist Feu'r und Herd,
Messias die Tinktur, die Leib und Seel verklärt.

8. Die Rose
Die Rose, welche hier dein äuss'res Auge sieht,
Die hat von Ewigkeit in Gott also geblüht.

9. Bei Gott ist nur sein Sohn
Mensch, werd aus Gott gebor'n: bei seiner Gottheit Thron
Steht niemand anders als der eingebor'ne Sohn.

10. Die geheime Jungfrauschaft
Wer lauter wie das Licht, rein wie der Ursprung ist,
Derselbe wird von Gott für Jungfrau auserkiest.

11. Gott ist mir, was ich will
Gott ist mein Stab, mein Licht, mein Pfad, mein Ziel, mein Spiel,
Mein Vater, Bruder, Kind, und alles, was ich will.

12. Das Licht besteht im Feuer
Das Licht gibt allem Kraft: Gott selber lebt im Lichte,
Doch wär er nicht das Feu'r, so würd es bald zu nichte.

13. Die geistliche Arch' und's Manna-Krügelein
Mensch, ist dein Herze Gold und deine Seele rein,
So kannst du auch die Arch' und's Manna-Krüglein sein.

14. Gott ist nichts (Kreatürliches)
Gott ist wahrhaftig nichts, und so er etwas ist,
So ist er's nur in mir, wie er mich ihm erkiest.

15. Der Mensch ist's höchste Ding
Nichts dünkt mich hoch zu sein: ich bin das höchste Ding,
Weil auch Gott ohne mich ihm selber ist gering.

3. Body, Soul, And Godhead
The soul a crystal is, the Godhead is its shine,
The flesh in which you live is of them both the shrine.

4. Each In His Own
The bird rests in the air, the stone rests on the land,
In water lives the fish, my spirit in God's hand.

5. The Treasure Lies In The Cornerstone
Why do you rack the ore? The cornerstone alone
Does call good health and gold and every art its own.

6. Whoever Has Become All Divine
Who is, as if he weren't and ne'er had even come,
He is, oh blessedness, a purest God become.

7. The Spiritual Alchemy
The metal I, the soul the hearth, the blaze that warms.
Messiah is the dye, that flesh and blood transforms.

8. The Rose
The rose, regarded here by your external eyes,
In God eternally has blossomed on this wise.

9. Only His Son Is With God
Oh man, be born of God: for at His Godhead's throne
None other than His Son, there born, a place may own.

10. The Secret Virginity
Who pure as light and chaste as origin has stayed,
That man has been by God elected as His maid.

11. God Is To Me What I Desire
God is my staff, my path, my goal, my game, my fire,
My father, brother, child, and all that I desire.

12. The Light Exists In The Fire
To all things light gives force; God dwells Himself in light,
Yet were He not the fire, then it would soon be night.

13. The Spiritual Ark And The Manna-Vessel
Man, if your heart is gold, and if your soul is pure,
Then you can be the ark and manna hold secure.

14. God Is Nothing (Physical)
Now God is truly naught, and if He aught may be,
He's it in me alone, as He for Him takes me.

15. Man Is The Highest Thing
I think naught great: I am the highest thing of all,
Since lacking me e'en God before Himself is small.

16. Je aufgegebener, je göttlicher
Die Heiligen sind so viel von Gottes Gottheit trunken,
So viel sie sind in ihm verloren und versunken.

17. Die Sünde
Der Durst ist nicht ein Ding und doch kann er dich plagen;
Wie soll denn nicht die Sünd den Bösen ewig nagen.

18. Der Glaube
Der Glaube, Senfkorn gross, versetzt den Berg ins Meer:
Denkt, was er könnte tun, wenn er ein Kürbis wär.

19. Die Abscheulichkeit der Bösheit
Mensch, solltest du in dir das Ungeziefer schauen,
Es würde dir für dir als für dem Teufel grauen.

20. Zufall und Wesen
Mensch, werde wesentlich; denn wenn die Welt vergeht,
So fällt der Zufall weg, das Wesen, das besteht.

21. Die geistliche Schwängerung
Ist deine Seele Magd und wie Maria rein,
So muss sie augenblicks von Gotte schwanger sein.

22. Nimm also, dass du hast.
Mensch, nimm du Gott als Trost, als Süssigkeit und Licht,
Was hast du dann, wenn Trost, Licht, Süssigkeit gebricht?

23. Der Tugend Ziel ist Gott
Gott ist der Tugend Ziel, ihr Antrieb, ihre Kron,
Ihr einziges Warum und ist auch all ihr Lohn.

24. An St. Augustin
Halt an, mein Augustin, eh du wirst Gott ergründen,
Wird man das ganze Meer in einem Grüblein finden.

25. Die Liebe
Die Lieb ist wie der Tod, sie tötet meine Sinnen,
Sie brichet mir das Herz und führt den Geist von hinnen.

26. Ein's jeden Element
Im Wasser lebt der Fisch, die Pflanzen in der Erden,
Der Vogel in der Luft, die Sonn im Firmament,
Der Salamander muss im Feu'r erhalten werden,
Im Herzen Jesu ich, als meinem Element.

27. Die Tiefe, Höhe, Breite, und Länge Gottes
Durch Weisheit ist Gott tief, breit durch Barmherzigkeit,
Durch Allmacht ist er hoch, lang durch die Ewigkeit.

16. The More Abandoned, The More Divine
The saints are in such wise from God's own godhead drunk,
As they in Him are lost, as they in Him are sunk.

17. Sin
Thirst is no thing and yet it cruel can torment you:
Should then eternally sin not on evil chew?

18. Belief
Belief, great mustard seed, sends mountains to the sea:
But think what it could do, could it a pumpkin be.

19. The Abomination Of Evil
Man, could you in yourself the vermin all behold,
Then, as 'twere Satan, you would at this sight grow cold.

20. Chance And Essence
Become essential, man, for if the world should flee,
The chance will know decay, the essence constancy.

21. The Spiritual Impregnation
If maiden is your soul, like Mary undefiled,
Then it will instantly from God have got a child.

22. Take Therefore That You May Have
Man, if you God as balm, as light, and sweetness take,
What have you then when balm, light, sweetness you forsake?

23. Virtue's Goal Is God
God does for virtue goal and urge and crown afford,
He is its single cause and is its whole reward.

24. To St. Augustine
Stop, my Augustine, stop: ere you will God explain,
A little dimple will the mighty sea contain.

25. Love
Love is a twin to death; it makes my senses dead;
By it my heart is broke, my soul from hence is led.

26. Each Its Own Element
In water lives the fish, and plants live in the earth,
The bird in air, the sun within the firmament,
The salamander must in fire alone take birth,
In Jesus' heart I dwell, as in my element.

27. The Depth, Height, Breadth, And Length Of God.
Through wisdom God is deep, and broad through charity,
High through omnipotence, long through eternity.

28. Maria

Maria wird genannt ein Thron und Gotts Gezelt,
Ein Arche, Burg, Turm, Haus, ein Brunn, Baum, Garten, Spiegel,
Ein Meer, ein Stern, der Mond, die Morgenröt, ein Hügel,
Wie kann sie alles sein? sie ist ein andre Welt.

29. Seufzer zu Gott

Gott ist ein starker Strom, der hinnimmt Geist und Sinn;
Ach, dass ich noch nicht gar von ihm verschwemmet bin.

30. Die Welt ist ein Sandkorn

Wie, dass denn bei der Welt Gott nicht geschaut kann sein?
Sie kränkt das Auge stets, sie ist ein Sandkörnlein.

Wenzel Scherffer von Scherffenstein

DER MUSIC LOB

Du Zeitvertreiberin/ Freund aller Gasterey/
Du Bannerin und Zwang der tollen raserey/
Du Kummerwenderin/ Du Kind der Pierinnen/
Du Dämpferin des Zorns/ Du Labsal unser Sinnen/
Du Freudenmehrerin/ der Ohren liebste Kost/
Du Göttliches Geschenk/ des Hertzens wehrte Lust/
Du süsse Musica/ der Engel ewigs üben/
Du Gottes dienerin/ wer wollte dich nicht lieben/
Du liebens-würdigste? die Du mit deiner Kunst
bey Keiser/ Königen und Fürsten findest gunst/
ob dir woll alle nicht ihr' Huld und gnade gönnen/
so sind es doch nur Die/ die nicht emfinden können
dein' hohe liebligkeit........
Du bist von solcher art/ die aller Menschen Sinnen/
und innerstes Gemütt' erschleicht und kan gewinnen/
durch welcher krafft ein Mensch dermaassen wirdt bewegt/
dass sich auch Traurigkeit zu seinen Füssen legt.
Du kanst die böse feucht'/ als Artzeney zertreiben/
die Lebens-Geisterlein der Freuden einverleiben/
bist aller Menschen art/ wes Standes auch die seyn
sehr nützlich und beqwäm'; und setzest in gemein
der Frommen andacht zu; den Weisen du vermehrest
ihr' hohe Wissenschafft; voraus auch Du gehörest
zur Labsal denen/ welch' ein einsam leben führn;
Du kanst in Regiment: und Wirtschafften gebiern
die rechte mässigung des Menschlichen Gemüttes;
Du führst nicht wenig auch des träglichen Gebittes
in unsern schwachen Leib/ gesundheit zuvermehrn;
Dich traurige so wol als frölische verehrn.

28. Mary

A throne is Mary called, and Heaven's tent unfurled,
An ark, keep, tower, house, a spring, glass, garden, tree,
A star, the moon, a hill, the rosy dawn, the sea:
How can she be all this? She is another world.

29. Sigh To God

God is a mighty stream, who captures soul and sense;
Oh, that I have not yet by it been carried hence!

30. The World Is A Grain Of Sand

How then that in the world God cannot be discerned?
The world's a mite of sand, by which the eye is burned.

Wenzel Scherffer von Scherffenstein

PRAISE OF MUSIC

You conqueress of time, friend to festivity,
You conjuress and yoke of madness' malady,
You monitress of woe, you child Pieridine,
You mistress stern to wrath, our senses' cooling wine,
You augmentress of joy, dear banquet of the ear,
You Heaven's charity, the heart's high-treasured cheer,
Sweet music, evermore the angels' exercise,
You serving maid of God, who then would you despise,
You most benignant queen! That open with your art
The way to emperor's and king's and prince's heart.
Though some deny to you their grace and reverence,
The recreants are those, who have not soul to sense
You noble loveliness.......
You're of that order which each sense of human kind
And its most inner soul can bring to bay and bind,
And through whose might a man is moved to such extent
That vanquished at his feet lies even black lament.
You can as medicine the evil damp destroy,
And make incorporate the vital sprites of joy.
You are to every man, whatever class he be,
Most useful and most fond, and nourish commonly
The prayers of pious folk; high wisdom has increased
For wise men by your strength, nor is your part the least
Within the balm of those who lonely lives must lead.
You can for government of house or cohort breed
A proper temperance within the human breast.
You bear no little load of salutary rest
Into our failing flesh, our healthiness to raise.
You harvest merry's thanks and melancholy's praise.

David Schirmer

Er liebet

Mein liebster Freund ist wund/ mit mir hats nun Gefahr/
weil meine Marnia so plötzlich sich erwecket/
und ümb mein Hertz herümb ihr Bildnis aufgestecket.
Mein liebster Freund ist wund/ ich brenne gantz und gar.
   Wo bistu Freiheit nun/ die mein so zartes Haar
mit ihres Goldes Glantz hielt allezeit verdecket?
Wo bistu Phöbus hin? Wer hat dich so erschrecket?
Bleib hier/ verlass mich nicht/ bleib hier mit deiner Schaar.
   Apollo/ ja du bleibst auf meinem Helicon.
So kom und setze dich zu Venus kleinem Sohn/
und meiner Marnien/ die meine Feder reitzen.
   Auf! Schönste von der Welt/ dir geb ich einzig mich/
Apollo bleibt mir hold/ mein Vers steigt über sich.
Nun mag ich Eulen nicht/ ich kan mit Falcken beitzen.

David Schirmer

Uber Ihr Grab

Hier lieget Marnia begraben gar allein.
Doch auch alleine nicht/ weil Venus leichter Knabe
ihr zum Begräbnis noch den Pfeil und Bogen gabe/
den Köcher/ und was sonst stets seine Waffen seyn.
   Der Hals/ der rothe Mund/ der Augen heller Schein/
der Lippen süsse Gluth/ des Hauptes Zier und Habe/
das Purpur-braune Haar liegt auch mit ihr zu Grabe/
und ihre zarte Schos bedeckt der Leichenstein.
   Ziert/ Nymphen/ diese Gruft mit den bethauten Rosen/
bringt Amaranthen her/ und Liljen/ eure Lust/
setzt einen Mytrenstrauss auf ihre weisse Brust/
und deckt den leichten Staub mit Schönheit der Zeitlosen.
   Schont keiner Blume nicht/ des Lentzens beste Zier/
Die eine Blume war die lieget nun alhier.

David Schirmer

He Loves

   My dearest friend is struck, and I must stern beware,
Since she, my Marnia, does suddenly awaken,
Her image round my heart has guardian service taken.
My dearest friend is struck, and I am flame and flare.
   Where, freedom, have you fled, whose shine my tender hair
Once with its gold concealed and now has me forsaken?
Where, Phoebus, do you go? And with what terror shaken?
Stay here with all your troupe, nor leave me in despair.
   Apollo, you will stay upon my Helicon.
So come and sit you down by Venus' little son
And by my Marnia: they've roused my writing feather.
   Come! Fairest of the world, you are my queen alone;
My verse outdoes itself, Apollo stays my own.
Now I'm no friend of owls but hunt with hawks at tether.

David Schirmer

On Her Grave

   Here Marnia alone and in her grave-place lies.
And yet not all alone, since Venus' graceful knave
Her at the burial his bow and arrow gave,
His quiver and what else his weapons may comprise.
   The throat, the ruddy mouth, the bright shine of the eyes,
The lips' sweet glow, the head where wit and wiles were slave,
The hair of purplish-brown lie with her in her grave,
Her lap's fragility the tombstone fortifies.
   Oh nymphs, go hence and deck with dewy rose the tomb,
Go gather amaranths and lilies of your best,
Put down a myrtle bough upon her snowy breast
And hide the tender dust with saffron's fairest bloom.
   Spare not a flower of all the springtide's finest ware,
For she too was a flower who now lies covered there.

David Schirmer
An Seine Neue Buhlschafft

Sie/ meine Marnia/ kam an das todte Meer/
der Charon solte sie mit andern überführen/
du/ Schöne/ wer du bist/ rief er/ hier gilt kein zieren.
Leg deine Schönheit ab/ und denn kom wieder her.
    Sie that/ was er befahl. Was ich nicht mehr begehr/
sprach sie/ das nim nur hin. Hier liegt des Hertzens rühren/
hier liegt der Wangen Blut/ hier liegt der Pracht dupliren/
hier liegt mein gantzer Leib/ ja hier/ hier lieget er.
    Mercur der sah ihr zu/ und sprach: soll denn dein lachen/
der Mund/ der Hals/ diss Haar so gar verdorben seyn?
nein/ Edle Marnia/ nein/ Edle Nymphe/ nein/
sie sollen deinen Schatz noch oftermals anlachen.
    Drauf hub er alles auf/ und bracht es/ Nymphe/ dir.
Nun lieb ich dupelt dich von wegen dein und ihr.

Benjamin Schmolck
Gebet vor dem H. Abendmahl
Um die heilsame Würckung des Leibes und Blutes Jesu Christi

Heyland Jesu/ voller Heil/ lass mich deine Wunden küssen/
Und bey diesem Gnaden-Mahl deines Todes Krafft genüssen:
    Deinen Leib hast du gegeben zu Bezahlung meiner Schuld/
    Und dein Blut hast du vergossen zu Erwerbung Gottes Huld.
Dieses weiss und glaub ich nun/ will mich auch darauf verlassen/
Und was du mir schenckst und gibst/ suchen und zu Hertzen fassen;
    Gib mir nur/ dass ich das alles würdiglich und fruchtbarlich
    Finde/ habe und behalte/ so erquick und lab ich mich.
Lasse deinen theuren Leib meiner Seelen Hunger stillen!
Lass dein Blut als einen Tranck meines Hertzens Durst erfüllen!
    Hülle mich in deine Wunden/ gib/ dass deines Leidens Krafft
    In der letzten Todes-Stunde lauter Labsal mir verschafft.
Durch dies Opffer mache mich rein von allen meinen Sünden/
Durch die Artzney lasse mich geistliche Gesundheit finden;
    Gib/ dass dieses Brod des Lebens Stärck und Nahrung bey mir hat;
    Und durch dieses süsse Manna mache meine Seele satt.
Dieses Labsal müsse mich durch und durch mit Lust erquicken/
Und diss theure Heiligthum meines Hertzens Tempel schmücken.
    Zünde durch diss Gnaden-Zeichen lauter Eifer in mir an;
    Hilff/ dass dis Erlösungs-Mittel mich zum Himmel bringen kan.

David Schirmer

To His New Paramour

My Marnia did come unto the dead sea's tide,
Where she with others should try Charon's navigation.
"Whoe'er you, beauty, be, here helps no affectation;
Come this way once again, with beauty put aside."
　She did as she was told: "What is no more my pride,"
She said, "That take away. My heart's wild palpitation,
The roses of my cheeks, my splendor's duplication
Lie here, and even here does all my flesh abide."
　Her Mercury beheld and said: "Shall then your smile,
Your mouth, your throat, your hair all to their ruin go?
No, noble Marnia, no, noble dryad, no!
Again and often they shall on your lover smile."
　Then he her parts did find and brought them, nymph, to you,
To whom for Marnia's sake and yours I'm doubly true.

Benjamin Schmolck

Prayer Before Holy Communion
For the Healing Influence of the Body and the Blood of Jesus Christ

Savior Jesus, You Who save, let my lips Your wounds embrace,
And the power of Your death savour at this meal of grace.
　You have yielded up Your flesh in a payment of my debt,
　And have cast away Your blood that I might God's favor get.
This I know, this I believe, on this thing I will depend,
And will seek and take to heart what to me you give or send.
　Grant me but that all these things worthily and fruitfully
　I shall find and have and keep: thus I'll bathe and freshen me.
Let Your precious body now make my spirit's hunger still!
Let Your blood as beverage this my thirst of heart fulfill!
　Hide me deep within Your wounds. Grant me, that Your passion's
　　　　　　　　　　　　　　　　　　　　　　　　　might
In death's final moment will give to me sheer balm's delight.
Through this sacrifice make me purified of every sin,
Let me health of spirit find through this spirit-medicine.
　Grant me that this bread of life bring me strength and nourishment,
　And that this sweet manna-food will my spirit make content.
Let this balsam through and through bring to me joy's freshening,
Deck the tempel of my heart with this dear and holy thing.
　Through this marking-badge of grace light in me that purest zeal:
　Aid, that this redemption-means Heaven will to me reveal.

Johann Matthias Schneuber

MORGENGESANG

Jetzund hebt es an zu tagen
Die taunasse Morgenröt,
Welche vor der Sonn hergeht
Eilt mit ihrem Purpurwagen
Und macht dem den Weg bereit,
Der die Welt mit Licht bekleidt.

Durch das lieblich Vögelsingen
Ist die stille Ruh der Nacht
Aufgelöset und erwacht,
Berg und Tal und Wäld' erklingen
Auch steht jetzt der Himmel leer,
Man sieht nicht viel Sternen mehr.

Allbereit hab ich erblicket,
Wie das gülden Aug der Welt
Tausend Strahlen auf das Feld
Über das Gebirg herschicket
Und vertreibet ganz und gar
Was zu Nacht stockfinster war.

Jesu, du mein Trost und Leben,
Sonne der Gerechtigkeit,
Ich bin auch voll Dunkelheit,
Will mich aber dir ergeben:
Ach! zünd in mir an dein Licht,
Mach, was finster ist, zunicht.

Johann Georg Schoch

ER BRENNT

Ich bin der Aetna-Berg/ Enceladus sein Schrein/
Der in Sicilien fürdessen war zufinden/
Er fängt an allgemach in mir sich zu entzünden/
Und sprudelt tausend Weh durch den zerknirschten Stein/
    Die Augen wollen mir geflammte Funcken seyn.
Der ungesunde Dampff schlägt durch mit Seufftzer-Winden.
Ich spreng mich selbsten offt aus meinen tieffsten Gründen/
Und schling mich wiederumb selbst in mich selbsten ein.

Johann Matthias Schneuber

MORNING SONG

Presently there starts its reign,
Wet with dew, the rosy dawn,
Which before the sun has gone,
Galloping with crimson wain,
And for him the way prepares
Who this planet's light-dress bears.

By the bird-song's lovely sound
Is the darkness' still repose
Brought to waking and to close:
Peak and dale and woods resound.
Now the heavens too are bare,
And we see small starlight there.

I already did descry
How a thousand beams were sent
Cross the mountains, earthward bent,
From creation's golden eye:
These have driven all away
What pitch-black in darkness lay.

Jesus, You my life and aid,
Sun of very righteousness:
I too walk in darkness' dress,
Yet I would Your slave be made:
Oh, light then Your light in me,
Let what's black no longer be.

Johann Georg Schoch

HE BURNS

Enceladus's [80] vault I am and Etna's throne,
Which peak in ancient times did lie in Sicily:
In me it slowly starts to set its flaming free,
And spits a thousand woes out through the shattered stone.
   To sparklets hot with flame my very eyes have grown,
With sighing winds the steam sets loose its villainy;
I burst myself from out the deepest vaults of me,
And let myself once more into myself be blown.

Mein ausgebrandtes Hertz bleibt wol die Feuer-Schmiede/
In welcher Mulciber erhitzte Gluten blösst/
Es wird zu Tag und Nacht in hämmern nimmer müde/
　Weil stündlich eine Glut die ander' abelösst.
Ihr Hertz ist zwar der Stahl/ so täglich wird getrieben;
Doch klag' ich/ dass an Ihm die Härte stetz geblieben.

Justus Georg Schottel

Donnerlied

　Schwefel, Wasser, Feur und Dampf
wollen halten einen Kampf.
Dicker Nebel dringt gedickt,
Licht und Luft ist fast erstickt.

　Drauf die starken Winde bald
sausen, brausen mit Gewalt,
reissen, werfen: Wirbelduft,
Mengen Wasser, Erde, Luft.

　Plötzlich blickt der Blitz herein,
macht das Finstre feurig sein;
Schwefelklumpen, Strahlenlicht,
Rauch und Dampf herein mit bricht.

　Drauf der Donner brummt und kracht,
rasselt, rollet hin mit Macht,
prallet, knallet grausamlich,
puffet, summsend endigt sich.

　Bald das Blitzen wieder kommt
und der Donner rollend brummt.
Bald hereilt ein Windesbraus
und dem Wetter macht Garaus.

My fire-dark heart will sure that fiery smithy stay
In which old Mulciber [81] his heated fires lays bare,
It of its hammering tires not by night or day,
   Since every hour one flame relieves the other there.
Her heart indeed is steel which every day is drawn,
And yet its durity (I weep) holds steady on.

Justus Georg Schottel

Thunder Song

   Sulphur, water, fire, and reek
Will a savage battle seek.
Thick mist thick will penetrate,
Light and air near suffocate.

   Thereupon the strong winds soon
Whirl and swirl their mighty tune,
Tumbling odors pull and tear,
Spates of water, earth, and air.

   Sudden lightning glances in,
Sets aflame the gloomy din,
Balls of sulphur, bolts of day,
Smoke and vapor join the fray.

   Then does thunder growl and smite,
Rage and roll with all its might,
Smack and crack in horrid blend,
Puff, and humming come to end.

   Now the lightning comes once more,
Now does thunder roll and roar,
Now flies hence a boisterous breeze
And the storm brings to its cease.

Ernst Schwabe von der Heyde

SONNET

Ihr die ihr höret an/ wie mancher Sturmwind wehet/
   Durch seufftzen ohne zahl in meinen Reimelein/
   Und einen weiten Bach darin/ voll Threnelein/
   Und ein verletztes Hertz voll tausent Wunden sehet.
Erlernet wohl hierauss/ wass man in lieb' ausstehet/
   Darin die junge Zeit mich liess ergeben sein/
   Alss ich für wahre lust hielt' einen falschen schein/
   Darüber mich jetzund hertzliche rew' umbfähet:
Und fliehet solche brunst und jhre süsse Gifft/
   Der eiteln schönheit glantz/ die uns das Hertz schnell trifft/
   Und angst und schmertzen vol witzloss herummer leitet.
Ohn tugend ist schönheit nur ein triegliches Kleid/
   Wer solcher dienstbahr ist/ dem lohnet rew' und leidt:
   Auss tugent wahre lust allein wird zubereitet.

Sibylla Schwarz

SONETT

   Ist Lieben keusch? wo kompt denn Ehbruch her?
Ist Lieben guht/ nichts böses drinn zu finden/
Wie kan sein Feur dan so gahr viel entzünden?
Ist Lieben Lust/ wer bringt dan das Beschwär?
   Wer Lieben liebt/ fährt auff der Wollust Meer/
Und lässet sich ins Todes Netze binden/
Das nicht zerreist/ er lebet nuhr den Sünden/
Liebt Eitelkeit/ und ist der Tugend leer.
   Das ewig lebt/ dem stirbt er gäntzlich ab/
Sieht seine Noht erst/ wan er siht sein Grab.
   Wer dan nuhn wird in Liebes Brunst gefunden/
Der fliehe bald/ und hasse/ die er liebt;
Ist Lieb ihm süss? so werd er drümb betrübt;
Ist sie sein Brodt? so geb er sie den Hunden.

Ernst Schwabe von der Heyde

Sonnet

Oh you who think to hear how many a tempest sounds
   In these my tiny rhymes, devised of countless sighs,
   And see in them a brook, all swoll'n with weeping, rise,
   And see an injured heart which bears a thousand wounds:
Learn from this poem then how lovers love confounds,
   That love to which late time surrendered me as prize,
   When fickle pretence seemed true pleasure to my eyes,
   That love on whose account rue now my heart surrounds.
Oh hasten from such lust and from its poison sweet,
   From idle beauty's shine, which quick our heart does meet
   And it all witlessly in pain and fear ensnares!
For beauty, virtueless, is fraud's poor masquerade:
   Who in such service stands, with pain and rue is paid.
   For virtue's might alone true happiness prepares.

Sibylla Schwarz

Sonnet

    If love is chaste, what bears adultery?
If love is good, and does no evil own,
How can its fire so many flames propone?
If love is joy, why's it called cruelty?
    Who love adores, sails on a lustful sea,
And lets himself into death's net be sewn,
Which does not tear; he lives for sin alone,
Is stripped of virtue, worships vanity.
    For life eternal totally he dies,
And sees his grief but when his grave he spies.
    Whoever has been found in loving's fit,
Let him hate love and flee it in all haste.
Does love taste sweet? Let him despise its taste.
Is love his bread? Let him feed dogs with it.

Sibylla Schwarz

Sonett

Itzt wil ich in den Wald/ und mit Dianen jagen!
Ich lieb'/ und dass ich lieb'/ gefällt mir selber nicht;
Dan Lieb' ist solch ein Tuhn/ das alles guhte bricht/
Mein Elend ist zu gross; Ich muss mich damit plagen/
    Dass mein Gewissen krenckt/ und stets Verlangen tragen
Nach dem/ das mir nicht wird: die böse Liebes Gicht/
Die grimme Tobessucht/ hat mich so zugericht/
Dass ich nicht ich mehr bin; Itzt will ich ihr entsagen/
    So viel ich immer kan/ dan ungegründte Trew
Läst nimmer friedsam seyn/ und bringt zu späte Rew;
    Sie ist ein fressend Fewr/ und frisst sich nimmer satt/
Ist blind/ ist Wind/ und brent/ ist ein Verderb der Jugend/
Sie ist ein guhtes Bös' und lasterhaffte Tugend;
Doch sey sie/ wie sie wol/ mich macht sie faul und matt.

Sibylla Schwarz

Sonett

    Man sagt/ es sey kein Ort/ da Amor nicht zu finden/
Es sey kein öder Wald/ es sey kein Teil der Welt/
Da dieser grosse Fürst nicht seine Hoffstadt helt;
Man sagt/ es sey kein Man/ den er nicht könne binden:
    Noch hat er meinen Muht nicht können überwinden/
Weil mir sein schnödes Thun zu keiner zeit gefält;
Ob er schon noch so weit ihm bawet sein Gezelt/
Dass in Arabia man ihn auch stets kan finden.
    Europa ist zwahr sein/ er sitzt in Africa/
Er wohnt in Asia/ und kent America.
    In summ/ es ist kein Haus/ das er nicht innen hatt/
Es ist kein Menschlich Hertz/ das er nicht könte lencken/
Mich doch/ ob er schon nah mir ist/ kan er nicht krencken/
dan ist er auff dem Dorff/ so bin ich in der Stadt.

Sibylla Schwarz

SONNET

I will into the woods and hunt with Diane there!
I love and that I love does not find my consent:
For loving is a deed by which all good is bent;
My woe has grown too great, and I must know the care
    Of conscience injured, yet eternal yearning bear
For that I cannot have: the evil gout, love-sent,
The cruel pox of rage have so my spirit rent
That I am no more I; now love I shall forswear
    However much I can, for faith unbounded lets
No man know peacefulness, and tardy brings regrets.
    Love is a glutton-fire, and never eats its fill,
Is blind, is wind, and burns, makes youth ruin's sacrifice;
Love is good evilness, and virtue filled with vice:
Let love be what it would: it turns me slow and ill.

Sibylla Schwarz

SONNET

    Men say there is no place where Amour can't be found,
There is no part of earth, there is no desert wood,
To which this mighty prince has not held neighborhood.
They say no man exists who can't by him be bound,
    But yet he has no strength, my power to surround:
Since I his evil ways have ne'er considered good,
Though in such distant lands his canopy has stood
That in Arabia he always can be found.
    All Europe's surely his; he reigns in Africa,
He dwells in Asia and knows America.
    In short, there is no house which Amour does not own,
There is no human heart which he cannot command;
Yet me he does not harm, though he invade my land,
For if he's in the thorp, then I am in the town.

Jakob Schwieger

Sie ist sein Pol

Du bist mein lichter Pol, der mich zur Liebe führet,
Ach Adelmut mein Kind! du leitest mich allein
Zu deiner Schönheit Port; du bist es, die mich zieret,
Du bist es auch, du, du, die mir bringt Angst und Pein.
Mein Pohl bistu und willt mir doch nicht weiter dienen,
Nachdem du mich gebracht am Hafen deiner Zier
Da ich vor Anker lieg. Warüm bistu erschienen
Mein Nordstern, wenn du nicht willt ferner helfen mir.

Andreas Scultetus

Blutschwitzender und todesringender Jesus

Der Sternen Oberhaupt und schnelle Zeitenhalter
War längst vorbey gerückt; sein voller Amtsverwalter,
Des Monden Silber, gab dem Schatten seine Macht,
Und zierte die Gestalt der abgrundschwarzen Nacht
Mit Lichtfiguren aus: wie unser Seligmacher,
Der gegen Höll und Tod geschworne Widersacher
Den Kidron überschritt. Der klargekreisste Bach
Krystallte bis in Grund; das blaugewölbte Dach
Hatt', um den Höchsten recht in Augenschein zu fassen,
Mit allen Bildern sich in diesen Quell gelassen,
Und liess, o Heiland, dich in Gleichnissweise fast,
Wie du dich Himmel ab zu uns gesenket hast,
Durch dieses Werk verstehn. Du bliebst im Uebergehen,
Mein Jesus, eine Zeit, bey diesem Wasser stehen,
Erwugest, wie alldar der gleichgehaufte Sand
Jemehr unwandelbar am Boden sich befand,
Jemehr von obenher die Wellen sich bewegten,
Und auf den Grund hinzu die Wogen überlegten.
So wankt mein Todesschluss im allermindsten nicht,
Wie heftig Fleisch und Blut demselben widerspricht:
Gedachtest du, mein Herr, und giengest fort mit Beten
Vor Gottes Gnadenthron und Richterstuhl zu treten.
Wie folget aber ihr in solches Ungemach,
Das euren Meister drängt, so überdrüssig nach,
O hochgeliebten Drey? Wie dass ihr euch verweilet?
Nehmt wahr, wie euer Fürst ohn alles Halten eilet.

Jakob Schwieger

SHE IS HIS POLE

You are my shining pole, which love-ward pilots me,
Oh Adelmut, my child! For you alone can guide
Me to your beauty's port: you lead me winsomely,
And yet you torture bring and terror to my side.
My pole you are, and yet no more will serve me here,
Since you my ship have brought to your sweet harbor's bar,
Where I at anchor lie. Why did you then appear,
If you no further aid would give, my northern star?

Andreas Scultetus

JESUS, SWEATING BLOOD AND WRESTLING WITH DEATH

The chieftain of the stars and time's quick fugleman
Had long ago passed by; his full custodian,
The silver of the moon, gave to the shade its might,
And blazoned out the form of chasm-colored night
With figures of its shine: then He Who makes us blest,
The Foeman Who has sworn both death and hell to best,
Passed over Kidron's brook. The limpid-eddied stream
Was crystal to its floor; the blue-arched roof did seem
(So that it could our Lord into its vision bring)
With all its images to plunge into this spring,
And made You, Savior, then, almost in symbol's wise,
See how You had to us descended from the skies,
By means of this, its fall. In crossing, You did bide,
My Jesus, for a while along the water's side,
And thought "how in this place the even-layered sand
The more immovable did lie upon the land,
The more there stirred above the wavelets of the brook
And down into the floor their frantic passage took.
Thus nothing can disturb My firm resolve to die,
Though storms of flesh and blood do fierce My will belie."
You pondered there, my Lord, and left the place with prayer
To go before God's throne of grace and judgment-chair.
But yet, why do you go into that misery,
Which does your Lord beset, so hesitatingly,
Oh much-beloved trine? [82] Why do you seek repose?
Behold, how without pause your Master hasty goes.

Bis an den Himmel hat der Thabor euch entzückt,
Jetzt aber haltet ihr die Augen zugedrückt.
Ist, Peter, auch allhier gut Hütten aufzubauen?
Wir würden nimmermehr das Himmelreich beschauen,
Wie dein zur Zeit noch nicht erlauchter Sinn gedacht,
Hätt unser Heiland sich nicht auf den Weg gemacht,
Für uns genung zu thun. Wie hebt er an zu zagen,
Weil alle Missethat der Welt auf ihn geschlagen,
Bleycentnerwichtig hangt? Indem ihr stehen bleibt,
O Jünger, und für Schlaf die Augenbremen reibt,
Ist allbereit der Herr von euch hinweg gegangen,
Das Leiden mit der Angst des Todes anzufangen.
Sein Garteneintritt macht den Adamiten Raum,
Ins Paradies zu gehn. Er henkt in Lebensbaum
Durch seinen Blutschweiss auf, was Eva weggerissen
Und, in der bösen Lust verteufelt, angebissen.
Steig, mein Erlöser, steig den Oelberg immer an;
Ich folge dennoch dir, wie lang ich folgen kann,
Mit Sinnen emsig nach, die aber vor Erschrecken
In Schlafsucht eben auch, wie deine Jünger, stecken.
                                                (11.1.-46)

Justus Sieber

AN SEIN VATERLAND/
WELCHES ER IN SIEBENZEHN JAHREN
NICHT BESUCHEN KÖNNEN

Verzeih' es deinem Sohn/ du liebes Vaterland/
Dass er so lange dier hat keinen Kuss gegeben.
Es heist ihn Gott und Glück von dier entfernet leben/
Seit dass der Donner-Mars dich traff mit Feur und Brand.
Wie freudig würd' er dier sonst biethen Hertz und Hand/
Und seinen Fuss mit Lust in dein Gefild' erheben/
Wo vormahls Ceres pflag in Frölichkeit zu schweben/
Wenn sie gab ihre Frucht/ der Erden Liebes-Pfand.
Wollan! was er nicht thut/ das thun doch die Gedancken.
Die Lieb' in ihm zu dier kan und wird nimmer wancken.
Er giebt/ O Vaterland/ sich gantz zu eigen dier.
Gebrauche deinen Sohn/ und liebe deinen Treuen.
Du kennst ihn zwar nicht recht/ doch soll dichs nicht gereuen/
Weil ihn die Fremden auch ziehn ihren Kindern für!

Mount Tabor [83] lifted you in joy 'midst Heaven's kind,
But presently you hold your vision locked and blind.
Should, Peter, you lay here your tabernacle's floor?
The realm of Heaven we would visit nevermore
(As it did to your soul, still swathed in night, appear),
Had not our Savior set Himself to this career
Of wiping out our debt. How may He hesitate,
Since all the world's misdeeds hang like a hundredweight
On Him, and press Him down? While you your station keep,
Oh followers, and rub your eyelids dulled with sleep,
The Lord already has from you his parting made
To start His passion with the terror of death's blade.
His garden-entrance will the sons of Adam set
A way to Paradise, He will by bloody sweat
Hang in life's tree again what Eve of old did seize
And bite, by devils drawn her evil lust to please.
Make, my Redeemer, make the Olive-Mount's ascent,
And I shall follow you until my strength is spent,
With eager senses which do yet from sheer dismay
In wild desire for sleep, like You disciples, stay.

Justus Sieber

To His Fatherland
Which He Could Not Visit
for Seventeen Years

Forgive, forgive your son, beloved fatherland,
That he these many years has kept you from his kiss.
Both God and fortune did him far from you dismiss,
When Mars in thunder struck you down with flame and brand.
Else he would joyfully give you his heart and hand,
And take across your fields his sweet anabasis,
Where Ceres once was wont to hover in her bliss
And parcel out her fruits, love's pledge to earth's demand.
Well then! What he does not, that thing his thoughts will do.
His love ne'er can nor will turn fickle-heart from you.
He gives, oh fatherland, himself to you alone:
Love well your faithful son, use his accomplishment;
You know him not, yet you will not your choice repent,
Since foreigners would call him child and slight their own.

Johann Wilhelm Simler

SONETT/ ODER TRAURIGER TODTENKLANG/ ÜBER/
HERRN LANDS-HAUBTMANN MEINRAD BUOLEN
IHME SELIGES; DEM VATTERLAND /
HÖCHSCHÄDLICHES ABLEIBEN

Ach! armes Vatterland! des Vatters nun beraubet
   Durch den/ der allem fleisch versaget Audientz/
   Bey welchem weder Bitt/ noch Goldgeleiches Gläntz/
Noch auch die Tugend gilt; dieweil er keinem glaubet/
Und ihm der Schöpffer selb das Würgen hat erlaubet:
   Es mag ein König seyn/ in einem Purpur-Rok/
   Ein Bättler an der Strass/ auf halb verfaultem Stok/
Ein weiser oder thor/ er frissts unaussgeklaubet/
   Doch nur das Sterbliche/ Herrn Buolen Seele lebt/
   Und /selig/ Gottes Lob im Himmel hoch erhebt/
Erwartend auch des Leibs. Die Ehrgedächtnuss bleibet/
   Sein weltbekanntes Lob verschwindet nimmermehr/
   Wo seiner wird gedacht/ beschihets nur in ehr/
So/ dass der Ewigkeit sein Namm bleibt eynverleibet.

Friedrich Spee

DIE GESPONSS JESU KLAGET IHREN HERTZENBRAND

   Gleich früh wan sich entzündet
     Der silber weisse tag;
   Und uns die Sonn verkündet/
     Wass nachts verborgen lag:
   Die lieb in meinem hertzen
     Ein flämlein stecket an;
   Dass brint gleich einer kertzen
     So niemand leschen kan.

   Wan schon Ichs schlag in Winde/
     Gen Ost- und Norden brauss;
   Doch ruh/ noch rast ich finde/
     Last nie sich blasen auss.
   O wee der qual/ der peine!
     Wo soll mich wenden hin?
   Den gantzen tag ich weine/
     Weil stäts in schmertzen bin.

Johann Wilhelm Simler

SONNET, OR SAD SOUND OF DEATH, CONCERNING
GOVERNOR SIR MEINRAD BUOL'S [84] DEPARTURE
FROM THE FLESH, BLESSED FOR HIMSELF,
HIGHLY DAMAGING TO THE FATHERLAND

Oh wretched Fatherland! Of father now bereaved
  By death, who to all flesh denies an audience,
  Against whom neither plea nor gold does give defence,
Nor even virtuousness; since he no man's believed
And 'neath the Maker's hand his murderous task achieved.
  A monarch, it may be, wrapped in his purple dress,
  A beggar on the street, whose staff's half rotteness,
Wise man or fool: of all death has his feast conceived,
  Yet eats but mortal food: Sir Buol's spirit lives,
  And, blessed, praise of God the lofty Heavens gives,
Awaiting too his flesh. His honored fame remains,
  His world-wide eulogy will vanish nevermore,
  And when thoughts turn to him, they have but praise in store,
So that eternity his endless name contains.

Friedrich Spee

THE SPOUSE OF JESUS LAMENTS HER HEART'S FLAME

    All early, when the day
      In silver-white's revealed,
    And us the sun can say
      What nighttime had concealed:
    Love has within my heart
      A little flamelet lit;
    It takes a candle's part
      And none can smother it.

    Though I the flame bore 'round
      'Gainst East- and Northwind's shout,
    Nor rest nor respite found,
      No wind has blown it out.
    Let woe these worries cry!
      Now whither shall I turn?
    I always weep since I
      Fore'er in torments burn.

Wann wider dann entflogen
  Der Tag zur Nacht hinein/
Und sich gar tieff gebogen
  Die Sonn/ und Sonnenschein;
Dass Flämlein so mich queelet
  Noch bleibt in voller glut;
All stundt/ so viel man zehlet/
  Michs je noch brennen thut.

Dass Flämlein dass ich meine/
  Ist JESU süsser nam;
Ess zehret Marck und Beine/
  Frisst ein gar wundersam.
O süssigkeit in schmertzen!
  O schmertz in süssigkeit!
Ach bleibe doch im Hertzen/
  Bleib doch in Ewigkeit.

Ob schon in pein/ und qualen
  Mein Leben schwindet hinn/
Wann JESU Pfeil und Stralen
  Durchstreichet Muth und Sinn;
Doch nie so gar mich zehret
  Die Liebe JESU mein/
Alss gleich sie wider nehret/
  Und schenckt auch frewden ein.

O Flämlein süss ohn massen!
  O bitter auch ohn ziel!
Du machest mich verlassen
  All ander Frewd/ und Spiel;
Du zündest mein gemüthe/
  Bringst mir gross Hertzen leidt/
Du kühlest mein Geblüthe/
  Bringst auch ergetzligkeit.

Ade zu tausent Jahren/
  O Welt zu guter nacht:
Ade lass mich nun fahren/
  Ich längst hab dich veracht.
In JESU lieb Ich lebe/
  Sag dir von Hertzen grund:
In lauter Frewd Ich schwebe/
  Wie sehr ich bin verwund.

When once again has fled
   The day down night's decline,
And sleepwards bend their head
   Both sun and sunlight's shine:
The gnawing flamelet stays
   In me at fullest force,
Ignores the hour's swift ways,
   And burns me in its course.

The flame of which I think
   Is Jesus Christ's sweet name
And bone and marrow sink
   All strangely in its flame.
Oh loving born of pain!
   Oh pain born lovingly!
Oh in my heart remain
   For all eternity!

Although in wrack and rue
   My life does swiftly go,
When Jesus wanders through
   My heart with bolt and bow:
Yet love does never eat
   My soul to such degree,
Unless she gives me meat,
   And pours out joy for me.

Sweet fire from endless founts!
   Oh boundless bitter flame!
You cause me to renounce
   Each other joy and game!
You set my soul afire
   And bring me heart-born woes,
You cool my blood's desire
   And bring me glad repose.

A thousand years' good-night,
   Oh world, is my farewell:
Now free me from your sight,
   I long have scorned your spell.
In Jesus' love I lie,
   From heart's vault tell the news:
In sheerest joy I fly
   Despite my cruel abuse.

Friedrich Spee

ANDERS LOB AUSS DEN WERCKEN GOTTES

Ein liedlein süss wolt stimmen an/
  Ihr wolgespante seiten/
Ihr Lauten/ Geigen/ Dulcian/
  Ihr Cymbel/ harpff/ und fleuten/
Posaun/ Cornet/ Trompeten klar/
  Auch hörner krum gebogen/
Gott loben sollet jhr fürwar
  Sagt an wass euch will frogen.

Wer hat in gold- und silber-stück/
  Die Sonn/ und Mon gekleidet?
Wer hats gemacht so schnell/ und flück/
  Dass nie kein pfeil erleidet?
Wer hat die sternen zündet an?
  Wer hats gezehlt mit namen?
Wer hats mit wesen angethan!
  Da sie von nichten kamen?

Wer läret auss den vollen Mon?
  Wer schleiffet ihm die spitzen?
Wer heisst die flüss von felsen gahn?
  Wer macht die brünlein spritzen?
Wer wicklet hoch in wolcken ein/
  Die spitz der wilden bergen?
Wer thut den lieben Sonnenschein/
  Mit schwartzer nacht verhergen.

Wer färbet uns die morgenröth/
  Mit purpur zart gerieben?
Wer thut/ wass uns die nacht getödt/
  Ans liecht bald wider schieben?
Wer heisst von wolcken springen ab
  Die blitz in eyl entflogen?
Wer zuckt die wind in vollem trab?
  Wer spannt den regen-bogen?

Wer wirfft auss beyden händen voll
  Reiff/ hagel rund gefroren?
Wer spinnet uns die winter-woll/
  Den schnee so rein geschoren?

Friedrich Spee

ANOTHER PANEGYRIC FROM THE WORKS OF GOD

    A measure sweet you will begin,
        You strings in fair dispute,
    You dulcian, lute, and violin,
        You cymbal, harp, and flute,
    Trombone, cornet, and trumpet clear,
        And horns bent in a bow,
    God shall indeed your praises hear.
        Speak out, what you would know.

    Who has in silver and in gold
        The moon and sun adorned?
    Who's made them swift of wing, so bold
        That they the bolt have scorned?
    Who set the starry hosts afire?
        Who has their titles taught?
    Who did them with a self inspire,
        When they emerged from naught?

    Who empties out the swollen moon?
        Who grinds away its tips?
    Who has the rocks for rivers hewn?
        Who parts the fountains' lips?
    Who wraps around with lofty clouds
        The savage mountain tops?
    Who with the ebon evening's shrouds
        The treasured sunlight stops?

    Who paints for us the rosy dawn
        With purple, tender made?
    Who has into the morning drawn
        The victim of the shade?
    Who bids from off the cloudy tier
        The hasty lightning spring?
    Who halts the winds in full career?
        Who can the rainbow bring?

    Who portions out from fingers full
        Round hail and hoarfrost's sheen?
    Who spins for us the winter-wool,
        The snow, all clipped and clean?

Wer zäumet auff mit eyss und kält
   Die stoltze wasser-wogen?
Wer ist ders meer in züchten hält/
   Wans komt in grimm gezogen?

Wer gibt der erden lebens krafft
   Dass nie von alter sterbe?
Wer träncket sie mit wolcken safft/
   Dass nie von hitz verderbe?
Wer nehret wild/ und zahmes vieh?
   Wer sorget jhn die speisen?
Dass endlich doch noch manglet nie/
   Wie deutlich steht zu weisen?

Allein/ allein ist unser Gott/
   Der thaten gross verrichtet:
So bald nur schallet sein gebott;
   All streit ist schon geschlichtet.
Da lauffens ihm in eyl zuhand
   Geschöpff nach seinen sinnen;
Voll seiner krafft wird alles land/
   Viel wunder da beginnen.

Sein will/ und werck im selben schritt/
   Im selben glid passiren/
Kein härlein eins vors ander tritt/
   Mag ihm ja nichts falliren.
Wass er dan wil/ thut er behendt
   In gleichem punct verrichten:
Was er auch wil/ thut unverwendt
   In gleichem punct zernichten.

Drumb nur zu loben fanget an
   Ihr wolgespante seiten/
Ihr lauten/ geigen/ dulcian/
   Ihr cymbel/ harpff/ und fleuten/
Posaun/ cornet/ trompeten klar/
   Auch hörner krum gebogen/
Gott loben sollet jhr fürwar/
   Wass wil man weiters frogen?

Who bridles with the ice and cold
    The billows in their pride?
Who can the sea to order hold,
    When it in rage does ride?

Who has the earth with life endowed,
    That it ne'er die of age?
Who nurses it with milk of cloud,
    That ne'er it know heat's rage?
Who feeds the tame- and wild-heart beast?
    Who gives to them their food,
That ne'er unto this day has ceased
    Our patent plenitude?

It is Our Lord, alone, alone,
    Who does these deeds perform;
If but the trumps His word make known,
    Peace follows on the storm.
Then hasty run toward His hand
    The creatures of His mind,
Full of His might will every land
    Rich birth of marvels find.

His will and work in equal pace,
    In equal rank pass by;
No hair may take the other's place,
    And naught may go awry.
What then He will, He with sure speed
    That self-same moment makes;
And if He will, His every deed
    That self-same moment slakes.

Thus with your praises now begin,
    You springs in fair dispute,
You dulcian, lute, and violin,
    You cymbal, harp, and flute.
Trombone, cornet, and trumpet clear,
    And horns bent in a bow;
God shall indeed your praises hear:
    What further would you know?

Josua Stegmann

SEI wohlgemut, lass trauren sein,
Auf Regen folget Sonnenschein.
Es gibt doch endlich noch das Glück
Nach Toben einen guten Blick.

Wenn hat der rauhe Winter sich
An uns erzeiget zorniglich,
Bald wieder die Sonn höher steigt,
Und alles fröhlich sich erzeigt.

Favonius, der zarte Wind,
Auf harten Frost sich wieder findt;
Das Eis muss alsdenn ganz zergehn,
Und kann der Schnee nicht mehr bestehn.

Die Vöglein, so sich in die Bäum
Verkrochen hatten in geheim,
Sich wieder in die Lüfte schwingen,
Und ihrm Schöpfr ein Liedlein singen.

So stell da auch dein Trauren ein,
Mein Herz, und lass dein Zagen sein;
Vertraue Gott und glaube fest,
Dass er die Seinen nicht verlässt.

Caspar Stieler

Der Hass küsset ja nicht

1

Die ernstliche Strenge steht endlich versüsset,
  die qweelende Seele wird einsten gesund.
Ich habe gewonnen, ich werde geküsset,
  es schallet und knallet ihr zärtlicher Mund.
    Die Dornen entweichen,
    die Lippen verbleichen,
indehm sie die ihren den meinen auffdrükkt.
Ich werd' auss der Erde zun Göttern verschikkt.

Josua Stegmann

Be happy, put your grief aside,
For sunbeams after rain do ride,
And fortune surely will at last
Give pleasure when the storm is past.

If savage winter-time has shown
To us what anger it does own,
Soon will the sun ascendant go,
Each thing in merriment to show.

Favonius,[85] the tender breeze
Once more does steely frosts displease;
The ice must hasten all away,
The snow no more can keep its sway.

The little birds that in the tree
Themselves had hidden secretly
Again into the heavens swing,
Their Maker there a song to sing.

See that you stem lamenting's tide,
My heart, and put your fear aside;
Trust God, and with the faith be girt
That he will ne'er His folk desert.

Caspar Stieler

Hatred Surely Does Not Kiss

1

At last earnest sternness is transformed to sweet,
   The pain-spitted spirit must some day turn sound.
Now I have my triumph, I kisses do meet,
   Her delicate mouth does re-echo, resound:
      Her thorns, they do fail,
      Her lips, they grow pale,
In that she her lips' fit on mine does essay,
I'm sent to the gods from this planet away.

2

Ihr klagende Plagen steht jetzo von fernen,
   es fliehe der ächzende krächzende Neid!
Mein Gang ist gegründet auch über die Sternen,
   ich fühle der Seeligen spielende Freud'.
      Es flammen die Lippen.
      Die rösslichte Klippen
die blühen und ziehen mich lieblich an sich.
Was acht' ich dich Honig! was Nektar-wein dich.

3

Durch dieses erwiess es ihr süsses Gemühte,
   sie wolle, sie solle die Meinige sein.
Nu höhn' ich der Könige Zepter und Blüte,
   mich nimmet der Vorraht Eufrates nicht ein.
      Kan ich sie nur haben:
      was acht' ich der Gaben
der siegenden Krieger im Kapitolin,
die durch die bekränzeten Pforten einziehn!

4

Ich habe die Schöne mit nichten gewonnen
   mit Solde von Golde, mit Perlenem Wehrt,
und scheinenden Steinen in Bergen geronnen,
   den Tyrischen Purpur hat sie nie begehrt.
      Die Zeilen, die süssen
      aus Pegasus Flüssen
die haben ihr härtliches Hertze gerührt:
Nu stehet mein Lorber mit Myrten geziert.

Caspar Stieler

Vergisst mich Sie nur nicht

1

Was frag' ich nach den Trauer-fahnen,
was nach den Wapen vieler Ahnen,
   und ob mich denn ein Marmor ziert:
Wenn einsten zu den blassen Schaaren
mein Geist ist übern Fluss gefahren,
   wor uns der Ehre Sucht nicht rührt.

2

You plagues with your nagging must presently fly,
  Let envy's moans, groaning, to exile be pressed.
My coursing ascends o'er the stars of the sky,
  I feel now the dallying joy of the blest.
    Her lips' flaming coals,
    Those rosy-hued shoals,
  They bloom and their blooming does fair me entwine:
  What care I for honey, for you, nectar-wine!

3

Her sweet mood did prove I had wooed me her bond,
  She would be, she should be my mistress alone,
I mock at the monarchs, their glory and wand.
  I would not Euphrates' reserves make my own.
    If I her but hold,
    What care I for gold
  Of conquering troops on the Capitol's height,
  Who march through the wreath-covered arches their might.

4

Nor did I with prizes her loveliness win:
  Gold's weight in full holding, pearl's worth in full fire,
Nor glittering jewels, to mountains poured in;
  The Tyrian purple she ne'er did desire.
    The sweet lines that course
    From Pegasus' source,
  These lines have her heart in its hardness suborned:
  My laurel stands now with the myrtle adorned.

Caspar Stieler

IF SHE DOES BUT NOT FORGET ME

1

What do I for black banners care
Or what my fathers' scutcheons bear,
  Or whether marble me adorns,
When someday to death's pallid team
My soul is brought across the stream
  Where man at last ambition scorns.

2

Es mag mich wer da will beklagen,
mag sauer sehn, und Leide tragen;
  ich achte nicht dess Pöfels Spiel.
Hin Filidor, nur hingestorben,
bleibt nur dein Nachruhm unverdorben
  bey Rosilis, der Reime Ziel.

3

Ich weiss, es werden deine Zeilen
bey ihr nicht zum vergessen eilen.
  Sie wird dich lesen Tag und Nacht,
und sagen: was ist hier geschrieben,
hat Filidor auss treuem lieben
  auff unser beyder Brunst erdacht.

Ernst Stockmann

Christus ist auferstanden

Die Sonne fängt vor Freuden an zu tanzen,
Der Engel steigt herab
Und stellt sich hin zu seines Herren Grab;
Die Wache stutzt, verlässet Helm und Lanzen,
Der schwache Boden bebt,
Als Jesus sich aus seiner Gruft erhebt;
Die Totengräber zittern,
Maria kömmt mit Salben an den Ort
Und höret diese Wort:
Wen suchet ihr? Der Herr ist auferstanden,
Er ist nicht mehr vorhanden,
Beschaut die Stätte selbst,
Denn was die Augen sehen,
Das lässt das Herz geschehen.

2

Whoever will, may me lament,
Have lemoned face, dark ornament:
  I care not for the people's game.
Die, Filidor, die then away,
If but your fame unharmed may stay
  With Rosilis, your rhyming's aim.

3

I know it sure, your lines will not
By her so quickly be forgot,
  For she will read you day and night;
And she will say: What here is writ,
My Filidor did join and fit
  From our twin passions, blazing bright.

Ernst Stockmann

Christ Is Risen

The sun in happiness begins to dance,
The angel does descend,
There at his Master's grave his march to end.
The guard is stunned, and helmet leaves and lance;
The earth in weakness shakes,
When Jesus from His sepulcher awakes;
The sextons quake for fear.
And Mary, come with ointments to that ground,
Hears how the words resound:
The Lord is risen! Whom then search you for?
He is at hand no more.
Behold the place yourself,
For what the eyes behold,
The heart will let unfold.

Gottlieb Stolle

Die verliebte Verwandlung

Du hast, o Liebe, mich erst in ein Reh verkehrt,
Das seines Jägers Pfeil in zarter Brust getragen;
Hernach in einen Schwan, der sich zu Tode singt;
Und dann in eine Blum, in die die Flamme dringt,
So von der Sonne kommt und allen Saft verzehrt;
Hierauf verlor ich mich in einen Tränenregen,
Und jetzund muss ich, mir zur Pein,
Ein Salamander sein,
Der in der Strahlenglut, so Daphnens Augen hegen,
Verschmachtet, und doch auch sein schmachtend Herze nährt.
Jedennoch wollt ich mich im mindsten nicht beklagen,
Wenn deine Wundermacht,
Die mir bisher nichts Süsses zugedacht,
Mir endlich noch die Gunst gewährte,
Und mich vor meinem Tod in Daphnens Schatz verkehrte.

Gottlieb Stolle

Auf den Herrn von Hoffmannswaldau

Dein kiel, berühmter Mann! so nur von honig rinnt,
Und amber-tropffen führt, hat nirgend seines gleichen:
Es muss Marini dir die sieges-crone reichen,
   Weil deine lieblichkeit der seinen abgewinnt.
   Sagt, dichter! sagt es aus! was seine lieder sind?
Ob ihre kräffte nicht ein stählern hertz erweichen?
Es mag Amphion nur die stoltzen seegel streichen,
   Denn seiner harffe krafft ist fabel, dunst und wind.
Dass itzt die lieblichkeit so wenig Musen nähret,
Macht deine poesie, die sie gantz ausgeleeret.
   Apollo sieht dich selbst mit neid und eyfer an:
Er hätte dir zwar längst den lorbeer-krantz geraubet;
Doch er getraut sich nicht, dieweil er selbst nicht glaubet,
   Dass seine laute dir die wage halten kan.

Gottlieb Stolle

The Enamored Transformation

You did me first, oh love, into a roebuck make,
In whose soft breast a bolt is by his huntsman sent,
Thereafter to a swan, who sings himself to death,
And then into a bloom that's seared by flaming breath
Which comes down from the sun and every juice does take.
Next I did lose myself within a weeping rain;
And, to my pain, must presently
A salamander be,
Who in the bath of fire that Daphne's eyes contain,
Does yearn and nonetheless his yearning heart may slake.
However I would not in smallest wise lament,
If but your wondrous might,
That granted me no sweetness in my plight,
Would me at last its favor give
And let me ere my death as Daphne's lover live.

Gottlieb Stolle

Concerning Master Hofmannswaldau

   Your quills, oh famous man, which pure with honey run
And write in amber ink, nowhere a peer possess:
Marino [86] must to you the the victory-crown address
   Since your sweet quality from him the prize has won.
   Tell, poets! Tell us true of what his songs are spun
And if their strength cannot steel heart to softness press:
Sir Amphion [87] must strike his canvas' haughtiness,
   For fable, haze, and wind are his harp's benison.
Your verses are to blame that Muses benefit
But rare from loveliness, for you have emptied it.
   Apollo looks on you with eager envy's fire,
And long ago he would from you the laurel thieve,
But still he does not dare, since he cannot believe
   That, placed in balance, he can best you with his lyre.

Johann Peter Titz

AUFF REINHOLD FRIEDRICHS UND
HEDWIG TÖNNIESSINS HOCHZEIT

Der raue Herbst ist hier: der Winter wird sich finden.
  Wie habt Ihr, Edles Par, es doch so wol bedacht,
  Dass Ihr Euch unterwerfft der Liebe starcken Macht,
Und Eure Hertzen lasst durch diese Flamm' entzünden!
Die angenehme Lust dess Sommers mag verschwinden:
  Der Felder schöne Zier, der Garten edle Pracht,
  So uns bissher ergetzt, mag geben gute Nacht;
Ihr werdet doch bey Euch den Sommer stets empfinden.
  Zeucht gleich die Sonn' itzund die Krafft der Strahlen ein:
  Bey Euch wird dennoch Hitz' und lauter Sonne sein.
Liegt alles gleichsam todt: bei Euch wird alles leben.
  Muss alle Blumen-Lust; muss Laub und Grass vergehn,
  So bleibet Ihr doch stets in voller blüthe stehn,
Und werdet mit der zeit gewünschte Früchte geben.

Andreas Tscherning

EIN BAUM REDET DEN MENSCHEN AN

  Was mir hat der Herbst genommen
Kan ich wieder neu bekommen/
Wann dess Frülings Vater bläst;
Mensch/ du kriegest auff begehr
Deinen Geist nicht wider her/
Wann er einmal dich verläst.
  Meine starcke Wurtzeln machen
Dass ich mag der Winde lachen:
Du hingegen sinckest hin/
Wann nur etwan uber Feld
Sud nicht gleiches Wetter helt/
Oder böse Dünste ziehn.
  Bin ich einmal gut beklieben/
Und für schaden frey geblieben/
So besteh ich' lange frist:
Aber du wirst abgemeyt
Offt in deiner Frülingszeit/
Wann du kaum gebohren bist.

Johann Peter Titz

ON THE MARRIAGE OF
REINHOLD FRIEDRICH AND HEDWIG TÖNNIES

The cruel fall has come; soon winter will be here.
  How have you, noble pair, so set your plan aright
  That you submit yourselves to loving's sinewed might
And do allow this flame your hearts to catch and sear!
The summer's soothing joy may pale and disappear;
  The garden's noble growth, the meadow's fair delight,
  Which pleased us hitherto, must bid us now good night.
Yet you will feel in you the summer ever near.
  The power of its beams the sun must now restrain,
  And yet in you will heat and sheerest sunshine reign.
In you all things will live, when all lies deathly still.
  Though flowers' joy and leaves and grass must meet their doom,
  Yet you eternally shall keep your fullest bloom,
And shall, with flight of time, produce what fruits you will.

Andreas Tscherning

A TREE ADDRESSES MAN

  What the autumn took from me,
All renewed again will be,
When the Springtime's father blows;[88]
Man, you'll not, at your command,
Get your soul again to hand,
When at last it from you goes.
  In my roots such power lies
That I may the winds despise;
You however sink away
If perchance across the fields
Fickleness the south wind yields
Or inclement vapors play.
  When my roots are tightly laid,
And I free from harm have stayed,
I'll a long delay have won.
You, however, fall to earth
Hardly past your hour of birth,
Often ere your springtime's done.

Venus-Gärtlein

Du Beherrscher unsrer Sinnen,
O du kleiner Liebes-Gott,
wer wird deine Macht nicht innen?
Und wem bringstu nicht in Noth,
    mit dem Pfeil, damit du offt
    uns verletzest unverhofft.

Jupiter, sampt seinen Pletzen,
sampt der starcken Donners-Macht,
weicht dir kleinem Bogen-Schützen,
du hast jhn dahin gebracht,
    dass er muss, aus Liebes-Pein,
    in ein'm Schwan verwandelt seyn.

Alle Götter und Göttinnen,
alle Wasser-Nymphen Heer,
die gelehrten Pierinnen,
Himmel, Helle, Erd, und Meer,
    und was man nur finden kan,
    ist dir Amor unterthan.

Unter diesen aber allen,
muss am meisten, sonderlich,
Venus dir zu Fusse fallen,
die doch hat geboren dich,
    die dich hat ans Liecht gebracht,
    hastu selbst verliebt gemacht.

Nu, du Zwinger harter Hertzen,
hast mich auch gebracht dahin,
durch den süssen Liebes-Schmertzen,
dass ich gäntzlich meinen Sinn
    auff ein Cavalier gericht.
    Ach was kann die Liebe nicht.

Venus-Gärtlein

You, our senses' little king,
You, our tiny loving-god,
Whom do you no trouble bring?
Who knows not your power's prod
    And the bolt, by which you've made
    Wounds in us by ambuscade.

Zeus's lightning-armory
And his awful thunder-might
From this little bowman flee.
You have brought him to such plight
    That he must, from loving's pain,
    E'en the swan's disguise obtain.

All the gods and goddesses,
All the water-nymphs' command,
Pierus' learned priestesses,
Heaven, hell, and sea, and land
    And what else men here can find,
    Amour, you do take and bind.

Specially, and most of all,
In the realm of the sky and earth,
Venus at your feet must fall,
She who gave you very birth.
    You have placed in loving's way
    Her who brought you to the day.

Now, you tamer of hard hearts,
You have brought me to this end
Through sweet loving's pleasant smarts
That my sense I wholly send
    Searching for a lover too:
    Oh, what things can love not do!

Venus-Gärtlein

Die weltliche Nonne

Wie muss ich meine Zeit verschlüssen,
  ich armes Kind,
ich muss von keinen Frewden wissen,
  die Weltlich sind:
Wie lieber möcht ich einen Knaben,
Als eine grawe Kappen haben.

Pfy diesem Kleyd unnd Nonnen-Leben,
  hinweg mit dir,
mir ist kein Nonnen-Fleisch gegeben.
  Ist niemand hier,
der mich auss meinem Joch' ausspannt,
unnd meinen frischen Leib bemannt.

Man hat mich Jung hieher getrieben,
  war so schlecht,
dass ich nicht wuste, was das Lieben,
  was linck, was recht:
Nun mich die Jahre Mannbahr machen,
gedenck ich auch an Mannes-Sachen.

Mein Dencken ist in einen Orden,
  da man sich küsst,
ich bin der Nonnen müde worden,
  dann mich gelüst:
Ein Weib kan Gott so wol gefallen,
als nun aller Nonnen-Psalter lallen.

Georg Rudolf Weckherlin

Von dem Cardinal de Richelieu

Frankreich, dein ist der Sig. Du bist der Reichest Ort,
  Das beste Reich der Welt, gleichloss durch Gottes seegen;
Zwar nicht, weil fruchtreich du der frembden trost und hort,
  Auch nicht weil deine leut, wie du, gut zu thun pflegen:
Nicht weil du der Lieb sitz; der sturmleydenden port,
  Nichts deines weisen Rahts, und dapfern Adels wegen;
Nicht weil dein König gross durch seine werck und wort
  Bezeuget, dass ihm nichts dan dein hayl angelegen.

Venus-Gärtlein

The Worldly Nun

Shall I, a wretched child, thus go
    My time to end?
I never shall those pleasures know
    Which earth does spend.
How much the more I'd think it good
To have a boy than gray-dipped hood.

Would that this garb, this life of nun
    Might disappear.
No nunly flesh have e'er I won:
    Is no one here
Who will me from my yoke unspan
And then my blooming body man?

So young and simple to my plight
    They banished me,
That I knew not what left, what right,
    What love might be.
Since years for men do make me fit,
My thoughts do also men admit.

An order calls my thoughts its own,
    Whose members kiss,
For I of nuns have weary grown;
    My passion's this:
A woman God as well can please
As nuns who mouth their psalteries.

Georg Rudolf Weckherlin

Concerning the Cardinal de Richelieu

Oh France, the victory's yours; you are the richest court,
    The world's best empire: free of like through Heaven's grace;
    But not since fruitful France is exile's kind resort,
    Nor since good deed's the wont of land or populace.
Nor since you're love's domain, the storm-tossed seaman's port,
    Nor for your wisdom's sake nor your brave nobles' race,
    Nor since your king may prove, through works and word's support,
    That he does care for naught save your salvation's case.

Nein. Sondern weil dir wehrt ein solcher Cardinal,
    Dass ihm auch an verdienst sunst kein mensch gleich zu finden,
    Wan in der weitten welt dir Got schon geb die wahl.
Darumb lass weder forcht noch hoffnung dich verblinden,
    Dieweil gantz seelig du, durch Got und ihn zu mahl
    Kanst, so du wilt, die welt, dich kein feind überwinden.

Georg Rudolf Weckherlin

AN BRISSACH VON HÖCHSTERMELTEM HELDEN BERNHARD HERTZOGEN ZU SACHSEN EINGENOMMEN

Ja, Brissach, dein verlust ist dein gewin und preyss;
    Du hast, in dem du dich verloren, dich gefunden;
    Du hast, von disem schwert erobert überwunden;
Und uneinnehmlich nu wirst du auff dise weiss.
Dan diser Fürst, Held, Mars (dein Siger) ist so weiss,
    So gütig, mächtig, gross, dass dein verdruss verschwunden,
    Alsbald dich seine faust zu seinem dienst verbunden,
Darumb mit frewd und danck gehorsam dich erweiss.
Sih doch, bedenck und merck, wie herrlich Er dich zieret,
    Und du mit nichten Ihn; wie durch ihn Got in dir,
    Als durch Got über dich Er (sigreich) triumfieret!
So lern nu seine lehr (und gib inm danck darfür)
Weil Got den Fürsten selbs, wie der Fürst dich, regieret,
Dass ihm allzeit der Sig, und Got die ehr, gebihr.

Georg Rudolf Weckherlin

VON DEM KÖNIG VON SCHWEDEN

O König, dessen Haupt den Weltkreis zu regieren
Und dessen Faust die Welt zu siegen allein gut,
O Herrscher, dessen Herz, Herr, dessen grossen Mut
Gottsforcht, Gerechtigkeit, Stärk, Mass und Weisheit zieren;

O Held, für dessen Schwert die Verfolger die Wut,
Ihr Klagen, Forcht, Gefahr die Verfolgte verlieren,
Mars, göttlichen Geschlechts, von der Erretter Blut,
Wert, über Tyrannei und Stolz zu triumphieren!

No! rather since you have so good a cardinal
    That you in worthiness could ne'er his equal find,
    If God did let you search through the world's wide ball.
Let not your eyes be turned by hope or terror blind:
    Since you, all blest, at once on God and him may call,
    No foe can make you slave, yet you the world can bind.

Georg Rudolf Weckherlin

To Breisach,[89] Taken by That Supremely Celebrated Hero, Bernhard, Duke of Saxony

Yes, Breisach, your decrease is profit yet and prize,
    You are, in loss of self, unto that self restored,
    And win the victory, defeated by the sword:
    Impregnable you are become upon this wise.
For this prince-hero-Mars, your victor, is so wise,
    So kind, great, mighty, that your rage became accord,
    The moment his strong hand you to his service warred;
    Therefore with joyful thanks him of your faith apprise.
Behold, consider, mark your splendid ornament
    (Though you are none to him); how God through him in you,
    And he through God o'er you his winning passage went.
So learn this lesson now and give him thanks anew,
    (Since God the prince's will, as he your own, has bent)
    That victory may be his and praise God's constant due.

Georg Rudolf Weckherlin

Concerning the King of Sweden

Oh king, whose head alone can rule Earth's company,
Whose hand alone the world in victory can embrace,
Oh chief, whose heart, oh lord, whose courage knows the grace
Of fear of God, restraint, strength, wisdom, equity!

Oh hero, at whose sword the hunter halts the chase,
The hunted halt their wails, their fears, their misery,
Oh Mars of blood divine and of the saviors' race,
A worthy conqueror o'er pride and tyranny!

Des Feinds Zorn, Hochmut, Hass, durch Macht, Betrug, Untreu,
Hat schier in Dienstbarkeit, Unrecht, Abgötterei
Des Teutschlands Freiheit, Recht und Gottesdienst verkehret,

Als Euer Haupt, Herz, Hand ganz weis, gerecht, bewehret,
Die Feind bald ihren Wohn und Pracht in Hohn und Reu,
Die Freind ihr Leid in Freud zu verkehren gelehret.

Georg Rudolf Weckherlin
Sie ist die gröste Reichthumb

Das prächtigste Kriegsschiff, dem ie das Meer war kund,
    Hat keinen mast so hoch, als hoch ist mein begehren;
Kein äncker halb so starck und beissend in den grund,
    Als meine lieb und trew, die unaufhörlich wehren.
So knüpfet auch kein sayl noch leyn ein solchen bund,
    Als die zart krause haar, die meinen gaist beschweren;
Kein wind bliess jemahl auff die seegel stoltz und rund
    Als mich die süsse lufft des rothen munds bethören.
Kein Schiffman hat iemahls in einer schwartzen nacht
    Ein halb so klares liecht oder gestirn erblicket
    Als hell seind die augstern, mein trost und Amors pracht:
So hat auch noch kein schiff, nach langer fahrt beglicket,
    Ein Kleinoth so viel werth zu uns von Ost gebracht,
    Als dises Kleinoth ist das alle welt erquicket.

Georg Rudolf Weckherlin
An eine, sich alt zu werden beklagende, Schönheit

Nein. Ihr seit noch nicht alt. So zart, so schön, so klar,
    Pfleg ich stehts ewer flaisch, farb und aug zuerfahren,
Dass ihr mir billich jung. Frisch, hurtig, süss ist zwar
    Der glatten jugend Lieb, und Früling unsrer jahren.
Dass unser Sommer auch gantz liebreich sey, ist wahr;
    Doch ist die hitz so gross, dass sein gedranck zu spahren
    Ihm kaum kan möglich sein: Daher er matt und bahr
    Durch der Lieb starcke brunst in taussenten gefahren.
Wan nu, weil noch zu jung, fruchtloss die Frühlings zeit;
    Der Sommer vil zu heissz: Ist weder zu verschweigen,
    Noch zu erhöben gnug des Herbsts lust-reiche beut.
Dan Er ergötzet Uns mit so Lieb-reiffen Feigen,
    Mit solcher Wollusts frucht, dass er ohn allen streit
    Die ander übertreff, ihm gnug an zweyen Zeugen.

By falseness, force, deceit had hate, pride, rage of foe
Almost to slavishness, injustice, idol's show
The freedom, rights, and faith of German nations brought,

When your hand, heart, and head, tried, just, and wise in thought,
Your foe's vain dream and pomp a change to scorn and woe,
The suffering of your friends a change to gladness taught.

Georg Rudolf Weckherlin
SHE IS THE GREATEST WEALTH

The grandest ship-of-war which e'er to sea was known
    Has not a mast that climbs as high as my desire,
    No anchor does such strength or biting fluke-arms own,
    As do my faith and love which never will expire.
Nor is from rope or cord so strong a rigging sewn,
    As from those tender locks which hold my soul in hire,
    And ne'er a wind the sails so proud and round has blown,
    As I'm to madness puffed by her red mouth's sweet choir.
No seaman who his way through murky night has sought
    Has half so clear a light or constellation spied
    As those eye-stars, Love's pride, my comfort, bright are wrought.
No vessel has, at last upon the homeward tide,
    So dear a jewel to us from Eastern reaches brought,
    As is this gem wherein the world's delight resides.

Georg Rudolf Weckherlin
TO A BEAUTY COMPLAINING THAT SHE GROWS OLD

No, you are not yet old: so fine, so fair, so clear
    I'm always wont your flesh, your hew, your eye to gauge,
    That you seem justly young. Fresh, hasty, sweet's the cheer
    Indeed of smooth youth's love, the springtide of our age.
And it is likewise true that summertime's most dear,
    But yet its wine to save, since such cruel heat does rage,
    Is hardly possible: thus it, worn out and sere
    From love's fierce flame, must war 'gainst thousand dangers wage.
Now then, since, still too young, the springtime lacks in fruit,
    The summer's much too hot, no one may dare suppress
    Nor fail to praise enough the autumn's joyful boot;
For with such tasty figs it can our taste caress,
    With such gay crop, that it without the faintest bruit
    Outstrips the others: two this truth will glad profess.

Georg Rudolf Weckherlin

Die Lieb ist Leben und Tod

Das Leben, so ich führ, ist wie der wahre Tod,
Ja über den Tod selbs ist mein trostloses Leben.
Es endet ja der Tod des Menschen Pein und Leben,
Mein Leben aber kann nicht enden dieser Tod.

Bald kann ein Anblick mich verletzen auf den Tod,
Ein andrer Anblick bald kann mich wiedrum beleben,
Dass ich von Blicken muss dann sterben und dann leben,
Und bin in einer Stund bald lebendig bald tot.

Ach, Lieb! Verleih mir doch nunmehr ein anders Leben,
Wenn ich ja leben soll, oder den andern Tod:
Denn weder diesen Tod lieb ich, noch dieses Leben.

Verzeih mir, Lieb, ich bin dein lebendig und tot.
Und ist der Tod mit dir ein köstlich süsses Leben,
Und Leben, von dir fern, ist ein ganz bittrer Tod.

Georg Rudolf Weckherlin

An das Teutschland

Zerbrich das schwere Joch/ darunder du gebunden/
O Teutschland/ wach doch auff/ fass wider einen muht/
Gebrauch dein altes hertz/ und widersteh der wuht/
Die dich/ und die freyheit durch dich selbs uberwunden.

Straf nu die Tyranney/ die dich schier gar geschunden/
Und lösch doch endlich auss die (dich verzöhrend) glut/
Nicht mit dein eignem schwaiss/ sondern dem bösen blut
Fliessend auss deiner feind und falschen brüdern wunden.

Verlassend dich auf Got/ folg denen Fürsten nach/
Die sein gerechte hand will (so du wilt) bewahren/
Zu der Getrewen trost/ zu der trewlosen raach:

So lass nu alle forcht/ und nicht die zeit hinfahren/
Und Got wirt aller welt/ dass nichts dan schand und schmach
Des feinds meynayd und stoltz gezeuget/ offenbahren.

Georg Rudolf Weckherlin

Love is Life and Death

The life which now I lead is as a perfect death,
Yea, even worse than death is my unhappy life,
For death indeed can end a creature's pain and life,
But yet my life is not concluded by this death.

A glance can deal me wounds unto the point of death,
Another glance can bring me back again to life,
That I from glances first must die and then have life,
And be within the hour now living, now with death.

Oh love, grant me instead another way of life,
If I shall live at all, or then that other death:
For I love not this death, nor this my present life.

Forgive me, love, that I am yours in life and death.
For death becomes with you a sweet and precious life,
And life, far from your side, a more than bitter death.

Georg Rudolf Weckherlin

To Germany

   Destroy the heavy yoke beneath which you are bound!
Oh Germany, awake! Again your courage claim!
Employ your time-tried heart and seek the rage to tame
Which by your aid yourself and freedom would confound!

   Let now on tyranny its hangman's arts redound!
At last the fire put out which eats you with its flame!
And let it in the blood from wounds of evil fame,
Of foe and fickle friend (not in your sweat) be drowned!

   Entrusting you to God, go at those princes' side
Whose course (just as you will) His righteous hand will chart,
The faithful to console, the faithless to deride.

   So let now every fear but not the hour depart,
And God will show the world that, out of hostile pride
And foeman's false-sworn oaths, but shame and pain may start.

Christian Weise

Auf die Geburt eines jungen und hoch-verlangten Sohnes

Das ist der beste Schatz/ der Kern von allen Gaben/
Die wir aus Gottes Hand hier zu geniessen haben;
   Wenn ein geliebtes Weib/ als ein Oliven-Baum/
   Mit steter Fruchtbarkeit den all zu weiten Raum
Am Tische kleiner macht. Denn die bewehrten Früchte
Sind unser Ebenbild; des Vaters Angesichte
   Steht in der zarten Reih so klärlich abgemahlt/
   Dass sein Gedächtnüs auch den blassen Todt bestrahlt/
Und in der Nach-Welt lebt. Das sind dieselben Stützen/
Die Kirch und Regiment mit neuer Krafft beschützen/
   Wenn wir verblichen sind: Ja das ist unser Geld
   Und unser höchstes Gut/ das auch in jener Welt
Die volle Währung hat. Hingegen andre Schätze/
Geld/ Acker/ Hauss und Hoff/ sind alle dem Gesetze
   Der Eitelkeit verknüpfft/ und können nicht bestehn/
   Wenn dieses gantze Rund durchs letzte Feuer gehn
Und sich verzehren wird. Ein Baum verliert die Blätter/
So bald ein rauher Nord das kalte Winter-Wetter
   In unsre Gräntzen bläst: Jedennoch in der Frucht
   Da lebt des Samens Krafft/ dadurch man solche Zucht
Noch weiter bringen kan. Wolan des Höchsten Güte
Hat diesen Stamm bissher mit einer schönen Blüte
   Belieblich angesehn: Nun kömt die beste Zeit/
   Und krönet solchen Glantz mit voller Fruchtbarkeit.
Willkommen kleiner Sohn/ du/ deines Vaters Leben;
Der dir das Leben giebt/ dem solt du künfftig geben/
   Dass er nicht sterben kan; du bist das Ebenbild
   Darein er ietzo zwar sein Angesicht verhüllt:
Doch künfftig wird sein Geist durch deine Seele dringen/
Da wirstu neben ihm den Gipfel höher schwingen/
   Als keine Ceder thut: worinn er uns gefällt/
   Da wirstu mit der Zeit der künfftig-klugen Welt/
Nicht minder kostbar seyn. Schau wie die Musen lachen/
Und dir in ihrer Schoss ein süsses Lager machen;
   Schau wie der Sternen Licht auff deinen Wirbel blickt/
   Und einen stillen Fluss biss in das Hertze schickt/
Das uns erfreuen sol. Ja Gott der allen Samen
Am liebsten fruchtbar macht/ wenn er in seinem Nahmen
   Hinaus gestreuet wird/ der giebt den Willen drein/
   Du solst in allem Thun ein andrer Vater seyn.

Christian Weise

Upon the Birth of a Young and Highly-Desired Son

This treasure is the best, of all those gifts the grain
Which we from Heaven's hand do to our pleasure gain;
   When a beloved wife, all in the olive's ways,
   With constant fruitfulness, the yawning space allays
Around the family board. For proven heritance
Are our small likenesses: the father's countenance
   Stands in the tender row designed with such clear brush
   That memory of him brings pallid death to blush,
And fills posterity. These pillars are the same
Which guard (with might renewed) both church and ruler's fame
   When we have passed away. Yes, these our moneys are
   And highest properties, which on that distant star
Their proper value keep. For other treasures: gold,
Fields, mansion, and estate, are subject to the hold
   Of vanity's decree, and can no longer last
   Than when this rounded globe through final fire has passed,
And has devoured itself. A tree its bareness shows
As soon as Boreas cold winter-weather blows
   Rough 'cross our boundaries: and yet the force of seed
   Still lives within the fruit, and through this force the breed
Can still be carried on. Now, Heaven's kindliness
Has deigned until this day with handsome bloom to bless
   Our family tree: at last there comes the finest time
   And crowns such splendor with its full and fertile prime.
Oh welcome, little son, who are your father's spark:
Who gives that spark to you, you'll rescue from the dark
   Of death by future gift: his image you reveal,
   Since in you recently his face he did conceal.
Yet henceforth will his soul your spirit penetrate:
Then you (next him) will lift your height to higher state
   Than any cedar might; the world does deem him dear,
   And you, with time's course, will to wisdom's world appear
No less desirable. See how the Muses smile
And in their lap prepare your couch of gracious style.
   See how the starry light upon your crown descends
   And deep into your heart a silent river sends,
Which carries our delight. Yes, God, Who seed does make
Most gladly fruitful when that seed for His name's sake
   Is in the furrow sown, will with this aim agree:
   You shall in every act another father be.

Christian Wernicke

ABRISS EINES WELTMANNS,
UNTER DEM GEMÄLD' VON POMPONIUS
ATTICUS

Sieh Atticus' Gemäld' in diesen Zeilen an:
Er war ein schlauer mehr als tugendhafter Mann,
Er hatt' im Überfluss das, was die ganze Welt
Zu des Besitzes Ruhm verblendet: Witz und Geld;
Er hatte keinen Trieb, der ihn gewaltsam führt'
Zu dem, was sich zu thun und nicht zu thun gebührt,
So dass er heimlich hier und dorten offenbar
Der Tugendhaften Schutz, der Frevler Zuflucht war
Und, weil Pompejus das, was Cäsar von ihm meint,
Zugleich zwei grosse Feind' ihn nannten einen Freund.

Christian Wernicke

AN UNSRE DEUTSCHE POETEN

Ihr Tichter, wenn ein Vers aus eurer Feder quillt,
Um eure Phillis zu bedienen,
So zeigt sich gleich ein Marmorbild,
Ihr Aug' ist von Achat, die Lippen sind Rubinen,
Die Adern aus Saphir gemacht,
Und eure Buhlschaft wird, weil ihr sie preist, verlacht.
Die Welschen sind zwar auch nicht klug,
Weil sie in einem weiten Flug
Mit einer Göttin stets bis an die Sterne fliegen;
In Frankreich macht man sie von lauter Geist und Witz,
Der Freundschaft fähig und verschwiegen,
Kurz, ein Gefäss ohn' eine Ritz';
In England, wo sie schalt- und walten,
Da werden sie vor nichts als Blut und Fleisch gehalten;
Ihr aber wollt verkehrt Pygmalions alle sein,
Denn eure Phillis ist ein Bild und Bild von Stein.

Christian Wernicke

Sketch of a Cosmopolite, under the Portrait of Pomponius Atticus [90]

Behold within these lines our pictured Atticus:
He may be called a man more sly than virtuous.
He had in plenty what the owner needs to blind
The world entire: he had much gold and subtle mind.
He had no secret lust, which him by force had won
For that which man should do and that which man should shun, [91]
So that he hidden here, and there all openly
A shield to virtue was, yet sheltered blasphemy;
Of him Sir Pompey thought and Caesar thought the same,
So that two mighty foes at once him friend could name.

Christian Wernicke

To Our German Poets

You poets, when a verse comes rushing from your pen
To give your Phyllis fresh supply,
A marble bust is fathered then:
Her lips are ruby-stone, and agate is her eye.
Her veins of sapphire gems are tooled;
And your amour is, since you praise her, ridiculed.
Nor are, indeed, Italians wise,
Since in a mighty arc they rise,
Their goddess at their side, the very stars to meet.
In France men make her out of wit and intellect,
In friendship talented, discreet,
A vessel thus without defect.
In England, where she rules and reigns,
She naught but flesh and blood in poet's eye remains.
But you have in reverse Pygmalion's lesson learned:
For Phyllis at your hands has into statue turned.

Christian Wernicke

FUROR POETICUS

Wie glücklich ist der Mann/ der sich vom Wind' ernährt/
Und Wolle von dem Schnee/ gleich wie von Schafen/
   schert;
Der zu Dukaten-Gold der Sonnen Strahlen schlägt/
Und in ein Spinngeweb' ein Bild der Tichtkunst pregt;
Der Marmor und Albast aus Brüst- und Händen haut/
Und ein Escurial dem Ruhm zur Wohnung baut;
Der Edelstein' und Stern aus seiner Feder spritzt/
Und dessen Muse nichts als Musck und Amber schwitzt;
Der in dem Aug' Achat/ in Thränen Perlen findt/
Und aus den Disteln Zeug der Lust zum Schlaffrock spinnt;
Der dem Betrug aus Rauch/ Helm/ Schild/ und Pantzer
   schmiedt/
Und wie ein Sonntags Kind/ Nichts in Person/ offt sieht:
Wie glücklich ist der Mann/ der seine Noht vergisst/
Nicht Durst noch Hunger fühlt/ weil er von Sinnen ist.

Philipp von Zesen

KLÜNG-GETICHTE AUF DAS HÄRZ SEINER TRÄUEN

   O trautes härts! was härts? vihl härter noch als hart/
o! stahl? mit nichten stahl; es lässt sich bässer zühen.
wi dan magneht? o nein; ihm ist vihl mehr verlihen.
   ist's dan ein deamant? auch nicht; dan diser ward
im schäzzen nahch-gesätzt däs härzens wunder-ahrt.
wi! ist es dan kristal? durch dehn di strahlen sprühen/
wan izt di sonne stäht in follem glanz' und glühen.
   o nein. wo-durch würd dan sein währt rächt offenbahrt?
indähm es mehr als hart/ mehr zühglich ist und zühet
   als stahl und libes-stein; mehr währt als deamant/
dehn sonst di blinde wält fohr täuer-währt ansihet;
   vihl reiner als kristal/ vihl klährer von verstand
als er am blohssen schein. noch hält däs Folkes hal
dein härze gleich magnet/ stahl/ demant und kristal.

Christian Wernicke

Furor Poeticus

How happy is the man who food from wind can reap,
And shear wool from the snow, as though he sheared from
   sheep,
Who beats to ducat-gold the arrows of the sun,
And in a spider web the poet's stamp has spun,
Who makes from breast and hands white alabaster fall
And marble, building thus his fame's Escurial,
Who squeezes from his pen fine gems and starry fire,
Whose Muse can naught but musk and amber-sweat perspire,
Who finds in tears the pearl, in eyes the agate-stone,
And weaves from thistles stuff for pleasure's sleeping gown,
From smoke he's, 'gainst deceit, shield, helm, and armor
   pried,
And like a Sunday child sees Naught personified.
How happy is the man who to his needs is blind,
Nor thirst nor hunger feels, since he has lost his mind.

Philipp von Zesen

Sonnet on the Heart of His Faithful Lady

   Beloved heart! if heart, it's harder still than hard.
Or steel? Steel not at all; this may be better drawn.
Or then a magnet? No: it has still more in pawn.
   A diamond? Nor that: the diamond was barred
   From besting this strange heart on treasure's racing card.
Or is it crystal then, which light-beams burst upon
When now the sun into its fullest splendor's gone?
   Oh no! How may one then its perfect worth regard?
Since it is more than hard, more quickly drawn and draws
   More than love's stone and steel, lasts more than diamond,
(Which as a precious thing the blind world elsewise awes),
   More pure than crystal's rays, in clear wit set beyond
That crystal's simple gleam. And yet to people's mind
   Your heart's of diamond-, steel-, magnet-, crystal-kind.

Phillipp von Zesen

Schertzlied an die truebseelige... Roselinde

Wie von den Maehren schreibt Virgil/ dass sie der wind macht
        schwanger;
so schwaengert manche Jungfer auch die luft vom Bluhmenanger.
Die Biene kent den beischlaf nicht/ und haekt doch Jungen
        aus/
wan sie im suessen eifer kuest den zahrten Bluhmenstraus.

So kraeftig war die Rosenluft/ mit eifer eingesogen/
dasz Roselinde sich befand/ das suesse Kind/ betrogen.
Woher doch komt mir dis? sprach sie: Ich weisz von keinem
        Man;
und gleich wol seh' ich/ dass man mich bald Mutter nennen kan.

Der Nahme komt Ihr nun auch zu. Doch wer sie Fraue nennet/
der tuht/ wie sie selbst spricht/ zu viel; weil sie kein Man
        erkennet.
Ists wahr? So habt ihr euch gewisz/ ihr Jungfern/ vorzusehn:
es moecht' euch von der Bluhmen luft sonst auch ein schimpf
        geschehn.

Heinrich Anselm von Zigler und Klipphausen

Aus der asiatischen Banise

  Wahr ists, die schönheit ist Achillens spiess und schwerdt,
    Die einen Telephus verletzt und wieder heilet,
  Die schönheit ist ein gifft, das tödtet und ernehrt,
    Ein blitz, der ruhe störht, und unmuth doch zertheilet,
  Ein brand, der städte tilgt, und länder doch erhält,
    Ein pfeil, der wunden macht, und gleichwol lust erwecket,
  Durch sie ward Troja grauss, doch Rom das haupt der welt:
    Ein wein, der wermuth ist, und doch wie zucker schmecket.

Philipp von Zesen

Mocking Song to the Melancholy Roselinde

As Vergil writes of mares that wind to them a foal will
                          yield, [92]
So many a chaste maiden swells from air of flowered field.
The bee knows not the sleep of love, and yet it young can
                          bear,
If it to kiss the tender bloom has, zealot, cleaved the air.

So mighty was the rose's air she, zealot, gobbled in,
That Roselinde, the lovely child, was tricked to her chagrin.
"Whence does this come?" she said, "For I did ne'er with men
                          commune,
And nonetheless I see that men will call me mother soon."

That name indeed is hers. Yet he who her his wife would name,
But lies, as she herself does say, since she no man can
                          claim.
'Tis true? Then, maidens, you must be forever vigilant,
Lest flower's breath would in you too a like misfortune
                          plant.

Heinrich Anselm von Zigler und Klipphausen

From the Asiatic Banise

It's true that beauty is Achilles' spear and sword,
    Which injures Telephus and makes him whole again, [94]
And beauty is a bane, where death and food are stored,
    A bolt, which ends repose, and yet cuts woe in twain,
A fire which razes towns, and nations whole does keep,
    An arrow, which deals wounds, yet wakens joy with haste;
It made of Rome our head and Troy a rubbish heap:
    A wine which wormwood is, and yet has sugar's taste.

Heinrich Anselm von Zigler und Klipphausen

AUS DER ASIATISCHEN BANISE

Phocas singt folgende worte:

1

JEde Nymfe, jede Göttin, bleibet meine lust und freude,
Jedes antlitz, jede brüste, werden meiner augen weide.
Ich bin gleichsam eine motte, die bey jedem licht sich findt,
Und ein Phönix, dessen asche wird von aller glut entzündt.

2

Es kan mein verliebtes hertze einem Protheus sich vergleichen,
Welcher jeder zu gefallen an sich nimmt der liebe zeichen.
Doch es bringet ruhm und ehre, wenn bald die, bald jene labt,
Weil der nackte liebes-schütze auch mit flügeln ist begabt.

Julius Wilhelm Zincgref

AN DIE TEUTSCHEN

Ihr klagt, ihr habt vor euch noch einen schweren Berge
Zu steigen, bis ihr kompt zu des Luftpferds Herberge,
Und zu der Ewigen Gedächtnus güldnem Thron,
Uff dem bewahret liegt die edle Lorbeerkron;
Wohlan, wie dass ihr dann so still hienieden sitzet,
Und vor Teutschlands Ehr nit auch ein wenig schwitzet.
Je weiter ist der Weg, je reicher ist der Lohn:
Ist dann der Weg gering, je grösser ist eur Hohn.

Heinrich Anselm von Zigler und Klipphausen

From the Asiatic Banise

Phocas sings the following words:

1

Every nymph and every goddess do my lust and joy remain,
Every face and every bosom gratify my eye-light's twain.
I'm a moth, in way of speaking, which is drawn to every light,
And a phoenix-bird, whose ashes every flame can quick ignite.

2

My enamoured heart resembles that old Prothean design,
Which, to bring each maiden pleasure, does appropriate love's sign.
Yet it carries fame and honor, though now she, now she gives aid,
Since the naked bowman also with a pair of wings is made.

Julius Wilhelm Zincgref

To the Germans

You moan that you must still a cruel mountain win
Before you climbing come unto the air-steed's [93] inn,
And to the golden throne of evergreen renown
On which there lies preserved the noble laurel's crown.
Now then, why do you sit so quiet here below,
Nor will a drop of sweat for German honor show?
The gain's the richer by the distance to be borne:
And if the way be brief, the more your pay in scorn.

Julius Wilhelm Zincgref

Epigramma
Vom Thurn zu Strassburg/
warumb der andere darneben
nit auffgebawet worden

Ihr seyt unrecht daran/ Zuseher/ die ihr schauet
    Diesen herrlichen Thurn/ das achte Wunderwerck
    Dess Irrdischen bezircks/ und uber alle Berg
Denselben hoch erhebt/ weil er köstlich erbawet
Biss an die Wolcken reicht/ dass jhr darbey wolt klagen/
    Es mangelt jhm noch eins/ diss nemlich/ dass der grundt
    Seins Bruders neben jhm leer/ der uff diese stundt
Nur halb geführet auff. Nicht lasset euch misshagen
Dieses geheimnus gross. Natur hats eingestelt
    Dass neben diesem Thurn noch einer solt gefallen/
    Dann so ist er allein der schönst und höchst vor allen/
Und hat seins gleichen nicht in dieser weiten Welt.

Julius Wilhelm Zincgref

Epigram
Concerning the Tower at Strassburg:
Why the Other One
Has Not Been Erected Beside It

Spectators, you are wrong, who standing here do see
   This steepled majesty, of our terrestial state
   The octave wonderwork, and high it elevate
Above the mountain-tops, since it, built preciously,
Unto the clouds ascends: you err, when you lament
   That it's still got a fault: to wit, its brother's seat
   Beside it empty stands, a work but half complete
Until this very hour. Do not in pique resent
This mighty mystery. For Nature'd not allow
   That, by this tower placed, a twin might us enthrall;
   For it alone's the best, the highest thing of all,
And in the vasty world has not its equal now.

BIOGRAPHICAL INDEX

ABRAHAM A SANTA CLARA (Johann Ulrich Megerle) (1644-1709). The youngest of a Baden innkeeper's eight children, Megerle attended the Latin school at Messkirch, the Jesuit college at Ingolstadt, and finally the Benedictine college at Salzburg. In 1622, he entered the Augustine Order (discalced) and spent his novitiate at Mariabrunn near Vienna; four years later he was ordained a priest. After an apprenticeship as "Sunday and holiday preacher" at Cloister Taxa in Upper Bavaria, Megerle was called to Vienna; there Leopold I named him "imperial preacher." During the pestilence of 1679-1680, Megerle won great popularity with the Viennese populace; three years later, at the time of the Turkish peril, he boldly made his way to the outpost city of Graz. It is in connection with the Turkish invasion that he wrote his most famous sermon, "Auf, auf, ihr Christen" ("Awake, awake, you Christians"). In his later years, matters pertaining to his order called him three times to Rome.

A master of colorful language, Megerle failed when, as in his satirical novel, *Judas der Erzschelm* (*Judas the Arch-Rogue*), he attempted to use a larger canvas. However, despite his artistic shortcomings, he has long been admired by German poetry and criticism; Schiller has left him a lasting monument in the figure of the Capuchin in *Wallensteins Lager*.

ABSCHATZ, HANS ASSMANN VON (1646-1699). Orphaned early in life, like his fellow Silesian Gryphius, Abschatz was nonetheless able to obtain a good education, first at Breslau, then at the Universities of Strassburg and Leyden; a "cultural journey" took him through France, Holland, and Italy. Upon his return to Silesia, he was appointed stadholder in the principality of Liegnitz and selected as representative to the Princely Diet at Breslau, in which capacities he had frequent contact with the court at Vienna. Abschatz is perhaps best remembered for his translations of Adimari's (*Scherz-Sonette: Jest-Sonnets*); he also rendered Guarini's classic *Pastor Fido* into German. His original poetry is distinguished by its simplicity.

ALBERT, HEINRICH (1604-1651). Born at Lobenstein in the Vogtland, Albert studied law at Leipzig, but abandoned that pursuit in order to devote himself to music. In 1629, after training with his uncle, Heinrich Schütz, the famous Dresden Kapellmeister, Albert went to Königsberg in East Prussia; two years later, he was made organist of the Königsberg cathedral. A member of the Königsberg circle of lyricists, Albert not only set the songs of his friends to music but composed poetry of his own.

ALBINI, JOHANN GEORG (1624-1679). A Saxon from Unternessa (near Weissenfels), Albini was trained in theology at Leipzig; in 1653 he became rector of the cathedral school at Naumburg, and, in 1657, minister at Saint Ottmar's Church in that city. Some of Albini's hymns are still to be found in the *Common Service Book* of American Lutheranism.

ANTON ULRICH, Duke of Brunswick-Wolfenbüttel (1633-1714). After having been excellently tutored, by Johann Georg Schottel and Sigmund von Birken, Anton Ulrich made the baroque gentleman's usual journey through South Germany, France, Holland, and Italy. Upon his father's death, he was first (in 1667) named stadholder by his elder brother, then (in 1685) co-regent. In the War of the Spanish Succession, Anton Ulrich favored the French cause; on this account Leopold I deprived him of his co-regency in 1703; but a year later, on his brother's death, he became undisputed ruler of his little land. Five years before his own decease, he was converted to Roman Catholicism. A Maecenas of both the arts and the sciences, Anton Ulrich was also an important artist in his own right: a member of the *Fruit-Bringing Society*, the author of two gigantic courtly novels, *Die durchläuchtige Syrerin Aramena* (*The Illustrious Syrian, Aramena*, 1669-1673) and *Octavia, Römische Geschichte* (*Octavia, A Roman Story*, 1677; later revised as *Die römische Octavia*, 1711 and 1712), and a composer of spiritual songs.

ARNOLD, GOTTFRIED (1666-1714). Arnold, a Saxon from the Erzgebirge, studied at the Lutheran stronghold of Wittenberg, but, strongly influenced by Philipp Spener, underwent a conversion to pietism at Dresden. It was Spener's doing, too, that he got a tutorship at Quedlinburg, where he came into further contact with pietistic circles. In 1698, Arnold caused a public furor by his abandonment of his newly acquired chair in history at Giessen; he had come to believe that the holding of any "worldly position" was incompatible with true Christianity. The literary products of Arnold's pietistic crisis are his spiritual songs and the *Unparteyische Kirchen- und Ketzer-historie* (*Impartial History of Churches and Heretics* (1699ff.). Returning to Quedlinburg, Arnold underwent a second "conversion" to a more tolerant viewpoint: now he was able to accept a church appointment, and did so, becoming "castle-preacher" of the Duchess of Saxe-Weimar. However, a conflict of conscience compelled him to give up this post also. At last he found refuge under the forbearing sceptre of the Prussian king, and spent the remainder of his days as pastor at Werben and superintendent at Perleberg, defending himself against orthodox Lutheran theologians on the one hand, and his former friends of the radical pietistic persuasion on the other.

AUGSPURGER, AUGUST (c. 1642). Nothing is known of Augspurger's life, save that he published his poetry, pastoral and spiritual, at Dresden.

BESSER, JOHANN VON (1654-1729). After having completed his studies at the University of Königsberg, Besser proceeded to Leipzig as the companion of a scion of the Kurland nobility. When the young nobleman was killed in a duel, Besser went on to Berlin. In Brandenburg he became an important functionary, serving, among other things, as emissary in London and master of ceremonies at the Berlin court. These offices, and his promotion to the nobility, Besser owed in great measure to his panegyrics on the House of Hohenzollern. Unfortunately, he was stripped of his duties when the miserly Frederick William I came to the throne in 1701, but, after a poverty-stricken interim, he found a rewarding place as councillor of war and master of ceremonies for Augustus II ("the Strong") at Dresden.

BIRKEN, SIGMUND VON (1626-1681). Birken's father, Lutheran pastor at Wildenstein near Eger (in the north Sudetenland), was compelled by the Counter Reformation to flee to Nürnberg with his little son, Sigmund. The youth's university studies at Jena were cut short by lack of money, and he returned to his adopted city, only to become tutor at the Wolfenbüttel court, where Anton Ulrich was his pupil. This good fortune he owed to the recommendation of Georg Phillipp Harsdörffer, who had already brought him – as "Floridan" – into the *Society of Pegnitz Shepherds*. After a second tutorial appointment, at Dannenberg in Hannover, Birken settled in Nürnberg, and played there a major role in arranging the festivities which marked the end of the Thirty Years' War. For Octavio Piccolomini he composed an allegorical festival-play, which, like his other dramas, he presented with the sons of Nürnberg patrician families. Birken's dramas and his pastoral novels must take second place to his artfully constructed lyrics, subtle, serene poems representative of the best in the Nürnberg school.

BROCKES, BARTHOLD HEINRICH (1680-1747). Brockes, whose works form a watershed between the baroque and the "age of enlightenment," was born in Hamburg. He studied at the new, pietistically oriented University of Halle; then was briefly employed, like Goethe later on, in the imperial courts of justice at Wetzlar. Having made his tour through the Rhineland, Italy, France, and Holland, he came back to Hamburg in 1704, and devoted himself entirely to the arts: his most important public deed was the founding, together with König and Richey, of the *Teutschübende Gesellschaft* (the *German-Using Society*). Election to the Hamburg Senate in 1720 put an end to Brockes' idyll, during which, under the influence of Thomson and Pope, he had written many of those simple, "un-formalized" nature poems on which his fame rests. As the Senate's ambassador, Brockes was sent to Vienna, Copenhagen, Berlin, and Hannover; his grateful Hamburgers rewarded him for his services by giving him the lucrative post of customs-administrator at Ritzebüttel (at the Elbe's mouth).

CANITZ, FRIEDRICH RUDOLF LUDWIG VON (1654-1699). A native Berliner, Canitz, after studies in Leipzig and Leyden and travels in England, France, and Italy, became chamberlain to the Great Elector and accompanied him on the Pommeranian campaigns against the Swedes. He occupied a series of important administrative and diplomatic posts in Prussian service, and was, as a crowning glory, made Baron of the Empire by Leopold I. Illness caused his retirement in the spring of 1699, and he died a few months later. Canitz is remembered as one of the keener satirists of the late baroque; for his immediate successors in German poetry, such as König, he was both model and inspiration.

CZEPKO, DANIEL VON (1605-1660). Czepko, on his father's side, came from a long line of Lutheran pastors; his mother, née Anna von Krestinki-Mohra, was of Polish ancestry. The boy wrote his first poetry while attending the Latin school at Schweidnitz; after his father's death he began the study of medicine at Leipzig, but soon changed both university and faculty, going, in 1626, to Strassburg to study law. Upon his return to Silesia, Czepko became tutor for several families belonging to the Silesian-Polish country nobility; literarily, his most fruitful tutorship was that spent at Dobroslawitz, the estate of Baron Czegan von Slupska (1633-1635). With his marrigage, he became the owner of four farms in the vicinity of Schweidnitz, but, despite his duties as landowner and official (in the Brieg government), Czepko was able to devote considerable time to his mystical and literary pursuits; in these happy years his *Sexcenta Monodisticha Sapientium*, that important collection of epigrams on mystical and earthly subjects, came into being, although it was not published until 1655. With Silesia's invasion by General Torstenson (1640), Czepko's fortunes changed for the worse: he was saddened in particular by the religious conflicts which, apart from the mere military campaigns of the Lutheran and Imperial forces, were laying waste his fatherland. His death was bizarre; serving as a mine inspector in Reichenstein, he fell prey to pit-gasses.

DACH, SIMON (1605-1659). Dach was from Memel, in the Baltic East, and was sent for his secondary education to Königsberg, Wittenberg, and Magdeburg. His university years were spent at Königsberg; not very well-to-do, he supported himself by tutoring and the composition of occasional poetry. From 1633 until 1639 Dach was preceptor at Königsberg's cathedral school; he left this post to become professor of poetry at the university. As "professor poesis" Dach was compelled to a constant use of the skill in occasional verse he had learned in his youth: he managed to give life to a remarkably large number of productions in that least inspired area of poetic endeavor. A man whose natural melancholy was perhaps increased by the requirements of his position, Dach was nevertheless convivial enough to take great pleasure in his membership in the "Pumpkin-Hut" group, with Heinrich Albert and Robert Roberthin.

ELTESTER, C. (died after 1732). Eltester (C.E. in the Neukirch collection) has been described by König in his introduction to Besser's *Schriften*: "Mr. Eltester... who is still alive... possesses more strength, not only in his extensive reading... but also in the art of poetry itself, than he, out of modesty, lets one notice; however I could easily convince my readers of it if I wanted to betray him and to name here those many witty pieces of his, which are to be found in the first parts of the Hofmannswaldau [i.e. Neukirch] collection."

FINKELTHAUS, GOTTFRIED (1610-after 1647). Finkelthaus' birthplace of Lützen was so ravaged by the military operations of the early 1630's that the young poet was forced to flee to Hamburg. A friend of Paul Fleming, Finkelthaus seems to have been infected by Fleming's adventurous spirit, for he spent some years in Brazil: he ended his days as city clerk in Leipzig. He wrote under the pseudonym "Gregor Federfechter von Lützen."

FLEMING, PAUL (1609-1640). Still another of the many German poets born in the manse, Fleming early left his home village of

Hartenstein (Harteise) in the Erzgebirge, first to attend primary school at Mitweida, then the famous Thomasschule at Leipzig (where the Thomaskantor, Johann Hermann Schein, was one of his teachers), and at last the medical faculty of Leipzig's university. In 1633, he made his away across Germany to obtain a post with the expedition which Frederick III of Holstein-Gottorp was planning to send to the Czar of Russia. In Moscow, Frederick's ambassadors obtained permission to prepare a second mission which, passing through South Russia's Cossack-infected reaches, would persuade the Shah of Persia to allow the establishment of a trade route from the shores of the Caspian Sea to the Baltic ports. This far more dangerous expedition, in which Fleming also took part, set out from Travemünde in 1635, paid Moscow a brief visit, and then went on to distant Ispahan. Coming back to the West in 1639, Fleming settled down with a will to his medical studies, which he completed at Leyden in 1640. He set up practice in Hamburg, only to be carried away almost immediately by an illness. The loss was a most serious one to German letters; Fleming's *Teutsche Poemata*, published posthumously in 1642, show that their author possessed one of the strongest lyric talents of his time.

FRANCK, JOHANN (1618-1677). While a student at Königsberg, Frank came under the influence of Simon Dach, who remained thenceforth his model. After completing his studies, Frank returned to his native town of Guben in the Niederlausitz, which he served as council member and mayor. He is one of the baroque's better religious lyricists in the simple vein.

FÜRER VON HAIMENDORF, CHRISTOPH (1663-1732). A Franconian, Fürer studied at the University of Altdorf; meanwhile, at the tender age of seventeen, he was elected a member of the *Society of Pegnitz Shepherds* at Nürnberg (three decades later he functioned as the society's chairman). Following lengthy journeys through France, England, Holland, Italy, and his native country, Fürer was deemed worthy of becoming a member of the Nürnberg goverment. An imitator and translator of Boileau, he also put Corneille and Tasso into German.

GERHARDT, PAUL (1607-1676). Gerhardt was born in the little Saxon town of Gräfenhainichen, where his father was mayor. The gifted boy was sent to the "Prince's School" at Grimma; at the age of twenty-one he enrolled in the University of Wittenberg, and imbibed there the uncompromising Lutheranism which was to prove so fateful in his career. For many years he served as a tutor to various families; it was only in 1651 that he obtained a pastorship at Mittenwalde near Berlin. Four years later he married Anna Maria Berthold, whose father, a Berlin lawyer, had once employed Gerhardt to instruct his children. With his appointment, a few years after his marriage, as dean of St. Nicolai-Church in Berlin, Gerhardt seemed to have reached the pinnacle of success; however he sacrificed his career to the narrowness of his religious beliefs. In 1666 Gerhardt refused to respect the religious edict of Frederick William, by which the Great Elector (who no doubt had conceived the plan in a moment of the most extreme optimism) had hoped to make the Lutheran and the Reformed ministers of his realm cease their practice of mutual recrimination. The good-hearted monarch was persuaded to allow Gerhardt to stay in office, but the latter, feeling that his conscience could not be wholly free under such conditions, insisted upon laying down his charge. Not long thereafter, the Duke of Merseburg summoned Gerhardt to Lübben a.d. Spree (Niederlausitz); there, sheltered from the breath of tolerance, he lived out his days. Gerhardt is generally conceded to be the greatest of the Protestant hymnists of the baroque; yet he is certainly not the seventeenth century's greatest writer of religious poetry: he floated above religious depths, while Greiffenberg and Scheffler plumbed them.

GREFLINGER, GEORG (c. 1620-1677). Greflinger seems to have had a childhood like that of Grimmelshausen's Simplicius; a shepherd boy from the countryside near Regensburg, he lost his parents in an attack by marauding soldiery. He fled to Regensburg, where generous souls among the town's citizenry made it possible for him to attend the gymnasium. After juristic studies, military service, and wanderings throughout the whole German East, from Vienna to Danzig, Greflinger settled in Hamburg. Through the friendship of Johann Rist he became a member, under the name "Seladon," of the *Order of the Elbe Swan*. Apart from his activities as lyricist and epigrammatist, he published a journal in Hamburg, *Der nordische Merkur*, and translated from the Spanish (Lope de Vega), Dutch, and French.

GREIFFENBERG, CATHARINA REGINA VON (1633-1694). Greiffenberg was born in her family's castle of Seyssenegg, in Lower Austria (although Greiffenberg has always been called an Upper Austrian poet). Little is known of her youth; she was her parents' only child and her father died when she was but eight years old. Her uncle, Hans Rudolf von Greiffenberg, directed her education; one must conclude that he was a splendid tutor, for Catharina Regina knew French, Italian, Spanish, Greek, and Latin, and was well acquainted with Holy Scripture, classical mythology, history, and, last but hardly least, astronomy. At the age of thirty-one she married her uncle, Hans Rudolf, in Nürnberg; presumably, her good friend, Sigmund von Birken, obtained the agreement of church and civic authorities to the semi-incestuous match. Two years before the wedding, Catharina Regina had established her literary reputation with *Geistliche Sonette, Lieder, und Gedichte* (*Spiritual Sonnets, Songs, and Poems*), and it is only natural that Nürnberg, where she was not exposed to difficulties because of her Lutheran faith, was more attractive to her than Vienna or her lonely Austrian castle. After some years of alternate residence in Franconia and the Ybbs Valley, the couple sold Schloss Seyssenegg to a certain Baron von Riesenfels, (1674), but the poetess did not make her permanent residence in Nürnberg until 1679, subsequent to her husband's death. In the same year she also became a member, "Die Tapfere" ("The Doughty One"), of Zesen's *Teutschgesinnte Genossenschaft* (*German-Minded Company*): despite her friendship with Birken, she could could never join the Pegnitz Shepherds. From Birken's death on, Catharina Regina lived in retirement, working at her contemplations on the life of Jesus, the second volume of which appeared just before she passed away.

GRIMMELSHAUSEN, HANS JAKOB CHRISTOFFEL VON (1622-1676). Grimmelshausen, it seems, lost both his home (at Gelnhausen in Upper Hessia) and his parents during the Thirty Years' War. The orphaned boy served with the Saxon and the Imperial troops in various theaters of the conflict, became regimental clerk to a Colonel Elter, and then, secretary to the Count von Schauenburg, upon whose Baden estates, at the close of hostilities, he was appointed steward. In 1661 he took a position as manager of the properties of a Strassburg jurist, Johann Kiefer, on the Ullenberg near Gaisbach (Baden), where he had earlier served Schauenburg, and from 1665 until 1667 was innkeeper at the "Silver Star" in Gaisbach. He left these positions to enter the service of the Strassburg bishop, Egon von Fürstenberg; however, he had apparently been converted to Catholicism some time before this last appointment. In his final years he was mayor of the Black Forest village of Renchen. Not long before his death he returned to the military calling of his youth, serving with the Imperial forces during Turenne's invasion of Baden (1674). Grimmelshausen's *Der abenteuerliche Simplicissimus*, together with its pendants (*Die Landstörzerin Courasche, Der seltsame Springinsfeld*, and *Das wunderbarliche Vogelnest*), are no doubt the greatest literary works inspired directly by the Thirty Years' War; his heroic-gallant novels are infinitely less effective.

GROB, JOHANN (1643-1697). From Canton Sankt Gallen, Grob, after schooling in Zürich, joined the company of Swiss halberdiers which George II of Saxony hired for service at his court. Upon completing his term of enlistment, Grob traveled through England, Holland, France, Italy, and Germany: in Switzerland once more, he entered the linen trade, and, having achieved commercial success, was named episcopal commissioner by the Abbot of Sankt Gallen. Difficulties with the good Abbot, however, caused him to move to the neighboring canton of Appenzell, where his success in negotiations with Leopold I won him ennoblement by the Emperor and honorary citizenship in the Appenzell town of Herisau. Because of Grob's wide range of experience and vigorous sense of humor, his epigrams surpass at times even those of Logau.

GRYPHIUS, ANDREAS (1616-1664). The Greif or Gryphius family came from Thuringia; Gryphius himself was born at Glogau in Silesia, at which town his father was pastor. In 1621 he lost his father, and his mother made an unhappy choice of a second husband; nevertheless, Gryphius managed to obtain a first-rate education, becoming thoroughly acquainted with nine languages and their respective literatures. After studies at the Danzig gymnasium (1634-1636), he became tutor to the sons of a wealthy Fraustadt jurist, Georg von Schönborn, in whose library he spent some of the happier hours of his otherwise unhappy youth. Upon the death of his patron, Gryphius received an inheritance which enabled him to undertake university studies at Leyden. He arrived in Holland on July 22, 1638, and by 1639 he had begun to hold his own lectures in various fields. It was in the same year that he published his *Sonn- und Feiertags-Sonette* (*Sunday and Holiday Sonnets*). In 1643 Gryphius returned briefly to Glogau, but soon set out on a journey through France and Italy as the traveling companion of a Pommeranian nobleman, Wilhelm Schlegel. After two years of traveling, Gryphius and Schlegel separated in Strassburg, where the former stayed for some time; then, by way of Amsterdam and Stettin, he went home to Silesia. Refusing calls to the universities of Frankfurt a.d. Oder, Uppsala, and Heidelberg, he opted for public life instead, and was elected, in 1650, as syndic of the diet of the principality of Glogau, in which capacity he served until his death. Most of Gryphius' tragedies, *Leo Armenius, Catharina von Georgien, Carolus Stuardus,* and *Cardenio und Celinde,* were composed in the period from 1646 until 1649, when the plays of Vondel were still fresh in his mind; only *Aemilius Paulus Papinianus* had its conception in the later Glogau period. The three comedies were written at various times: *Peter Squenz* around 1648, *Horribilicribrifax* around 1650, and *Verliebtes Gespenst* (*The Ghost in Love*), with its musical section,

Die geliebte Dornrose (*Beloved Dornrose*), in 1660. However, Gryphius' gloomy genius is best revealed not in his dramas nor in his numerous translations, but in his lyrics: orthodox Christian beliefs have seldom found better poetic expression.

GRYPHIUS, CHRISTIAN (1649-1706). The eldest son of Andreas Gryphius, Christian attended the gymnasium at Gotha and the universities of Jena and Strassburg. In 1674, a year after his return to his Silesian homeland, he was appointed professor of Greek at the Elisabethanum in Breslau, and, fourteen years later, was made rector of the city's Magdalenen-Gymnasium. Like his father, Christian Gryphius died of a stroke. Poetically, he outstripped his father in a single field, that of occasional poetry.

GÜNTHER, JOHANN CHRISTIAN (1695-1723). While a student of medicine at Wittenberg, Günther (from Striegau in Silesia) became so involved in poetic pursuits and in the wilder amusements of student life, that he was refused any further financial support by his father. Going to Leipzig, Günther came under the protection of the historian and poet, Johann Burkhard Menke, but here too he soon fell prey to drink and evil comrades, and, because of his careless behavior, lost a position as Dresden court poet which Menke had succeeded in obtaining for him. Back in Breslau, Günther's plight once more aroused the sympathy of friends, but it was too late to save him: he spent his remaining years as a wretched hedge-poet. His romantic fate, together with his undeniable genius, have caused him to be treated again and again in creative literature; some of the better-known works based upon his life are the drama of Laura Marholm and the novels by Robert Hohlbaum and Enrica von Handel-Mazzetti.

C.H.(?). The riddle of C.H.'s indentity has not been solved. Arthur Hübscher, in "Die Dichter der Neukirch'schen Sammlung" (*Euphorion*, 1922), lists, and demolishes, theories that C.H. is Hofmannswaldau, Hunold, and Hallmann.

HALLMANN, JOHANN CHRISTIAN (1647-1704). A Breslauer who studied law at Jena, Hallmann did not attain the security of a civic post like those held by his fellow Silesian dramatists and poets. A convert to Catholicism, he spent his later years in poverty; having become completely déclassé, he tried to support himself and his family by acting. In his martyr-plays, *Mariamne* (1670) and *Sophia* (1671), he reveals himself as a close student of Gryphius and the Jesuit dramatists.

HANKE, MARTIN (1633-1709). Hanke, a pastor's son, followed the usual path of a Silesian youth destined for a learned or a public career; he attended the Elisabethanum in Breslau and the University of Jena, in which latter academy his brilliance attracted widespread attention. Called back to the Elisabethanum in 1661, he became the school's rector in 1688. Several years before, he had been offered a post as imperial librarian in Vienna but refused it, not wishing to become Catholic. Apart from his poetic work, for which he was made *poeta laureatus*, he was a prolific writer on historical subjects, and, in particular, on the past of his native Silesia.

HARSDÖRFFER, GEORG PHILIPP (1607-1658). A member of a Nürnberg patrician family, Harsdörffer was educated at Altdorf, Strassburg, and on a five-year journey through the favorite lands of the baroque traveler, England, France, Holland, and Italy. In Nürnberg once more, he became an important figure in the courts and council halls of his native city, but he devoted his chief energies to poetic and linguistic undertakings. A member of the *Fruit-Bringing Society* and Zesen's *German-Minded Society*, he was a founder, with Johann Klaj, of the *Society of Pegnitz Shepherds*. Harsdörffer developed his poetic theories in his bizarre *Poetischer Trichter, die deutsche Dicht- und Reimkunst in sechs Stunden einzugiessen* (*Poetic Funnel for the Pouring-In of the Art of German Poetry and Rhyme in Six Hours*, 1647). His other important work is the *Frauenzimmer-Gesprächspiele* (*Ladies' Conversation-Games*, 1641-1649), an encyclopedic work intended to polish the minds and tongues of the well-born.

HAUGWITZ, AUGUST ADOLF VON (1645-1706). A nobleman from the Upper Lausitz, who spent his maturity as stadholder of the same region, Haugwitz wrote one of the most stageworthy dramas of the late baroque, the tragedy *Maria Stuarda*.

HEERMANN, JOHANN (1585-1647). A Silesian furrier's son, Heermann attended the Latin school at Fraustadt (today Wszowa in Poland), in which institution he met Valerius Herberger, one of Lutheranism's most effective spokesmen (the so-called "Protestant Abraham a Santa Clara"). After further studies at Breslau and Brieg, he took appointment as tutor to the sons of a Freiherr von Rothkirch, accompanying them to the universities of Leipzig, Jena, and Strassburg. An eye disease compelled him to give up his charge, but Rothkirch obtained a pastorate for him at the Silesian village of Köben. He stayed in Köben, which was frequently raided by troops during the Thirty Years' War, for twenty-six years; then he retired to Lissa, near Posen, where he died. One of his songs, "Treuer Wächter Israel," has turned up in some strange places in German literature: Clemens Brentano used it for his poem, "Die Gottesmauer," which Fontane, in turn, employed in the seduction scene of *Effi Briest*.

HÖCK, THEOBALD (1573-1618). Höck spent his life in two regions destined to be laid waste by the great wars of the baroque century. Born at Limbach in the Rhenish Palatinate, Höck became secretary to Peter Wok von Rosenberg, at the Rosenberg's ancestral castle of Wittingau in the Bohemian Forest. (A prominent ancestor of the Rosenbergs has been described by Adalbert Stifter in *Witiko*.) Höck's collection of worldly poetry, *Schönes Blumenfeldt* (*Beautiful Field of Flowers*, 1601), helped to create the lyric style of the early baroque.

HOFMANNSWALDAU, CHRISTIAN HOFMANN VON (1617-1679). Hofmannswaldau, son of an official in the Breslau government, was sent to the Danzig gymnasium, where he met and was encouraged by Martin Opitz. University studies at Leyden followed; then the young Silesian, as a member of the retinue of a Prince de Tremonville, made the grand tour through the Netherlands, England, France, and Italy, and so became well acquainted with the splendors of the baroque world. Through his father's aid he then became (in 1646) councillor in his native city, despite the fact that he had not yet reached the legal age for such a dignified post. He served Breslau admirably during the thirty-three years remaining to him, undertaking an embassy to Vienna and being elected to the presidency of the city council. Nonetheless, he found time to compose the erotic poetry, so characteristic of the high baroque, which made him famous; he is Marino's chief student in Germany.

HOMBURG, ERNST CHRISTOPH (1605-1681). From Mihla near Eisenach, Homburg spent the most of his life at Naumburg, working as lawyer and court-clerk. A follower of Opitz, a member (under the name, "The Chaste One") of the *Fruit-Bringing Society* and the *Order of the Elbe Swan*, the modest Homburg was highly regarded by his contemporaries.

HUDEMANN, HEINRICH (died before 1629). A precursor of Opitz, Hudemann studied at Rostock and was pastor at Wewelsfleth in Stormarn (Holstein). His publications were *Divitiae poeticae* (1625) and *Hirnschleifer, das ist Auserlesene teutsche Emblemata oder Sinnbilder* (*Brain-Grinder, that is: Selected German Emblems or Symbols*, 1626).

HUNOLD, CHRISTIAN FRIEDRICH (1680-1721). Hunold, who became known under the pseudonym "Menantes," was born at Wandersleben in Thuringia, received his university education (and wasted his father's fortune) at Jena, and then went to Hamburg, in the literary feuds of which he directly became involved. Eventually compelled to leave the Elbe city because of these difficulties, he won – after intervals at Arnstadt and Rudolstadt – a docentship at Halle; he lectured on "morals, German oratory, poetry, and style." Hunold is one of the so-called "gallant poets": indeed, he wrote a handbook for the would-be "galant homme", *Die allerneuste Manier höflich und galant zu schreiben* (*The Very Newest Method of Writing Politely and Gallantly*, 1702), and called his collection of verses *Edle Bemühungen müssiger Stunden in Galanten, Verliebten, Sinn-, Scherz-, und Satyrischen Gedichten* (*Noble Efforts of Idle Hours in Gallant, Amorous, Thoughtful, Jesting, and Satirical Poems*, 1702). Students interested in examining the decay of the baroque will turn to Hunold's *Satyrischer Roman* (1705).

KIRCHNER, CASPAR (circa 1624). Kirchner, a fellow student of Opitz, saw five of his own poems printed in the appendix to Zincgref's *Martini Opicii Teutsche Poemata*; as an adviser to the Liegnitz court, Kirchner sought to aid his friend Opitz both in the latter's artistic and political career.

KLAJ, JOHANN (1616-1656). A Saxon from Meissen, Klaj went to Wittenberg to study theology, but found his attention captured by the university's professor of poetry and oratory, August Buchner, "The Nightingale of the Elbe." Going to Nürnberg, Klaj earned his bread first as a private teacher, then as an instructor at the Sebaldus School; he became fast friends with Georg Philipp Harsdörffer, and, together, the two enthusiasts founded the *Pegnesischer Blumenorden* (*Pegnitz Flower-Order*) or the *Pegnitzer Hirtengesellschaft* (*Pegnitz Society of Shepherds*). Called to the pastorate at Kitzingen in 1650, Klaj survived but six years of exile from Nürnberg's sociable atmosphere. Embedded in Klaj's oratorios are numerous small gems of the German baroque lyric.

KNORR VON ROSENROTH, CHRISTIAN ANTON PHILIPP (1636-1689). Knorr's father was a pastor in the Silesian principality of Liegnitz; however, the family had been given the patent of nobility by Maximilian I. The boy's secondary schooling was unusual in that, instead of being sent to Breslau, he was enrolled in schools in Fraustadt and far-away Stettin. Knorr's universities were Leipzig and Wittenberg; after obtaining the master's degree, he undertook a long trip through Holland, France, and England, in the course of which he became familiar with the alchemistic and cabalistic arts. His choice of interests was fortunate: when Knorr returned to Germany, he was chosen chief minister of Christian August von Sulzbach, the ruler of a principality in the Upper Palatinate whose enthusiasm for things mystical had led him to embrace Catholicism. Knorr served Christian August, as adviser and alchemist, from 1668 until his death.

KÖLER, CHRISTOPH (1602-1658). Christoph Köler (or Colerus), born in Bunzlau and trained in Frankfurt a.d. Oder and Strassburg, was, from 1624 on, co-rector of the Elisabethanum at Breslau. Here he interested many of his gifted students in the Optizian "learned art" of poetry, and Titz, Scultetus Mühlpfort, and Hofmannswaldau are among the poets who profited from his tutelage.

KÖNIG, JOHANN ULRICH VON (1688-1744). A Swabian, from Esslingen, König studied at Tübingen and Heidelberg. After a trip to Brabant, as secretary of a count whose son he had been tutoring, he went to Hamburg. He played an active role in the cultural life of that city, founding, with Brockes and Richey, the *Teutschübende Gesellschaft* (*German-Using Society*), and providing librettos for the Hamburg opera. In 1719, following stays in Leipzig and Weissenfels, König went to Dresden; there he became court poet, confidential secretary, and after Besser's death, master-of-ceremonies. Probably his most characteristic work is an incomplete epic portrait of his lord, Augustus the Strong: it is called *Augustus im Lager*.

KUHLMAN, QUIRINUS (1651-1689). Kuhlmann was a Breslauer in whom the mystical urges of the Silesian early got the upper hand. While a student at Jena, Kuhlmann became convinced that the humanistic universities and the dogmatic churches were equally untrue to Christianity. Next, Kuhlmann proceeded to Leyden, read Jakob Böhme, and fell in with a Dutch religious figure, Johannes Rothe, who helped convert him to a chiliastic way of thought. Kuhlmann and Rothe planned a religious renaissance for all of Europe, but difficulties arose between them; and Kuhlmann, now convinced that he was the Son of God, set off by himself to establish his new and purified world-empire, "das Kuhlmannstum." His travels in service of this project took him to England, France, Rome, Constantinople, and, finally, to Russia, where, upon the direction of the patriarch of Moscow, he was burned at the stake. His first important collection of religious poetry is *Himmlische Liebes-küsse* (*Heavenly Kisses of Love*, 1671), in whose sonnets God is still regarded as an entity outside the soul of man; *Der Kühlpsalter* (1684) leads the reader into the madhouse created by Kuhlmann's religious egotism – but a madhouse, nonetheless, constructed with unusual poetic power.

LAURENTIUS VON SCHÜFFIS (Johann Martin) (1633-1702). Johann Martin was born at Schnüffis (Schnifis) in the Vorarlberg; after an adventurous life as a wandering student, as a player in Vienna, and as court actor to Archduke Karl Ferdinand of the Tyrol, Martin studied theology and entered the Capuchin order. He died as a member of the Capuchin community at Constance. Martin employed an anagram on his patronymic in the titles of most of his works: in his autobiography, *Des Miranten... wunderlicher Weg* (*Mirants' Wondrous Way*, 1678), and in his collections of poetry (*Mirantische Waldschallmey: Mirant's Forest Shawm*, 1688, and others), where he, in the tradition of Spee, uses the paraphernalia of pastoral poetry for religious ends.

LEIBNIZ, GOTTFRIED WILHELM (1646-1716). A Leipzig professor's son, Leibniz became the greatest philosopher of his age and the most important German thinker before Kant; his ideal of a synthesis of reason and faith grows out of the baroque, although, because of its optimism, it is scarcely characteristic of the baroque. However, Leibniz was not only important as a philosopher: a poet himself, he judged German literature with remarkable acuteness (see his judgment on Spee), and was also, like Zesen, Logau, and many other figures in the German baroque, much concerned with the purification of his mother tongue – this despite the fact that he wrote his philosophical works in French or Latin.

LIST, G. (circa 1720?). Seventeen poems in Neukirch's collection bear the initials, G.L., and one the name, G.List. Hübscher (*Euphorion*, 1922) surmises that the poet may be the Gottfried List mentioned in the continuation of Jöcker's *Gelehrtenlexikon*: "from Reichenbach in the Vogtland, master of philosophy, went to Warsaw in 1720 as field-chaplain with Electoral Saxony's mounted Garde de Corps, and after his return became pastor at Niederseefeld."

LÖWENSTERN, MATTHÄUS APELLES VON (1594-1648). Löwenstern is one of those literary musicians so common in the baroque: compare Heinrich Albert, Johann Hermann Schein, Johann Beer, W.C. Printz, and Johann Kuhnau. From Upper Silesia, Löwenstern began his career as a teacher, became Kapellmeister in Bernstadt, married money, and then – a step into a still higher world – was named councillor to Duke Karl Friedrich von Münsterberg-Oels. Nor did these honors make his cup overflow: he was subsequently appointed imperial councillor and raised into the nobility by Ferdinand III.

Löwenstern had a double importance for the German lyric: he was both a spiritual poet in his own right and the patron of Andreas Tscherning.

LOGAU, FRIEDRICH VON (1604-1655). Logau was born on his family's estate, Brockut near Nimptsch in Silesia; his studies at the Brieg gymnasium seem to have been interrupted by the early campaigns of the Thirty Years' War. Having studied at Frankfurt a.d. Oder, Logau assumed the management of Brockut, no easy task, since the family's lands had been ravaged by soldiery. In 1644 Logau obtained a position as councillor to Duke Ludwig of Brieg, whose parents had been fond of Logau when he was a gymnasium student; when, a decade later, Duke Ludwig received the principality of Liegnitz, Logau followed him to his new seat, and died there in July of the following year. Logau had tried his wings as an epigrammatist in 1638, with the publication of two hundred epigrams under the pseudonym, "Salomon von Golau"; in 1654 he brought out the collection, *Salomons von Golau Deutscher Sinn-Gedichte Drei Tausend* (*Three Thousand German Epigrams of Salomon von Golau*), which established him as the greatest epigrammatist, on secular matters, of his century. A witty and a tolerant writer, Logau has achieved the widest and most lasting popularity of all the baroque poets.

LOHENSTEIN, DANIEL CASPAR VON (1635-1683). Young Caspar (his family received the patent of nobility and the name "Lohenstein" in 1670). was like young Lessing, a "horse that needed double fodder". Born at Nimptsch in Silesia, he began the Brieg gynmasium at seven and the University of Leipzig af fifteen, later going on to Tübingen. His "educational trip" took him not only through Holland but through other countries seldom visited by the baroque's gentlemen-travelers – Switzerland, Austria, and Hungary. Upon his return to Silesia, he married profitably and became, at thirty-one, an official for the princely house of Württemberg-Oels (which Johann Scheffler had served as physician a decade before). Later, the city council of Breslau summoned him to be its syndic, and he was often sent to Vienna on the difficult task of defending the rights of Silesian Protestants. The author of the massive courtly novel, *Grossmüthiger Feldherr Arminius* (*The Magnanimous General Arminius*, 1689), Lohenstein also wrote the most important German tragedies of the later baroque, *Ibrahim Bassa*, *Cleopatra*, *Agrippina*, *Epicharis*, *Sophonisbe*, and *Ibrahim Sultan*. The object, ever since Gottsched, of critical attack because of his bombast, Lohenstein is nevertheless a poet whose genius, though perhaps perverse, has proved itself to be authentic.

LUDWIG, FÜRST ZU ANHALT-KOETHEN (1597-1650). Literary history remembers Ludwig for accomplishments having little to do with his abilities as a sovereign. He was co-founder, with Caspar von Teutleben, marshal of the Weimar court, of *Die fruchtbringende Gesellschaft* (*The Fruit-bringing Society*, later also called the *Palmenorden*). The model for the society was the Florentine *Accademia della crusca*, of which Ludwig had become a member during his years in Italy (1598-1604). The *Fruit-Bringing Society* was formally founded at Castle Hornstein on August 24, 1617; Ludwig followed von Teutleben in the society's chairmanship, and held the post until his death.

LUND, ZACHARIAS (1608-1667). Lund is that *rara avis*, a Slesvig poet of the baroque. Lund's education was entirely German: he attended the gymnasium in Hamburg and the universities of Leipzig, Wittenberg, and Königsberg; but, as a Danish subject, he spent his maturity in various educational and governmental posts north of the Eider. He was rector of the Latin school at Herlufsholm on Sjælland, then librarian to Count Jörgen Seefeldt (whose collection of 26,000 volumes was reputed to be one of the finest in Scandinavia), and finally "Royal Danish Court-Secretary" and vicar of the bishopric of Aarhus.

MELISSUS (actualy SCHEDE), PAUL (1539-1602). Melissus, a precursor of the baroque, was born in Franconia; a humanist and a good Latin lyricist, he was crowned *poeta laureatus* by Emperor Ferdinand I in 1564, and often served as an envoy for Ferdinand's successors, Maximilian and Rudolf. In such official capacity Melissus appeared, in 1582, at the court of Elizabeth of England. Melissus is notable in German letters for his translations of *Die Psalmen Davids in Teutische Gesangreymen* (*The Psalms of David in German Song-Rhymes*, 1572), in which the influence of the Pléiade can be observed. Five of Melissus' poems are included by Zincgref in the appendix to *Martini Opicii Teutsche Poemata*.

MOSCHEROSCH, HANS MICHAEL (1601-1669). An Alsatian, from Wilstädt near Strassburg, Moscherosch was descended from a family of Aragonese extraction. When he had completed his law studies at Strassburg, Moscherosch made the obligatory journey to France; upon his return, he earned his keep as a tutor and an official in various public positions. Like Grimmelshausen and Greflinger, Moscherosch suffered severe personal misfortunes during the Thirty Years' War: he lost two wives, was thrice plundered, and stood on the brink of starvation. In the post-war years he successfully administered a number of important charges, but made himself unpopular by "writing and telling too much truth." His final service was as councillor to the Countess of Hesse-Kassel. In his *Wunderliche und wahrhaftige Gesichte Philanders von Sittewald* (*Wondrous and True Visions of Philander von Sittewald*, 1640), based on the *Sueños* of Quevedo Villegas, he gave the baroque one of its major satires; as "Der Träumende" ("The Dreamer") he was made a member of the *Fruit-Bringing Society*.

MÜHLPFORT, HEINRICH (1639-1681). A Breslauer of manifold talents, Mühlpfort began as a painter, then became a druggist, then studied medicine at Leipzig, and at last ended this apprentice stage of his career by winning a doctorate of law at Wittenberg. A friend of Hofmannswaldau, he spent the years between the completion of his academic training and his death (presumably of gout) in his native city, employed as a notary and devoting his leisure hours to the composition of occasional poetry.

NEANDER, JOACHIM (1650-1680). Neander, the most important song-writer of the Reformed Church, was born in Bremen. His employment, as tutor-companion to five young men from Cologne and Frankfurt mercantile houses, enabled him to go to Heidelberg, the academic center of German Calvinism; his own father, a teacher at Bremen's Latin school, was of course unable to finance his son's university education. At the age of twenty-four he became rector of the Latin school at Düsseldorf; not long before his death he was appointed "third preacher" at Bremen's Martinikirche. Neander was a man with a double artistic gift: he composed music for a good many of his songs and psalms.

NEUKIRCH, BENJAMIN (1665-1729). Neukirch, from Upper Silesia was educated at Breslau and at the universities of Frankfurt a.d. Oder, Halle, and Leipzig. Growing bored with his Breslau law-practice, he set himself up a teacher of poetry and eloquence in Frankfurt. After some years as a tutor in noble houses he became professor at the newly founded *Ritterakademie* (*Knights' Academy*) in Berlin; and, upon the academy's dissolution, went, as tutor and councillor, to the little Ansbach court of the "Franconian Hohenzollerns." A good epigrammatist, translator, and imitator of Boileau, Neukirch's best deed for German literature was his collecting and editing of the lyrics of the later Silesians; the fruits of his labors were published in the seven volumes of *Des Herrn von Hofmannswaldau und anderer Deutschen auserlesene und bisher ungedruckte Gedichte* (*Selected and, Until Now, Unprinted Poems of Herr von Hofmannswaldau and Other Germans*, 1695-1727).

NEUMARCK, GEORG (1621-1681). A Thuringian, Neumarck set out in 1640 on his way to the University of Königsberg, but a series of misfortunes (including an attack by robbers on the Garleber Heath) brought him instead to Kiel, where he worked for two years as a tutor. On April 12, 1643, he was finally able to sail from Lübeck on the last leg of his journey; in Königsberg, apart from law studies, he devoted himself to poetry under the tutelage of Simon Dach. There followed interludes in Warsaw, Thorn, Danzig (where he became a friend of Johann Peter Titz), and Hamburg; in 1653, he was appointed librarian at Weimar by Wilhelm II of Saxe-Weimar, chairman of the *Fruit-Bringing Society* and leading patron of the arts. Later, Neumarck was made archival secretary of the duchy; his master also saw to it that he was granted several distinguished posts within the noblest of all the German language-societies. Neumarck's "Wer nur den lieben Gott lässt walten" had the distinction of becoming one of the most popular spiritual songs of the seventeenth century.

OMEIS, MAGNUS DANIEL (1646-1708). A Nürnberger, Omeis studied law at the University of Altdorf; following further studies at Strassburg, Omeis went to Vienna as tutor in the house of the Brandenburg ambassador. In 1674, returning to Altdorf as the tutor of two Bohemian noblemen, he suddenly found himself raised to academic glory: his old university named him to the professorship of poetry and eloquence. Elected a member of the *Society of Pegnitz Shepherds* in 1667, he became its "chief shepherd" in 1697. Both practicing lyricist and theoretician, Omeis attempted to combine the virtuosity of the Pegnitz poets with the sober theories of Christian Weise.

OPITZ, MARTIN (1597-1639). Opitz, whose father was a well-to-do butcher, was born at Bunzlau in Silesia. He attended the Magdalenen-Gymnasium in Breslau, then, after a brief period at Beuthen, immatriculated at the University of Frankfurt a.d. Oder. Dissatisfied with life at Frankfurt, Opitz went on to Heidelberg, where he made many friends, among them Julius Zincgref and Caspar Barth. The dissolution of the Heidelberg University in 1620 (its patron had, of course, been the unlucky Frederick V) forced Opitz to flee to Holland, whose great Latin poet, Daniel Heinsius, had been favorably impressed by the German's translations of his poems. Next, Opitz visited his Danish friend, Hamilton (a colleague from Heidelberg) in Jutland; returning to Silesia, he soon became the recipient of an appointment as professor of philosophy and poetry at the newly founded gymnasium in Weissenburg (Transylvania). Upon giving up his teaching post, he found a new refuge at the court of Duke of Liegnitz: during this period he wrote (in five days) *Das Buch von der deutschen Poeterei*, the basic poetic of the German baroque. A year later, in 1625, he published his collected poems (basing his edition upon that published by his friend Zincgref in Strassburg in 1624); at the same time he was crowned *poeta laureatus* by Emperor Ferdinand II in Vienna. From 1626 until 1632, Opitz, although a Lutheran, served as secretary to Burggraf Karl Hannibal von Dohna, president of the imperial chamber at Breslau and a fanatic opponent of Protestantism. It was at Karl Hannibal's request that the Emperor ennobled Opitz, giving him the appellation, "von Boberfeld"; and the Burggraf did Opitz a second good turn by sending him on a secret mission to Paris, where he came into contact with Hugo Grotius, the Dutch jurist and humanist. In 1632, when Breslau's indignant citizens drove out Karl Hannibal, Opitz entered the diplomatic service of the Dukes of Liegnitz-Brieg, in which capacity he visited the headquarters of the Swedish leader, Oxenstjerna; he also accompanied another Swede, Banér, on his Bohemian campaign. The Imperial troops re-entered Silesia in 1634, and Opitz hastened with his master, Johann Christian von Brieg, to Thorn in West Prussia. In 1637, having settled in Danzig, Opitz was chosen historiographer by Vladislav IV of Poland; yet there is reason to believe that he acted simultaneously as a Swedish agent against the Poles. On August 20, 1639, even as he enjoyed these well-paid positions, he was carried off by the plague. An industrious translator, of Heinsius, Grotius, Sophocles, Seneca, Barclay, Rinuccini, and the psalms, the author of a work (*Schäferei von der Nymphen Hercinie*) that helped to found German pastoral literature, Opitz's greatest importance lies in his poetic theories and in his lyrics. A poet of rather mediocre gifts, he was able, nonetheless, to put his stamp on the whole of German baroque poetry.

OPPELT, JOANNES (1673-1729). Oppelt was born at Pilau in Bohemia. His admission to the Jesuit order took place in 1690; he was active first as a teacher of the humanities, rhetoric, and Hebrew, and later in the public ministry. His single poetic work is the *Geist- und Sinnreiche Gedanken über Verschiedene aus der Natur, Kunst, und Wissenschaften vorgestellte Sinnbilder* (*Clever and Ingenious Thoughts Concerning Various Symbols, Presented from Nature, Art, and the Sciences*), published posthumously in 1749.

PLAVIUS, JOHANNES (circa 1630). Plavius, or Plauen, is another of the baroque poets about whose life little is known. He seems to have come from Danzig, or, at any rate, to have spent his poetic career there, since the single sections of his *Trauer- und Treugedichte* (*Poems of Lamentation and Faithfulness*, 1630), as well as many of the occasional poems included therein, are dedicated to inhabitants of the old Baltic seaport. In the poetics of the second half of the seventeenth century, Plavius became a proverbial figure of fun because of his use of diminuitives for rhyming; yet, despite his stylistic oddities, he was technically one of the most able poets in a period that had many virtuosi.

RICHEY, MICHAEL (1678-1761). The scion of a Hamburg mercantile family, Richey distinguished himself at Wittenberg by the variety of his interests. Fragile health prevented him from seeking an academic post at his *alma mater*; the same condition – which is belied by the high years he attained – kept him from accepting a call to Greifswald. Later on, feeling himself stronger in wind and limb, he became rector of the gymnasium at Stade, but during the Great Northern War, when Stade (which had become Swedish by the Peace of Westphalia) was about to be besieged by the Danes, he fled to Hamburg. There Richey played an active part in the city's educational and cultural life, teaching Greek in the gymnasium and founding, with Brockes and König, the *German-Using Society*.

RINCKART, MARTIN (1586-1649). Known to all Lutherans for his "Nun danket alle Gott," written for the centenary celebration of the Augsburg Confession, Rinckart had come from the very heart of the Luther country, from Eilenburg in Saxony. Following studies at Leipzig, in the course of which Rinckart supported himself with his musical abilities, Rinckart was made cantor, then deacon, at Luther's birthplace of Eisleben. In 1613 he became pastor at Erdenbirn and, four years later, "Archidiakonus" in his native town. Rinckart wrote not only songs for the church but spiritual comedies, like *Der Eislebische Christliche Ritter* (*The Christian Knight of Eisleben*, 1613).

RIST, JOHANN (1607-1667). Rist's father was pastor at Ottensen near Hamburg, and young Johann had no other thought than to follow in his father's footsteps. He studied at the universities of Rinteln and Rostock (and perhaps at Leipzig and Leyden), and, at the age of 28, was named pastor at Wedel, not far from his birthplace. In 1645 he was made *poeta laureatus* by Emperor Ferdinand III, and, not forgetful of his debt to even that distant Catholic patron, he wrote two festival dramas concerning the end of the Thirty Years' War, *Das friedewünschende Teutschland* (*Germany Longing for Peace*, 1647) and *Das friedejauchzende Teutschland* (*Germany Rejoicing in Peace*, 1653). A member of the *Fruit-Bringing Society* and *Society of Pegnitz Shepherds*, Rist himzelf founded, in 1656, the *Elbeschwanenorden* (*Order of the Elbe Swan*). A poet who possessed a gift for simple and powerful expression, Rist is the author of the wonderful hymn, "O Ewigkeit, du Donnerwort," of which Wilhelm Riehl makes such good use in his story, *Gespensterkampf*.

ROBERTHIN, ROBERT (1600-1648). Roberthin, East Prussian and cosmopolitan, gave his colleagues in the Königsberg poetic circle a link with the outside world. He studied at Königsberg, Leipzig, and Strassburg; at the last university he met Opitz, with whom he later carried on a lengthy correspondence. Like many baroque poets, Roberthin was afflicted with wanderlust; in tutorial and secretarial capacities he repeatedly left his native city, traveling to Holland, England, France, and Italy. His appointment, in 1637, as secretary of the Prussian high court in Königsberg and his marriage, two years later, seem at last to have tamed his passion for travel. Roberthin's peregrinations and his official duties kept him from publishing his own poetry; Heinrich Albert included his friend's poems in his *Arien*, and so preserved them for posterity.

ROMPLER VON LÖWENHALT, JESAIAS (1605-after 1672). Little is known of Rompler's life. It is assumed that he was born at Wiener Neustadt (Austria); he claims to have accompanied the Dukes Leopold Friedrich and Georg von Württemberg on their travels, and, by his lack of a fixed abode, to have avoided provincialisms in his language. He aided Schneuber in founding the anti-Opitzian *Aufrichtige Gesellschaft von der Tanne* (*Upright Society of the Fir*, 1633) in Strassburg; in 1645 he was admitted by Zesen to the *Rosenzunft* (*Rose-Guild*) of the *Deutschgesinnte Genossenschaft* (*German-Minded Fellowship*).

SCHEFFLER, JOHANN, called "ANGELUS SILESIUS" (1624-1677). At Breslau's Elisabethanum, young Scheffler was led by Christoph Köler to make his first attempts at verse. He began his university studies with a year at Strassburg (medicine and history), then went to Leyden, at which city he read both Ruysbroeck and Böhme – a strong concern with theological problems is already evident. In 1647 he proceeded to Padua, and a year later was graduated as "dr. phil. et med." Back in Silesia, Scheffler fell in with Daniel von Czepko, who introduced him to the writings of Valentin Weigel; becoming personal physician to Duke Silvius Nimrod von Württemberg-Oels, he got to know Abraham von Frankenberg, and was led still further into the realm of mystic thought. Upon Frankenberg's death (and following an argument with the Oels court-preacher, who had forbidden the printing of a religious tractate by Scheffler), Scheffler returned to Breslau. In 1653 he caused a great scandal in

Breslau Protestant circles by becoming (with considerable ostentation) a member of the Roman Church. Called "Johannes Angelus" at his new baptism, he added the designation "Silesius" to avoid confusion with a like-named theologian. Eight years after his conversion he was consecrated a priest at Neisse, and shortly thereafter, by means of his connections in Vienna, forced Breslau's city fathers to allow a public Corpus Christi procession, something that had been illegal since 1525. For a time Scheffler served the Prince Bishop of Breslau, Sebastian von Rostock, and is said to have written fifty-five polemical tracts against the Lutherans during this period; his last years he spent as a recluse in the Sankt Matthias cloister in the Silesian capital. Ironically, Scheffler, who once had sought a supra-confessional, mystical Christianity, and had given this desire classical expression in *Geistreiche Sinn- und Schlussreime* (*Ingenious Rhymes of Wit and Conclusion*, 1657) – later published as *Der cherubinische Wandersmann* (*The Cherubical Wanderer*) – became the most bitter defender of extreme orthodoxy. In this dogmatic spirit he wrote his final work, the sometimes grotesque, sometime majestic *Sinnliche Beschreibung der vier letzten Dinge* (*Sensuous Description of the Four Last Things*, 1675).

SCHERFFER VON SCHERFFENSTEIN, WENZEL (1603-1674). Another of the baroque's poet-musicians, Scherffer, from Leonschütz in Upper Silesia, was at once castle organist and court poet for the Dukes of Brieg.

SCHIRMER, DAVID (1623-1683). A minister's son from Poppendorf near Freiburg (Saxony), Schirmer attended secondary school in Halle (where his talents aroused the interest of Christian Gueintz, the orthographer); his universities were Leipzig and Wittenberg. In 1674 he was made a member of Zesen's *German-Minded Fellowship*; three years later he was called to Dresden as court poet. In 1656 he also became the librarian of the electoral prince, Johann Georg II, who was determined to turn his city into a German Athens. Dismissed from his librarianship in 1682, Schirmer, one of the most charming light poets of the baroque, died the following year.

SCHMOLCK, BENJAMIN (1672-1737). Schmolck, whose father was pastor at Brauchitschdorf in Silesia, was destined from his tenderest years for a career in the church. After attending the gymnasia at Liegnitz and Lauban, Schmolck proceeded to Leipzig, where, instead of losing his faith at that gallant university, he found himself strengthened in it. Rising rapidly in the hierarchy of the Lutheran church, Schmolck became "first pastor" and inspector of schools and churches at Schweidnitz before a series of strokes put an end to his career. A most fecund poet on the spiritual vein, Schmolck is also noteworthy for the training in verse-writing which he gave his young friend, Johann Christian Günther.

SCHNEUBER, JOHANN MATTHIAS (1614-1665). Schneuber, from Mühlheim in Baden, is an important figure in the development of baroque literature in southwestern Germany. Director of the gymnasium at Strassburg, Schneuber – with the aid of the mysterious Jesaias Rompler von Löwenhalt – founded, in 1633, the *Aufrichtige Gesellschaft von der Tanne* (*Upright Society of the Fir*), the second oldest, after the *Fruit-Bringing Society*, of Germany's language societies.

SCHOCH, JOHANN GEORG (1627-after 1688). A Leipziger who studied at his home city's university, Schoch appears to have practiced law at Naumburg. Little is known of his career: in the summer of 1666 he was an official at Westerburg (Hesse-Nassau); in 1688 he was in the service of the Dukes August Wilhelm and Ludwig Rudolf at Brunswick. Schoch enriched baroque drama with his *Comoedia vom Studenten-Leben* (*Comedy of Student Life*, 1657), a drastic satire on student life; many of the numbers in his *Neu-Erbauter Poetischer Lust- und Blumen-Garten* (*Newly Built Poetic Garden of Joy and Flowers*, 1660) became folksongs in the course of time.

SCHOTTEL, JUSTUS GEORG (1612-1676). Schottel lost his father, pastor at Einbeck in Hannover, when he was only a boy; his mother, impoverished, was compelled to apprentice him to a merchant, but young Schottel was able, after a year in the shop, to find the necessary means to continue his education. He attended the secondary school at Hildesheim, the gymnasium at Hamburg, and the universities at Leyden and Wittenberg. In 1638 the University of Wittenberg was temporarily closed by the misfortunes of war, and Schottel went to Brunswick, becoming there the tutor of the children of Duke August, among them the gifted Anton Ulrich. He received his doctorate of laws at Helmstedt in 1646, and thus equipped, occupied a number of important posts at Wolfenbüttel. Schottel's fame rests upon his theoretical and grammatical works; his *Ausführliche Arbeit von der Teutschen Haubt-Sprache* (*Extensive Work Concerning the German Literary Language*, 1663) is the first German grammar written in accordance with "scientific" principles. A member, "Der Suchende" ("The Searcher"), of the *Society of Pegnitz Shepherds*, Schottel's verse has the playful elegance characteristic of that school (to which he gave a poetic with his *Teutsche Vers- oder Reimkunst*: *Art of German Verse or Rhyme*, 1635).

SCHWABE VON DER HEYDE, ERNST (circa 1616). Schwabe von der Heyde is known only through the references made to him by other poets. He is said to have published a small book of verse at Frankfurt a.d. Oder in 1616, but Zincgref, in 1624, says that he has attempted in vain to obtain a copy of the work (in which Schwabe is supposed to have used the first German Alexandrines and to have called attention to the sonnet form). Several of Schwabe's poems are preserved in Opitz's argument for the literary possibilities of the German language, *Aristarchus sive de contemptu Teutonicae Linguae* (1617).

SCHWARZ, SIBYLLA (1621-1638). Sibylla Schwarz, the "Pommeranian Sappho," spent her brief life at Greifswald, where her father, Christian Schwarz, was a member of the city government. Her poems were published by Samuel Gerlach in 1650.

SCHWIEGER, JAKOB (1624-after 1667). A native of Altona who first studied, then preached at Wittenberg, Schwieger returned to Hamburg in 1654, and there devoted himself to literary undertakings. In 1657 he joined the Danish army in its campaign against the Swedish garrisons in Poland, and it was long presumed that Schwieger composed *Die geharnschte Venus* (*Venus in Armor*, 1660) while a member of the Danish force. However, in 1897 Albert Köster robbed Schwieger of this brightest star in his literary crown by proving that Caspar Stieler was the true author of the collection.

SCULTETUS, ANDREAS (c. 1622-1647). A Bunzlau shoemaker's son and a relative of Andreas Tscherning, Scultetus was a student of Christoph Köler at the Elisabethanum in Breslau. Lessing, who rediscovered him and published his poems, praised his artistry in warmest terms: "One of the chief beauties in our author is his language, which is so rich, so strong, so picturesque, that it deserves comparison only with Opitz's. Fleming, Tscherning, and all the others who in those days emulated Opitz, fall far shy of being [Scultetus'] equals in this respect."

SIEBER, JUSTUS (1628-1695). Born at Einbeck in Hannover, an advocate's son, Sieber studied at Helmstedt, Leipzig, and Wittenberg. In 1659 he became pastor at Schandau in "Saxon Switzerland."

SIMLER, JOHANN WILHELM (1605-1672). A Züricher and the most prominent of Opitz's Swiss imitators, Simler was trained for the ministry. Having proved, in pastorates at Urtikon and Herliberg, that he was incompetent as a public speaker, he obtained a school inspectorship at Zürich, and kept the post with honor for the rest of his days. In his lifetime he published four editions of his *Teutsche Getichte*; he became so beloved of his Swiss compatriots that they fearlessly called him the equal of Opitz.

SPEE, FRIEDRICH VON (1591-1635). Spee was the scion of a noble Rhenish family, but he possessed a nobility of heart more important than that of birth. The recipient of a careful education at his home (at Kaiserswerth near Düsseldorf) and at the Jesuit gymnasium at Cologne, Spee himself entered the Society of Jesus on September 22, 1610. Following the novitiate at Trier, studies at Würzburg, and teaching at Speyer, Worms, and Mainz, Spee was ordained a priest in 1622. In 1627-28 he served in Würzburg as father-confessor to criminals condemned to death; among these unfortunates were more than two hundred persons sentenced to be burnt for witchcraft. So horrified was Spee by what he saw and learned that he wrote the *Cautio criminalis* (1631) in which he attacked witch-hunting, a practice to which Spee's Würzburg superior, Bishop Adolf von Ehrenburg, was passionately devoted. Among Spee's later accomplishments as a man of God were his reconversion of the Hannoverian town of Peine to Catholicism – his success so annoyed certain local Protestants that they attempted to murder him – and his exemplary conduct during the siege of Trier by Imperial and Spanish troops in 1635. Worn out by his humanitarian efforts, in particular as a nurse, Spee died on August 4 of that year. Spee's greatest literary work is, of course, his *Trutz-Nachtigall* (*Better than the Nightingale*, first published in 1649), which Spee wrote while convalescing at Falkenhagen from the attempt upon his life.

STEGMANN, JOSUA (1588-1632). Stegmann, a Lutheran pastor's son, studied at Leipzig. Several years after his appointment as a teacher in the gymnasium at Stadthagen, Stegmann became a university professor almost inadvertently: by fiat of the Duke of Schaumburg, the gymnasium was moved to Rintelen and transformed into a university. (The life of Rintelen's university was also ended by fiat: Jerome Napoleon ordered it closed in 1809.) Stegmann's spiritual songs were published under the title *Erneuerte Herzen-Seufzer in neuen Reimen* (*Renewed Heart-Sighs in New Rhymes*) by Andreas Gryphius in 1644.

STIELER, CASPAR (1632-1707). Stieler, the poet of *Die geharnschte Venus* (*Venus in Armor*, 1660), was of a changeable disposition: after studying theology and medicine at Leipzig, Erfurt, Marburg, and Giessen, he entered military service. Later, tiring of camp life and of travels which had brought him as far as distant Königsberg, he returned to Jena, where he studied law. Next, he became secretary to the Dukes of Schwarzburg, then "secretary of title deeds" at Eisenach. The last decades of his life he spent without public office. A member of the *Fruit-Bringing Society*, Stieler bore the name "Der Spate," "The Late Comer."

STOCKMANN, ERNST (1634-1712). Paul Stockmann, Ernst's father, had served Gustav Adolf as chaplain on the Swedish king's first continental campaigns, and had indeed been called to Norrtälje (in Uppland) as pastor of a German congregation there. Ironically enough, Paul Stockmann, upon his return to German soil, became minister at Lützen, and there Ernst was born some eighteen months after the battle which brought death to his father's patron. Ernst Stockmann himself was a shining example of a Lutheran clergyman, a good preacher and a good man, closely concerned with the welfare of his congregation. His virtues were eventually rewarded with a superintendentship at Allstedt (in Saxe-Weimar).

STOLLE, GOTTLIEB (1673-1744). Stolle, who wrote under the pseudonym, "Leander aus Schlesien" ("Leander from Silesia"), had the typical career of the baroque poet. Born at Liegnitz, scholar at Breslau, student of law at Leipzig, he had to discontinue his studies for lack of funds; following service as a tutor in Schweidnitz and Leipzig, he took up his academic work once again at Halle. From 1714 until 1717 Stolle was director of the gymnasium at Hildburghausen in the Harz Mountains; in 1717 he was called to a professorship at Jena. Despite the sobriety of his calling and his character, he named his collection of poems, which appeared in 1699, *Deutsche Gedichte und galante Gedichte* (*German Poems and Gallant Poems*).

TITZ, JOHANN PETER (1619-1689). Titz, or Titius, was from Liegnitz in Silesia. In the Elisabethanum at Breslau, Christoph Köler is supposed to have interested Titz in the poet's calling, an interest furthered by Martin Opitz at Danzig, where Titz went to complete his secondary education. Following five years of university studies at Rostock, Titz found his way to Königsberg, becoming there a close friend of Dach, Alberti, and Roberthin. He returned to Danzig in 1645 as a teacher (later co-rector) of the Marienschule; in 1651 he became professor at the Danzig gymnasium.

TSCHERNING, ANDREAS (1611-1659). The brutal measures of Opitz's master, Karl Hannibal von Dohna, compelled the youthful Tscherning to flee his Silesian birthplace of Bunzlau. He found refuge in Görlitz, the mayor of which gave the fugitive a place as tutor in his home. After studies in the gymnasia at Görlitz and

Breslau (whither he had gone after Karl Hannibal's deposal), he went north to the university of Rostock. Forced to abandon his university work after two years, for lack of funds, he returned to Bunzlau, but once again religious persecutions prompted him to try his fortunes elsewhere. He managed to support himself by giving private lessons at Breslau, where, in 1642, he established his literary reputation by publishing the collection, *Deutscher Getichte Frühling* (*Springtide of German Poems*). The book won him the patronage of Matthäus Apelles von Löwenstern, whose financial support then enabled him to complete his master's degree at Rostock. In 1644 he succeeded his teacher, Peter Lauremberg, as professor of poetry at Rostock, a post he retained until his death.

Venus-Gärtlein (*Venus' Small Garden*). The most popular song-book of the seventeenth century, put together by an anonymous hand and published in 1656.

WECKHERLIN, GEORG RUDOLF (1584-1653). Weckherlin, after studying at Tübingen, made a lengthy journey through Germany, France, and England, in the course of which he became convinced that German verse lagged far behind that being produced by French and English pens. Upon his return to his home city of Stuttgart, he was made secretary and court-poet to the Duke of Württemberg (1610). During this Stuttgart period, Weckherlin published his *Oden und Gesänge* (*Odes and Songs*, 1618-1619), in which he attempted to correct some of the besetting sins of the German muse. The Thirty Years' War brought Weckherlin good fortune: after the defeat of the Protestants at the Battle of White Mountain, Frederick V, son-in-law of James I of England, fled to London, where a chancellory for German affairs was established. Weckherlin, who had tired of life at the Stuttgart court, became secretary of the new chancellory; King James and his successor, Charles, were so impressed by Weckherlin's abilities that they encouraged him to enter English service, in which he remained until Cromwell's accession to power. In 1641 Weckherlin published his second collection of poetry, *Geistliche und Weltliche Gedichte* (*Spiritual and Secular Poems*), which offered more than ample proof of Weckherlin's ability to capture his noteworthy contemporaries, and their deeds, in impressively bombastic verse. Although looked down upon by Opitz and his followers (and it is true that Weckherlin could not, or would not, follow the Opitzian practice of using natural word accent in verse), Weckherlin nonetheless possessed a baroque grandeur of spirit which the "swan of Boberfeld" never attained.

WEISE, CHRISTIAN (1642-1708). Weise's father, like Birken's, had been forced to leave Bohemia for religious reasons, but in literary matters Weise was the very opposite of the skillfully frivolous Nürnberg poet. While at the University of Leipzig, Weise interested himself in almost every field of learning, and thus qualified himself for positions as secretary to one nobleman and tutor to another. In 1670 he became professor at the newly founded gymnasium in Weissenfels; eight years later he was called to the rectorship of the gymnasium at Zittau, his home city. During the thirty years of Weise's administration, the Zittau gymnasium came to be one of the best institutions of its kind in Germany. Weise, who was determined to provide his students with suitable dramatic material (he regarded the theater as a "school for life"), turned out fifty-five dramas for amateur players; although he used many typically baroque subjects, he despised the thunderous Alexandrines of Gryphius and Lohenstein, preferring sober prose. In his novels, too, Weise revealed himself as the sworn foe of the baroque spirit. One suspects that Weise, in his accentuation of stylistic (and emotional) moderation and his praise of "healthy common sense," was making virtues of his shortcomings; whatever his motivation may have been, he helped to prepare the demise of the baroque and the coming to power of the enlightenment.

WERNICKE (also WARNECKE, WERNIGKE), CHRISTIAN (1661-1725). Wernicke was born at Elbing in West Prussia, the son of a Saxon father and an English mother. As a university he chose the new institution at Kiel, founded in the year of his birth; there he studied with the polyhistor and poet, Daniel Georg Morhof, under whose direction he laid the foundation for his future skill with the epigram. For a time he belonged to the service of the vicious Kristian Detlev Rantzau, stadholder of Schleswig-Holstein; then, after travels in England and France, he settled in Hamburg, only to become involved in acrimonious literary feuds with Hunold and Postel. From 1708 until 1723 Wernicke was Danish envoy in Paris. Intimately acquainted with the "gallant world," Wernicke described it with the mordancy of a Juvenal.

ZESEN, PHILIPP VON (1619-1689). The most prolific of all the baroque poets, Zesen was born in a village near Dessau as the son of a Lutheran pastor. Even as a gymnasium student at Halle, Zesen began to write poetry, a passion in which he was later encouraged by his professor at the University of Wittenberg, the famed August Buchner. After further studies at Leyden, Zesen went to Hamburg, where, on May 1, 1643, he founded the poetic society called *Die teutschgesinnte Genossenschaft* (*The German-Minded Fellowship*); he had already begun to fight for the purification of the German tongue with the poetic, *Deutscher Helikon*

(*German Helicon*, first edition, 1640). Zesen, who received the appropriate name "Der Färtige" ("The traveler") from his society, soon left Hamburg; his journeyings took him to London, Paris, Amsterdam, Rotterdam, Utrecht, Leyden, Nürnberg, and Regensburg; in the last-named city he was crowned *poeta laureatus* by Ferdinand III, and raised into the nobility. From 1655 until 1667 he maintained residence in Holland, there becoming a friend of the great Czech pedagogue, Amos Comenius. His last years were spent in Hamburg. Zesen's theories led him to absurd extremes: he spelled German in a most original way, and, being dissatisfied with a "foreign" word like "Fenster" (from Latin "fenestra"), he demanded that "Tagesleuchter" ("day-lighter") be put in its place. Nevertheless, Zesen was a literary figure of indisputable importance. His *Adriatische Rosemund* (1645) is a novel remarkable for its emotional sensitivity and its lack of religious bias; his *Assenat* (1670), on Joseph's love for Potiphar's daughter, is that rarity in the baroque, a tightly constructed novel; his *Simson* (*Samson*, 1679) treats a favorite baroque figure allegorically. As a lyricist, Zesen demonstrated almost incredible ingenuity, but not poetic genius.

ZIGLER UND KLIPPHAUSEN. HEINRICH ANSELM VON (1663-1697). Zigler und Klipphausen had the good fortune to be born the son of wealthy landowner in the Upper Lausitz. Having completed his education at the Görlitz gymnasium and the University of Frankfurt a.d. Oder, the young man returned home, to administer his father's lands and to devote the remainder of his time to literary pursuits. At the age of twenty-five he published one of the most popular novels of the late baroque, *Die asiatische Banise, oder das blutige, doch mutige Pegu* (*Asiatic Banise, or Bloody yet Brave Pegu*, 1689). His activity as councillor in Wurzen prevented him from undertaking any serious literary work during the last years of his short life.

ZINCGREF, JULIUS WILHELM (1591-1635). A native of Heidelberg and a student at its university, Zincgref made an educational tour of Switzerland, England, France, and Holland in the halcyon days before Frederick of the Palatinate accepted Bohemia's crown. The first years of the Thirty Years' War found Zincgref as executive officer of the Heidelberg courts-martial, but when Tilly besieged the city in 1622, the "General-Auditeur" had to flee, first to Frankfurt and then to Strassburg. In the Alsatian city, Zincgref served as secretary-interpreter of the French envoy, Marescot: while thus employed, he oversaw the publication of the *Teutsche Poemata* of Martin Opitz, whom he had known and admired at Heidelberg. The appendix of the *Poemata*, the *Auserlesene Gedichte anderer teutscher Poeten* (*Selected Poems of Other German Poets*), contains, among other things, twenty-two poems by Zincgref himself. The remainder of Zincgref's life was unhappy; while accompanying Marescot to Stuttgart, he came down with an illness that compelled him to abandon his secretaryship. For brief periods he held posts in Worms, Kreuznach, and Alzey; after the Protestant defeat at Nördlingen, he fled northward to join his father-in-law at Sankt Goar but was robbed during the journey. He died of the plague a little more than a year later.

(The reader interested in further bibliographical and biographical information about the poets listed above is referred to Curt von Faber du Faur, *German Baroque Literature: A Catalogue of the Collection in the Yale University Library*, New Haven, 1958.)

NOTES

1. Leo Villiger has pointed out that Seyssenegg actually lies just inside Lower Austria, near Viehdorf an der Ybbs.
2. Naso: Ovid; Nasica: Scipio Nasica; Nasamo-folk: the Nasamones, a people of ancient Libya (Cyrenaica), mentioned by Herodotus in his *Histories* II, 32 and IV, 172, 182, 190.
3. In his garden, Albert had a so-called "pumpkin-hut," where, from 1631 until 1640, the members of the Königsberg circle – among them Simon Dach, Johann Peter Titz, and Robert Roberthin – were accustomed to hold their summer assemblies. Eventually, the artistic friends came to call their group after its meeting-place. In 1645, Albert published a series of verses, set to music by himself (he was the cathedral organist in Königsberg), in which he celebrated the various members of the circle; this collection too was called the "Musikalische Kürbis-Hütte."
4. Bellona: Roman goddess of war.
5. June 28th by the Gregorian Calendar.
6. Fabius, the Roman appointed dictator after the defeat of Rome's troops at Lake Trasimene during the Punic Wars. His policy of harassing Hannibal's force while refusing a battle earned him the nickname of Cunctator, "the Delayer."
7. Marcus Claudius Marcellus was the Roman general who distinguished himself by his promptitude and determination in the period following the defeat at Cannae.
8. Carl Emil died of dysentery during the Alsatian Campaign of 1674; his death occurred in Strassburg on December 7th.
9. Rathenow fell to electoral troops on the night of June 25th, 1675. The town was commanded by the Swedish colonel Wangelin; the famous Fieldmarshal Derfflinger (Dörfling) was second in command to the Great Elector, while Major-General Götze and Colonel Dönhof were infantry officers.
10. Waldemar von Wrangel was in command of the Swedish troops in the field at Fehrbellin; his brother, Carl Gustav Wrangel, was the marshal of the Swedish force. It is the former whom Besser means here.
11. Prince Friedrich von Homburg, whose disobedience won the day at Fehrbellin for the Great Elector, and literary immortality – in Kleist's great play – for himself.
12. The Ostrogothic Regiment, which had been opposite the Mörner Regiment in the line of battle, had been decimated; its commander, Baron Adam von Wachtmeister, had been killed; the Swedish infantry regiment of Colonel Dalvig (Delwig) was completely wiped out by the Prussian cavalry.
13. Birken was born in 1626 at Wildenstein near the town of Eger, through which flows the river of the same name. He came to Nürnberg, on the "slender Pegnitz-tide," in 1645, eleven years after the murder of Wallenstein in Eger's council hall had given the little northern Sudeten town a certain gruesome fame. Even in the final years of the Thirty Years' War

the region saw heavy military activity on the part of both Lutheran and Imperial forces, and it is to this seemingly endless misery of his birthplace that Birken refers.

[14] Charles the Great, as everyone knows, was crowned emperor at Rome on Christmas Day, 800, by Pope Leo III.

[15] Louis the Pious (778-840) divided the Carolingian Empire among his sons, Lothar, Pepin, and Louis "the German," in the celebrated *divisio imperii* of 817.

[16] Lothar (795-855), after having divided his realm among his sons, retired to Cloister Prüm in the Eifel Mountains.

[17] Louis II (822-875), the eldest son of Lothar I, had the task of defending Southern Italy against the Arabs. A weak ruler, he was the last of the Carolingian monarchs of Italy.

[18] Charles the Bald (823-877), who in 875 assumed the imperial title which by rights belonged to his brother, Louis the German, was called to Italy by Pope John VIII (who had offered him the empire's crown), there to fight against the Saracens. However, made uneasy by the appearance of his nephew. Cardoman, in Italy, and distressed by the pleas of his noblemen that he return to fight against the Romans, Charles hastened back toward France. He died on the way, poisoned, perhaps, by his Jewish physician, Zedekiah.

[19] Otto the Great (912-975) did in fact re-establish the importance of the German Imperial throne.

[20] Otto II (955-7-983) died in Rome while preparing a campaign against the Greeks and their Saracen allies in Southern Italy.

[21] Otto III (980-1002) apparently died of natural causes; yet a story sprang up that Stefania, the widow of Crescentius, a Roman patrician whom Otto had had executed, first seduced Otto, then murdered him by some magical device.

[22] Henry the Saint (973-1024) in 1022 dealt the Byzantine armies in Apulia and Calabria a crushing blow. His marriage to Kunigunde is supposed to have been one in name only.

[23] Conrad II (c. 990-1039) saw it to that Burgundy was rejoined to the Empire during his reign.

[24] Henry III (1017-1056) had little difficulty with papal encroachments; as a matter of fact, he disposed of three rival claimants to the papacy (1046), and saw to it that his own appointments held the papal throne. However, it was one of these, Leo IX, who laid the foundations for the papacy's future strength.

[25] Henry IV (1050-1106) indeed had difficulty with the "papal ban"; his great opponent, Gregory IX, five times hurled the ban at him; but it was probably the defection of Henry's son to the enemy camp which broke his father's heart.

[26] Frederick William I, "the Great Elector" to be (1620-1688), held his solemn entrance into Königsberg, at whose university Dach was a professor, on November 30th, 1641.

[27] On October 10th, 1645, Louise Charlotte, the sister of Frederick William, was married to the Duke of Curland.

[28] Frederick III of Holstein-Gottorp sponsored the expeditions which took Fleming on his journeys to Russia and Persia.

[29] Perm was formerly the name of both a city and a governmental district in Russia; the city is now called Molotov.

[30] The River Kam (or Kamo) is a tributary of the Volga.

[31] One of the many appelations of Hecate-Cybele: after Mount Berecyntus in Phrygia, which was sacred to the goddess.

[32] Delos was celebrated as the natal island of Apollo and Artemis (Diana).

³³ A special name of Artemis-Diana as moon-goddess. Note that Fleming uses all the names applied in classical times to the moon-goddess: he does not distinguish between such very different goddess "constellations" as Hecate-Cybele and Artemis-Diana.
³⁴ The word derives from the oracle of Apollo of Klaros, or from Zeus Klarios as a god of fate. Thus, "deutsche Clarien" would mean "German gods of fate."
³⁵ Greflinger lived in Danzig from 1639 until 1642; in 1643 he went to Frankfurt am Main, where his first works were printed. In the spring of 1644, he was invited to return to Danzig, and it was on this occasion that he wrote the above poem. According to his biographer, Wolfgang von Oettingen, his arrival was spoiled by the discovery that Flora had been unfaithful to him.
³⁶ Greiffenberg is thinking of Cyrus the Elder, the wise prince of Xenophon's *Cyropaedia*, not the foolhardy Cyrus the Younger of the *Anabasis*.
³⁷ Isaiah, 42 : 3: "A bruised reed will he not break, and a dimly burning wick will he not quench." Matthew, 12 : 20: "A bruised reed shall he not break, and smoking flax shall he not quench...."
³⁸ Thetis, the sea-nymph who by Peleus became mother to Achilles, was an extremely hospitable divinity: she gave shelter to Dionysus on his flight from Lycurgus, and to Hephaestus when, as a sickly babe, that god was cast out of Olympus.
³⁹ Mercury, the god of merchants, was a heraldic device of Amsterdam, that most mercantile of cities.
⁴⁰ The great jurist of the baroque, Samuel Pufendorf (1632-1694), left his post at the University of Heidelberg to become professor first at the newly established University of Lund (1670), then, in 1678, official historiographer and secretary of state in Stockholm. Returning to German soil in 1686, he was appointed the historiographer of Brandenburg.
⁴¹ Hans Rudolf Werdmüller (1614-1677), a heroic and a colorful professional soldier of the baroque age, is well-known to readers of German literature through his appearance in Conrad Ferdinand Meyer's *Der Schuss von der Kanzel* (1878).
⁴² The "Sunday and Holiday Sonnets" were written before Gryphius left Silesia for Holland.
⁴³ Chach Abas is the villainous Persian king in the face of whose lusts and cruelty Gryphius' tragic heroine, Catherine of Georgia, stands adamant.
⁴⁴ The Byzantine emperor Leo Armenius (in Gryphius' tragedy of the same name) is murdered before the altar of a church in which mass is being celebrated:
  And as he fell, they stabbed him two times through the breast:
  I saw myself how he a fire on that cross pressed
  On which his body fell, and with the fire did die.
⁴⁵ Salem here means Jerusalem.
⁴⁶ Gryphius spent the first months of 1646 in Rome.
⁴⁷ Sailing from Danzig to Holland in June, 1638, Gryphius passed through a violent storm off the coast of the island of Rügen.
⁴⁸ Surname of Artemis as moon-goddess.
⁴⁹ The Danube.
⁵⁰ The mountain of the curse; cf. Deuteronomy 27.
⁵¹ Rübezahl is the mythological giant who inhabits the Riesengebirge of Silesia and Bohemia.
⁵² The Zobtenberg is a mountain to the southwest of Silesia's capital, Breslau.
⁵³ The Riesenkoppe is one of the highest peaks of the Riesengebirge.
⁵⁴ Caspar von Schwenckfeld (1489-1561), a Silesian nobleman and religious figure, the founder of a Protestant sect, whose members held to principles

of tolerance, pacifism, and freedom of conscience. The "Schwenckfelder" placed special emphasis on the free action of the spirit, and thus fell into opposition to the Lutherans, who retained the intermediary instruments of the sacraments and the Holy Scripture.

[55] Hallmann's poem was published in 1672, thus in the fifteenth year of Leopold's reign and eleven years before Leopold's hasty withdrawal from Vienna made the Holy Roman Emperor seem somewhat less than invincible. Nonetheless, the indomitable courage of Count Starhemberg in the presence of Kara Mustafa's Turkish hordes allowed Leopold to keep his reputation of invincibility.

[56] Hallmann means Poland and Sweden; in the Northern War of 1655-1660, Leopold had supported the Poles against the Swedes.

[57] The Ottoman Empire, against which (from 1662 until 1664) Leopold had waged an unsuccessful war in Transylvania.

[58] On February 27, 1670, influenced by his Spanish wife, Margareta Theresa (who attributed the death of her first-born child to her husband's toleration of the Jews), and by Graf Kollonitsch, Bishop of Wiener Neustadt, Leopold ordered the expulsion of the Jews from Vienna and from Upper and Lower Austria.

[59] Members of the "Fruit-bringing society": see the sonnet of Ludwig von Anhalt-Koethen, below.

[60] Harsdörffer's "Zinken" does not, of course, refer to a modern cornet, but to the cornett, or "cornett à bouquin," a conical bore instrument played with a cup mouthpiece, and pierced with lateral holes. Anyone who has heard the distressing tone of this hybrid instrument, half brass and half woodwind, will appreciate the aptness of Hardörffer's adjective, "shuffling"; the cornett's virtue was that it provided a soprano "brass" instrument capable of producing a diatonic scale. During the eighteenth century the cornett lost favor, making its last orchestral appearance in the Vienna production of Gluck's *Orfeo* (1772).

[61] Hofmannswaldau is probably referring to Berenice (Bernice), the daughter of Agrippa I, whose beauty caused such confusion in the heart of Titus, Roman emperor-to-be.

[62] The east wind.

[63] Theodore Beza (1519-1603) was the most distinguished of Calvin's followers; upon Calvin's death he became the leader of the Reformed Church.

[64] Zanzibar.

[65] Count Carlo Serini (properly Sereni): a lieutenant of Ernst von Starhemberg during the siege of Vienna. Sereni later on took an outstanding part in the campaign against the Turks which ended with the capture of Belgrad (September 2, 1688).

[66] Maria Theresa entered Prague on April 28, 1734, and was crowned Queen of Bohemia in Saint Wenzel's Cathedral on May 12. The situation was a dramatic one, since Prague had recently been taken by Prussian troops (December 25, 1742), then freed from them by the peace which Maria Theresa concluded with Frederick II.

[67] Irus: Cf. *The Odyssey*, XVIII, 11.5 ff. "Then up came a common beggar, who was wont to beg through the town of Ithaca, one that was known among all men for ravening greed, for his endless eating and drinking, yet he had no force or might, though he was bulky to look on. Arnaeus was his name, for so had his good mother given it him at birth, but all the young men called him Irus, because he ran on errands, whensoever any might bid him" (Butcher and Lang's translation).

[68] A pointed remark about an abuse common during the baroque age, the bestowal of nobility through the letter patent.

⁶⁹ The sonnet celebrates the marriage of Arminius (Herman), the hero of Lohenstein's gigantic courtly novel, with his beloved Thusnelda.
⁷⁰ The daughter of Oceanus and Thetis, the wife of her brother Nereus, and the mother of the Nereides: Doris' name is sometimes used to mean the sea itself.
⁷¹ The most important of the baroque "language societies", the "Fruchtbringende Gesellschaft" was founded in 1617 by Prince Ludwig of Anhalt-Koethen. Among its members were Opitz, Harsdörffer, Schottel, Rist, Zesen, Logau, Neumark, and Birken.
⁷² "Therefore be ye also ready; for in an hour that ye think not the Son of man cometh."
⁷³ It perhaps had been, as Neukirch surmises, an aim of the Great Elector, Frederick William, to win for himself the title, "King in Prussia"; however, his chief goal was a far more important and less selfish one – to make Brandenburg-Prussia the leading Protestant power of the Holy Roman Empire. The accomplishment of Frederick III of Brandenburg, the Great Elector's son and the subject of this poem, was actually much less substantial than Neukirch makes out: for his support of the Emperor Leopold in the War of the Spanish Succession, he was allowed to assume the title, "King Frederick *in* Prussia"; the title, "King Frederick *of* Prussia," would have been diplomatically impossible, since West Prussia still belonged to Poland.
⁷⁴ Frederick's son, who succeeded to the throne twelve years later (as King Frederick William I), happily was able to undo much of the damage done by his wastrel father.
⁷⁵ The claims of nineteenth and twentieth-century France to be a "protector fidei" against the Moslem world are more than a little amusing. Since the days of Francis I, France had pursued, to its own advantage and the marked discomfort of Central Europe, a pro-Turkish policy, a policy which in the seventeenth century, with the rise of Austrian power, became ever more overt. The army of Kara Mustafa, as it besieged Vienna in 1683 – and threatened the heart of Europe –, had an active ally in Louis XIV, the "most Christian sovereign of France."
⁷⁶ Hercules, tormented by the wounds which he had received from the shirt of Nessus, immolated himself on Mount Oeta, from whence he was carried up into Olympus and there made immortal.
⁷⁷ Opitz was a student at Heidelberg, when, on September 25, 1619, Frederick V of the Palatinate left his land to become the unhappy "winter king" of Bohemia. The young Silesian poet there had the chance to see the last of those happy days which Frederick spent in Heidelberg with his high-spirited wife, Elizabeth, the "worthy nymph" of this poem.
⁷⁸ Oppelt confuses two related Cretan myths: Daedalus constructed the Labyrinth at Cnossus, out of which Ariadne guided Theseus by means of that famous thread. Daedalus, it would seem, should know his way through his own Labyrinth.
⁷⁹ Charles XII was noted for the plainness of his dress.
⁸⁰ Enceladus, the son of Tartarus and Ge, was one of the hundred-armed giants who made war upon the gods. Zeus slew him and buried him under Etna.
⁸¹ Mulciber is a surname of Vulcan.
⁸² Matthew 17, 1-5: "And after six days Jesus taketh with Him Peter, and James, and John, his brother, and bringeth them up into a high mountain apart. 2. And he was transfigured before them; and his face did shine as the sun, and his garments became white as the light. 3. And behold, there appeared unto them Moses and Elijah talking with him. 4. And Peter answered and said unto Jesus, Lord, it is good for us to be here: if thou

wilt, I will make here three tabernacles; one for thee, and one for Moses, and one for Elijah. 5. While he was yet speaking, behold, a bright cloud overshadowed them: and behold, a voice out of the cloud, saying: This is my beloved Son, in whom I am well pleased; hear ye him."

[83] Since Origenes, Tabor has been regarded as the mount of the transfiguration.

[84] Meinrad Buol (1588-1658), the Swiss general and statesman, who, both in war and in negotiation, successfully defended the Grisons against Austrian encroachments.

[85] The Latin equivalent of Zephyr, the west wind.

[86] Giambattista Marino (1569-1625), the creator of the literary baroque style in Italy ("Marinism").

[87] Amphion, the son of Zeus and Antiope, learned to play with such magic skill on his lyre, a gift from Hermes, that he could move stones and enchant savage beasts. Wilhelm Riehl (1823-1897), in his novella "Amphion," has drawn a splendid picture of a Baroque musician who attempts to emulate his mythical rival.

[88] Favonius (or Zephyrus), the west wind, is usually associated with the springtime.

[89] In 1638, the town of Breisach (in Baden), was besieged and captured by Bernhard, Duke of Sachsen-Weimar (1604-1639), after Gustav of Sweden perhaps the most brilliant Protestant general of the Thirty Years' War.

[90] Pomponius Atticus (109-32 B.C.) is that urbane and unimpassioned friend to whom Cicero's *Epistolae ad Atticum* are addressed.

[91] Wernicke's note on these lines runs as follows: "Whoever, according to the present make-up of the world, intends to rise high in it, must be by nature given over neither to virtue nor vice, but must know how to exercise now the one, now the other according to the opportunity of the time and to people's spirits, without force and to his own profit. The world is too evil for one to progress in it through sheer virtue, and too skillful for one to progress in it by public vices. Men of cold mind have in this case all the gods, and, if they are at the same time sly, hell itself at their service."

[92] Cf. *Georgics*, III, ll. 274-275: "They snuff the light airs and often without being mated, conceive, for the wind – astounding to tell – impregnates them" (C. Day Lewis's translation).

[93] Pegasus.

[94] Telephus, King of Mysia, attempted to prevent the Greeks from landing in his kingdom. Caused by Dionysus to stumble over a vine, he was wounded by Achilles. The wound refused to heal and, upon consulting an oracle, Telephus learned that only he who had dealt the wound could make it close again. The Greeks, having consulted their own oracle in quite a different matter (the attack upon Troy), had in their turn discovered that they could not reach Priam's capital without the aid of Telephus. Thus Achilles was persuaded to heal Telephus with the rust of the spear by which the King had been wounded.

INDEX OF POEMS AND SOURCES

Abbreviations:

LVS: *Bibliothek des Literarischen Vereins in Stuttgart* (Tübingen/ Leipzig/ Stuttgart, 1843-   ).

ND: *Neudrucke deutscher Literaturwerke des 16. und 17. Jahrhunderts*, begründet von Wilhelm Braune (Halle/ Saale, 1876-   ).

DNL: *Deutsche National-Literatur*, begründet von Joseph Kürschner (Berlin und Stuttgart, 1882-1899).

CvFdF: *Deutsche Barocklyrik: Eine Auswahl aus der Zeit von 1620-1720*, herausgegeben von Curt von Faber du Faur (Salzburg-Leipzig, 1936).

Cysarz: *Deutsche Literatur in Entwicklungsreihen: Reihe Barock: Barocklyrik*, herausgegeben von Herbert Cysarz (Leipzig, 1937).

C & M: *German Lyrics of the Seventeenth Century: A Miscellany*, compiled and edited by A. Closs and W.F. Mainland (London, 1940).

Wehrli: *Deutsche Barocklyrik*, herausgegeben und mit einem Nachwort versehen von Max Wehrli (Basel, 1945).

Milch: *Deutsche Gedichte des 16. und 17. Jahrhunderts (Renaissance und Barock)*, herausgegeben von Werner Milch (Heidelberg, 1954).

DBL: *Deutsche Barock-Lyrik*, herausgegeben und eingeleitet von Herbert Cysarz (Stuttgart, 1954).

Hederer: *Deutsche Dichtung des Barock*, herausgegeben von Edgar Hederer (Munich, 1955).

INDEX OF POEMS AND SOURCES

Introduction 1-45
Abraham a Santa Clara
Der Mond 46
The Moon 47
    (Milch, p. 111)
Hans Assmann von Abschatz
Das schöne Kind 46
The Beautiful Child 47
    (DNL, XXXVI: *Die zweite schlesische Schule*, herausgegeben von Felix Bobertag, Berlin und Stuttgart, n.d., I, 363)
Die schöne Kleine 48
The Lady, Fair and Small 49
    (DNL, XXXVI, 363-364)
Die schöne Blatternde 48
The Pimpled Beauty 49
    (DNL, XXXVI, 364)
Die Schöne mit hohem Rücken 50
The Beauty with the Hunchback 51
    (DNL, XXXVI, 364-365)
Die schöne Hinckende 50
The Beauty Who Limps 51
    (DNL, XXXVI, 365)
Die schöne Gross-Nase 52
The Beauty of Great Nose 53
    (DNL, XXXVI, 366)
Die schöne Schwangere 52
The Lady, Fair and Pregnant 53
    (Hans Assmann von Abschatz, *Poetische Übersetzungen und Gedichte*, Leipzig und Breslau, 1704, II, 233)
Heinrich Albert
Musicalische Kürbs-Hütte 54-56
Musical Pumpkin-Hut 55-57
    (Cysarz, I, 217-219)

JOHANN GEORG ALBINI
Englische Anredung an die Seele 58
Angelic Address to the Soul 59
 (Cysarz, III, 224)
UNBEKANNTER DICHTER (ANONYMOUS)
Allegorisch Sonnet 58
Allegorical Sonnet 59
 (Cysarz, II, 260)
ANTON ULRICH, HERZOG VON BRAUNSCHWEIG-
 WOLFENBÜTTEL
Sterblied 60
Dying Song 61
 (Milch, p. 166)
GOTTFRIED ARNOLD
Gedoppelt Licht 62
Doubled Light 63
 (Wehrli, p. 189)
AUGUST AUGSPURGER
Arte & Marte 62
Arte & Marte 63
 (Cysarz, I, 194)
JOHANN VON BESSER
Beschreibung der Schlacht bei Fehrberlin 64-68
Description of the Battle at Fehrbellin 65-69
 (Cysarz, III, 90-92)
SIGMUND VON BIRKEN
Hirtengedicht 70
Shepherd-Song 71
 (CvFdF, pp. 133-134)
Traur-Hirten-Spiel 70
Play of the Shepherd's Lament 71
 (Sigismund Betelius [Sigmund von Birken], *Todes-Gedanken und Todten-Andenken*, Nürnberg, 1670, p. 3)
Hirtengedicht 72
Shepherd-Song 73
 (CvFdF, pp. 132-133)
Ihr Blätter/Wetterspiel 72
You leaves, you weather-game 73
 (Sigmund von Birken, *Fortsetzung der Pegnitz-Schäferey*, Nürnberg, 1645, p. 83)
Des ehrliebenden Floridans lustiges Herbst- und
 Liebeslied 74-76
A Merry Autumn- and Love-Song of Honor-Loving

Floridan	75-77
(Milch, pp. 133-134)	

BARTHOLD HEINRICH BROCKES

Kirschblüte bei der Nacht	76
Cherry Blossoms at Night	77
(DNL, XXXIX: *Die Gegner der zweiten schlesischen Schule*, herausgegeben von Ludwig Fulda, Berlin und Stuttgart, n.d., II, 351-352)	
Geteilte Sinnen.	78
Separated Senses	79
(DNL, XXXIX, 364-365)	

FRIEDRICH RUDOLF LUDWIG VON CANITZ

Sinn-Schrifften Auf einige Teutsche Käyser. . . .	78-82
Epigrams Concerning Some German Emperors. . .	79-83
(Cysarz, III, 87-89)	

DANIEL VON CZEPKO

Spiele wohl! Das Leben ein Schauspiel	84
Act Well! Life is a Play	85
(Wehrli, pp. 45-46)	
Angst und Hohn der Liebe Lohn	84
Scorn and Dismay the Lover's Pay	85
(Cysarz, I, 169)	
Aus den *Monodisticha*	86-88
From the *Monodisticha*	87-89
(Cysarz, III, 165-168)	

SIMON DACH

An Regina Voglerin, verwittibte Oederin zum Namenstage	90
To Regina Vogler, the Widowed Madam Oeder, on Her Name-Day	91
(Simon Dach, *Gedichte*, herausgegeben von Walther Ziesemer, Halle/Salle, 1936-37, I, 117)	
Über den Eingang der Schlossbrücke	90
Over the Entrance of the Castle-Bridge	91
(Dach, *Gedichte*, II, 168)	
Über der Schloss-Pforte, da Ihr Fürstliche Durchl. auff dero Beylager einzogen, zu lesen	92
To be Read above the Castle-Gate, when His Princely Highness Rode in to His Marriage Bed. . . .	93
(Dach, *Gedichte*, II, 168)	

C. ELTESTER

Als sie ein Lied in die darzu gespielte theorbe sang . .	92
When She Sang a Song to the Theorbo's Accompaniment	93
(C &M, p. 54)	

GOTTFRIED FINKELTHAUS
Der Soldate. 94-96
The Soldier 95-97
    (Gottfried Finkelthaus, *Teutsche Gesänge*, Leipzig,
PAUL FLEMING   [1642 n.p.])
Er redet die Stadt Moskaw an, als er ihre vergüldeten
    Türme von Fernen sahe   96
He Addresses the City of Moscow, as He Sees Her
    Guilded Towers from Afar   97
    (LVS, LXXXII-LXXXIII: Paul Fleming, *Deutsche Ge-
    dichte*, herausgegeben von J. M. Lappenberg,
    Tübingen, 1865, 525)
An die grosse Stadt Moskaw, als er schiede   98
To the Great City of Moscow, as He was Leaving . .   99
    (LVS, LXXXII-LXXXIII, 472-473)
Über den Zusammenfluss der Wolgen und Kamen. .   98
On the Confluence of the Volga and the Kama. . .   99
    (LVS, LXXXII-LXXXIII, 476-477)
Von sich selber 100
Concerning Himself 101
    (Cysarz, II, 12)
An den Mon 100
To the Moon 101
    (Wehrli, pp. 134-135)
Über Herrn Martin Opitzen auf Boberfeld Sein Ableben 102
Concerning the Demise of Mr. Martin Opitz of Boberfeld 103
    (Wehrli, p. 14)
An Sich 102
To Himself 103
    (Wehrli, p. 15)
Herrn Pauli Flemingi Der Med. Doct. Grabschrift. . 104
Epitaph of Mr. Paul Fleming, Med. Doct. 105
    (Wehrli, p. 16)
JOHANN FRANCK
Aus der *Vater-Unser-Harffen* 106
From the *Lord's Prayer Harp* 107
    (CvFdF, p. 241)
CHRISTOPH FÜRER VON HAIMENDORF
Streit des Fleisches wider den Geist 108-110
Battle of the Flesh Against the Spirit 109-111
    (Cysarz, II, 168)
PAUL GERHARDT
Geh aus, mein Herz, und suche Freud 110-112
Go out in this dear summertide 111-113
    (Paul Gerhardt, *Dichtungen und Schriften*, heraus-

gegeben von Eberhard von Cranach-Sichart, Munich, 1957, pp. 119-120, strophes 1-8)
Der 121. Psalm Davids 112-114
The 121. Psalm of David 113-115
(Gerhardt, *Dichtungen und Schriften*, pp. 161-162)

GEORG GREFLINGER
An eine vortreffliche schöne und Tugend begabte Jungfrau 114-116
To a Splendid, Beautiful, and Virtuous Maiden. . . 115-117
(Cysarz, II, 45)
Gegensatz: An eine sehr hässliche Jungfrau . . . 116-118
The Opposite: To a Very Ugly Maiden 117-119
(Cysarz, II, 46)
Auf die Zurückreise 118-120
Concerning His Return 119-121
(Milch, pp. 158-159)

CATHARINA REGINA VON GREIFFENBERG
Göttlicher Anfangs-Hülfe Erbittung 120
Plea for Heaven's Initial Help 121
(Leo Villiger, *Catharina Regina von Greiffenberg: Zu Sprache und Welt der barocken Dichterin*, Zürcher Beiträge zur deutschen Sprach- und Stilgeschichte, Nr. 5, Zürich, 1952, p. 99)
Über Gottes unbegreifliche Regierung / seiner Kirchen und Glaubigen 120-122
On God's Incomprehensible Rule of His Churches and His Faithful 121-123
(Villiger, p. 100)
Auf Christus Mensch-werdige Wunder-Tat 122
Upon Christ's Wonder-Deed: Becoming Man . . . 123
(Villiger, pp. 101-102)
Auf die übernatürliche Meerwandelung des Herrn. . 124
Concerning the Supernatural Walk of Christ Upon the Sea 125
(Villiger, p. 102)
Das VI. Wort: Es ist vollbracht 124
The VI. Word: It is Finished 125
(Villiger, p. 103)
Auf die fröhlich- und herrliche Auferstehung Christi . 126
Concerning the Joyous and Splendid Resurrection of Christ 127
(Villiger, p. 104)
Gott lobende Frühlingslust 126
Spring-Joy Praising God 127
(Villiger, p. 105)

Verlangen nach der herrlichen Ewigkeit	128
Desire for Splendid Eternity	129
(Villiger, pp. 40-41)	
Auf die verfolgte, doch ununterdrückliche Tugend. .	128
Concerning Persecuted, Yet Indomitable Virtue . .	129
(Wehrli, p. 28)	
Brünstiges Weissheit Verlangen	130
Fiery Desire for Wisdom	131
(Cysarz, II, 192)	
Eifrige Lobes vermahnung	130
Zealous Admonition to Praise	131
(Cysarz, II, 193)	
Über Gottes gnädige Vorsorge	132
Concerning God's Gracious Care	133
(Cysarz, II, 193)	
Auf meinen Vorsatz / die Heilige Schrifft zulesen . .	132
Concerning My Resolution to Read Holy Scripture .	133
(Cysarz, II, 193-194)	
Auf die Thränen	134
On Tears	135
(Cysarz, II, 195)	
Gott-lobende Frülings-Lust	134
Spring-Joy Praising God	135
(Cysarz, II, 197)	
Auf die Fruchtbringende Herbst-Zeit	136
Concerning the Fruit-bringing Autumn-season. . . .	137
(Cysarz, II, 197)	

HANS JACOB CHRISTOFFEL VON GRIMMELSHAUSEN

Komm Trost der Nacht, o Nachtigal	136-138
Come, balm of night, oh nightingale	137-139
(Cysarz, II, 197-199)	

JOHANN GROB

Epigrame	138-140
Epigrams	139-141
1. Von dem Bertramen	138
1. Concerning Bertram	139
(LVS, CCLXXIII: Johann Grob, *Epigramme, nebst einer Auswahl aus seinen übrigen Gedichten*, herausgegeben von Axel Lindquist, Leipzig, 1929, 115)	
2. Amsterdam.	140
2. Amsterdam.	141
(LVS, CCLXXIII, 120)	
3. Die Schweiz	140
3. Switzerland	141
(LVS, CCLXXIII, 121)	

4. Samuel Pufendorf	140
4. Samuel Pufendorf	141
(LVS, CCLXXIII, 186)	
5. General Werdmüller	140
5. General Werdmüller	141
(LVS, CCLXXIII, 188)	
6. Auf einen kurzweiligen Ostindienfahrer . . .	140
6. Concerning an Amusing Traveler from the East Indies	141
(LVS, CCLXXIII, 190)	
7. Prag	140
7. Prague	141
(LVS, CCLXXIII, 192)	

ANDREAS GRYPHIUS

Ueber seine sonntag- und feiertags-sonnette . . .	142
Concerning His Sunday and Holiday Sonnets . . .	143
(LVS, CLXXI: Andreas Gryphius, *Lyrische Gedichte*, herausgegeben von Hermann Palm, Tübingen, 1884, 92-94)	
An Gott den heiligen Geist	142
To God the Holy Ghost	143
(LVS, CLXXI, 98)	
Uber die Geburt Christi	144
On the Birth of Christ	145
(LVS, CLXXI, 99)	
Menschliches elende	144
Human Misery	145
(LVS, CLXXI, 103)	
Thränen des vaterlandes, anno 1636	146
Tears of the Fatherland, anno 1636	147
(LVS, CLXXI, 113-114)	
An einen unschuldigen leidenden	146
To an Innocent Sufferer	147
(LVS, CLXXI, 117)	
An die sternen	148
To the Stars	149
(LVS, CLXXI, 118)	
An Eugenien	148
To Eugenia	149
(LVS, CLXXI, 121-122)	
An sich selbst	150
To Himself	151
(LVS, CLXXI, 125)	
An die welt	150

To the World 151
    (LVS, CLXXI, 125-126)
Morgen sonnet 152
Morning sonnet 153
    (LVS, CLXXI, 130)
Mittag 152
Midday 153
    (LVS, CLXXI, 130-131)
Abend 154
Evening 155
    (LVS, CLXXI, 131)
Mitternacht 154-156
Midnight 155-157
    (LVS, CLXXI, 131-132)
Einsamkeit 156
Solitude 157
    (LVS, CLXXI, 133)
Auf die letzte nacht seines XXV. jahres 156-158
Concerning the Last Night of His XXV. Year . . . 157-159
    (LVS, CLXXI, 138-139)
Als er aus Rom geschieden 158
When He Departed From Rome 159
    (LVS, CLXXI, 152-153)
Das letzte gerichte 158
The Final Judgment 159
    (LVS, CLXXI, 156)
Die hölle 160
Hell 161
    (LVS, CLXXI, 156-157)
Andencken eines auf der see ausgestandenen gefährlichen sturms 160
Remembrance of a Perilous Storm, Endured Upon the Sea 161
    (LVS, CLXXI, 173-174)
Auf einen in der heiligen Pfingst-nacht entstandenen brand 162
Concerning a Fire Which Arose in the Holy Night of Pentecost 163
    (LVS, CLXXI, 174-175)
Über Nicolai Copernici bild 162
Concerning Nicolaus Copernicus' Picture 163
    (LVS, CLXXI, 393)

CHRISTIAN GRYPHIUS
Ungereimtes Sonett 164

Unrhymed Sonnet 165
    (Milch, p. 300)
Auf einen angenehmen Hund 164
Concerning a Pleasant Dog 165
    (DNL, XXXVI, 394)
Wienerisches Sieges-Lied (1683) 166
A Viennese Song of Triumph (1683) 167
    (Cysarz, II, 243)

JOHANN CHRISTIAN GÜNTHER

An seine Magdalis 166
To His Magdalis 167
    (LVS, CCLXXV: Johann Christian Günther, *Sämtliche Werke*, herausgegeben von Wilhelm Krämer, Leipzig, 1930, I, 58)
Als sie an seiner Treu zweifelte 168
As She Doubted His Faithfulness 169
    (LVS, CCLXXV, 56)
Abschiedsaria 168-170
Departure-Aria 169-171
    (LVS, CCLXXV, 84-85)
Trostaria 172
Consolation-Aria 173
    (LVS, CCLXXVII: Johann Christian Günther, *Sämtliche Werke*, herausgegeben von Wilhelm Krämer, Leipzig, 1931, II, 9)

C. H.

An eine liebens-würdige Schlesierin 174
To a Lovable Silesian Girl 175
    (Cysarz, II, 257)

JOHANN CHRISTIAN HALLMANN

Der Unüberwindliche Leopoldus 174
Leopold the Invincible 175
    (Cysarz, II, 229)

MARTIN HANKE

Von der letzten Zeit 176
Concerning the Final Time 177
    (Wehrli, pp. 43-44)

GEORG PHILIPP HARSDÖRFFER

Die Liljennymphe 176
The Lily-Nymph 177
    (Wehrli, p. 143)
Aus den *Gesprächspielen* 178
From the *Conversation-Games* 179
    (Cysarz, II, 137)
Alcaische Ode 178

Alcaic Ode 179
    (Cysarz, II, 137)
AUGUST ADOLF VON HAUGWITZ
An seine Bücher 180
To His Books 181
    (Cysarz, II, 229-230)
An seiner Freundin übelgetroffenes Bildnüss . . . 180
To the Ill-struck Portrait of His Mistress 181
    (Cysarz, II, 230)
JOHANN HEERMANN
In Krieges- und Verfolgungsgefahr 182
In Peril of War and Persecution 183
    (Wehrli, pp. 99-100)
THEOBALD HÖCK
Von der Welt Hoffart und Bossheit 182-184
Of the World's Pridefulness and Spite 183-185
    (Cysarz, I, 109-110)
CHRISTIAN HOFMANN VON HOFMANNSWALDAU
Er liebt vergebens 186
He Loves In Vain 187
    (Wehrli, p. 80)
Vergänglichkeit der Schönheit 186
Beauty's Transitoriness 187
    (Wehrli, p. 83)
Beschreibung vollkommener schönheit 188
Description of Perfect Beauty 189
    (Cysarz, II, 200)
Er ist gehorsam 188
He Is Obedient 189
    (Cysarz, II, 201)
Grabschrifft Grafens Serini 190
Epitaph of Count Serini 191
    (Benjamin Neukirch, *Herrn von Hofmannswaldau und anderer Deutschen auserlesener und bissher ungedruckter Gedichte erster Theil*, Leipzig, 1697, I, 234-235)
Sonett: er schauet der Lesbie durch ein Loch zu . . 190
Sonnet: He Observes Lesbia through a Hole . . . 191
    (Neukirch, I, 13)
ERNST CHRISTOPH HOMBURG
Was ist die Liebe 192
What Is Love? 193
    (Wehrli, p. 48)
HEINRICH HUDEMANN
Von der Zeit 192

Concerning Time 193
    (Cysarz, I, 140)
CHRISTIAN FRIEDRICH HUNOLD
Auf die unmässige Hunde Liebe 192
Concerning the Immoderate Love of Dogs 193
    (Cysarz, II, 281-282)
CASPAR KIRCHNER
Frawenlob H. Michael Bartschen und Frawen Helene
    Burkhardin zu Ehren entworffen 194
A Praise of Woman Composed in Honor of Master
    Michael Bartsch and Mistress Helene Burkhard . 195
    (ND, XV: *J. W. Zincgrefs und anderer deutscher Poeten auserlesene Gedichte: 1624*, herausgegeben von W. Braune, Halle/Saale, 1879, p. 24)
JOHANN KLAJ
Auf! güldenes Leben! glückliche Nacht! 194
Oh, golden life, waken! Fortunate night! 195
    (Milch, p. 129)
Die Soldaten Luzifers singen 196
The Soldiers of Lucifer Sing 197
    (Milch, pp. 129-130)
Spazierlust 196
Stroll-Joy 197
    (DBL, p. 32)
CHRISTIAN ANTON PHILIPP KNORR VON ROSENROTH
Abends-Andacht 198
Evening Devotions 199
    (Cysarz, III, 240-241)
CHRISTOPH KÖLER
An die Bienen 200
To the Bees 201
    (Cysarz, I, 164)
JOHANN ULRICH VON KÖNIG
Auf Ihro Königl. Majestät Der regierenden Königin
    von Ungarn und Böhmen Krönungs-Fest zu Prag 200-202
Upon the Coronation Festival of Her Royal Majesty,
    the Ruling Queen of Hungary and Bohemia, at
    Prague 203-205
    (Cysarz, III, 94-95)
QUIRINUS KUHLMANN
Der Wechsel menschlicher Sachen 202-204
The Change of Human Things 203-205
    (Milch, pp. 249-250)
Aus tiefster Not 204-206

From Deepest Need 205-207
   (Wehrli, pp. 178-179)
Der 15. Kühlpsalm 206-208
The 15th Kühl-Psalm 207-209
   (Cysarz, III, 187)
LAURENTIUS VON SCHNÜFFIS
Die achte Mirantische Wald-Schallmey 208-212
The Eighth Mirantian Forest-Shawm 209-213
   (Cysarz, III, 149-152)
GOTTFRIED WILHELM LEIBNIZ
Auf die Nachahmer der Franzosen 212-214
Concerning the Imitators of the French . . . 213-215
   (Cysarz, III, 86)
G. LIST
Auf die liederlichen vers-verderber 214
Concerning the Lewd Corrupters of Verse . . . 215
   (Cysarz, II, 251)
MATTHÄUS APELLES VON LÖWENSTERN
Alkaische Ode 214-216
Alcaic Ode 215-217
   (Wehrli, p. 96)
FRIEDRICH VON LOGAU
Epigramme 216-220
Epigrams 217-221
   1. Die unartige Zeit 216
   1. Our Naughty Time 217
   (DNL, XXVIII: *Die erste schlesische Schule*, herausgegeben von H. Osterley, Berlin und Stuttgart, n.d., II, 145)
   2. Trunckenheit 216
   2. Drunkenness 217
   (DNL, XXVIII, 152)
   3. Der Arzte Glücke 216
   3. The Physicians' Fortune 217
   (DNL, XXVIII, 152)
   4. Die Geburt ist der Tod; der Tod ist die Geburt . 218
   4. Birth is Death; Death is Birth 218
   (DNL, XXVIII, 157)
   5. Frantzösische Kleidung 218
   5. French Dress 219
   (DNL, XXVIII, 162)
   6. Glauben 218
   6. Faith 219
   (DNL, XXVIII, 166)
   7. Beute aussm deutschen Kriege 218

7. Booty from the German War	219
(DNL, XXVIII, 171)	
8. Weiber-Herrschung	218
8. Women's Rule	219
(DNL, XXVIII, 175)	
9. Wasser und Wein	218
9. Water and Wine	219
(DNL, XXVIII, 175)	
10. Ein Frosch	218
10. A Frog	219
(DNL, XXVIII, 179)	
11. Seele und Leib	218
11. Soul and Body	219
(DNL, XXVIII, 182)	
12. Narren und Kluge	218
12. Fools and Wise Men	219
(DNL, XXVIII, 183)	
13. Alter Adelstand	218
13. The Old Nobility	219
(DNL, XXVIII, 192)	
14. Die Freyheit	220
14. Freedom	221
(DNL, XXVIII, 194)	
15. Göttliche Rache	220
15. Divine Revenge	221
(DNL, XXVIII, 195)	
16. Ein Glaube und kein Glaube	220
16. One Faith and No Faith	221
(DNL, XXVIII, 203)	
17. Mächtige Diener	220
17. Powerful Servants	221
(DNL, XXVIII, 203)	
18. Die deutsche Sprache	220
18. The German Language	221
(DNL, XXVIII, 207)	

DANIEL CASPAR VON LOHENSTEIN

Sonette aus *Arminius*	220-222
Sonnets from *Arminius*	221-223
I. Komm Sonne / Brunn des Lichts	220
I. Light-spring, oh sun, in light	221
(Daniel Caspar von Lohenstein, *Grossmüthiger Feldherr Arminius*, Leipzig, 1689-1690, VIII, 1173)	
II. Hier liegt der weiseste	222
II. The wisest of all men	223
(Lohenstein, *Arminius*, V, 684)	

III. Allhier liegt Spartacus 222
III. Here lies the noble flesh 223
    (Lohenstein, *Arminius*, VI, 954)
Nacht-Gedancken über einen Traum 224
Night-Thoughts Concerning a Dream 225
    (Daniel Caspar von Lohenstein, *Himmel-Schlüssel oder geistliche Gedichte*, Leipzig, 1733, p. 44)
Die Augen 224
Her Eyes 225
    (C & M, p. 52)

LUDWIG, FÜRST ZU ANHALT-KOETHEN
Kling-Gedichte Auf die Fruchtbringende Geselschaft . 226
Sonnet Concerning the Fruitful Society 227
    (CvFdF, p. 46)

ZACHARIAS LUND
An die Liebste 226
To His Dearest One 227
    (C &M, p. 19)

PAUL MELISSUS
Sonett: Jörgen von Averli und Adelheiten von Grauwart 228
Sonnet: To Jörgen von Averli and Adelheit von Grauwart 229
    (ND, XV, 13-14)

HANS MICHAEL MOSCHEROSCH
Aus den *Gesichten Philanders von Sittewald* 228-230
From the *Gesichte Philanders von Sittewald* 229-231
    (DNL, XXXII: Hans Michael Moscherosch: *Gesichte Philanders von Sittewald*, herausgegeben von F. Bobertag, Berlin und Stuttgart, n.d., pp. 146-147)

HEINRICH MÜHLPFORT
Sechstinne 230-232
Sestina 231-233
    (Cysarz, II, 248-249)

JOACHIM NEANDER
Der Muntere 234
The Man Who Wakes 235
    (Cysarz, III, 231-232)

BENJAMIN NEUKIRCH
Auf die Krönung Friedrich I., Königes in Preussen: 234
Concerning the Coronation of Frederick I, King in Prussia: 1701 235
    (DNL, XXXIX, 502)
Auf das Bündnis des Königs in Frankreich mit den Türken 236

Concerning the Alliance of the King of France with the
Turks 237
(DNL, XXXIX, 503)

GEORG NEUMARCK

Sonnet: Als ich zu Lübekk im 1643sten Jahre den 12.
Aprill zu Schiffe / üm nach Königsberg auff die
Universitet zu reisen / gieng 236
Sonnet: When I went on board ship in Lübeck, on
April 12 of the 1643rd year, in order to journey
to Königsberg to the university 237
(Cysarz, I, 204)

MAGNUS DANIEL OMEIS

Wenn du etwas Liebliches hörest 238
Whenever You Hear Something Sweet 239
(Hederer, p. 204)

MARTIN OPITZ

An diss Buch 238
To This Book 239
(Cysarz, I, 153)
Ich will diss halbe mich 238-240
I'll lay this halfway me 239-241
(Cysarz, I, 154)
Ich gleiche nicht mit dir 240
With snowy light of moon 241
(Cysarz, I, 155)
Du güldne Freyheit, du 240
You golden freedom, both 241
(Cysarz, I, 155)
Vom Wolffsbrunnen bey Heidelberg. 242
Concerning the Wolffsbrunnen near Heidelberg. . . 243
(ND, CLXXXIX-CLXXXXII: Martin Opitz, *Teutsche
Poemata*, herausgegeben von Georg Witkowski,
Halle/Saale, 1902, pp. 111-112)
Folgen underschiedliche Grabschrifften 242-244
A Series of Various Epitaphs 243-245
(ND, CLXXXIX-CLXXXXII, 135-136)

JOANNES OPPELT

Daedalus 244
Daedalus 245
(Cysarz, III, 160)

JOHANN PLAVIUS

Sey verschwiegen 246
Be of Close Council 247
(*Danziger Barockdichtung*, herausgegeben von
Heinz Kindermann, Deutsche Literatur in Ent-

wicklungsreihen: Reihe Barock: Ergänzungsband, Leipzig, 1939, p. 154)
MICHAEL RICHEY
Ueber das Bildniss Sr. Königl. Majestät von Schweden,
   Carls, des Zwölften   246
Concerning the Portrait of His Royal Majesty of
   Sweden, Charles XII   247
   (Cysarz, III, 92)
MARTIN RINCKHART
Das Uhralte: Domine respicere digneris   248
The Age-Old: Domine respicere digneris   249
   (Cysarz, III, 203-204)
JOHANN RIST
Auf die Winterzeit 248-250
Concerning the Wintertide 249-251
   (Milch, p. 146)
Als die wunderbahre / oder vielmehr ohnverhoffte
   Zeitung erschallete / dass der Hertzog von Friedland zu Eger wehre ermordet worden   250
When the Marvelous, or, on the Contrary, Unexpected
   News Sounded Out that the Duke of Friedland
   Had Been Murdered at Eger   251
   (Cysarz, I, 236)
Sie rühmet ihre Beständigkeit   252
She Boasts of Her Constancy   253
   (Cysarz, I, 248-249)
ROBERT ROBERTHIN
Frühlingslied 252-254
Spring Song 253-255
   (Hederer, pp. 50-51)
JESAIAS ROMPLER VON LÖWENHALT
Zu einer Leich 254-256
For a Wake 255-257
   (Cysarz, I, 182)
Gaistliche Spiegelberaitung   250
Spiritual Mirror-making   257
   (Cysarz, I, 188)
ANGELUS SILESIUS (JOHANN SCHEFFLER)
Aus dem *Cherubinischen Wandersmann* 256-262
From the *Cherubical Wanderer* 257-263
   1. Man weiss nicht, was man ist   256
   1. One Knows Not What One Is   257
   (Angelus Silesius, *Sämtliche poetische Werke*, herausgegeben und eingeleitet von Hans Ludwig Held, Munich, 1922, II, 3)

2. Ich bin wie Gott, und Gott wie ich	256
2. I Am As God, and God As I	257
(AS, II, 4)	
3. Leib, Seele, und Gottheit	258
3. Body, Soul, and Godhead	259
(AS, II, 10)	
4. Ein jedes in dem Seinigen	258
4. Each In His Own	259
(AS, II, 13)	
5. Im Eckstein liegt der Schatz	258
5. The Treasure Lies In The Cornerstone . . .	259
(AS, II, 14)	
6. Wer ganz vergöttet ist	258
6. Whoever Has Become All Divine	259
(AS, II, 14)	
7. Die geistliche Goldmachung	258
7. The Spiritual Alchemy	259
(AS, II, 16)	
8. Die Rose	258
8. The Rose	259
(AS, II, 16)	
9. Bei Gott ist nur sein Sohn	258
9. Only His Son Is With God	259
(AS, II, 20)	
10. Die geheime Jungfrauschaft	258
10. The Secret Virginity	259
(AS, II, 22)	
11. Gott ist mir, was ich will	258
11. God Is To Me What I Desire	259
(AS, II, 26)	
12. Das Licht besteht im Feuer	258
12. The Light Exists In The Fire	259
(AS, II, 27)	
13. Die geistliche Arch' und's Manna-Krügelein .	258
13. The Spiritual Ark And The Manna-Vessel .	259
(AS, II, 27)	
14. Gott ist nichts (Kreatürliches)	258
14. God Is Nothing (Physical)	259
(AS, II, 28)	
15. Der Mensch ist's höchste Ding	258
15. Man Is The Highest Thing	259
(AS, II, 28)	
16. Je aufgegebener, je göttlicher	260
16. The More Abandoned, The More Divine . .	261
(AS, II, 29)	

17. Die Sünde 260
17. Sin 261
(AS, II, 30)
18. Der Glaube 260
18. Belief 261
(AS, II, 31)
19. Die Abscheulichkeit der Bösheit 260
19. The Abomination Of Evil 261
(AS, II, 31)
20. Zufall und Wesen 260
20. Chance And Essence 261
(AS, II, 48)
21. Die geistliche Schwängerung 260
21. The Spiritual Impregnation 261
(AS, II, 58)
22. Nimm also, dass du hast 260
22. Take Therefore, That You May Have . . . 261
(AS, II, 61)
23. Der Tugend Ziel ist Gott 260
23. Virtue's Goal Is God 261
(AS, II, 119)
24. An St. Augustin 260
24. To St. Augustine 261
(AS, II, 120)
25. Die Liebe 260
25. Love 261
(AS, II, 121)
26. Ein's jeden Element 260
26. Each Its Own Element 261
(AS, II, 121)
27. Die Tiefe, Höhe, Breite und Länge Gottes . 260
27. The Depth, Height, Breadth, And Length Of
God 261
(AS, II, 122)
28. Maria 262
28. Mary 263
(AS, II, 123)
29. Seufzer zu Gott 262
29. Sigh To God 263
(AS, II, 234)
30. Die Welt ist ein Sandkorn 262
30. The World Is A Grain Of Sand 263
(AS, II, 237)
WENZEL SCHERFFER VON SCHERFFENSTEIN
Der Music Lob 262

Praise of Music	263
(Cysarz, I, 177-178)	
DAVID SCHIRMER	
Er liebet	264
He Loves	265
(Cysarz, II, 53)	
Uber Ihr Grab	264
On Her Grave	265
(Cysarz, II, 53)	
An Seine Neue Buhlschafft	266
To His New Paramour	267
(Cysarz, II, 54-55)	
BENJAMIN SCHMOLCK	
Gebet vor dem H. Abendmahl	266
Prayer Before Holy Communion	267
(Cysarz, III, 232)	
JOHANN MATTHIAS SCHNEUBER	
Morgengesang	268
Morning Song	269
(Hederer, pp. 132-133)	
JOHANN GEORG SCHOCH	
Er brennt	268-270
He Burns	269-271
(Cysarz, II, 59)	
JUSTUS GEORG SCHOTTEL	
Donnerlied	270
Thunder Song	271
(DBL, p. 31)	
ERNST SCHWABE VON DER HEYDE	
Sonnet: Ihr die ihr höret an	272
Sonnet: Oh you who think to hear	273
(Cysarz, I, 140-141)	
SIBYLLA SCHWARZ	
Sonett: Ist Lieben keusch	272
Sonnet: If love is chaste	273
(Sibylla Schwarzin, *Ander Teil deutscher Poetischer Gedichten*, Danzig, 1650, p. 12)	
Sonett: Itzt wil ich in den Wald	274
Sonnet: I will into the woods	275
(Schwarzin, p. 13)	
Sonett: Man sagt / es sey kein Ort	274
Sonnet: Men say there is no place	275
(Schwarzin, p. 13)	
JAKOB SCHWIEGER	
Sie ist sein Pol	276

She is His Pole 277
  (Milch, p. 165)
ANDREAS SCULTETUS
Blutschwitzender und todesringender Jesus . . . 276-278
Jesus, Sweating Blood and Wrestling with Death . . 277-279
  (Gotthold Ephraim Lessing, *Werke*, herausgegeben von Julius Petersen und Waldemar von Olshausen, Berlin-Leipzig-Stuttgart-Vienna, 1925-35, XVI, 314-315)
JUSTUS SIEBER
An sein Vaterland 278
To His Fatherland 279
  (Cysarz, II, 61)
JOHANN WILHELM SIMLER
Sonett / oder Trauriger Todtenklang / über / Herrn Lands-Haubtmann Meinrad Buolen / ihme seliges; dem Vatterland / höchstschädliches Ableiben 280
Sonnet, or Sad Sound of Death, concerning Governor Sir Meinrad Buol's Departure from the Flesh, Blessed for Himself, Highly Damaging to the Fatherland 281
  (Johann Wilhelm Simler, *Teutscher Getichten die Vierte, vom Ihme selbsten und auss hinterlassenen Schrifften um einen Viertheil vermehrt- und verbesserte Ausfertigung*, Zürich, 1688, p. 60)
FRIEDRICH SPEE
Die gesponss Jesu klaget ihren hertzenbrand . . . 280-282
The Spouse of Jesus Laments Her Heart's Flame . 281-283
  (ND, CCXCII-CCCI: Friedrich Spee, *Trutznachtigall*, herausgegeben von Gustave Otto Arlt, Halle/Saale, 1936, 7-9)
Anders lob aus den werken Gottes 284-286
Another Panegyric from the Works of God . . . 285-287
  (ND, CCXCII-CCCI, 144-147)
JOSUA STEGMANN
SEI wohlgemut, lass trauren sein 288
Be happy, put your grief aside 289
  (Milch, p. 225)
CASPAR STIELER
Der Hass küsset ja nicht 288-290
Hate Surely Does Not Kiss 289-291
  (ND, LXXIV-LXXV: Caspar Stieler, erroneously attributed to Jakob Schwieger, *Geharnschte Venus*, herausgegeben von Theodor Raehse, Halle/Saale, 1880, pp. 21-22)

Vergiesst mich Sie nur nicht 290-292
If She Does But Not Forget Me 291-293
   (ND, LXXIV-LXXV, 27-28)
ERNST STOCKMANN
Christus ist auferstanden 292
Christ Is Risen 293
   (Hederer, p. 139)
GOTTLIEB STOLLE
Die verliebte Verwandlung 294
The Enamored Transformation 295
   (Wehrli, pp. 49-50)
Auf den Herrn von Hoffmannswaldau 294
Concerning Master Hofmannswaldau 295
   (C & M, pp. 51-52)
JOHANN PETER TITZ
Auff Reinhold Friedrichs und Hedwig Tönniessins
   Hochzeit 296
On the Marriage of Reinhold Friedrich and Hedwig
   Tönnies 297
   (*Deutsche Lyrik des siebzehnten Jahrhunderts*, herausgegeben von Paul Merker, Bonn, 1913, p. 20)
ANDREAS TSCHERNING
Ein Baum redet den Menschen an 296
A Tree Addresses Man 297
   (Cysarz, I, 198)
VENUS-GÄRTLEIN
Du Beherrscher unsrer Sinnen 298
You, our senses' little king 299
   (ND, LXXXVI-LXXXIX: *Venus-Gärtlein: ein Liederbuch aus dem XVII. Jahrhundert*. Nach dem Drucke von 1656 herausgegeben von Max Freiherrn von Waldberg, Halle/Saale, 1890, p. 139)
Die weltliche Nonne 300
The Worldly Nun 301
   (ND, LXXXVI-LXXXIX, 179)
GEORG RUDOLF WECKHERLIN
Von dem Cardinal de Richelieu 300-302
Concerning the Cardinal de Richelieu 301-303
   (LVS, CXCIX: Georg Rudolf Weckherlin, *Gedichte*, herausgegeben von H. Fischer, Tübingen, 1894, p. 431)
An Brissach von Höchstermeltem Helden Bernhard
   Hertzogen zu Sachsen eingenommen 302
To Breisach, Taken by That Supremely Celebrated

Hero, Bernhard, Duke of Saxony 303
    (LVS, CXCIX, 430)
Von dem König von Schweden 302-304
Concerning the King of Sweden 303-305
    (Wehrli, p. 13)
Sie ist die gröste Reichtumb 304
She is the Greatest Wealth 305
    (LVS, CXCIX, 464-465)
An eine, sich alt zu werden beklagende, Schönheit . 304
To a Beauty, Complaining That She Grows Old . . 305
    (LVS, CXCIX, 475)
Die Lieb ist Leben und Tod 306
Love is Life and Death 307
    (Wehrli, pp. 63-64)
An das Teutschland 306
To Germany 307
    (Cysarz, I, 131)
CHRISTIAN WEISE
Auf die Geburt eines jungen und hoch-verlangten
    Sohnes 308
Upon the Birth of a Young and Highly-Desired Son . 309
    (Cysarz, III, 9)
CHRISTIAN WERNICKE
Abriss eines Weltmanns, unter dem Gemäld' von
    Pomponius Atticus 310
Sketch of a Cosmopolite, under the Portrait of Pomponius Atticus 311
    (DNL, XXXIX, 530)
An unsere deutsche Poeten 310
To Our German Poets 311
    (DNL, XXXIX, 533)
Furor Poeticus 312
Furor Poeticus 313
    (C &M, p. 78)
PHILIPP VON ZESEN
Klüng-getichte auf das Härz seiner Träuen 312
Sonnet on the Heart of His Faithful Lady 313
    (Cysarz, II, 90)
Schertzlied an die truebseelige... Roselinde . . . 314
Mocking Song to the Melancholy Roselinde 315
    (CvFdF, pp. 144-145)
HEINRICH ANSELM VON ZIGLER UND KLIPPHAUSEN
Aus der *Asiatischen Banise* 314-316
From the *Asiatic Banise* 315-317
    Wahr ists, die schönheit ist 314

It's true that beauty is	315

(DNL, XXXVII: *Die zweite schlesische Schule: Ziglers Asiatische Banise nebst Proben aus der Prosa des 17. und 18. Jahrhunderts*, herausgegeben von Felix Bobertag, Berlin und Stuttgart, n.d., II, 229)

JEde Nymfe, jede Göttin	316
Every nymph and every goddess	317

(DNL, XXXVII, 424)

JULIUS WILHELM ZINCGREF

An die Teutschen	316
To the Germans	317

(Milch, p. 65)

Epigramma Vom Thurn zu Strassburg	318
Epigram Concerning the Tower at Strassburg . . .	319

(Cysarz, I, 134)

BIOGRAPHICAL INDEX	320-350
NOTES	351-356
INDEX OF POEMS AND SOURCES	357-380